THE BOOKS OF
SAMUEL
VOLUME ONE

THE SOVEREIGNTY OF GOD ILLUSTRATED IN
THE LIVES OF SAMUEL, SAUL, AND DAVID

CYRIL J. BARBER

A Devotional Commentary
on First Samuel

LOIZEAUX
Neptune, New Jersey

Unless otherwise stated, all translations and paraphrases of Scripture in this
book are the author's. The chapter and verse divisions cited in parentheses
correspond to those found in most English Bibles.

In this book occasional references are made to the Apocrypha of the Old
Testament. These are to show the usage of a particular word or to draw the
reader's attention to some tradition or belief. Neither the author nor the
publisher equate the Apocrypha with the canonical Scriptures, even though
some Bibles have the Old Testament Apocrypha in them.

The Hebrew letter that appears on the title page and also encloses each
chapter number is the first letter in the Hebrew spelling of *Samuel.*

Library of Congress Cataloging-in-Publication Data

Barber, Cyril J.
The books of Samuel / Cyril J. Barber.
Includes bibliographical references and index.
ISBN 0-87213-027-4
1. Bible. O.T. Samuel—Commentaries. I. Bible. O.T. Samuel.
English. Barber. 1994. II. Title.
BS1325.3.B37   1994
222'.4307—dc20   94-337

Printed in the United States of America
10 9 8 7 6 5 4 3 2 1

To

Gary Strauss,

a friend who is closer to me

than a brother.

CONTENTS

FOREWORD

How I wish this book had been available years ago when I as a young minister tried to preach on the life of King Saul. My intentions were noble, but my preparation was inadequate. I shudder even today when I think of those sermons.

But Dr. Cyril Barber has now solved the problem for all of us! He has given us a commentary on 1 Samuel that balances dependable information, spiritual interpretation, and practical application. I predict that in years to come this volume will be a standard reference work for serious Bible students and careful expository preachers.

The author has amassed so much relevant scholarly material that I am amazed at his breadth of learning. But there is no dull academic atmosphere in these pages. The book is a joy to read. Dr. Barber writes with spiritual sensitivity and fervor, and his desire is only to magnify the Lord. Dr. Barber makes ancient history exciting and practical, and he does so without spiritualizing the text.

I especially appreciate the way he has integrated the data from Judges and 1 Samuel to show how key persons and events affected the history of Israel. As for the difficult problems in the text, he has ventured some explanations that are both bold and sensible. For this I commend him.

You will enjoy using this book. It will open up new facets of truth for you to receive and apply in your own life and then share with others. The author has done for 1 Samuel what the scribe Ezra and his associates did when they expounded the law: they "gave the sense, and caused them to understand the reading" (Nehemiah 8:8, KJV). And like the ready steward our Lord described in Matthew 13:52, Dr. Barber has brought forth out of his treasury things new and old.

What more can a Bible student want?

Warren W. Wiersbe

PREFACE

Many years ago I had the privilege of studying the Bible under Dr. Howard G. Hendricks. He impressed upon me two essentials: (1) the need for thorough research when studying the Biblical text and (2) the importance of relevancy when applying the text. In this book I have tried to follow Professor Hendricks's counsel. The notes at the end of the book give some indication of the thoroughness of my preparation. It will be up to my readers to determine the degree to which I have succeeded in applying the teaching of each passage to life.

I believe that in this latter area I am in a fortunate position, for I have never been in the ministry per se. I have always worked as a layman in the church and church-related organizations. Let me explain. Because of a difficult family situation I was compelled in my teens to take up a career I did not enjoy: I became an accountant. Then after twelve years of balancing other people's books, the opportunity came for me to take courses in Biblical studies and library science. These subjects I thoroughly enjoyed. I began teaching in a school in southern California, but after about eight years the institution was forced to merge with another college. I was faced with a mid-life career change and new studies—this time in marriage and family counseling.

The hours I put in are long and the work is demanding. And so I have much in common with other people who work hard all day and come home tired at night. My time for Bible study is limited to an hour in the morning and a few hours each evening. In spite of this limitation, I trust that the thoughts contained in this book will stimulate new ideas and a fresh consideration of a portion of God's Word.

I regret that some important resources I would have liked to consult were not available to me. Among these are the writings of E. P. Dhorme and R. deVaux on the life of Samuel.

Volume 1 of W. G. Hupper's *An Index to English Periodical Literature on the Old Testament and Ancient Near East* was published as I was concluding my comments on 1 Samuel 10. I have not repeated any of his entries in this study, but rather have made reference to him so that those who wish to research some facet of the Biblical text further may consult his listing without fear of unnecessary duplication.

My book, a very simple treatment of 1 Samuel, is designed for those who wish to take a careful look at the old familiar stories of the Bible. Unsophisticated and unadorned, this study follows the format established previously in my expositions of the books of Judges and Ruth. My sole purpose in sharing my thoughts with readers has been to contribute in some small way to their edification. Having desired to write only a devotional commentary, I may perhaps be forgiven for emphasizing some areas of application that I feel have either been ignored or glossed over by other commentators. To avoid making the book too extensive, I have made only brief references to certain portions of the text that are self-explanatory. I hope, however, that what I have written will stimulate interest in the events that occupied the Biblical historian's attention and the narrative that is so deserving of close scrutiny. In order to keep each chapter a reasonable length, there have been times when I have only hinted at areas of practical application; I trust that readers will further develop these trends of thought themselves.

I am painfully aware that concepts of God's sovereignty vary considerably. I am not able to engage scholars in technical debate, and even if I could, the purpose of this study would then be lost. I know of the tensions that exist between those who clamor loudly for a belief that appears to favor determinism and rule out man's freedom of thought and action, and those in the opposing camp who have imbibed deeply the waters of humanism which tend to deify man and emphasize his ability to create his own destiny.

Personally I like the illustration of the late A. W. Tozer. He described God's sovereignty in terms of an oceangoing liner bound from New York to Liverpool. The passengers on board never doubted for one minute that their eventual destination would be the port specified on their tickets. While on the ship they were free to engage in different forms of recreation, use the lounges, eat on deck or in the dining room, and get up or go to bed when they pleased. They had freedom of choice within the parameters established by the size of the ship and their assigned destination.

In the beginning man was created with genuine freedom. Adam and Eve were free to choose where they would work in the garden, what food they would eat, and how they would spend their leisure time. They were also free to obey (or disobey) God.

But because of their fall we are born "into captivity to the law of sin" (Romans 7:23, KJV). Unless enlightened by the Holy Spirit (John 16:8-11) each one of us will remain in our lost state. Once redeemed, however, we are set free from the law of sin and death (Romans 8:2). We are able to relate meaningfully to God. Our destination is sure. God is honored as we voluntarily submit our wills to His will (2

Corinthians 10:5) and do those things that are pleasing in His sight. This is the essence of the doctrine of redemption.

As Dr. Charles C. Ryrie pointed out in his masterful condensation of Bible doctrine, *Basic Theology,*

> Sovereignty/freedom forms an antinomy (a contradiction between two apparently equally valid principles or between inferences correctly drawn from such principles). Antinomies in the Bible, however, consist only of apparent contradictions, not ultimate ones. One can accept the truths of an antinomy and live with them, accepting by faith what cannot be reconciled; or one can try to harmonize the apparent contradictions in an antinomy which inevitably leads to overemphasizing one truth to the neglect or even denial of the other. Sovereignty must not obliterate free will, and free will must not dilute sovereignty.[1]

We will find that in the books of Samuel the three leading personalities—Samuel, Saul, and David—all acted with complete freedom (even choosing, as in the case of Saul, to disobey God's explicit command or, as in David's experience, to lie or feign madness to gain certain ends). All the while God may be observed behind the scenes orchestrating events for the good of His people.

I want to express my sincere thanks to Mr. Donald Pugh, former editor of Gospel Light/Regal Books, for so kindly giving me permission to use and quote from *Always a Winner* (a commentary on 1 Samuel coauthored with my colleague John Carter) which was widely used in their curriculum series.

Since the publication of *Always a Winner* several notable studies have appeared. These include the works of Klein, McCarter, and Mauchline. In re-examining the text of 1 Samuel I have read these volumes together with other monographs on the ark narrative, the life of Saul, and David's rise to prominence. One of the most useful and balanced studies is the late Leon Wood's *Israel's United Monarchy.* Among other commentaries I have found indispensable are the works of William G. Blaikie, William Deane, and Thomas Kirk. My indebtedness to these writers is evident throughout.

A brief word needs to be said about the case histories in this book. They are all factual. Names and identities have been altered, however, to protect the privacy of those who sought my counsel. I wish to express my gratitude to each person who has graciously allowed me to share his or her experiences.

Special thanks are due Dr. Warren W. Wiersbe—for many years the senior pastor of the Moody Memorial Church in Chicago—for so kindly reading the manuscript and writing the Foreword.

Finally, I hope that those who use this commentary will experience a measure of the blessing that has enriched my life as I have been privileged to interact with this portion of God's Word.

INTRODUCTION

Denis Waitley in his *Secrets of Greatness* told an interesting story of the way traditions are passed from one generation to the next. A young newlywed was preparing a meal for her husband. She had carefully selected a ham from the local supermarket, and before putting the ham into the pan, cut off both ends. Her husband was watching her and asked the reason. "Oh, my mother always did it that way," was the reply.

Several months later while dining at the home of his in-laws, the young man was reminded of the incident when his mother-in-law served them roast ham. Without wishing to offend either his bride or her mother, he asked why she had cut off the ends of the ham before cooking it. His mother-in-law shrugged her shoulders nonchalantly and commented that this was what her mother had always done.

Finally the day came when he asked the grandmother why she had always cut the ends off the ham. She looked at him suspiciously and then replied tartly, "Because my baking dish was too small!"[1]

TRADITION AND INTERPRETATION

God's people have their traditions too. Some believe that the Bible is inerrant. Others hold to varying degrees of Biblical authority, but not to its plenary inspiration. The text of the books of Samuel forces us to grapple with this issue, for the manuscripts that have come down to us are not as well preserved as other portions of the Old Testament canon. In fact many Bible scholars have pointed to the "poor state of the Masoretic text,"[2] and have taken liberties in emending it.

Let me say at the outset that I believe in the inerrancy of the Bible. I know that this statement immediately places me with the minority. The doctrine of inspiration, however, has to do with the original manuscripts, not the copies that were made of them. The original documents were composed under the superintendence of the Holy Spirit. Using the individual personalities of the original human authors, He caused these penmen to compose and record without error God's revelation to man.[3]

None of these original writings remain. It seems likely that in the course of time they either wore out or were lost. Copies of them, however, have survived and are available in sufficient quantity for us to reconstruct the original text. The science of textual comparison is an exacting one, and we can be assured that our present Bible of sixty-six books translated from the original Hebrew, Aramaic, and Greek languages accurately preserves what God desired to communicate to us.

But other traditions cloud the issues and make the theme of these books more difficult to understand. These traditions include the commonly accepted views of the authorship and purpose of these books.

In addition there are the traditional interpretations of those who purport to understand the strengths, weaknesses, successes, and failures of Samuel, Saul, and David. Such views are to be found in the indictments handed down condemning Samuel for being a bad father; in the explanations offered for the statement, "And God gave Saul another heart"; in the comments made about Saul's prophesying with the young men from the schools of the prophets; in the opinions given on the real relevance to us of David's conflict with Goliath; in the questions raised about the true nature of the love David had for Jonathan; in the debates started over how David could be a "man after the heart of God" and yet repeatedly consort with the Philistines who were the enemies of God's people; and in the doubts expressed about how the Bible's teaching on monogamy is to be sustained when David had several wives at one time.

Other traditions have grown up around the opinions of some popular writers and preachers. These opinions have been so widely accepted that to tamper with them is regarded by some as tantamount to heresy. However, an uncritical acceptance of erroneous theories has led some Christians to develop unsound views of what the Bible really teaches. Well-established principles of interpretation must be followed if we are to arrive at the truth. The text of Scripture must be studied inductively with an unbiased mind, and the literal-cultural-textual laws governing sound hermeneutics must be adhered to if we are to ascertain with as much accuracy as possible the real meaning of a passage. Deduction (where the human element enters into matters of interpretation to a greater extent than with induction) allows us to offer at best only tentative solutions to interpretative problems.

Unfortunately there has been a tendency on the part of a segment of the Christian church to test a person's orthodoxy by the answers given to certain questions. Only those who follow the traditional interpretation, free of independent thought, are then given the right hand of fellowship.

The real issue facing us as men and women who desire to handle God's Word faithfully is, Can the traditions we have accepted be supported or do they fall into the category of the ham that had to be accommodated to the size of the baking dish? In other words, does the popular interpretation of events conform to the laws of hermeneutics or have its contours been determined by other criteria?

TITLE

Another ancient tradition has to do with the names assigned to the books of the Bible. The two books of Samuel originally formed one scroll. With the two books of Kings, they comprise a complete history of the kingdoms of Israel and Judah. The division into four books began with the Septuagint (commonly referred to as LXX and dated about 250 B.C.). In the Hebrew Bible the single book was referred to as *Sh^emū'ēl*.

In the Greek translation made of the Old Testament by "the seventy" (that is, the septuagint), the books we know as 1 and 2 Samuel and 1 and 2 Kings were given the title, "The Books of Kingdoms" *(bibloi basileioñ)*. The reason for the increase in the number of books may be traceable to the fact that the Greek version, containing vowels, required one and three-quarters more space than the unpointed Masoretic text (which did not contain vowels until after A.D. 600). Two scrolls were sufficient for Samuel and Kings in Hebrew, whereas four were needed for the Greek version. Jerome, writing in the fourth century, preserved this fourfold division but substituted the title "Books of Kings" *(libri regnōrum)*. Only in 1516-1517, when Daniel Bomberg provided a new edition of the Hebrew Bible, were 1 and 2 Samuel and 1 and 2 Kings incorporated into the Hebrew Bible as four separate books.

AUTHORSHIP AND DATE

Even though the majority of people in our churches are convinced that Samuel wrote the books of Samuel, we can only speculate as to their origin. Some think the books were named after Samuel because he was the chief person in the story. But if Samuel wrote the books, then both of them must have been completed prior to his death (c. 1013 B.C.). This is not possible, for 1 Samuel closes with the death of Saul (1011 B.C.) and Samuel died prior to Saul's demise and before David became king over God's people. Samuel could not have written of events that transpired after his death.

Authorship

The Talmud may be largely responsible for ascribing to Samuel the authorship of these books. There we read that "Samuel wrote the books that bear his name."[4] Charles C. Ryrie in the *Ryrie Study Bible* said:

> Though the two books of Samuel are named for the key figure of the early chapters, Samuel could not have written more than a part of 1 Samuel since his death is recorded in chapter 25. That he did in fact write a book is attested in 1 Samuel 10:25.[5]

It is unlikely that our 1 Samuel is the book referred to. But even if Samuel did write chapters 1–24, we still must ask who wrote the other portions.

Rejecting all thought of unity,[6] some modern scholars have posited a variety of authors, sources, and stages of development. The more conservative approaches see Abiathar the priest (1 Samuel 23:6-12; 30:7-8) or Seraiah the scribe (2 Samuel 8:17) or Ahimaaz the son of Zadok (2 Samuel 15:27; 1 Chronicles 6:8,53) as possible authors.

The most probable view (though certainly not without its problems, as will be explained below) is that initially Samuel worked with Nathan and Gad and one of these men continued the work after Samuel's death (2 Chronicles 9:29). Whoever compiled the final book had access to other sources, as is evident from 2 Samuel 1:18 and 1 Chronicles 27:24. Such a view of the authorship of the books of Samuel is rejected by liberal scholars as too simplistic.

Most liberal writers see in the narrative supposed duplicate accounts and, building on the documentary theory adopted for the study of the Pentateuch, claim justification for a Jahwistic and an Elohistic author.[7] Otto Eissfeldt adds a Levitical writer,[8] though his views have not been widely accepted. To these authors is added a Deuteronomic redactor who reworked the entire narrative around 550 B.C. Critical research led A. R. S. Kennedy to distinguish five separate stages in the development of the narrative, each contributed by a different literary tradition.[9]

The books of Samuel possess unity as well as a clear plan and purpose, and there is nothing to be gained by introducing such speculation about numerous authors and their supposed sources or about redactors and their supposed revisions. The critics have been ably answered by modern conservative scholars[10] and no further refutation is needed.

Date

Questions of authorship have a direct bearing on the date of these books. Many able students of the Word assign a time for their composition to a period much later than is warranted by the Biblical evidence. Even among conservative theologians there is considerable disagreement. Gleason L. Archer, for example, holds to an early date—soon after the death of Solomon. Others allow for compilation at various times throughout the period of the divided kingdom (though all but the most ardent adherents to the Deuteronomic view will concede that inasmuch as there is no evidence or hint of the fall of the northern kingdom, the books must have been completed before 722 B.C.).

The period covered by the books of Samuel (c. 1105-971 B.C.) is a long one.[11] Of crucial importance is the statement that "Ziklag belongs to the *kings of Judah* to this day" (1 Samuel 27:6, italics added). C. F. Keil and F. J. Delitzsch, evaluating with their usual thoroughness the Biblical data pertaining to the date of the writing of these books, conclude that the book of Samuel (that is, our 1 and 2 Samuel) could not have come into its final form until after the falling away of the ten tribes from the house of David.[12] Keil and Delitzsch admit that the distinction between the tribes of Israel and Judah cannot be pressed too far, for such a distinction had existed for centuries before the division of the kingdom (Joshua 18:5 where Israel is spoken of as the "house of Joseph"; 19:9; Judges 10:9; 1 Samuel 11:8; 17:52; 18:16; 2 Samuel 3:10; 24:1), and that any advocacy of a date in the period of the divided kingdom must be counterbalanced by the fact that 2 Samuel closes *without* an obituary to the man whom later generations looked back on as an ideal king. This omission argues for an early date— soon after Solomon ascended the throne—and warns us that a late date cannot be presumed.

The style of writing and expressions used are indicative of an early period in Israel's history. The selectivity in presenting information (many events of apparently trifling importance are given extended treatment, whereas events of major significance in the lives of Samuel, Saul, and David are passed over with considerable brevity) argues for an eyewitness who was thoroughly familiar with the times. In spite of this selectivity the book of Samuel is complete. The reader does not get the impression that the accounts have been pieced together. The book of Samuel follows the literary pattern of the books of Judges and Ruth. Each concludes with an appendix: Judges 17–21; Ruth 4:18-22; 2 Samuel 22–24.

Because no single person could have lived long enough to complete a work covering more than a century and a quarter, Keil and Delitzsch conclude that the writings of Samuel, Nathan, and Gad form the book of Samuel.

> It is very evident from the character of the work before us, that the author had sources composed by eye-witnesses of the events at his command [2 Samuel 1:18; 1 Chronicles 27:24], and that these were employed with an intimate knowledge of the facts and with historical fidelity, inasmuch as the history is distinguished by great perspicuity and vividness of description, by a careful delineation of the characters of the persons engaged, by great accuracy in the accounts of localities, and of subordinate circumstances connected with the historical events.[13]

Who brought the books of Samuel into their final form we have no means of knowing. No vital doctrine of Scripture is affected by our ignorance, however, and although the Septuagint and Dead Sea scrolls are longer and more detailed in places,[14] both confirm the essential accuracy of the Masoretic text.

OUTLINE

Elaborate outlines of the books of 1 and 2 Samuel are to be found in nearly all introductions, study Bibles, and the better commentaries. These outlines invariably deal with the leading characters: Samuel, Saul, and David. The major headings are usually similar to what follows:

> I. Samuel, Israel's Last Judge, 1 Samuel 1:1–8:22
> II. Saul, Israel's First King, 1 Samuel 9:1–31:13
> III. David, Israel's Ideal King, 2 Samuel 1:1–24:25

While easy to remember and useful in keeping in mind the main thrust of these books, such outlines are not necessarily accurate. Samuel did not die when Saul became king (1 Samuel 9). Saul did not abdicate the throne after David was anointed as his successor (1 Samuel 16). The lives of these men overlapped, and if prominence in the Biblical narrative is to be the criterion in the outline, then it should be pointed out that relatively little is mentioned of King Saul's reign following his rejection in 1 Samuel 15, while much is recorded about David. Furthermore, as was pointed out above, Judges, Ruth, and 2 Samuel end with an appendix. In most cases the biographical outlines given for the books of Samuel do not readily lend themselves to such anomalies.

John Bright, following Keil and Delitzsch, has pointed to a "very definite pattern of organization" on the part of the Biblical writer.[15] It follows a cycle: A leader is introduced and played off against an older leader, whose career is then brought to a climax before he is set aside. At this point a summary of his achievements is given and a new leader is introduced. The process is then repeated.

For example, in 1 Samuel 1–7 Samuel is introduced. His birth is recorded and he is dedicated to the service of the Lord. Samuel is compared and contrasted with Eli and his sons, who are then rejected. Judgment comes upon them (many years later in a strict chronology), and in the end they are removed and Samuel comes to prominence. Chapter 7 passes over twenty years of ministry in a single verse (7:2), records the high point of Samuel's career (the convocation on the summit of Mizpah), and closes with a summary of his activity. In point of fact, Samuel continues to minister through at least two decades of Saul's reign.

In 1 Samuel 8–15 the cycle begins again. Samuel's administration is rejected and a new man, Saul, is introduced. He is played off against Samuel and the high points of Saul's career are summarized. He is then rejected and in chapter 16 David is introduced. Saul continues as king for about another fifteen years, but it is David who comes into prominence. The kingdom begins to disintegrate under Saul until he kills himself after a battle against his archenemies, the Philistines, in chapter 31.

There is a struggle for the throne of Israel, with Saul's son Ish-bosheth attempting to lead the northern tribes of Israel. His reign is summarized in 2 Samuel 3:1, which records a "long war" between the house of David and the house of Saul. Ish-bosheth is assassinated by two of his guards (4:5-7) and David is then made king over Israel and Judah. In 1 Kings Solomon is played off against his brothers. He is crowned king and serves as coregent until David dies. "And the kingdom was established in the hands of Solomon" (1 Kings 2:46).

From the foregoing it would appear as if an outline of the books of Samuel should allow for the overlapping of lives and administrations of the principle characters. As unconventional as it may appear, the books may be diagramed as follows:

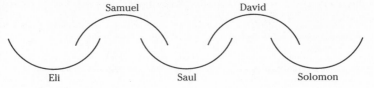

Samuel · David

Eli · Saul · Solomon

THEME

Traditional Views

Some theories, based on the history of the times, have looked upon 1 Samuel as the record of the transition from the disunity of the period of the judges to the unity achieved by the monarchy.[16] Second Samuel is then seen as a story of David's triumphs and, following the incident with Bathsheba, his trials.[17] However, inasmuch as 1 and 2 Samuel were originally a unit, to assign them separate purposes subjectively (quite apart from the intent of the Biblical writer) does not do justice to this portion of God's Word.

It is true that Saul's main task was to unify the tribes. Through Samuel's ministry a measure of spiritual oneness had prevailed, and Saul, therefore, was faced with the task of winning over the confidence of the people, establishing his administration, and giving the people a common sense of purpose. But only three out of thirty-one chapters in 1 Samuel (13–15) deal with Saul's rule. And the theme of the book cannot properly be regarded as transitional, for greater disunity prevailed at the time of Saul's death than before he ascended the throne. Plainly, a better explanation is called for.

Another view I feel is erroneous sees the theocracy coming to an end with the institution of the monarchy.[18] Actually the theocracy continued. As the Holy Spirit had clothed Himself with the different judges to equip them for service, so He came upon Saul. This special enduement enabled him to be the leader of God's people. Saul's appointment, therefore, was by God (1 Samuel 9:17; 10:24; 15:1,23; 16:1). His anointing by Samuel was at God's command (10:1), and Samuel instructed Saul in his responsibilities on the roof of his house (9:25). All of these facts indicate a continuation of the theocracy. Saul was God's regent.

David likewise was anointed with oil and endued with divine power (1 Samuel 16:13). The "Spirit of Yahweh" left Saul and rested on David. The young shepherd then stood in the line of the theocracy.

At no time was the king a law unto himself. Scripture knows nothing of the divine right of kings. When Saul disobeyed the Lord, he forfeited first his dynasty (1 Samuel 13:8-14) and then his right to rule (15:17-23,28). He could not do as he pleased, but was subject to the One who had appointed him. The same was true of David. When he committed adultery with Bathsheba and then had Uriah murdered, Nathan rebuked him in the name of the Lord (2 Samuel 12:7-12). He could not sin with impunity. He was responsible to uphold God's law.

Rather than allowing the theocracy to be replaced by a monarchy, it was God's intent for Israel's kings to foreshadow the reign of the Lord Jesus Christ. He will combine in His person the offices of prophet, priest, and king and will rule as God's anointed (1 Corinthians 15:24,28; Psalms 2:7-9,11-12; 110:1-3,6-7; Revelation 19:16). The books of Samuel do not chronicle the end of the theocracy.

The theme of Samuel is further obscured by those who wish to discern some facet of God's covenant in each book of the Bible. Covenantal as well as dispensational issues are present in every book of the Bible. *However, each canonical work has a distinct emphasis and reveals something new about the character of God. Each is a separate part of His self-revelation, disclosing some new aspect of His person and work.* In Deuteronomy, for example, the theme is God's love for His people and His desire that they respond to Him in loyal obedience. In Joshua the theme is the faithfulness of God in fulfilling His promises to Abraham, Isaac, and Jacob by giving the people the land. In Judges the theme is the power of God in delivering His people from their enemies. In Ruth the theme is the grace of God in providing for the needs of those who trust in Him. And so we could go on.

In place of the usual theories pertaining to the purpose of the books of Samuel, I would like to offer the suggestion that they, more so than any other portion of the Bible, illustrate the sovereignty of God.

The Sovereignty of God

Objective Criteria. For the first time in all of God's Word thus far, we come across the divine name *Yahweh Ṣĕbāʿôt,* "Creator of the (heavenly) armies"—a name implying God's omnipotence and recognizing His right to rule over the whole earth.[19] As we read further, we find that God had prevented Hannah from conceiving. Later He graciously answered her prayer and gave her a son. Her psalm of praise (1 Samuel 2:1-10) shows that she rejoiced in His sovereign goodness toward her. He had caused the impossible to happen. The prophetic thoughts behind her words (so reminiscent of the expressions of worship of Elizabeth and Mary in Luke 1:41-55) underscore facts reiterated throughout the books of Samuel. In addition we note God's further blessing of Hannah with other children (1 Samuel 2:21).

God also unilaterally set aside Eli's house and predicted that both his sons would die on the same day (1 Samuel 2:27-36). He sovereignly chose Samuel; allowed the ark of the covenant to be captured by the Philistines and then plagued the Philistines until it was returned; destroyed the people of Beth-shemesh for their lack of reverence; blessed the house of Abinidab for showing loyalty to His cause; defeated the Philistines at Mizpah in answer to Samuel's prayer; selected Saul as Israel's first king and led him to Samuel; gave Saul his first victory over the Ammonites; empowered Jonathan and his armorbearer so that they were able to rout the Philistine garrison; commissioned Saul to destroy the Amalekites and punished him for his disobedience; anointed David in Saul's place and bestowed on David the gift of the Holy Spirit; enabled David to kill Goliath; preserved David from Saul's jealous anger; increased David's strength by sending men to him while he was in the cave of Adullam; gave David the victory over the Philistines in the battle of Keilah; miraculously spared David's life when Saul pursued him and nearly caught him; helped David and his men rescue their wives and children after they had been forcefully abducted from Ziklag; and gave David grace in the eyes of the people so that they willingly made him their king.

A casual summary of 2 Samuel supports the belief that these books emphasize the sovereignty of God. We note for example God's strengthening of David's kingdom while Ish-bosheth grew weaker and weaker; giving David two significant victories over the Philistines; increasing David's fame among the surrounding nations; promising David an enduring dynasty (in contrast to Saul's which was taken away from him); prospering David in his wars against his enemies on every hand; and punishing David for his wrongdoing. It is hard, therefore, to escape the realization that in these books we have illustrated for us (more so than in any other book of the Bible) God's sovereignty over the affairs of His people.

To this evidence must be added the testimony of Asaph and Ethan the Ezrahite. Asaph described God's actions as decisive: "He chose David...took him...brought him" (Psalm 78:70-72). Ethan likewise portrayed God's initiative behind the events that are recorded: "God spoke...exalted...chose...found...anointed...established ...strengthened" (Psalm 89:19-21). God promised David that his dynasty would never pass away (Psalm 89:28-29; 2 Samuel 7:9-16). All of these statements presuppose a God who is sovereign and able to work all things after the counsel of His will.

David was not a self-made man. He was no empire builder carving out a kingdom for himself. He was totally dependent on the Lord for his success. Israel's enemies were stronger than the combined tribes of Israel and Judah. Only as the Lord worked in and through the nation's appointed leaders were they victorious. I concur, therefore, with David Payne that four related principles may be discerned in these books of Samuel:

• God's providence in national affairs, small and great, and His active involvement in the lives of His people.

- God's relationship with His people in which He always acts in their best interest. While He may chasten them when they are disobedient to His will, His ultimate purpose is for their well-being.

- God's purposes for His people are achieved through appropriate leadership. (David has provided a model for leaders and also prefigures the Messiah.)

- God's presence with His people in revealing His will to them and protecting them from their enemies.[20]

Subjective Application. But what practical value is there in all of this discussion for God's people today? What can we learn from the lives of Samuel, Saul, and David? Don't we run the risk of confusing the distinction between Israel and the church by applying principles from these Old Testament narratives to our lives today?

In addressing these concerns let us look first at King Saul. His successes are passed by almost without notice, and instead we have presented to us his weaknesses. In spite of a good beginning, he never became a man of God in the same way Samuel and David did. In contrast to Saul, Samuel and David had strong internal God-consciousness. Saul's life, viewed from the human plane, seems to confirm the observation of the French philosopher Jean-Paul Sartre, who wrote: "Man can count on no one but himself; he is alone, abandoned on earth in the midst of his infinite responsibilities, without help, with no other aim than the one he sets himself, with no other destiny than the one he forges for himself on earth."[21]

We cannot, however, allow the statement of Sartre to pass unchallenged. It is significant that the Bible corrects such a pessimistic outlook on life. The difference between Sartre's view and what is possible for us is to be found in our Godward relationship. The key lies in the development of what psychologists call an *internal locus of control*. When we are motivated by our vertical relationship with the Lord, rather than intimidated or controlled by our horizontal relationships with other people, we are able to bring all our thoughts and actions under the lordship of Christ (Romans 14:7-8). In other words, we can either be motivated from without (as was Saul), or we can be motivated from within (as were Samuel and David).

God's blessing upon Samuel and David was possible because they walked in reverential awe of Him. As a result of their fear of the Lord, they were proactive. Their beliefs established their values and their values regulated their goals. Saul, by contrast, gave evidence from the second year of his reign of being reactive. He was motivated by fear. To be sure, the Philistines were a powerful foe, but having begun to rely on himself, he succumbed to external pressures.[22]

In the way Samuel was reared we see how a powerful internal force (that is, an internal locus of control) can grow into a strong commitment to spiritual principles. Then as we follow Samuel's career, we learn from him how we can handle life's inequities.

Saul, by contrast, demonstrates the dilemma of those who have *not* been reared with a commitment to Biblical values. Although the Lord equipped him with everything he needed in order to be a good king, he relied on the flesh and refused to submit to the will of God. As the Scriptures reveal to us more and more of the inner workings of his heart, we see how the fear of man brought about his downfall. In the end he failed ignominiously.

In David—as shepherd, warrior, "outlaw," and eventually king— we see how, in spite of several lapses (caused by giving way to improper fears), a man was able to rise above circumstances that threatened to engulf him. The Psalms David wrote reveal his spiritual growth and demonstrate his submission to the will of God.[23]

In the lives of these men—and the positive as well as the negative examples they set—we see clearly the conflict between the flesh and the Spirit. We also note how their lives illustrate the truths the apostle Paul described in Romans 8:5-9:

> For those who live according to [that is, are motivated by] the flesh have their minds oriented toward the things of the flesh, but those who live in accordance with the Spirit [have their minds set on] the things of the Spirit. For the mind oriented toward the flesh is death, but the mind [controlled by] the Spirit [leads to or results in] life and peace. Wherefore the mind [oriented toward] the flesh is in enmity against God; for it is not subject to the law of God [that is, does not acknowledge His sovereignty], neither indeed can it be; and those [who, like Saul, are] controlled by the flesh cannot please God. But you are not in [that is, controlled by) the flesh, but by the Spirit, since the Spirit of God dwells in you.[24]

Romans 8:12-14 enlarges upon this theme. It stresses the need for us to bring all of life into conformity to the will of Christ. This confirms the teaching of Galatians 5:16-26 where the emphasis is again on the importance of believers submitting to the controlling power of the Holy Spirit. He then makes possible the growth of a strong internal God-consciousness (which in time produces the fruit of the Spirit).

These reciprocal truths underscore the importance of a knowledge of who God is and a proper response to His revelation. The books of Samuel reveal the sovereignty of God; the teaching is *objective* and our response is *subjective.*

HISTORY OF THE TIMES

To understand this period of Biblical history properly, we need to consider briefly the religious, social, and political milieu. Such an approach will provide a fitting backdrop for a consideration of the lives of Samuel, Saul, and David. It is important to remember that Eli and Samuel ministered in the *era of the judges.*

Samson (c. 1108-1049 B.C.) and Samuel (c. 1105-1013 B.C.) were contemporaries. Samson's judgeship lasted for only twenty years, whereas Samuel served the nation from the time he was three (when he was left at the temple in the custody of Eli) until he died. Samuel succeeded Eli as the religious leader of God's people following the defeat of Israel by the Philistines in the battle of Aphek (c. 1069 B.C.).

Because Samson was able to keep the Philistines at bay on Judah's western border, Samuel had relative freedom of movement and could engage in a "Bible teaching" ministry. He ministered to the spiritual needs of the people at Ramah, Bethel, Gilgal, and Mizpah (1 Samuel 7:15-17). During the same period, and as a result of Jephthah's victory over the Ammonites, the Israelites to the east enjoyed a degree of peace and prosperity under Ibzan, Elon, and Abdon (1081-1058 B.C.; Judges 12:7-15).

The book of Judges (chapters 17-21) closes with two illustrations of the spiritual ignorance and moral confusion that prevailed from the time of Othniel (1373 B.C.) to the inauguration of the monarchy (1043 B.C.). This period included the administrations of Eli and Samuel.

Religious Condition of the People

Eli (c. 1165-1067 B.C.) served as high priest *and* judge. The latter office he held for a period of forty years (1 Samuel 4:18). As Leon Wood observed, this was a significant honor.

> Those whom God chose to serve as judges were extraordinary people. They did not receive the position by inheritance...but by special selection. Therefore, when a person, who already held

such an honored position as high priest, was also chosen to fill one of these special appointments, it can have been only a commendation that was indicated.[25]

Eli's sons, Hophni and Phinehas, perhaps born in their father's later years, did not share Eli's commitment to the Lord. They came to the office of priest as a result of heredity. With the shameful practices of the heathen deities saturating the minds of the people, Hophni and Phinehas did nothing to stem the tide but flagrantly violated every principle of sanctity and worship Moses had established (1 Samuel 2:12-16; Leviticus 7:32). They may possibly have suspended the work of other priests and Levites, for the regular courses (1 Chronicles 23:6) were not in operation, and Elkanah (a Levite according to 1 Chronicles 6:22,27,34) does not appear to have had any responsibilities in the temple. Perhaps Hophni and Phinehas excused their act on the grounds that few came to the central sanctuary to offer sacrifices and only a handful of selected individuals were needed to take care of the work. The conduct of the sons of Eli turned many God-fearing Israelites away from the worship of the Lord (1 Samuel 2:17).

For centuries pagan nations had dedicated both male and female prostitutes to the service of some local shrine. "Sacred" prostitution was a way of life. The sons of Israel participated in these shameful practices (Judges 10:6) but periodically, after a time of severe chastening, the people would repent and turn to the Lord. Now, however, Hophni and Phinehas sought to incorporate these debasing practices of the heathen into the ceremonies of God's temple in Shiloh (1 Samuel 2:22).[26] Walter C. Kaiser, Jr., wrote:

> Rarely has immorality, injustice, and corruption of every sort achieved greater freedom...The offerings of the Lord were distorted, and Eli's sons exceeded every boundary of good taste, morality, and common decency. They insisted on having the sacrifice done to their specifications rather than God's (1 Sam. 2:12-17), and they brazenly lay with the women who served at the entrance to the tent of meeting (1 Sam. 2:22).[27]

Further evidence of the low spiritual state of the people may be seen in their attitude toward the ark of the covenant. Remembering stories associated with the exodus, they looked on the ark as a talisman that would bring them success (1 Samuel 4:3-8). In this they were no better than the heathen, for while they thought of the Lord in times of crisis, in reality their hearts were far from Him. They soon saw their mistake, for they were defeated in battle and the ark was captured (4:11). It was kept by the Philistines for seven months, during which time God demonstrated His sovereignty over Israel's enemies (1 Samuel 5:1–6:18; Psalm 115:2-8). On being returned to Israel, however, the men of Beth-shemesh showed no respect for the ark. Their inquisitiveness caused them to look upon the sacred vessel with a lack of true reverence. As a result a large number of them died.

Although there is no mention of divination and witchcraft in the early chapters of 1 Samuel, these practices must have prevailed also, for later we read that Saul banished all who practiced spiritism from the land (1 Samuel 28:3-7; Deuteronomy 18:10-12).

During the spiritual nadir of this era, Samuel continued to teach the people. After twenty long years their hearts began to "lament after Yahweh" (1 Samuel 7:2). Samuel then convened a convocation on the summit of Mizpah and led the people in a renewed commitment of themselves to the Lord.[28]

It was only under David that Jerusalem became the center of worship. He restored the priestly and Levitical courses; and the people, being righteously governed, gladly followed the man on whom the hand of God rested. David also made plans to bring the ark to Jerusalem, and while he did not build the first temple, he made provision for its construction so that Solomon could proceed with its erection without hindrance.

Social Conditions of the People

The scale of social fortunes (or misfortunes) accurately reflected the degree of religious commitment among the people. The two were intimately intertwined. When God disciplined Israel for their apostasy by allowing surrounding nations to oppress them, it was only with difficulty that they were able to meet their basic physiological (that is, food and shelter) and safety needs. The people had to hide in ravines and caves. They had no real freedom. Whatever crops they raised on level ground soon fell into the hands of their enemies (Judges 6:1-6; 10:8; 1 Samuel 23:1). The Israelites lacked unity and so were unable to take a stand for what was rightfully theirs. It was only with difficulty that they were able to survive.

A society cannot sustain itself for very long if it does not give its people a sense of security and stability; the benefit of protection from marauders; freedom to grow and develop in accordance with their individual gifts; just law enforcement so that those who do not act in accordance with God's ordinances are speedily punished;

and wise and capable leaders who give balance and a sense of direction.

With these basics lacking during major portions of the period of the judges, and there being no king in Israel, it is not surprising that "every man did what was right in his own eyes" (Judges 17:6; 18:1; 19:1; 21:25). Only during periods of relative peace could the people really begin to benefit from the blessings God was so ready to bestow on them. Only then could love again flourish and laughter be heard in the streets. Only then did affection and a sense of cohesion strengthen the fiber of family life.

In any society certain individuals earn the respect of their peers. In Israel's case those who distinguished themselves as leaders of local militia and protected their villages from Bedouin bands intent upon plundering them, often became wealthy and were looked up to and respected. Judges 11:1, Ruth 2:1,[29] and 1 Samuel 9:1 give examples of men who were held in high esteem. For the most part, however, the deep-seated satisfaction that comes from feelings of confidence, a sense of success, a realization of one's intrinsic worth, and the joy of accomplishment were not widely shared. Succeeding generations therefore suffered from a certain ingrained sense of weakness and feeling of helplessness evident, for example, in Judah's readiness to hand over Samson to the Philistines. The result of such attitudes may be seen in the ease with which different tribes accepted the suzerainty of a foreign power (Judges 14:4; 15:11; 1 Samuel 11).

Add to these social conditions the fact that the nation had twice suffered the reverberating blows of civil war (Judges 12:1-7; 20–21) and you begin to realize how difficult it was for Israel to build any kind of solidarity, inner cohesion, and strength. Rarely, therefore, were the people in a position to develop their potential. They lagged behind other nations who were more advanced in commerce and industry (Judges 1:19; 1 Samuel 13:19-21). And the Lord and His will only became the topic of conversation around their campfires when adversity drove them to the limit of their resources.

Disunity among the tribes was compounded by the topography of the land. The Jordan river effectively separated the tribes of Reuben and Gad and the half tribe of Manasseh from their brethren to the west. Fewer and fewer attended the annual festivals during which the males particularly were to gather before the Lord (Exodus 23:14-17; 34:21-24; Deuteronomy 16:16). The people suffered the consequences of their isolation. And during times of war or oppression, the valley of the Esdraelon made it easy for the invading army to overrun the tribes of Issachar and Zebulun and separate Asher, Naphtali, and Dan from their brethren.

Saul faced a formidable task when he became king, and it is to his credit that to a large extent he succeeded in infusing the sons of Israel with a sense of national unity. It was only under David, however, and following the assassination of Ish-bosheth, that the people of Israel really felt themselves to be significant.

Political Conditions of the People

During the period of time covered by the books of Samuel (1105-971 B.C.) Israel's neighbors played a significant role in the outworking of God's providence. These nations included those adjacent to Israel's borders as well as those still living in the land (that is, the Canaanites and Amorites). We will touch briefly on the most significant.

The Philistines. The Philistines[30] were Israel's chief threat. From their pentapolis of Gaza,[31] Ashkelon,[32] Ashdod,[33] Gath,[34] and Ekron[35] they controlled the southwest part of Palestine. They were a warlike race and perhaps aimed at the conquest of all of Palestine and Syria.

The Hittites had known the secret of smelting iron for centuries. It may well have been through contact with them that Jabin learned of the process (Judges 4:2-3,13). The Philistines also mastered the art, and with their superior weapons they oppressed Israel for forty years.

The Ammonites. Ammon[36] was the half brother of Moab (Genesis 19:33-38). Ammon's descendants settled east of the Jordan river on the edge of the Arabian desert (Deuteronomy 2:37; Joshua 12:2; 13:10,25). The Ammonites had been defeated by Jephthah (Judges 11:32-33) but by the time of Saul had regained sufficient military strength to oppose Jabesh-gilead (1 Samuel 11:1-5).[37] It was partly due to the threat of the Ammonites that Israel came to Samuel and asked for a king (1 Samuel 12:12).

The Edomites. The Edomites[38] were descendants of Jacob's brother Esau. Their stronghold was mount Seir and the territory they controlled lay directly south of the Dead Sea. The Arabah valley was fertile and at one time had boasted fields of crops, vineyards, and wells of water (Numbers 20:17). The area had previously been inhabited by the Horites (Hurrians) but when Esau and his descendants began to occupy the area, the Horites were gradually dispossessed (Deuteronomy 2:12).

During the period of the judges there was apparently little contact with Edom. We do know that Saul fought against them (1 Samuel 14:47) and David put garrisons within their border (2 Samuel 8:14; Psalm 60).

The Moabites. Immediately north of Edom was the territory of

Moab[39] (Numbers 21:11,13; cf. Joshua 13:15-23). At one time the land
had been occupied by Emim (Deuteronomy 2:10-11). Later Eglon had
led his armies against Israel and Ehud had secured Israel's deliverance (Judges 3:12-30). Peaceful relations must have existed between
Israel and Moab in the years that followed, for David sought safety
for his parents in Moab when he was forced to flee from the wrath of
Saul (1 Samuel 22:3-4).

The Assyrians. By the time of the united monarchy in Israel, the
Assyrians[40] had had a long and eventful history. Their kings had ruled
from Assur on the Tigris river and had extended the sphere of their
influence throughout the ancient Near East. For a period of time they
had come under the control of the Sumerians (c. 2130-2030 B.C.), but
after regaining their independence the Assyrians made the surrounding nations their vassals.

During the period when Othniel judged God's chosen people,
Assyria established diplomatic relations with Egypt (c. 1365-1330 B.C.).
In the next two centuries they brought all of northern Mesopotamia
and also Babylon under their control. Then during the judgeships of
Jair, Elim, and Jephthah (1118-1078 B.C.) the Assyrians extended their
domain all the way to the Mediterranean. This growth must have
caused considerable anxiety to the Israelite tribes. In the providence
of God, however, Assyria soon began to decline politically and did
not constitute a threat to Saul as he began to rule in Gibeah.

Egypt. Thutmose III, the pharaoh of the oppression, had extended
Egypt's borders as far as the Euphrates river. When he died (c. 1450
B.C.), Amenhotep II, the pharaoh of the exodus, was unable to maintain Egypt's control over these lands. From 1445 B.C. until Seti I (1317-
1301 B.C.) re-established Egypt's supremacy, the land of the Nile languished. Then, following the vainglorious reign of Ramses II (1301-
1234 B.C.), Egypt entered an era of political confusion and vacillation
that lasted through the reigns of Saul and David. Even though some
show of strength was made at maintaining the empire, the pharaohs
had no real interest in foreign affairs.[41] Israel was therefore free from
interference.

All of these races controlled land outside Israel's borders. We now
turn to consider the major ethnic groups who possessed territory
inside the promised land and who constituted a threat to the people's
spiritual well-being.

The Canaanites and Amorites. Descended from Noah's son Ham,
the Canaanites had occupied Palestine for a long time before Abraham arrived in 2090 B.C. (Genesis 10:6; 12:6). Toward the close of the
third millennium B.C., Amorites had migrated from Upper Mesopotamia, and large numbers had displaced the local Canaanites from

such places as Megiddo, Jericho, and Ai. In some areas the Amorites mingled with the Canaanites, and in others the Canaanites forced the Amorites into the hill country (Numbers 13:29; Joshua 11:3; Judges 1:34-36; 3:5; 6:10; 10:8; 11:21-23).

A second group to migrate from the north to Canaan were the Horites (Hurrians). They were of Indo-Aryan descent. On entering Palestine they settled in the south and gradually intermarried with the Canaanites (Genesis 14:6; 36:20,29; Deuteronomy 2:12,22).[42]

As a result of the influence of the Amorites and Horites, the Canaanites imbibed many Mesopotamian social mores (Deuteronomy 7:1-6). These were deemed to be detrimental to the well-being of the Hebrews as they took possession of the land.[43]

NATURE OF THE MONARCHY

Relatively little space is given in the Biblical record to the kind of monarchy instituted by Samuel. When the elders of the people came to Ramah, they asked for a king to judge them in order that they might be like the other nations (1 Samuel 8:5). During this period of history the nations round about them had monarchs who ruled in regal splendor and maintained prestigious courts. All of this was pleasing to those who were prone to make evaluations solely on the basis of appearance.

Later, after Samuel had prayed about the matter, the leaders refined their demands. They wanted someone to rule over them, serve as a judge in civil matters, lead them in times of war, and give them a sense of permanence through the establishing of a dynasty. They did not want a city-state form of government such as their forefathers found when they entered Canaan. The elders also desired to avoid the "divine kingship" of other monarchies in which a king would claim to be either the embodiment of their deity or his son. God's people were aware of their unique relationship to the Lord (1 Samuel 10:1). They wanted a king who would assume responsibility for leading them in the path of righteousness. Based on Judges 17:6, 18:1, 19:1, and 21:25, the people must have expected the king to control sin through legislation—something the judges could not and did not do (Psalm 101:4-5,7-8).

Along with the benefits of a strong king, there were also some disadvantages. Under the judges each tribe assumed responsibility for administering the law. With the inauguration of the monarchy, legal jurisdiction would gradually be assumed by a central administration (2 Samuel 15:2-3) and efficiency would decrease. In addition there would be problems associated with taxation in a monarchy.

Taxation was probably not a major issue during the reigns of Saul and David, but during Solomon's era it became a source of contention (1 Kings 12:1-15).

Having surveyed the background of the book of Samuel, we are now in a position to consider the teaching of the text.

THE REWARD
OF THE RIGHTEOUS

1 Samuel 1:1–2:11

We want quick easy answers. As a society we have become accustomed to microwaves and microchips, rapid romances and crimes solved on television in sixty-minutes. Many Christians tend to demand the same from the system of beliefs by which they regulate their lives: they want immediate solutions to difficult problems. Numerous earnest believers do not invest the time needed to develop a Biblical approach to life.

Some who are willing to invest the time live in parts of the country where devotional literature, practical "how-to" books, and inspirational prose interspersed with a few verses of Scripture are regarded as Bible study material. At best such writing gives the application of a text without personal exposure to it.

A further hindrance to developing a Biblical approach to life is the superficial teaching of certain church groups. Their slogans have replaced sound doctrine. Their catchy clichés have become commonplace: "Name it and claim it" (as if God is somehow obligated to give us whatever we ask); "If you don't use it, you lose it" (which places a person on a guilt trip if he or she is not actively using his or her spiritual gifts in the church seven nights a week); "Tough times don't last, but tough people do" (which is supposed to encourage those facing the constant onslaught of adversity).

Preachers who have used these trite statements have led countless people astray with their half-truths. Such would-be exponents of God's Word have also placed an emphasis on religious externalism with the result that many people today have developed the tendency to look only at outward temporal realities. This tendency

may be seen in the quest for satisfaction in life and freedom from
its trials. A religion of the senses prevails. Now, "if it feels good,
do it."

But what happens to those whose experiences fail to measure up
to the expectations of "the good life" they have been promised? Perhaps the most unkind thing that could be said to them is, "Your faith
is too small," or after they have prayed earnestly about a matter, "If
you regard iniquity in your heart, the Lord will not hear you."

Scripture is often used to back up these words of advice but when
the Biblical texts are examined in light of their context, they do not
support the teaching being given. A little knowledge then becomes a
dangerous thing. It can be the means of intensifying the pain from
which others suffer.

Consider for example the case of Janice. Her situation may be
unique, but her feelings of hurt, frustration, and bewilderment are
not. One of her friends had recommended that she come to see me
for counseling. In her mid-forties, Janice was neatly dressed though
her dark blue suit and pink blouse were faded. They had seen better
days. Her blonde hair was streaked with gray and gave no signs of
professional care. Her face showed lines of pain and sadness. She
was prematurely old.

As Janice sat down it was easy to see that she was very upset. As
I opened the conversation her lips began to quiver and tears welled
up in her eyes. I pushed forward a box of tissues and reassured her
that I was not embarrassed by her tears. When she had gained her
composure, I encouraged her to share with me the source of her
hurt. Janice's sentences were interspersed with sobs. It was evident
that she had carried a very heavy burden for a long time. She began
by blaming herself for her condition.

"I find myself living a yo-yo existence. I want to live for the Lord
but my emotions get in the way. My friends at church have told me
that my suffering is the result of my sins. Honestly, Dr. Barber, I've
searched my heart and I do not know of anything in my life that would
cause God to punish me like this."

Sensing that her well-meaning friends might fall into the same category as Job's comforters, I said, "Why don't you tell me what's trou-
bling you, and I'll make up my own mind."

"I've trusted completely in God's sovereignty ever since I received
Christ as my Savior twenty-plus years ago. When my husband and I
were first married, we established a Christian home. Our children
were dedicated to the Lord at birth, and we were a happy family. We
were diligent in our church attendance. Our sons and daughters all
went through the AWANA program and everything else the church

had to offer. My husband is a God-fearing man and worked long and hard to provide for us.

"About twelve years ago our world began to fall apart. First one tragedy and then another struck our home. Our younger son, barely in his teens, was drowned. A year later, almost to the day, one of our twin daughters was struck down by a car and killed. All of this so affected our older son that he tried to overdose on drugs. My husband, who was a deacon in the church, had a stroke that has left him paralyzed on one side of his body. Because he was in construction and this was not a job-related injury, his boss eventually had to lay him off. He's been unemployed ever since. And I, who had never worked a day outside of our home and had no marketable skills, had to get a job. My remaining daughter blamed God for the deaths of her brother and sister and the condition of her father. She turned her back on the Lord and began keeping company with the kind of young people of whom we did not approve. In the course of time she became pregnant. To the trials we already faced was then added the smell of diapers and the chore of late-night feedings.

"I've prayed and prayed for God's help, but nothing seems to change. Our lives have become a continuous struggle to survive from one paycheck to the next. I no longer have leisure time for the Bible study I once enjoyed. I used to be so happy. Now I'm almost always depressed. I feel as if I have failed the Lord…[then in a barely audible whisper she added] and I feel as if He's forsaken me."

Janice and I talked for over an hour. Throughout our discussion her genuine commitment to Christ shone through her tears. Finally when she had taken the last Kleenex from the box on my desk she said half jokingly, "Well, I've used up all your tissues. I suppose it's time for me to go." I arranged to see her again in a few days.

After Janice left I sat at my desk while my mind replayed the events of the last ninety minutes. I was stunned by the extent and severity of her suffering. She had been comforted, however, as we had taken one Bible character after another and drawn encouragement from the way God had used adversity to further His purpose in them.

In the two years that followed, Janice regained much of her former optimism and while her outward circumstances changed little, she was again happy in her trust in the Lord. As her feeling of depression lifted, she was surprised how many people came to her for comfort and encouragement. Instead of feeling forsaken by God, she found that He had given her a unique ministry among the hurting people in her area. Only as we learn the true purpose behind suffering can we really come to understand the importance of a strong godward relationship.

GOD'S SOVEREIGNTY
IN HIS CHOICE OF A SPECIAL COUPLE (1:1-2)

It is comforting to know that when God appears to deal harshly with us, His lovingkindness ultimately intends our suffering to work out for our good. In our study of 1 Samuel we find that Elkanah's problems and Hannah's desires became the means whereby the Lord furthered His purpose for them.

A Certain Man

The Biblical text is revealing. It begins abruptly with "Now there was a certain man...." As we read further we find that his name was Elkanah. He was not numbered among the mighty or the noble in Ephraim, but he was significant to the Lord.

When we compare the way in which Elkanah is introduced to us with what happens in the rest of the book, we realize that when God determines to do some mighty work, He often begins with an insignificant person. This was true of Moses, whose parents initially are not even named in the account of the exodus (Exodus 2:1). It was true of Caleb, whose father was a proselyte who had joined the tribe of Judah. It was true of David, who as the youngest of Jesse's children was not thought to be of sufficient importance to appear before Samuel. It was true of Elijah, whose only background was as a herdsman from the rocky hills of Gilead. It was true of Amos, whose sole claim to fame was that he was a picker of figs from Tekoa. And it was true of the Lord Jesus Christ, who was born to a peasant woman whose husband was a poor carpenter.

A great man like Samuel can be raised up from an obscure background. The simple faith of godly parents can be the means of laying a foundation that will ultimately redound to God's glory in the life of their child.

Elkanah was a Levite (1 Chronicles 6:26-27,34-35) from Ramathaim-zophim, a village in the hill country of Ephraim.[1] His genealogy is impressive,[2] for his ancestor Zuph was a descendant of Kohath, whose sons were responsible for taking care of the ark and the furnishings of the tabernacle (Numbers 3:31). At the time of our story, however, Elkanah does not appear to be carrying out any Levitical duties. It is possible that with the sanctuary being located in Shiloh[3] and with relatively few among Israel attending the regular feasts, Eli's sons found it unnecessary to have a rotation of Levites performing their traditional functions. Elkanah therefore may have found himself deprived of his God-appointed service as well as the legitimate income that would have come from such a ministry.

This deprivation might have made a man of lesser character and commitment to the Lord bitter and resentful. Elkanah, however, does not appear to have allowed outward circumstances or the conduct of others to control his Godward relationship. He persevered in doing what was right. In addition to attending the three mandatory feasts when all males were obliged to appear before the Lord (Exodus 23:15-17; 34:18-24; Deuteronomy 16:16) he and his family also went to Shiloh for another feast at a set time each year.[4] These feasts were intended by God to be joyous times (Nehemiah 8:9-11) for He is honored when His people are happy.

The special object of Elkanah's worship is said to be *Yahweh Sĕbā'ôt,* "the Lord of hosts."[5] This name for God appears here in Scripture for the first time. How this facet of God's character was revealed to Elkanah is not told us. We do know that he lived during a time of national apostasy when the godly in the land were few. Elkanah's faith is seen to be in the supreme Creator, the Almighty, the One who has the power to bring things in Heaven and on earth under the rule of His Anointed. And Hannah, who shared her husband's faith, likewise trusted in His sovereignty. Later on in our story she will compose a song of praise in which she will declare:

> Those who contend with Yahweh will be shattered;
> Against them He will thunder in the heavens,
> Yahweh will judge the ends of the earth;
> And He will give strength to His king,
> And will exalt the horn of His anointed.
>
> (1 Samuel 2:10)

A Certain Woman

Hannah was a very special woman. Her piety is notable. But perhaps on account of her infertility, Elkanah had found it necessary to take a second wife.[6] In any event, Hannah had suffered a great deal because of her inability to bear children. She had never known the joy of telling her husband that they were participating with God in the creation of a new life; she had only known the increasing bitterness of disappointment as each month witnessed her inability to conceive. And who can begin to tabulate the grief she experienced as she went to the market and saw other young women, increasingly younger than herself, giving evidence of their own maternity?

Dr. William G. Blaikie observed that "the trial which Hannah had to bear was particularly heavy...to a Hebrew woman. To have no child was not only a disappointment, but seemed to mark one out as dishonored by God."[7] Barren women were looked on as having broken His covenant and as a result He was withholding His blessing from them (Deuteronomy 7:14). Such sufferers had to endure the whispers of other women behind their backs and deal daily with unfulfilled maternal instincts. When Hannah saw children laughing and playing, or crying and being comforted by their mothers, her heart must have longed for offspring of her own to whom she could show similar love and attention.

To add insult to injury, Peninnah, Elkanah's second wife, had no difficulty conceiving...again and again and again. Though blessed with sons and daughters, she nevertheless intensified Hannah's suffering with her taunts and innuendoes. It is a mark of Elkanah's wisdom and discretion that he provided separate homes for his wives;[8] otherwise Peninnah's mockery, scoffing, and derision would have destroyed all family unity.

Hannah's gracious godliness stands in marked contrast to Peninnah's carping criticisms. Hannah had all the qualities of a good mother; Peninnah had none.

OUTLINE

In this "certain man" and his special wife we see God's sovereign selection of a couple to bear a son. Through the child they scarcely dared dream would be theirs, the Lord would advance His purpose for His people. Their suffering was not a result of God's disfavor. The trials they endured were designed to better fit them for the task of preparing one of Israel's great leaders for his life's work. In the experiences of Hannah and Elkanah we can see

- God's Sovereignty in His Choice of Means (1 Samuel 1:3-18)
- God's Sovereignty in Answering Prayer (1 Samuel 1:19-28)
- God's Sovereignty in the Praise Given Him (1 Samuel 2:1-11)

GOD'S SOVEREIGNTY IN HIS CHOICE OF MEANS (1:3-18)

A Godly Example (1:3)

It should not surprise us that those who most wish to honor the Lord and serve Him find innumerable obstacles in their paths. These obstacles may come from either external or internal sources—or both as in the case of Elkanah. As we have already seen, Elkanah had been deprived of his livelihood as a Levite, and within his family he was faced with problems beyond his ability either to explain (Hannah's barrenness) or control (Peninnah's malice).

Elkanah's devotion to the Lord, however, was not dependent on priests who were pleasing to him or a family situation that made visits to Shiloh enjoyable. He was internally motivated and his conduct was regulated by his knowledge of God's Word. He did what he believed was right according to God's revealed will. He overcame any discouragement he may have felt because he was committed to serving the Lord, not pleasing man. And he readily involved his family in his activities and in this way set his children an appropriate example.

An Unjust Provocation (1:4-8)

When Elkanah took his family to Shiloh to offer his thank offerings and peace offerings (Leviticus 2:1–3:17) he had to contend not only with the wickedness of the priests, Hophni and Phinehas,[9] but also with the unwarranted bickering and uncalled-for taunts of Peninnah. Jealous of Hannah, Peninnah doubtless felt that inasmuch as she had borne Elkanah children, she should replace Hannah as his principal wife.[10] Her sadism inflicted deep emotional wounds, and Hannah was at a loss to know why God was seemingly angry with her. Furthermore Peninnah appeared to be satisfied only when her rival was reduced to tears.

It is common for preachers to indict Elkanah for not reproving Peninnah. As a righteous man he had probably tried many times to reason with her. Sociopathic personalities such as Peninnah, however, are beyond reason. They are ill-natured, malicious, and vindictive. They delight in vicious, spiteful, and sarcastic attacks on those who have incurred their ire. They are masters of the art of accusation and denunciation. If they hear any tiny piece of gossip, they twist it, enlarge upon it, and accommodate it to their evil purposes (Psalm 37:12). When sufficiently aroused, such individuals are without mercy and beyond feeling. Their speech is acrimonious and they are resentful of all that appears to stand between them and their goals.[11]

Instead of allowing the negative traits of his malcontented wife to control his emotions, Elkanah sought to accent the positive and provide Hannah with appropriate reassurance of his love for her. However, on a particular visit to Shiloh Peninnah's vitriolic accusations reached a climax on the day when Elkanah was to offer his sacrifice.

Her vindictiveness could not have been more poorly timed. When Elkanah returned to his family and in accordance with custom gave portions of his sacrifice to each member, Peninnah and her children received an ample share. But a double portion[12] was given to Hannah. It was Elkanah's way of showing her that she was special—her rival would in no way replace her in his affections, no matter how many children she bore.

Of comfort to all who suffer is the fact that twice in these verses Hannah's childlessness is said to be the result of a direct act of the Lord (1 Samuel 1:5-6). Her condition was not a result of unconfessed sin in her life. Why the Lord chose for a time to act in contradiction to His covenant is not revealed. Hannah however was unaware of the reason her maternal desires remained unfulfilled, and so she was vulnerable to Peninnah's attacks. Most women Hannah's age had sons and daughters who would soon be getting married.

Feeling humiliated and hurt, Hannah declined to eat what Elkanah gave her. Sensing what had happened while he was away, Elkanah tried to encourage his distraught wife. He said to her in effect, "Isn't my love for you worth more than if you had ten sons?"

It is a testimony to Hannah's maturity that she did not allow her hurts to mar her relationship with Elkanah. She showed her appreciation of his love by eating the food he gave her. The text explicitly states it was *"after* eating and drinking" (italics added) that she went to the temple to pray. By her actions she preserved the unity of their relationship while also drawing strength and encouragement from her husband's love for her. As much as Hannah desired to have a child of her own, she realized that children are temporary and marriage is permanent.[13]

But what are we to make of Peninnah? All that is revealed of her is negative. She is graceless and tactless and devoid of those sensibilities that would commend her to others. The only good thing that came of her unrestrained animosity is that she drove Hannah to her knees.

A Model Prayer (1:9-18)

As Hannah made her way hurriedly to the small, low, stone building that housed the ark of the covenant and the tabernacle furniture, Eli the high priest was sitting at the doorpost[14] of the nave of the sanctuary. The rough simplicity of the building highlighted the quality of her faith. In this place, however it may have appeared on the outside, she would worship Yahweh and lay her petition before Him.

Hannah's prayer is significant because reference to it is made six times in this chapter (1 Samuel 1:10,12,13,16,26,27). In bitterness of soul she poured out her heart to the Lord. She pleaded with Him to remember her and give her a son. Her prayer, in which we can see the essence of real intercession, can be divided into five parts:

- *Submission to the will of God.* This submission is inherent in Hannah's repeated use of the word *maidservant* (1 Samuel 1:11). In her prayer there was an absence of all reliance on any merit of her own. Instead there was the kind of humility that honors God. Her submission to the will of God is reminiscent of the attitude of Christ (Matthew 26:39,42).

- *Identification with the purpose of God.* Hannah's use of the name *Yahweh,* "the LORD," shows that she placed herself under the provisions of the covenant He had made with His people. In effect she implored Him to act in accordance with His name (that is, His nature; John 14:13-14).

- *Fervency in pleading with God.* Hannah's prayer came from her heart. She poured out her soul to the Lord (1 Samuel 1:10; James 5:17-18). Like Jacob, her attitude implied, "I will not let You go unless You bless me" (Genesis 32:26).

- *Specificity in her request of God.* Hannah knew exactly what she wanted. She asked Yahweh for a son (literally, a seed of man). So many of our prayers are futile because they are nebulous and aimless. Hers had purpose. She knew what she wanted.

- *Perseverance in waiting upon God.* Hannah also "continued to pray before Yahweh" (1 Samuel 1:12). She prayed long before the Lord. She was not heard for her many words, but for the intensity of her resolve. In the mystery of God's sovereignty, He tests our resolve. Hers passed the test.[15]

Hannah's vow needs only passing comment.[16] So intensely did she desire a son that she promised to give him back to the Lord all the days of his life. He would be separated to God as were those who had taken upon themselves the obligations of a Nazarite (Numbers 6:5)[17] but with one exception: his dedication to the service of "Yahweh of hosts" would be lifelong. Such a vow of course would have to be ratified by Elkanah (Numbers 30:3-8).

It is interesting for us to note the way in which Hannah received unexpected confirmation that the Lord had heard her prayer. The confirmation came from the aged priest Eli. He was in his mid-seventies and his heart had grown heavy with the sins of the people. As he watched Hannah he presumed that because she did not utter audible sounds she must be drunk (1 Samuel 1:12-14). He reproved her and was himself reproved—though in an entirely different way. Hannah respectfully and quietly denied his accusation:

> No, my lord, I [am] a woman pained in spirit.... Do not conclude that [literally, put] your maidservant is [literally, for] a daughter of Belial [that is, wickedness], for from the abundance of my complaint and my provocation I have been speaking until now (1:15-16).

Eli recognized his error. He was also touched by her courtesy and moved by her sincerity. Without knowing for what she had been praying, and with befitting magnanimity, he said:

> Go in peace; and may Elohim of Israel give you your petition which you have asked of Him (1:17).[18]

By faith[19] Hannah received Eli's words as from the Lord Himself. She returned to the others. "And her face was no longer [sad]" (1:18). She had the assurance within her heart that the Lord had heard her prayer. The next day the whole family worshiped before the Lord and then returned home.

GOD'S SOVEREIGNTY IN ANSWERING PRAYER (1:19-28)

A Test of Faith (1:19-20)

"And Elkanah knew Hannah his wife, and Yahweh remembered her...and she conceived[20] ...and bore a son" (1:19-20). In actual fact, Hannah's faith was still to be refined. The response of God to her prayers did not come immediately. Two full months passed during which time her confidence in the lovingkindness of the Lord was tested. Only in the third month did she conceive. And shortly before the next annual visit to Shiloh[21] Samuel was born.[22]

A Vow Performed (1:21-28)

Elkanah's oneness with his wife in their desire for a son may be seen in the fact that he too entered into a vow. After Samuel was born, in thankfulness to the Lord for having rolled away the reproach of his wife Elkanah went to Shiloh to appear before the Lord (1:21). There he probably offered a special thanksgiving offering (Leviticus 7:12-15; 22:29).

Hannah however chose to remain behind. She determined to nurse[23] Samuel until he was three years old. Then she would take him to the temple and leave him there. His first visit to Shiloh, therefore, would be a memorable one.

Dorothy Zeligs in *Psychoanalysis and the Bible*[24] stated her belief that Samuel's separation from his parents when he was left at Shiloh could only have been construed as abandonment. She concluded that this had the usual shattering effects on his personality and stifled his emotional development. This view is entirely false.

During the three years Hannah nursed her son she instilled in him a unique realization of his *belonging*. He felt secure in his relationship with his parents as well as in his growing understanding of his godward relationship. He knew he was loved. He knew he was a special child. As Hannah and Elkanah spent time with him, he developed an inner sense of his *worth*. He was able to grow in those essential characteristics of personal esteem that would later enable him to withstand the vicissitudes of life. Through what his parents told him he was given a sense of *purpose*. It is no wonder therefore that when he went up to the temple for the first time he possessed a reverential awe of the One whom his parents honored.

In our homes we need to begin early to give our sons and daughters a feeling of *security* by demonstrating to them our unconditional love and acceptance. We need not be passive or indulgent toward our children.[25] Instead we will enhance their inner sense of well-being as we set appropriate standards for and just limitations on their behavior.

We also need to instill in our children a realization that as far as we are concerned they are *special*. They have intrinsic worth. This realization will help to develop the kind of confidence that will give stability to their lives and facilitate their growth toward maturity.

And finally we need to show our sons and daughters how to persevere so that they will be *successful*. We need to give them small tasks and reward their accomplishments with suitable praise and affection. Then in keeping with their growth we should assign tasks that are progressively more difficult. Ultimately our children will be able to take on difficult responsibilities without depending on others for approval.

This kind of parenting can only take place as we are prepared to be continuously involved in the lives of our children; to model before them our beliefs, values, and goals; and to instruct them in accordance with their individual "bents."[26] To the degree that our examples are sincere, consistent, and authentic we can trust God to mold the lives of our children as He did Samuel's.

When Samuel was three, Hannah went up to the temple with Elkanah, Peninnah, and her children. They took Samuel with them. The Biblical record is silent about anything Peninnah may either have said or done. The Lord had stopped her mouth.

On arriving at Shiloh, Elkanah and Hannah sacrificed a three-year-old bull.[27] The bull was a valuable animal and had probably been born at roughly the same time as Samuel. From the very first it had been set aside as the one that would be offered (perhaps as a whole burnt offering symbolizing Samuel's entire dedication) to the Lord. Their sacrifice was accompanied by other tokens of their gratitude: an ephah of flour and a skin full of wine. Dr. Joseph Hall commented that these sacrifices were "more in number and measure than the law of God required of [Hannah, but] too little for her God that had so mercifully remembered her affliction, and miraculously remedied it."[28]

The sacrifice over, Elkanah and Hannah brought Samuel to Eli. Neither Elkanah nor Hannah gave any thought to redeeming and keeping Samuel for themselves (Exodus 34:20; Numbers 18:16). If they had decided not to go through with their vow, Eli would not have known for he had only seen Hannah's lips moving and had not heard the promise of her heart. To Hannah, however, the highest calling of which she could conceive involved giving her dearest possession to the Lord. With such devotion on the part of his parents, it is no wonder that Samuel worshiped the Lord there (1 Samuel 1:28).[29]

We make a great mistake if we conclude that from this time onward Samuel was bereft of maternal affection. Jephthah's daughter[30] was serving at the sanctuary and she, together with other women (Exodus 38:8), may well have attended to Samuel's bodily needs and domestic training. Furthermore, as William J. Deane observed, Eli, who must have taught Samuel the law and the history of God's people, would also have taken better care of Samuel than his own sons and would have attended more scrupulously to his training.[31]

GOD'S SOVEREIGNTY IN THE PRAISE GIVEN HIM (2:1-11)

Where and when Hannah gave expression to her psalm of thanksgiving to the Lord is not told us. It may well have been formulating in her heart during her pregnancy and uttered soon after the birth of her son.[32] She attributed her good fortune solely to the Lord her God.

Her psalm gives evidence of sustained spontaneity and unity of purpose. The song can be divided into three segments: (1) the holiness of God, 1 Samuel 2:1-3; (2) the uniqueness or incomparability of God, 2:4-8; and (3) the trustworthiness of God, 2:9-10.[33] Verse 11 forms a postscript.

Segment one reveals that Hannah derived her joy from who God is. His nature is such that she could exult in His holiness, lovingkindness, strength (He is her "rock"), knowledge, and justice. Her critics had been silenced. Their arrogance had been reproved. The Lord, who keeps covenant with His people, had vindicated her.

In segment two Hannah saw the things on which evil people rely rendered ineffective and useless. The haughty, the self-sufficient, and the powerful are made impotent before the Lord. He alone is sovereign. There is none like Him.

Finally in segment three Hannah praised God for His trustworthiness. He is righteous and just. He guides and protects those who acknowledge His right to rule over them. All others face the inevitability of His wrath. Although no king ruled in Israel as yet, Hannah saw with prophetic insight the inauguration of the monarchy and may even have caught a glimpse of the reign of Christ as the Lord's Anointed.

Dr. Blaikie summarized the implications of Hannah's song:

> What is the great lesson of this song? That for the answer of prayer, for deliverance from trial, for the fulfillment of hopes, for the glorious things yet spoken of the city of our God, our most cordial thanks are due to Him alone.[34]

The passage concludes with Elkanah and his family returning to Ramah while Samuel remained in Shiloh. He now had the responsibility of "ministering to Yahweh before Eli the priest" (1 Samuel 2:11). "And the child Samuel went on [grew] in both stature and favor, both with Yahweh and also with men" (1 Samuel 2:26; cf. Luke 2:52).

POINTS TO PONDER

Among the Faithful

As we consider the timely lessons that lie latent in these chapters, we notice first of all God's choice of "a certain man" (1 Samuel 1:1). Whenever God begins to do a significant work through an individual, He usually begins with that person's parents. It was so in the case of Samuel. In spite of widespread apostasy, Elkanah had retained his integrity. He may have been insignificant as far as the leaders of

Ephraim were concerned, but he was known to the Lord (1 Corinthians 1:26-31). In the same way that Bethany was significant because it was the "town of Mary and Martha" (John 11:1), so Ramah is immortalized because it was the residence of Elkanah.

We can take comfort from the fact that Elkanah was known to the Lord. We live in a world of depersonalization. To an employer a man is a budgetary item, to the IRS a number, to the census bureau a statistic, and to the neighbors a person who mows the lawn on Saturday morning. But the Lord knows each of us by name. He is intimately acquainted with our lives (Psalm 139). He knows our secret sorrows and our disappointed hopes. And while He may seem remote from the place where we live or the environment in which we work, He is nevertheless cognizant of all that goes on in our lives.

It is important for us to realize that even though Elkanah could not understand why God's covenant promises were not being fulfilled, he still believed in the faithfulness of *Yahweh Sĕbā'ôt*. As a result he is a constant inspiration to those of us who find ourselves in similar situations.

Hopeless Nights, Dreamless Days

A second lesson in this passage is that God sometimes withholds His blessings from those who walk uprightly, but only for a time (Psalm 28). We cannot explain why but it appears that it was God's will for Hannah to be barren. Twice we are told that "Yahweh had closed her womb." She had probably prayed many times for a son. As the years passed she may have questioned why her prayers were not answered. Her earnest request "O Yahweh of hosts...remember me" (1 Samuel 1:11) was answered by "And Yahweh remembered Hannah" and she conceived (1:19-20).

Hannah's experience proves beyond question that the Lord is intimately acquainted with the things that concern us. He hears our prayers. While we cannot properly understand His providence, Hannah's example inspires us with confidence. Her prayer to the Lord was to reverse the condition of her body and in answer to her entreaty He gave her the desire of her heart (Psalms 20:4; 37:4). We are to persevere in our prayers and remember to thank Him when the desired answer is given (1 Samuel 2:1-10).

Peninnah's constant berating of Hannah could have led her to become angry. She could easily have lashed out at her tormentor but Hannah did not give way to this very human emotion. Sometimes we lash out at others, or when our trials are not resolved we are tempted to direct our pent-up emotions against the Lord. In the final analysis anger is very destructive. Hannah did not become angry because she trusted completely in God's sovereignty.

The Happy Result

The third lesson concerns vows. Though Hannah was supremely happy over the birth of her son, at no time did she go back on her vow. When the time came she gladly dedicated him to the service of the Lord. And Samuel, who had developed a strong Godward relationship at his mother's knees, became one of the great men of Israel (Psalm 99:6; Jeremiah 15:1).

The Bible has a lot to say about our vows.[35] When we are sincere in our desires we are encouraged to make vows to the Lord (Psalm 76:11). Vows, however, should not be entered into by those who are immature and do not have the means to carry out the intents of their hearts. Hannah was mature. She was also sincere. She did not make a shallow or hypocritical promise (Matthew 5:33) and then seek for a way out. What she vowed, she performed (1 Samuel 1:27-28; Ecclesiastes 5:4-5).

Hannah kept her vow and offered praise. Her praise underscores the New Testament teaching of thanksgiving (2 Corinthians 9:12; Philippians 4:6; Colossians 4:2; 1 Timothy 2:1). God is honored when we thank Him for His beneficence toward us. He is a God of knowledge. He knows the thoughts and intents of our hearts. By Him actions are weighed. He raises up the poor from the dust, and lifts up the needy from the ash heap. He establishes the way of those who honor Him, and silences the wicked in darkness.

Hannah and Elkanah were thankful for God's sovereign ways, but they did not neglect their human responsibility. A sensitive reading of the text shows that they gave to Samuel an awareness of the fact that he was unconditionally loved, a deeply ingrained sense of his uniqueness, and a knowledge of his destiny as one dedicated to the Lord.

A Christian couple whom I have known for a quarter of a century also took their responsibility as parents seriously. Having grown up during the depression era, their finances were limited as they married and began their family, but they did not allow their economic status to hamper them. One day they were reminiscing with me on the way in which they had reared their five children:

"We determined that whatever we did with our children, we would make it fun. We made sure that none of them felt left out. As each of our children grew through the various stages, they developed different interests. We never missed any of the plays or track meets they participated in. We preserved unity in our home, however, by being regular in our attendance at church and encouraging our children to participate in the young people's programs.

"Of course there were times when schedules conflicted. When this happened one of us would go to one event and the other to the other event. During the most active period of their teen years we seemed to be always on the go. Now that all of our children are grown and married and have children of their own, it is a comfort to see how the values which we modeled for them are being reproduced in their own homes."

What then is the reward of righteousness? Being blessed with children and seeing them follow the Lord (Psalm 127:3-5; Proverbs 20:7); receiving answers to prayer in fulfillment of God's Word (Psalm 66:19-20; Proverbs 15:8,29); and seeing God vindicate us so that our commitments, values, and goals are shown in the end to be the ones that honor Him (Psalms 7:8; 26:1; 119:74-76).

A STUDY IN CONTRASTS

1 Samuel 2:12–4:1a

What influence do parents have upon their children?

Some years ago a study was undertaken in which two families were compared with one another. The first was the family of Jonathan Edwards and the second was that of Max Juke.[1]

Among the more than four hundred descendants of Jonathan and Sarah Edwards were fourteen college presidents, more than one hundred college professors, almost an equal number of lawyers, thirty judges, sixty physicians, at least sixty authors, and more than one hundred clergymen, missionaries, and theology professors. When this study was first published, there was scarcely any great American industry that had not at one time or another had a member of Jonathan Edwards' family among its chief promoters.

By way of contrast, the family of Max Juke was said to have cost the state of New York millions of dollars. Murderers, rapists, prostitutes, paupers, and several suicides made up his two hundred eighty progeny. Sixty were habitual thieves, fifty-five died of social diseases, and only twenty learned a trade (and ten of them learned their skills in a penitentiary). In all of American history no family rivals that of Max Juke for profligacy and corruption.

This assessment of the effect of godly piety (or the lack of it) is of particular significance as we compare the children of Hannah and Elkanah with the children of Eli in our study of 1 Samuel 2:12–4:1a. The passage is important to all of us who are parents.

OUTLINE

This section of God's inspired record may be divided into five parts:

- When Religious Externalism Gives Way to Selfishness
  (1 Samuel 2:12-18)
- When Internal Godliness Is Rewarded
  (1 Samuel 2:19-21)
- When Parental Reproof Is Insufficient
  (1 Samuel 2:22-26)
- When Divine Chastening Becomes Necessary
  (1 Samuel 2:27– 3:1a)
- When the Old Order Gives Way to the New
  (1 Samuel 3:1b– 4:1a)

PREVIEW

We have in these verses a study in contrasts. The dividing line between righteousness and unrighteousness is clearly and forcefully drawn. We see how God honors those who honor Him and sets aside those who despise Him. Eli's sons are said to have failed in their service of the Lord (1 Samuel 2:12,17) whereas Samuel is described as ministering acceptably before Him (2:18,21). We read that Hannah, who never asked God for other children, was rewarded with three sons and two daughters (2:20-21) while Eli was told that his sons would be taken from him (2:34). Eli is portrayed as very old and no longer able to give proper leadership to God's people (2:22) while Samuel is presented as young and "growing in stature and in favor with Yahweh and with men" (2:26).

God had not revealed Himself through Hophni and Phinehas (1 Samuel 3:1b) but He began to make His will known through Samuel (3:19–4:1a). God reminded Eli that although He had sovereignly chosen the house of Aaron to be His priests while the people of Israel were still in Egypt, on account of the sins of Eli's sons his descendants would be set aside. In their place the Lord would raise up a faithful priest who would walk before His anointed always (2:30-31,35).

There is something very touching about the godliness of Samuel's parents and their influence on him. Here are a few specifics from 1 Samuel:

- Hannah resolved, "After the boy is weaned, then I will take him [to the temple], and he will live there forever" (1:22).
- And [Samuel] worshiped Yahweh there (1:28).
- And the boy ministered[2] before Yahweh under the watchful eye [literally, before the face] of Eli (2:11).
- And [Hannah] would make [Samuel] a little robe and bring it to

him from year to year when she would come up with her
husband to offer the yearly sacrifice (2:19).
* And Samuel grew and Yahweh was with him, and he let none of
His words fall (3:19).

Samuel was blessed with godly influences, but how were his physical and emotional needs met? William Deane wisely observed that
not all those officiating at the temple were men and women of lax
habits and doubtful piety. Quoting Philo, Deane said, "[The Hebrews
in general] looked on their laws as oracles inspired by God, and instructed in them from early childhood, carry the image of the com-
mandments in their very souls."[3] We can presume therefore that there
were some devout people at Shiloh who revered the Lord and honored
His name. They would have cared for Samuel until he was old enough
to care for himself.

The process of socialization, however, is complex. To what extent
did Samuel have contact with other boys and girls? Two features set
Samuel apart from other youths being reared in or near the temple
precincts: (1) he wore an ephod[4] and (2) his hair was longer than
theirs. While he must have freely mixed with them, it is doubtful that
he was ever fully accepted by them.

However as Samuel matured, his peers began to look up to him
and respect him for "all Israel from Dan [in the north] to Beersheba
[in the south] recognized that Samuel was attested as a prophet of
Yahweh" (1 Samuel 3:20). Dr. F. B. Meyer summarized Samuel's life:

> His life seems to have been one unbroken record of blameless
> purity, integrity, and righteousness. One purpose ran through
> all his years, threading them together in an unbroken series.
> There were no gaps nor breaks; no lapses into sensuality or
> selfishness; no lawless deeds in that wild, lawless age. Towards
> the end of his long life he was able to appeal to the verdict of
> the people in memorable words which attested his conscious-
> ness of unsullied rectitude (12:2b-4).[5]

Let us consider some of the circumstances Samuel faced during
his formative years.

WHEN RELIGIOUS EXTERNALISM GIVES WAY TO SELFISHNESS (2:12-18)

While Samuel was still young, a scandal rocked the community of
Shiloh. The scandal concerned the conduct of Eli's sons. They were

worthless[6] men and had no regard for the Lord. Their concern was for themselves, not the One whose services they performed. They were preoccupied with exploiting their position, not with serving the God in whom they were supposed to trust (1 Samuel 2:12-13). Their chief sin was not (as some preachers have maintained) that they had incorporated certain sensuous heathen practices into the religion of Israel, but that they did not know[7] the Lord (2:12) and handled holy things with unholy hands.

In this scandal there is a solemn warning for all of us. Because our megachurches, radio ministries, and TV empires require ever-increasing budgets to maintain themselves, and correspondingly large salaries are either expected or demanded by those who keep such "ministries" going, modern preachers face the same kind of threats to their spirituality as Hophni and Phinehas faced. It is easy for preachers to lose sight of the spiritual side of true worship and in its place emphasize the aspects that maintain their popularity, draw large crowds, or result in sizable offerings. It is easy to give attention to externals—aesthetics, organ music, choral anthems, set rituals—and develop a following that likes to be entertained rather than edified.

When externals are emphasized, there is a corresponding diminution of true worship "in spirit and in truth" (John 4:23-24) and of that growth "in grace and knowledge" which is essential if one's Christian life is to retain its dynamic quality (2 Peter 3:18). And when there is a lack of true worship, those who sit in the pew or participate vicariously from the comfort of their living rooms find it increasingly easy to be caught up in what appeals to the senses. In time personal zeal eventually gives way to spiritual inertia and the same kind of lassitude creeps over the soul as was experienced by the Israelites during the era of Eli and his sons.

First Samuel 2:13-17 supports and illustrates the claim that Hophni and Phinehas were greedy, dishonest, and profane. They put themselves in first place. They took their allotted portion of the sacrifice before the Lord had been given His.

According to the law of Moses a part of the sacrificial offering was to be given to the priests in lieu of remuneration. The remainder of the animal was returned to the offerer to be consumed by him and his family. The portion of the peace offering for the priests was strictly defined (Leviticus 7:29-34; cf. 1 Corinthians 9:13-14). It was the breast, or brisket, and the right shoulder. These were solemnly dedicated to the Lord by the offerer—the breast being "waved" (moved from side to side in the presence of the Lord) and the shoulder being "heaved" (lifted up once before the Lord)—and then given to the priests. Earlier the blood (symbolic of life) would have been poured on the north side of the altar, and the fat or suet (symbolic of a perfect and well-nourished body) would have been burned on the altar (Leviticus 3:17), typifying the dedication of the whole sacrifice to the Lord. No portion could be appropriated until these rites had been performed.[8]

The sons of Eli deliberately violated the law. They claimed more than their share and they demanded raw meat for roasting. They sent around their servant to poke a fleshhook (a large three-pronged fork) into the meat that worshippers were broiling to eat with their families. If any objected, the servant took what the priest wanted by force. It is no wonder that the sons of Eli aroused the indignation of God's people so that the people "abhorred the offering of the Lord."[9]

Dr. W. G. Blaikie drew the thoughts of 1 Samuel 2:13-17 together when he pointed out that in the case of Hophni and Phinehas the salt had lost its savor. It mattered nothing to them what regulations God had made. They sought only to please themselves. In the process they robbed God of His honor and those who came to worship Him of the benefits of their obedience. It appeared as if these priests could sin with impunity and when their sins against the Lord went unpunished, they threw off all moral restraints as well.[10]

WHEN INTERNAL GODLINESS IS REWARDED (2:19-21)

The contrast between Eli's sons and Hannah's son could not have been more strikingly drawn. Eli's sons were obviously callous and indifferent, while Samuel is depicted as bright and serene, growing physically, mentally, emotionally, relationally, and spiritually. He was content to serve the Lord in the temple and wore an ephod over his full-length, seamless, and sleeveless coat. This garb indicated that he was looked on as a priest-in-training.

Though separated from his parents, Samuel knew he was loved. He was the object of his mother's tender care. The coats she made for him had to be woven from materials she herself had prepared. As she plied her busy spindle her thoughts were of him.

At the annual festival when for a short time they were together, Hannah and Elkanah renewed those strong early ties that had prepared Samuel for his life's work. Wondering how the influences of the evil priests affected Samuel, Hannah and Elkanah probably noticed how the trials brought on by the conduct of Eli's sons were helping to develop in Samuel important qualities of character. Although his parents had no means of determining how his growing steadfastness of purpose, forbearance, courage, unselfishness, and complete confidence in the Lord would be used, they knew that the

One to whom they had given their son would perfect His work in his heart (cf. Philippians 1:6). They also observed the growth of other faculties that would become evident later in his life: wise administration, a keen capacity for righteous judgment, impeccable integrity, blamelessness, and moral purity.[11]

In God's preparation of Samuel for his life's work we see how He sovereignly molds us, tempers our trials, and strengthens us as a result of the sufferings we endure. Far from being a platitude to encourage those on the brink of despair, the truth of Romans 8:28 is intended to cast a ray of light over all of life!

On one of their visits to Shiloh, Elkanah and Hannah spent a few minutes with Eli. As they parted, Eli said to Elkanah, "May Yahweh give you seed by this woman in the place of the one asked for, whom you asked of Yahweh" (1 Samuel 2:20). Since Eli was God's theocratic representative[12] to His people, his blessing carried with it divine approval. The godliness and integrity of Elkanah and Hannah were rewarded "for Yahweh was gracious to Hannah; and she conceived and she bore three sons and two daughters" (2:21).

"And Samuel [whom Hannah and Elkanah had given to the Lord] grew up before Yahweh." The conduct of their firstborn stood in marked contrast to the perfidy of Eli's sons.

WHEN PARENTAL REPROOF IS INSUFFICIENT (2:22-26)

The years passed. How many we do not know. Eli, now in his eighties, is described as "very old" (1 Samuel 2:22). The conduct of his sons had polluted the sanctuary. Their iniquity was reflected in the attitude of those who looked to them for guidance. Hophni and Phinehas introduced into the worship of the Lord the obscene vices of the heathen, and the entrance to the temple itself was desecrated with exhibitions of unbridled lust and sensuality.[13]

Two distinct religious elements now emerged in Israel. The lawless and the godless followed the example of Hophni and Phinehas. They emulated the "liberal" lifestyle of the younger priests. But there were some who still feared the Lord. They reproved Hophni and Phinehas for their unbiblical ways. Only when their remonstrance failed did they approach Eli himself.

Eli's sons had probably been born when he was in his fifties. Inasmuch as there is no mention of his wife, it is possible that she had died leaving him to rear the children while also discharging his duties as high priest. In trying to be both father and mother to Hophni and Phinehas, Eli may well have indulged and spoiled them. Children learn quickly how to get what they want from their parent(s), and Eli's later conduct gives evidence of the fact that for too long he had been too permissive.

Eli reproved his sons, but as their father, not as the high priest. He did not remove them from office. Instead he satisfied himself with a few words of warning:

> I hear of your wicked deeds from all the people. No, my sons; for it is not a good report that I hear spreading [among] the people of Yahweh (1 Samuel 2:22-24).

Eli took no steps to put a halt to the wickedness that had been brought to his notice[14] but contented himself with a quotation from an ancient proverb:

> If one man sin against another man, Elohim [God] may mediate for him; but if a man sin against Yahweh, who will intercede for him? (1 Samuel 2:25).

In the case of wrong between man and man, God as arbitrator may settle the dispute; but when a man sins against the Lord, what human power can interpose on his behalf? God can no longer act as an impartial moderator.[15]

Unfortunately Eli's remonstrance had no effect. It did not touch the consciences of his sons. His reproof was necessary, however, for they had become judicially blind and needed to be made aware of God's displeasure before judgment fell (1 Samuel 2:25).

Sin works its own punishment. When persistently followed, it hardens the heart, deadens the conscience, atrophies faith, and plunges the sinner to ever-increasing depths so that repentance (except by a miracle of God's grace) becomes impossible. These are the natural consequences of waywardness, but they are also in accordance with God's eternal law. Eli's sons had grown up in a degenerate age. Their present condition, however, was the result of the choices they had made. They had allowed the evil tendencies around them to influence their thinking, warp their characters, and produce conduct unbecoming to those in the ministry.[16]

From Eli's warning of God's judgment (1 Samuel 2:23-25) we pass to a brief statement of His mercy (2:26). Like the oscillation of a fan we pass from the rehearsal of the sins of Eli's sons to a consideration of Samuel. He was not yet a teenager (probably between six and eight years of age) and yet the course of his life was clearly marked out. He had set his heart to know the Word of the Lord and to do it; as a result he was growing in favor with God and man (cf. Luke 2:52).

WHEN DIVINE CHASTENING
BECOMES NECESSARY (2:27–3:1a)

The obstinacy of Eli's sons is again brought to our attention. How much time elapsed between the warning Eli gave Hophni and Phinehas and God's sentence of judgment cannot be determined with accuracy. We do know that the Lord sent an unnamed prophet, an *'îš 'Elōhîm,* "a man of God," to the aged priest. This prophet of the Lord sternly denounced Eli's weakness[17] and foretold the judgment of God that was to come upon him and his house (1 Samuel 2:27-36).

The primary fulfillment of this prophecy, however, was to be found in the life and ministry of Samuel, "a faithful priest" who would thoroughly discharge the office as God's representative to His people. As with other prophetic utterances that have both immediate and later fulfillments, so this prophecy may look beyond the era of Samuel and possibly include Him who as King of kings and Lord of lords will reign over the nations for ever and ever.

Samuel was of the family of Kohath, a son of Aaron, whose duties involved the service of the sanctuary, but precluded priestly functions. Samuel did not come from the line of Phinehas through Eleazar (Numbers 25:10-13) as did Eli and his sons. Samuel seems to have been designated a priest by divine appointment.[18] Inasmuch as he does not appear to have been included in the service of the sanctuary once it was moved from Shiloh to Nob, it is possible that after Eli's death the priests of the Aaronic line excluded Samuel from their company. If so, then the words of the man of God to Eli look to a yet future time when the righteous dead will be resurrected and the full intent of 1 Samuel 2:35 will be fulfilled.[19]

The prophet foretold that while Eli's descendants would continue to minister, none would reach old age (1 Samuel 2:30-34). The high priesthood would be given to another family (also descended from Aaron, but through Ithamar). This prophecy was probably fulfilled when Abiathar was deposed (1 Kings 2:27,35) and Zadok replaced him (1 Chronicles 12:26-28). And so that Eli might know the veracity of this sentence, he was given a sign: both of his sons would die on the same day.

In reflecting on 1 Samuel 2:27–3:1a, we should not overlook God's method of dealing with those whom He must chasten. He gave Eli the reason for His actions and reminded him that "those who honor Me, I will honor, and those who despise Me will be lightly esteemed" (2:30). His grace was mingled with His message of judgment, for He reminded Eli of the good He was doing for Israel and assured him of a posterity even though none would enjoy longevity (2:32-33).

Having indicated God's disapproval of Eli's sons, the prophet compared them with the "faithful priest" whom the Lord was preparing for significant service to the nation. This priest would do according to what was in God's heart and in His soul (1 Samuel 2:35).

"And the boy Samuel was ministering [continuously] to Yahweh before Eli" (1 Samuel 3:1a). Thus the writer shifted the scene and indicated that the young priest's life bore the mark of consistency. Samuel's dedication to the Lord was real. There was no self-seeking or hypocrisy in the things he said or did.

While there were probably many in Israel who yearned and perhaps even prayed for a renewed spirit of commitment to the Lord, change came slowly. God, however, heard and answered the prayers of His people; and as the text reminds us, He was about to do something in private that would eventually become public knowledge (cf. 1 Samuel 3:1b,19-21).

WHEN THE OLD ORDER GIVES WAY TO THE NEW (3:1b–4:1a)

The Bible was in the process of being written. Only the books of Moses, Joshua, and (probably) Job had been penned to date. The people therefore were dependent on the priests for fresh revelation of God's will for them. Eli had been given the privilege of communicating God's words to His people, but because his sons were evil, God neither revealed Himself to them nor spoke through them. As Dr. Joseph Hall commented, "I marvel not, while the priesthood was so corrupted... [that there was] no public vision. It is not the manner of God to grace the unworthy."[20]

By contrast, Samuel was now ready to become the channel of divine communication. And although God's judgment would not fall on Hophni and Phinehas for approximately another eight to ten years,[21] it is evident from what follows that Samuel had been selected to succeed Eli as God's representative to His people.

It grieves us to find the old high priest passed over and his declining years clouded by the knowledge of God's disapproval. We would have preferred to read of his devoted service to the nation culminating in a happy and contented old age.

As we survey Eli's career, we see many times when he had stood seemingly alone against the fluctuating but strong and ever-present tide of apostasy. He had witnessed "all Israel" playing the role of a harlot and worshiping the golden ephod Gideon made (Judges 8:27).

As a priest as well as a judge, Eli had raised his voice against the popular clamor when God's people broke their covenant with the Lord and made Baal-berith their god (8:33). His heart had grown weary as he tried to fan the small flame of spiritual fervor that was almost extinguished when the people capitulated to the sensuous worship of the Canaanites and Amorites and bowed down before the gods of Syria, Phoenicia, and Philistia (10:6). And he had spent his energies unceasingly in trying to heal the wounds left by civil war (12:1-6) and the invasion of Israel's borders by enemies from both the east and the west (13:1).

In desperation, and with the priesthood becoming increasingly corrupt, Eli had turned to his sons—reared in his home—and made them his helpers at Shiloh. The last crushing blow came to him when he was made aware of their evil practices.

Amid this dark picture Samuel was presented as Eli's successor. Samuel's character had been tested and he had not been corrupted by the evil influences that surrounded him. The conduct of Hophni and Phinehas just made Samuel more resolute. He was now ready for the Lord to speak directly to him.

A New Awareness of God (3:1b-9)

Samuel was about twelve years of age. With Eli's sight failing, Samuel was entrusted with taking care of the lamp[22] (Exodus 27:20; 30:7-8) and opening and closing the door of the temple at the beginning and the end of each day.[23]

Late one night or else early one morning (for the lighted candlestick had not yet gone out, 1 Samuel 3:3) Samuel awakened at the sound of someone calling his name. Believing that the aged priest had called, Samuel immediately ran to Eli's side. But no, Eli had not called him and Samuel returned to his pallet.

Again he heard his name, and again he ran to where Eli was sleeping on the floor near the entrance to the temple. And again he was sent back with the same assurance.

Previously Samuel had not received communication directly from God (1 Samuel 3:7) but when he heard his name a third time, Eli realized that it was the Lord who was calling the lad. Eli sensed inwardly that he was being replaced. Pride and jealousy could easily have prevented him from giving his young protégé the information he needed, but Eli showed no resentment. Without the slightest trace of bitterness and knowing full well that the seals of sacred office were being taken from him and given to Samuel, Eli instructed Samuel in what he should do.[24]

A Solemn Revelation from God (3:10-14)

The message given Samuel was a terrifying one. It was a denunciation of the man whom he had grown to love. The words previously communicated to Eli by the man of God (1 Samuel 2:27-36) were to be carried out from beginning to end. Eli had neglected to discipline Hophni and Phinehas and had in effect subordinated his duties as high priest to his devotion as a father. He had failed to act decisively when God's honor was at stake and so had missed the mark both as a priest and as a parent.

There are three major styles of parenting: *authoritarian* (discipline is harsh and rigid and children are allowed little or no freedom); *authoritative* (love and responsibility are balanced); and *permissive* (children are indulged and discipline is lax).[25]

Eli was apparently permissive. In all probability he had pampered his children and yielded to their whims. The opportunity to restrain them had passed. God's indictment revealed Eli's culpability. When he was made aware of the iniquity of his sons, he did not stop them. Now their sins could not be atoned for either by sacrifice or offering (1 Samuel 3:14). Their fate had been sealed. Their persistent, perverse conduct was to reap its inevitable harvest (Jeremiah 2:19; Galatians 6:7-8; 1 Timothy 5:24-25).

We may be quite sure that Samuel did not sleep after receiving this revelation from the Lord. The next morning Eli prevailed on him to tell him what the Lord had revealed to him the night before. Eli listened patiently as the indictment was relayed to him point by point. His response is commendable: "It is Yahweh['s word]; let Him do to me what seems good to Him" (1 Samuel 3:18).

A. F. Kirkpatrick showed that Eli with all his faults was still at heart faithful to God. Eli submitted without a murmur to the divine sentence, leaving himself and his house in the hands of God (cf. Exodus 34:5-7; Leviticus 10:3; Job 1:21; 2:10; Isaiah 39:8). Eli's passive resignation appears to be the result of his will having grown weak through all the trials and opposition he had to face during his long judgeship.[26]

Retribution takes many forms. Jacob, for example, lied to his father, and in turn his sons lied to him (Genesis 27:1-46; 37:18-24,31-35). Saul, who was made king over God's people, nonetheless sought his own ends and finally had to admit that he had "played the fool" (1 Samuel 26:21). Belshazzar, vice-regent of Babylon, was noted for his pride and arrogance and in a single night, while at the height of his glory, his soul was required of him (Daniel 5:30). Herod the Great ruled Judea with an iron fist; his harsh policies and suspicious mind alienated his subjects as well as his supporters and in the end he died friendless and alone.[27]

Turning from sacred history to the medieval era we take note of Lorenzo de'Medici. The head of a large and powerful Florentine family, he lived a life of ruthless self-indulgence. When he was dying he called Savonarola to his bedside, hoping to be given assurance of eternal life. But the tentacles of his self-sufficiency had wrapped themselves so tightly around his heart that he could not divorce himself from his possessions and trust in Christ alone. He died in his sins.[28]

Cardinal Wolsey, to aid his own ambition, had "encouraged the wealthy to indulge in the luxuries and pleasures of life so as to keep them supple and in the palm of his hand. He had supported learning, but only so that he might train a clergy that would keep the laity in subservience. While outwardly he appeared virtuous, inwardly he was rapacious and corrupt. His life was characterized by oppression and greed. He even engaged in treason to further his own goals. In the end, the whole fabric of his life was torn apart."[29]

In the case of Eli's sons, it was inevitable that God's righteous judgment would come upon them. They neglected to follow the truth and instead devoted themselves to satisfying their own narcissistic desires. As their consciences became insensitive to the real issues of life, they alienated the godly remnant among their people. In the end they died at the hand of the Lord.

A Growing Reputation before Men (3:15–4:1a)

Once again the pendulum swung and this time again focused attention on Samuel, who was marked out as God's new mouthpiece. While 1 Samuel 3 begins with a statement to the effect that communication from the Lord was rare and visions were infrequent, the chapter closes with "all Israel" from Dan to Beersheba knowing that Samuel was the man through whom God had chosen to reveal His will (3:19-21).

Reading of dreams and visions, certain groups of people within the church actively seek for such phenomena. Dr. F. B. Meyer offered some wise words of caution.

> Let us not seek for revelations through dreams and visions, but by the Word of God. Nothing is more harmful than to contract the habit of listening for voices, and sleeping to dream. All manner of vagaries come in by that door. It is best to take in hand and read the Scriptures reverently, carefully, and thoughtfully, crying, "Speak, Lord, for Thy servant heareth." And

in response there will come one clear, defined, and repeated message, asseverated and accentuated with growing distinctness from every part of the inspired volume. "This is the way—walk in it; this is My will—do it; this is My word—speak it."[30]

LIFE'S TRUE VALUES

Pattern of Divine Blessing

We do ourselves a disservice if we fail to take note of the way in which God's sovereign goodwill and grace is brought out in the story of Samuel and Eli. God rewarded the faithfulness of Elkanah and Hannah, delayed His judgment on Hophni and Phinehas, and through it all was determined to bless His people (1 Samuel 2:32).

To Elkanah and Hannah the Lord gave other sons and daughters. Samuel's parents did not ask for these children, but God graciously gave them. As Psalm 128:1-4 says:

Blessed [is] everyone who stands in reverential awe of Yahweh, who walks in His ways. You shall surely eat the labor of your hands; you [will be] happy and all [will be] good to you. Your wife [will be] like a fruitful vine by the sides of your house; your sons like olive plants around your table. Behold, so shall the man be blessed who fears Yahweh.

God honors us when we walk in reverential awe of Him. His blessings upon Elkanah and Hannah illustrate for us how He delights to reward those who are faithful to Him (Ecclesiastes 2:24-26; 9:9; Psalm 127:3-4). Though His blessings may be delayed, we should wait patiently for them (Psalm 37:7). Afterward we will find that the trial through which we have passed has yielded the peaceable fruit of righteousness.

Principle of Spiritual Growth

While Samuel was growing up God was working in Samuel's life to will and to do His good pleasure. In much the same way that David was a "man after the heart of God" (Acts 13:22), Samuel was singled out by the Lord as a person who would do according to all that was in His heart and soul (1 Samuel 2:35).

Samuel is an illustration of the continuous, positive growth of a righteous man. He was trained at his mother's knee and given a sense of purpose for his life, so that when he was presented before the

Lord at Shiloh, his response was one of worship (1 Samuel 1:28). His progress from this time on was marked by diligence and the development of a strong internal God-consciousness. Before long God moved Eli to place an ephod on Samuel (2:18) and he was recognized as a priest.

In spite of the corrupting influences of Eli's sons, Samuel eschewed evil. He retained his integrity. His growth, however, was balanced, for he enjoyed favor with both God and man (1 Samuel 2:26; Proverbs 3:3-4; Luke 2:52). Walking in reverential awe of God prevented him from giving way to the extreme of negativism on the one hand and the extreme of ultraconservatism on the other.

As he grew older Samuel assumed more and more responsibility. He responded positively as additional duties were given him (1 Samuel 3:3,15). And when God chose to reveal His will to and through him (3:10-14) Samuel diligently observed all that the Lord told him (3:19). It is no wonder, therefore, that his reputation began to spread and that "all Israel" became aware of the fact that he had been marked out as a prophet of the Lord (3:20–4:1a).

The principle behind Samuel's growth toward spiritual maturity is clear. No matter what the issue, his response to the Lord was positive. As Jim Elliot pointed out in his *Journal:*

> One does not surrender a life in an instant. That which is lifelong can only be surrendered in a lifetime. Nor is surrender to the will of God (per se) adequate to fullness of power in Christ. Maturity is the accomplishment of years, and I can only surrender to the will of God as I know what that will is. Hence the fullness of God's Spirit is not instantaneous but progressive, as I attain fullness of the Word, which reveals [His] will.[31]

In the final analysis Samuel's life demonstrates that God honors those who honor Him and lightly esteems those who despise Him— those who treat Him as unimportant are themselves valued as of trifling worth (1 Samuel 2:30). In this thought there is encouragement for us as well as warning.

MIRROR OF THE PAST

1 Samuel 4:1b–7:1

When Marco Polo, Christopher Columbus, James Cook, and others went on their voyages of discovery, they encountered new races of people with new ideals and new systems of belief. Accustomed to the "five catholic (universal) truths" propounded by Edward Herbert in *De Veritate*—a system of doctrine supposed to unite Christendom—the explorers found that in these pagan cultures the pure and undefiled worship of God (Psalm 19:1-3; Romans 1:20) had been perverted. It had degenerated into sadistic rituals accompanied by all manner of perverse superstitions.

In each newly discovered country an order of priests had arisen who exercised a stranglehold over the people—a rule of fear. The will of the religious leaders was virtually absolute and was enforced through the *power to curse*. This enforcement took several forms, all of which resulted in harm to the person who did not conform to the will of the priest. Inherent only in Christianity—rightly understood and rightly practiced—is the *power to bless*. False beliefs are ever-present and constant vigilance is needed if we are to avoid the errors of the past.

Since the 1950s we have been living in what church historians have chosen to call the "post-Christian era of American history." In many respects our religious practices have become pedantic rituals. There is within our society an emphasis on externals. Formalism, coupled with faith in special objects or persons claiming to have special powers, has taken the place of a biblically-founded, strong, internal God-consciousness. Horoscopes and astrological charts appear in nearly every newspaper and are frequently consulted before decisions are made. Prescribed prayers are recited for different occasions or prior to special events. Candles are lit or incense is burned to obtain the favor of a deity whose blessings are sought. Special periods of meditation are encouraged to insure success. Charms are worn by both men and women to guarantee safety or prosperity.

While these practices may appear ludicrous in the cold light of reality, there are hundreds of thousands of people all across the country who (while reluctant to admit the true nature of their superstitious beliefs) nonetheless feel the need for something outside of themselves and stronger than themselves to help them achieve their goals or desires. And let us not ignore the fallacious, erroneous, and often mythical beliefs that are an integral part of many of the cults or oriental religions that have taken root in the West in recent years.

Regardless of its structure, *superstition* may be defined as "a belief or practice founded upon fear or ignorance." Its manifestations are many and often include fetishism, a false form of mysticism, and a belief in omens.

OUTLINE

As we study 1 Samuel 4:1b–7:1 we should not be surprised to find that even God's people Israel, as well as their pagan Philistine neighbors, had their superstitions. At the root of the matter lies the struggle between *natural* versus *revealed* religion. The truth is evident by the outcome. These chapters may therefore be analyzed as follows:

- God's Sovereignty amid the Crushing Disappointments of Life (1 Samuel 4:1b-22)
- God's Sovereignty in Vindicating His Name before Unbelievers (1 Samuel 5:1–6:12)
- God's Sovereignty in the Worship Due to Him (1 Samuel 6:13–7:1)

GOD'S SOVEREIGNTY AMID THE CRUSHING DISAPPOINTMENTS OF LIFE 4:1b-22

It has become the accepted practice of modern commentators to treat this section of Scripture as a separate or distinct part of Israel's folklore inserted here in the narrative by a later editor.[1] William Deane, however, places the events in the context of the times in which they occurred.

> While the evil priests [Hophni and Phinehas] were filling up the measure of their iniquity, and the muttering of the coming storm that was to overthrow Eli and his house were heard in the distance, the child Samuel ministered before the Lord. . . . In

sharpest contrast stand forth pure devotion and unbridled licentious [*sic*], [Samuel's] life of holiness and the life of shame [of Eli's sons] are set opposite each other....Hophni and Phinehas, in priestly robes, profaned the worship of the Lord whose ministers they pretended to be; Samuel, in his white ephod, served the Lord purely and reverently (cf. 1 Samuel 2:26).[2]

A Crushing Defeat (4:1b-11)

In 1 Samuel 4 the Biblical record moves from the *religious* to the *political* scene.

"And Israel went out to meet the Philistines in battle" (4:1b).[3] It appears as if God's people had grown tired of Philistine oppression and decided to attack their oppressors (cf. 4:9). They camped at a place called, proleptically, *Ebenezer* (possibly 'Izbet Ṣarṭah)—see 1 Samuel 7:12—while their enemies established their battle formation at Aphek (identified as Ras el-'Ain),[4] twenty-five miles west of Shiloh.

The leaders of Israel had not consulted the Lord to ascertain His will and now that they were on the field of battle, they did not ask Him as their commander-in-chief (Yahweh of hosts) what strategy they should use. We do not read that they offered sacrifices, as one might expect of a God-fearing people. Instead they appeared supremely confident in themselves. Morale was high as the militiamen from the different tribes gathered together and prepared for the offensive.

On the day of battle they were surprised when their poorly equipped militia was routed by the well-armed, highly disciplined Philistine army. In tattered disarray the Israelites returned to camp, where their leaders were pressed for an answer. How were they to explain this unexpected defeat?[5]

In the past when Israel fought against their enemies, God's presence had invariably ensured their success (Numbers 10:33; Deuteronomy 4:4; Joshua 6:6–7:25). Having been conditioned to think in terms of externals, the only variable they saw between past victories and present defeat was the absence of the ark of the covenant.

While Israel's leaders had some knowledge of history, a little knowledge is a dangerous thing. Without thinking of consulting the Lord by the urim and thummim or by some other means, they acted presumptuously and sent to Shiloh for the ark "that *it* may...deliver us from the power of our enemies" (1 Samuel 4:3, emphasis added). The leaders not only misused their knowledge of history but also succeeded in deluding themselves and those who looked to them for guidance.[6]

When the ark of the Lord of hosts[7] was brought into the camp, the Israelites were elated and expected an easy victory (cf. Numbers 10:35). Feelings however are very deceptive. A high degree of religious excitement is no guarantee of God's favor or blessing. As Dr. A. F. Kirkpatrick has shown, a form of belief that confuses the symbol of faith with the real presence of God is the natural result of the decay of religion.[8]

Nevertheless the shouts of confidence aroused consternation in the enemy camp (1 Samuel 4:6-8) because the Philistines were also knowledgeable of Israel's history (Exodus 7–12; Joshua 5:1). The hearts of the warriors melted with fear, but their leaders challenged them to courage and fortitude (1 Samuel 4:9). The Philistine leaders possibly used a play on the words 'bd, "serve," and 'br, "Hebrew,"[9] and said in effect, "Don't allow yourselves to become the *servants* of these ragtag *Hebrews* as they have been *servants* to you."

The next day the fighting was resumed and Israel's defeat was made complete. Thirty thousand men were killed (seven and a half times as many as in the previous battle). The ark was captured and in fulfillment of the prophecy made many years earlier, Hophni and Phinehas were among those slain (1 Samuel 2:27-36).[10] Never in the past had such a calamity befallen God's people. It was evident that His favor had been withdrawn from them. Israel's political independence had been precarious at best; now it was curtailed by Philistine suzerainty.[11]

A Bitter Disappointment (4:12-18)

The scene quickly shifts to Shiloh. Eli, now blind, was sitting on a backless seat beside the highway (1 Samuel 4:13). Soon those on the wall saw a runner as he sped toward the city.[12] With perspiration coursing down his body, the messenger from the battlefield breathlessly described the events of the day. Eli heard only the commotion as the people reacted to the fateful news. When he asked the reason for the noise, the messenger was brought to him. The aged priest could not see the signs of grief so evident in the Benjamite's torn clothes and the dust upon his head.

The messenger answered Eli with a concise summary of the day's events. Each item of information was like the blow of a hammer as it flattened the iron on the anvil of God's justice: there had been a complete rout of the army; thousands of young men had been killed; Eli's sons had been slain; and the ark had been captured (the ark contained, among other things, the tablets of the law; see Hebrews 9:4).

All of this news was more than Eli could bear. National defeat and disgrace and family bereavement were trifling compared to the loss of the ark. Overcome with grief, he lost his balance and toppled over backward. His neck broke and he died.[13]

A concluding statement sums up his life: Eli judged Israel for forty years (1 Samuel 4:18).

Samuel is not mentioned in the story (possibly because he was not in favor of any aggression against Israel's enemies at this time). He must have realized that the Philistines, encouraged by their success at Aphek, would march on Shiloh and destroy the city to demonstrate to their own satisfaction the superiority of their gods over Yahweh of Israel. Samuel must have been the one, perhaps aided by some members of the Eliad priesthood, who hid the sacred vessels of the temple and the records of the nation, for they were later found at Nob (1 Samuel 21).

When the Philistines attacked the city, the inhabitants who had not fled to other places for safety were too disheartened to offer much resistance and they were massacred. From Psalm 78:59-64 and Jeremiah 7:12 we know that Shiloh was totally destroyed. Other cities were plundered and the trophies of war were carried off to Philistia.

It is probable that following Israel's defeat the Spirit of the Lord began to move young Samson as he saw the plight of his people (Judges 13:25). We note once again God's grace toward those who bore His name: He did not leave them entirely in the hands of their enemies but through Samson gave them a measure of deliverance.

Hopeless Despair (4:19-22)

The crushing defeat suffered by the nation and the bitter disappointment with which Eli finished his course on this earth were not the only tragedies marking the battle of Aphek. We also read of the hopeless despair of Phinehas's pious wife.

Who can count the trials this good woman had already endured? Hers had been a troubled life; yet she stayed with her husband, bore his children, cared for him and them, and perhaps prayed often for the Lord to draw Phinehas to Himself. Her daily suffering had required that she draw daily on the Lord for strength. However, when she heard of the tragic defeat of her people, of the thousands of homes affected by the deaths of Israel's brave men, of the demise of her husband and her father-in-law, and of the loss of the ark, the shock was too much for her tired body. She succumbed to an overwhelming feeling of desolation.

Premature birth pangs took the last of her strength from her. Even while the Philistines were pillaging the villages and hamlets on their ascent to Shiloh, she gave birth to a son. Instead of rejoicing over the birth (John 16:21) and being concerned for the baby's safety, her spirit was too weak to respond. Shortly before death relieved her of her suffering, she named her son *'I kābôd,* "No-glory," and then explained, "Glory is gone from Israel" (1 Samuel 4:21).

The term *glory of God* denotes the presence and majesty of God (Exodus 40:34; Leviticus 9:23-24). Known in Israel as the *shekinah,*[14] it gave special privileges to the nation (Romans 9:4).[15] For the visible presence of God to be forcefully taken from them was a tragedy too great to be described in words. So concludes one of the darkest chapters in Israel's history.

GOD'S SOVEREIGNTY IN VINDICATING HIS NAME BEFORE UNBELIEVERS (5:1–6:12)

After carrying the spoils of war back to their own towns and villages, the Philistines assembled at Ashdod (Azotus in Acts 8:40),[16] thirty-three miles west of Jerusalem and two and a half miles from the sea, to celebrate their victory. Ashdod was one of the chief cities of their pentapolis (Joshua 15:47; 2 Chronicles 26:6; cf. Apocrypha, 1 Maccabees 10:84) and was widely regarded by the people of antiquity as an impregnable fortress. Chief among the trophies they paraded through the streets was the ark of the covenant.[17]

The Ashdodites were devotees of Dagon, whose worshipers had established lavish temples at Ebla, Mari, and Ugarit. In certain legends Dagon is spoken of as the father of Baal, and therefore Dagon is similar to or the same as El in the Canaanite pantheon.[18] He was the god of grain and supposedly ensured the abundant harvests of those who acknowledged his sovereignty.

Chastening of the Lord (5:1–6:1)

In celebrating their victory over the Hebrews, the Philistines placed their prized trophy, the ark of the covenant of Yahweh of hosts, Israel's protector and defender, in the temple of Dagon. From the description given in the text there appears to have been a raised platform in the temple, and on this elevated dais there may have been a pedestal on which was placed the large and imposing figure of the Philistines' god. The ark was placed on the side of the platform and beneath the figure of Dagon—a position symbolic of an inferior waiting on and ready to serve a superior.[19]

While the Philistines had indeed conquered Israel, they had not vanquished Israel's God. The next morning the priests of Dagon found the object of their veneration toppled from his pedestal and lying face down like a suppliant on the floor before the ark. Unwilling to accept this incident as an evil omen and trying inwardly to reassure themselves that there was nothing supernatural in this inauspicious event, the priests hastily restored Dagon to his position of eminence (cf. Isaiah 46:7).

The next morning, however, rising early and with ill-disguised concern, the priests checked on the well-being of their god. If word of the previous day's mishap had spread, then we can be sure they wanted to dispel any superstitious rumors that might result in hysteria among the people of Ashdod and ruin the celebrations. On entering the temple the priests found Dagon mutilated beyond cosmetic repair. His head and arms, the symbols of his wisdom and activity, had been broken from his body.

On finding their deity in this condition, the priests were confronted with a theological problem. Is Yahweh mightier than Dagon? Refusing to admit the superiority of Israel's God[20] they developed instead a new tradition (1 Samuel 5:5). From that day forward no priest or worshiper who entered the temple was to tread on the threshold, lest the place where fragments of the god had lain should be profaned by human feet (cf. Zephaniah 1:9).

So we see the Philistines' unswerving allegiance to their superstitious beliefs. Each new challenge was met with a further elaboration of doctrine. Theirs was not a revealed religion, but a manmade one. Because they believed Dagon to be capable of capricious passions, they did all they could to placate him.[21]

Added to the misfortunes of the Philistines was the fact that the hand of Yahweh[22] was heavy on the Ashdodites and the people in the area adjacent to the city (1 Samuel 5:6; cf. Joshua 15:47; Apocrypha, 1 Maccabees 10:84; 11:4). The New American Standard Bible states that He "ravaged" them and afflicted them with "hemorrhoids."[23] This is an unlikely translation.

Three Hebrew words aid our understanding of what happened. The first is *'opēl*. It has variously been translated "mound," "tumor," "boil." The most plausible explanation of the affliction, based on the mounting evidence of 1 Samuel 5:6,9 and 6:4-5, is that rodents (mice and rats were grouped into a single phylum by people of antiquity) began to decimate the area.[24] Accompanying this devastation was an outbreak of bubonic plague. Large numbers of people were stricken by the disease and its symptoms caused widespread fear. The Philistines were familiar with different fevers but they were unfamiliar with the kind that was so intimately linked with *'opēl,* "swellings" (usually in the groin), from which people now began to die.

The second Hebrew word that aids our understanding of what happened is *ṭeḥōr* (1 Samuel 6:11,17). According to 1 Samuel 5:9 God terrified the Philistines by smiting them with tumors under their skin. *Ṭeḥōr* further describes this painful swelling. In the case of bubonic plague, such swelling is accompanied by a high fever. The lymph nodes of the infected area become enlarged to produce visible rounded mounds the size of a hen's egg or a large walnut.

The third Hebrew word that is of interest to us is *sāṭar* (1 Samuel 5:9). It is used only here in the Hebrew Bible so we cannot appeal to its usage elsewhere to determine its meaning. It may mean "to be hidden, to break out." In languages cognate with Biblical Hebrew, the word means "to be hidden, to be inverted."[25] In the case of the bubonic plague most victims die within a week. The swellings then soften and discharge (break out) their contents through the skin, leaving a depression where the hardened lump had been.

It is easy to see how in a superstitious society these symptoms would result in panic, first in Ashdod (1 Samuel 5:6)[26] and then in Gath (5:9)[27] and finally in Ekron (5:11).[28] (Their panic parallels the hysteria spread by the Black Death in Europe in 1348 and by the plague in London in 1665.)[29] It is no wonder, therefore, that the people of Ashdod, Gath, and Ekron wanted to be rid of the ark. They equated its presence with death and destruction. Such was their fear of the ark that according to 1 Samuel 6:1 they even left it outside their cities in the *śādeh*, "open fields,"[30] while their leaders debated endlessly over what should be done.

Counsel from the Priests (6:2-12)

The lords of the Philistine pentapolis eventually acceded to the request of the people. The lords summoned the priests and diviners and inquired of them if and by what means the ark should be returned to Israel.

William Deane reminds us that there were three primary modes of divination practiced throughout the ancient Near East (Ezekiel 21:21-22). (1) Divination by arrows—an arrow was shot into the air and an omen was taken from the direction in which it fell. (2) Divination by teraphim—these images were supposed to speak and give oracular responses to those who consulted them, provided of course the devotees were in right standing with the god or goddess from whom they wished to obtain favors. (3) Divination by sacrifice—the entrails and liver of a sacrificed animal were examined to help the priest determine the will of the gods.[31]

The means used to reach a decision regarding the ark are not told us. The priests did warn the leaders of the catastrophes that might yet come upon the nation if the ark were not returned to Israel. They also recommended that to placate Yahweh, a guilt or trespass offering be given Him for the offense of removing Him from His land. This offering was to be five golden mice and five golden tumors, one for each principal city. So anxious were the people to have the effects of the plague lifted that even villages around the major metropolitan areas contributed (1 Samuel 6:18).[32] These expensive offerings were put in a box and placed next to the ark.

The diviners also suggested a strategy whereby they would not be held liable if the plague were not lifted. They were wise enough to make their suggestion in a manner that skillfully shifted the burden of proof off themselves. Their plan was as follows: The ark together with the offerings were to be placed in a new cart. This cart was to be drawn by cows that (1) had recently calved and (2) had never borne a yoke before. If the cows left their calves behind and without direction from their owners willingly took the road that led to Beth-shemesh, then the lords of the Philistines would know that the ark and the plague were connected.

The command was given and the cart was built. Cows meeting the description given by the priests were selected. The cows, protesting their separation from their calves, nevertheless pulled the driverless cart all the way from Ekron to Beth-shemesh. Furthermore, the lords of the Philistines, together with their retinue and people from the nearest cities, followed the cart, glad that the source of their troubles was soon to be removed from their land.[33]

GOD'S SOVEREIGNTY IN THE WORSHIP
DUE TO HIM (6:13–7:1)

Beth-shemesh[34] was a Levitical city (Joshua 21:16; 1 Chronicles 6:59; Judges 1:33). When the ark arrived the people were busy in the fields for it was the time of harvest—late May, early June (1 Samuel 6:13).

Dr. William M. Thomson, who spent more than four decades as a missionary in Palestine and Syria, described what he saw one morning as he approached this ancient village:

> The whole plain appeared to be dotted with harvesting parties, men reaping, women and children gleaning and gathering the grain into bundles, or taking care of the flocks which followed

closely upon the steps of the gleaners. All seemed to be in good humour.... There was singing alone and in chorus, incessant talking, homemade jokes, and [much] laughter.[35]

As the cart came up the winding hill, someone's attention was diverted from the task at hand to the lowing of the cows. His or her gaze was immediately riveted to the ark. It was overlaid with gold and the two cherubim with their wings overshadowing the mercyseat were unmistakable. Whoever saw it first immediately called out to the others to take note of what was happening. Then they saw the Philistines. A momentary twinge of fear mingled with their excitement. Then the full realization of the fact that the ark was being returned to them sank in. A shout went up from the happy throng and they were swept up in a frenzy of excitement. God had brought the ark back to His people. No ransom had been demanded and no blow struck. Instead the Lord had convincingly demonstrated His power over His people's powerful enemies.

The cows meanwhile stopped close to a large stone that was in the field of a man named Joshua. The Levites were immediately summoned to take the ark and the box containing the Philistine guilt offering down from the cart (Numbers 1:51). Using the rock as an altar, the cart for firewood, and the cows for a burnt offering, the Levites then led the people in an act of consecration and worship.

The law specifically required unblemished males for a burnt offering (Leviticus 1:3; 22:19) but this part of the Mosaic legislation was not adhered to by the people of Beth-shemesh. God apparently accepted the sacrifice of the cows though, for having borne the sacred ark they could not now be used for any other purpose.

After witnessing these proceedings the five lords of the Philistines, together with their bodyguards and those who had come out of curiosity, returned to their own cities. It had been a day they would never forget.

Meanwhile back in Beth-shemesh the priests, who should have covered the ark as prescribed by law (Numbers 4:5,19-20), failed to do so. Perhaps the prolonged disregard of God's Word had caused them to become negligent. With the smoke of the sacrifices still ascending into the clear afternoon sky, some of the residents of Beth-shemesh went down to the spot where the ark of the covenant had been placed. They gazed on this symbol of God's presence with curiosity instead of reverence.[36] And the Lord, who had vindicated His honor among the Philistines, was now compelled to vindicate His holiness in the midst of His own people. A large number[37] were struck down and died. They did not fall victim to the bubonic plague as did their enemies. Instead their deaths were a direct result of the judgment of God.

The reaction of the survivors is surprising. Instead of repenting of their sin, those who had so recently rejoiced at the return of the ark now acted like their pagan neighbors. They asked, "Who is able to stand before Yahweh, this holy God? And to whom shall *He* go up from us?" (1 Samuel 6:20, emphasis added; cf. Exodus 29:45-46; Leviticus 11:44-45) They blamed God for their misfortune and sought for a means whereby they could quickly be rid of Him (cf. Matthew 8:34).

It is true that one facet of the fear of the Lord is repulsion. When we sense that we are in God's presence, our first conscious realization is of our unworthiness. He is awesome in His holiness (2 Corinthians 7:1; 1 Peter 1:15-16). As with Adam and Eve when they knew themselves to be sinners, our first reaction is to hide from Him (Genesis 3:7-8). Isaiah's response was similar. When he had his vision of the glory of God filling the temple, his first thought was of his unworthiness (Isaiah 6:1-5). And when the apostle Peter became aware of who Christ really is, he fell at His feet and said, "Depart from me, for I am a sinful man, O Lord!" (Luke 5:8)

However, also inherent in the fear of the Lord is the element of attraction. While in and of ourselves we cannot stand before God, neither can we live without Him (Acts 17:28). His love and grace meet us in our need. As a consequence of the atoning sacrifice of Christ on our behalf, we who formerly were estranged from Him are now brought into His presence (Ephesians 2:4-7,13-18). We are accepted in the beloved!

The difference between a cold formal orthodoxy and a blending of doctrine with experience is illustrated for us in an incident from the life of the apostle John. He was "in the Spirit on the Lord's day" when Christ appeared to him. John's immediate response was to "fall at His feet as one who is dead" (Revelation 1:10,17). John did not retreat from Him or ask Him to leave but was overcome with awe at His majesty. The apostle showed proper reverence as well as recognition of his unworthiness.

The people of Beth-shemesh reacted to the holiness of God by wanting to be rid of the ark. As they reasoned among themselves, one of their number suggested that it be sent to Kiriath-jearim.[38] Kiriath-jearim was not a priestly or Levitical city but was the nearest city of importance on the road to Shiloh. The men of Beth-shemesh therefore invited the people of Kiriath-jearim to come down and fetch the ark. And the people of Kiriath-jearim, being more noble than those of Beth-shemesh, did so.

The ark was then lodged in the house of Abinadab, who was

probably of Levitical descent (1 Samuel 7:1). And there the ark remained for approximately ninety years (c. 1069-980 B.C.; see 2 Samuel 6). Abinadab truly reverenced the Lord and consecrated his son Eleazar to keep or watch over the ark. The blessing of the Lord (which the people of Beth-shemesh could have enjoyed) now rested on the house of Abinadab!

Proverbs 10:22 tells us that the blessing of the Lord makes one rich and that He adds no sorrow to it. He does not consider His state of unsullied happiness to be His prerogative (Philippians 2:5-8). Instead He bestows happiness on those who do not have it. Yet in the Bible Yahweh is never referred to as happy after the fashion of the gods of antiquity, and this difference indicates at once the gulf that separates the faith of Israel from the religions of that time. The pagan deity was a privileged being. He was to be envied, feared, and placated. Yahweh by contrast is a God who comes to His people. As the Creator He is the source of all life and happy is the person to whom He reveals Himself and with whom He makes His covenant (Psalm 25:14; Jeremiah 31:31-33; Hebrews 9:15; 10:16).

Conscious of their privilege as a nation, the people of Israel extolled the blessedness of the one who fears the Lord. Such fear was regarded as the beginning of wisdom and the surest means of avoiding the evils of life and receiving its blessings (Psalm 33:18-19; 34:11-14; 66:16-20; 103:11,13; Proverbs 1:7; 8:13; 16:6; 19:23; 22:4; cf. Proverbs 29:25). The person whose relationship with the Lord is characterized by reverential awe becomes increasingly aware of knowing the one true God. Such knowledge cannot come through mere religious observances; it can only be acquired through divine revelation.

The blessing of the Lord is unique. It is the portion of those who belong to Him. Such individuals have been delivered from the oppression of false beliefs. To them has been given the supreme privilege of praising and worshiping the Lord of glory, who is vitally interested in His people.[39]

TIME FOR REFLECTION

We have already noted several important themes in 1 Samuel 4:1b–7:1: (1) the presumption of the leaders of Israel;[40] (2) the false sense of security enjoyed only temporarily by the Philistines;[41] (3) the need for obedience to the revealed will of God so lacking in the people of Beth-shemesh; (4) the weighty issues surrounding the concept of the fear of the Lord; and (5) the nature of God in delighting to bless His people. Also of significance is the interplay between divine sovereignty and human freedom. Whether personally (as in the case of Abinadab) or corporately (as in the case of the people of

Beth-shemesh) or nationally (as in the case of Israel or the Philistines), we see the effects of human decision.

The Danger of Presumption

The leaders of Israel, for example, chose to make war on the Philistines. The Israelites should have sought God's counsel first, but followed instead their own misguided beliefs. Only when faced with failure did Israel think of the Lord. Needing the assurance of God's presence and partially understanding the Scriptures, they acted on their superstitious faith and brought the ark into their camp. Then they felt that God would surely be compelled to defend His honor and give them victory.

The Creator, however, is not subject to His creature's manipulations. As the Israelites found out, God cannot and will not allow Himself to be contained within the narrow scope of our finite conceptions (Isaiah 55:8-9).

Lest we be tempted to conclude that the principles illustrated for us in 1 Samuel 4:1b–7:1 are not operative today, let us consider some of the false beliefs that cause people in our churches to try to manipulate God into doing what they want. There are those, for example, who think that by fasting they can prevail on God to answer their prayers. Others, misquoting and misapplying Matthew 18:20, ask fellow Christians to agree with them in prayer, confident that God will grant their requests. Still others presume they can make a purchase or commit themselves to a course of action (marriage, for example) and then expect God to bail them out of debt or save an unconverted spouse for the sake of His honor and the testimony they either have or could have in the community.

If we are to avoid the hard lessons experienced by the Israelites, we must learn to subordinate our wills to His will and bring every thought captive to the obedience of Christ (2 Corinthians 10:5). Presumption only leads to trouble for us and those connected with us. Only by living in reverential awe of God and obeying His Word can we avoid this error.

The Danger of Ignorance

The Philistines also had freedom of choice, but when they fought their wars in the names of their gods and calamity befell them, they did not choose to acknowledge God's sovereignty. Instead they added to their superstitious rituals and determined to resist the truth. In the end their own priests did counsel the leaders to "give glory to the God of Israel" (1 Samuel 6:5) and offer guilt offerings to Him (6:3-9), but we may be sure that true to human nature such an acknowledgment of His right to be worshiped did not come until all other methods for relieving the distress of the people had been tried.

A God who has the right to be worshiped also has the right to be obeyed. The people of Beth-shemesh offered burnt offerings and thank offerings to the Lord, but they did not show Him due reverence. Their irreverence was the result of an unenlightened will. They failed to obey the part of divine revelation He had communicated to them. As a consequence they suffered under His sovereign displeasure.

The Blessing of the Godly

How different was the spirit of Abinadab. He did not fear either the plague or the judgment of God, but welcomed the ark into his house. Then he consecrated one of his sons (probably the oldest, his heir and therefore the one most important to him) to the service of the ark. By his acts Abinadab showed his deep and abiding respect for the Lord and a willingness to give Him top priority. He demonstrated the condition of his heart by honoring God over material or familial concerns. So it was that God sovereignly honored Abinadab and blessed him and his house.

The Place of Freedom

Examples of freedom of choice are to be found throughout Scripture (Matthew 23:37; John 7:17; Romans 7:18; 1 Corinthians 9:17; Philemon 14; 1 Peter 5:2). Our responsibility is to choose to obey God's Word and to treat each imperative as a supreme command. While we find it hard to harmonize God's sovereignty with our responsibility, we take comfort from the fact that He has established His throne in Heaven and His kingdom rules over all (Psalm 103:19; 1 Chronicles 29:11; Daniel 4:17,25,35; 5:21; 7:14; 1 Timothy 6:15; Revelation 19:16). He controls the destiny of men and nations (Acts 14:15-17; 17:24-28; Ephesians 1:11) and nothing lies outside the realm of His power (Mark 10:27; Luke 1:37).

Even the death of Christ on the cross links human decisions with God's predetermined counsel (Acts 2:23; 4:27-28). Of comfort to us today is the knowledge that the Lord Jesus possesses all authority in Heaven and earth (Matthew 28:18) and He displays His power in and through those who have been called into a unique relationship with Him (Romans 1:16; 1 Corinthians 1:24; Ephesians 1:18-22). It is part of His divine plan to use human means to accomplish His ends.

RECOVERY OF RIGHT-MINDEDNESS

1 Samuel 7:2-17

Benjamin Disraeli defined *success* as "constancy of purpose."[1] Let's look at the lives of four "successful" people to see if constancy of purpose was all they needed to reach their objectives.

The first success story concerns Sandra Day O'Connor. As a nation we were delighted when she was appointed to be the first woman to sit on the bench of the United States Supreme Court. We felt that Mrs. O'Connor was eminently qualified for this distinguished position. She had diligently prepared herself for a legal career by studying law at Stanford University. She had also proven herself capable of handling responsibility by serving as an assistant district attorney in Arizona and then as a judge in the Arizona State Court of Appeals. When her family, former teachers, and colleagues were interviewed following her appointment, all attributed her success to her devotion to detail, perseverance, tact, and commitment to doing what she believed to be right.

Several decades ago a man named Booker T. Washington saw the need to lift the veil of ignorance from his people and point the way to progress through education and industry. To do so, he first needed to secure an education for himself. He learned to read and write while working in coal mines, sawing wood, plowing fields, and serving alternately as a janitor and a waiter. Later he was chosen to start an institute to provide the form of education he had dreamed of. The task before him was herculean. It involved combining cultural awareness with vocational training. With courage, an understanding of human nature, patience, and confidence in himself and his cause, he pushed forward and in spite of much opposition ultimately accomplished his goal.

Who can forget Russian-born and American-educated Golda Meir? When she married Moshe Myerson, they determined to leave the

United States and join a kibbutz in Israel. There she worked hard in the fields, developed new skills, and taught young Israeli women the things she had learned. In a society that did not approve of women in public office and where political affairs were carried on by men, Golda's wisdom and boldness finally won her a hearing. Her speeches were characterized by simplicity and feeling. At age seventy she was appointed prime minister and led the state of Israel through one of the stormiest periods in its recent history. When asked what makes a person great and able to do great things, she replied, "A great ideal." But there was more to her success than that. She was a person of determination, intelligence, and character, and she possessed the ability to influence others.

And then there is Itzhak Perlman. Born in Tel Aviv at the end of World War II, he was stricken with polio at the age of four. His indomitable spirit, however, refused to be limited by his paralysis. He played soccer on crutches in the streets with his friends and, turning to music, practiced assiduously so that today he is one of the world's finest violinists. His irrepressible optimism, sense of humor, and constancy of purpose have given him a place of honor among music lovers around the world.

These men and women and countless others like them were not swept up to greatness. Because they persevered through their difficulties, they eventually achieved the objectives they had set for themselves. Samuel's success must likewise be attributed to his perseverance, for he labored for a full twenty years to bring the nation of Israel back to the Lord.

TOUCH OF REALISM

As we consider the information in 1 Samuel 7, we need to do so from the perspective of Samuel's era, not from our vantage point in the twentieth century with its almost impeccable hindsight. Samuel is today recognized as one of the great men of the Old Testament. At the time Shiloh was destroyed, however, he was barely twenty years of age and he was looked on by his peers as an intruder on whom Eli (the doting but senile high priest) had mistakenly placed the ephod. Now Eli was dead.

Ousted from the Ministry

It is possible that the remaining descendants of Eli, eager to remove the sentence of God against them (1 Samuel 2:30-33), determined to purify themselves and the priesthood. Long accustomed to thinking solely in terms of externals (cf. Joel 2:13), they may have thrust Samuel out of the ministry, for he was only a Levite by birth and not a descendant of Aaron through either Eleazar or Ithamar (Numbers 3:9-10). Their theology did not allow for any exceptions (cf. 1 Samuel 2:28 and 35).

After the destruction of Shiloh, Samuel returned to Ramah and was not at any time invited to resume priestly functions at Nob (only a few miles from his home) when the tabernacle was relocated there.[2] Instead he appears to have moved more into the role of judge (1 Samuel 7:6,15,17) and to have officiated as a priest only at Ramah, Bethel, Mizpah, and on occasion at Gilgal—without the approval of the descendants of Eli. As Paul's apostleship was denied by some and questioned by others (cf. 1 Corinthians 9:1-2; Galatians 1:1), so Samuel's ordination to the priesthood by God was questioned by those who felt they were in a position to judge matters of genealogy and appointment.

Because rejection faces all of us at one time or another, the words of Dr. F. B. Meyer are most apropos:

> The supreme test of character is disappointment and apparent failure.... Let the tide turn against us; let men avert their faces and refuse our counsels; let us be driven to stand on the defense against a world in arms—then our true metal is approved. We are now to see how Samuel bore himself in the face of keen disappointment.[3]

Perseverance with the Ministry

Without bitterness or regret Samuel set himself the task of rebuilding Israel's ruined state. He never doubted for one moment his call from the Lord. With no promise of eventual success, he faithfully ministered to the people through a dreary period of their history. Speaking particularly of the twenty years referred to in 1 Samuel 7:2, Dr. A. F. Kirkpatrick wrote:

> The period here passed over in silence was a dark page in Israel's history, politically and religiously. They were vassals of the Philistines, reduced apparently to abject submission.... The people sank into idolatry [1 Samuel 7:3-4]. But meanwhile Samuel was growing in strength and influence, and when the right moment came and the desire for better things sprang up as the fruit of his prophetic labours, he was ready to take his place as the leader of the nation.[4]

And so, through these long years of service, the word of Samuel came to all Israel (1 Samuel 4:1).[5]

Colleague in the Ministry

As Samuel served the needs of those in the highlands, Samson served as a judge on Judah's southern border (he ministered south of his home; see Judges 16:31). The times were dangerous and there can be no doubt that Samson's presence gave to Samuel a measure of protection as he moved about and ministered in different parts of the country.

The news of Samson's death may have helped to shock the nation into wakefulness and provide the catalyst for Samuel to call the people to a renewed commitment of themselves to the Lord. Keil and Delitzsch wisely observed:

> The statement that twenty years had passed [1 Samuel 7:2] can only be understood on the supposition that some kind of turning point ensued at the close of that time. The complaining of the people after Jehovah was no such turning point.[6]

It is likely that the news of Samson's solitary death at Gaza provided the emotional incentive for Israel to free themselves from Philistine domination.

OUTLINE

Outlining 1 Samuel 7 is made easy for us by certain repetitious statements: "And Samuel spoke"; "And Samuel said"; "And Samuel took"; and finally, "And Samuel judged". When we add the thoughts implied by the introduction, we can outline the passage in the following way:

- The Return to Ramah (1 Samuel 7:2)
- The Role of Repentance (1 Samuel 7:3-4)
- The Result of Recommitment (1 Samuel 7:5-11)
- The Reminder of Past Blessings (1 Samuel 7:12-14)
- The Review of a Noble Life (1 Samuel 7:15-17)

THE RETURN TO RAMAH (7:2)

Shiloh was in ruins. Having stored the sacred vessels of the temple and the records of his people in a safe place, Samuel felt compelled to return to the home he had left in much happier times. Who can imagine his nostalgia as he walked the streets he had formerly toddled along while holding his mother's hand? And who can adequately describe the pain he felt as he saw young women in widows' garb and observed the hopelessness and fear on the faces of those who scarcely had the will to live? It was a sad homecoming.

The village that had witnessed Samuel's remarkable birth twenty years earlier now became his residence for the rest of his life. Here he married, and here his sons were born. The names he gave them were an expression of his own faith during these troubled times: *Joel,* "Yahweh is God," and *Abiah,* "Yahweh is my Father."

Here in this hamlet on the top of a hill in the territory of Benjamin were gathered some ardent young mavericks who were the earliest students in the school of the prophets.[7] These men were carefully trained, and they in turn were sent out on short "preaching missions" to tell in the campfires and marketplaces of Israel the things they had learned.

Samuel's life, however, was a solitary one. No longer could he enjoy the company of those with whom he grew to manhood in Shiloh. Few appreciated his efforts in his new role as a reformer or judge.

In spite of the spiritual and moral discontinuity of the times, Samuel walked with the Lord. He was a man of integrity. He maintained a godly home and became known as a man of prayer (1 Samuel 9:6-9; Psalm 99:6; Jeremiah 15:1). Slowly but surely he gained the confidence of the people. But he had no steady income, and this uncertainty could only have placed a great strain on his young wife and their children.

From Ramah Samuel visited the cities of Bethel, Gilgal, and Mizpah annually. People from the surrounding areas came to these centers of worship to hear his judgment on personal as well as spiritual matters.[8]

THE ROLE OF REPENTANCE (7:3-4)

Through twenty long years Samuel remained in touch with the pulse of the people. As time passed he sensed a quickening of their spiritual aspirations. His persistent teaching of God's Word sowed the seeds that eventually caused them to begin to desire something better. Then, if our reconstruction of the chronology is correct, the death of Samson jolted the nation out of its complacency and inertia. Individuals here and there who had renounced their idolatry and recommitted their lives to the Lord were ready for a renewal of the covenant. Samuel likewise believed that the time had come for a national return to Yahweh as their real suzerain.

Dr. William G. Blaikie has drawn attention to the two phrases that illustrate for us Samuel's noble work: "all the house of Israel" and "lamented after the Lord." These phrases, he believes, point to the essential factors that Samuel brought together. First, all Israel heard the word of the Lord; and second, toward the close of the second decade of Samuel's ministry the people began to see how sad and desolate were their lives when deprived of the tokens of God's love and grace. Israel began to grieve over the sins that had caused Him to withdraw His blessings, and they longed for Him to return and be gracious to them.[9] To test the nation's true commitment, Samuel encouraged the people to renounce the worship of Baal and the Ashtaroth.

Putting away these false gods was a harder condition than we at first imagine. The temptation to worship these pagan deities was most subtle. The religious worship of Israel's neighbors was very attractive and appealed to the senses. Israel's own worship, prescribed by God through His servant Moses, had little to allure the human heart. The Jewish religion was simple and self-denying. By contrast, the worship of the pagans was lively and attractive. Entertainment and revelry characterized their festive occasions. Male and female religious prostitutes were readily available. The worship of these pagan deities was inherently pleasing to the carnal mind. To renounce such worship and devotion was to fall back on what was unattractive and somber.[10]

From Samuel's solemn admonition we learn that the first steps toward a renewal of right-mindedness and an enjoyment of the blessings of God on our lives must be (1) the forsaking of our sins (no matter how enjoyable they are) and the way of life that leads to them; and (2) a recommitment of ourselves to seek out and follow the truth as it has been revealed to us in God's Word (John 17:17). As the apostle Paul pointed out, it is through the renewing of our minds that we come progressively to appreciate and understand the good and acceptable and perfect will of God (Romans 12:2). Only by putting into practice what is taught in the Bible can we enjoy the rewards of righteousness.

What we need therefore is a greater sensitivity to the dangers of externalism (a false faith placed in people or rituals or dogmas that cannot be fully supported by Scripture). Then through diligent study of the Old and New Testaments we can begin to develop a comprehensive, consistent, and cohesive set of Biblical *beliefs* that will in turn develop Biblical *values* that will be seen in the establishing of Biblical *goals*. Such a cultivation of a strong internal God-consciousness will eventually result in our gladly giving the Lord His rightful place in our lives.

When he summoned the people to Mizpah, Samuel promised them deliverance: "Yahweh will deliver you from the hand of the Philistines" (1 Samuel 7:3). There can be no doubt that he believed that the Lord would cause Israel to be victorious over their enemies (1 Samuel 7:8-9; 12:8,10; Joshua 24:7; Judges 3:9,15; 4:3; 6:6-7; 10:10,12).[11]

THE RESULT OF RECOMMITMENT (7:5-11)

Mizpah is a mountain about five miles northwest of Jerusalem in the tribe of Benjamin. It has an elevation of 2935 feet above sea level. The view from its summit is breathtaking. One can see mount Gerizim to the north; the promontory of Carmel to the northwest; the cities of Jaffa and Ramleh; the coastline of the Mediterranean; Jerusalem and the mount of Olives to the south; the Jordan valley to the southeast; and beyond the region occupied in Old Testament times by the Ammonites and Moabites.[12]

By ones and twos, in families and in small groups, and from all points of the compass, the people began to converge on Mizpah. They brought their food with them, for this was not a convocation that would be over in a day. It took time for them to assemble. One ewe even gave birth to a lamb (1 Samuel 7:9) while the people were journeying on foot or by donkey to the place where Samuel, the man of God, had summoned them.

For Samuel it must have been a tense yet exciting scene. After his many years of patient persistent labor, would he see a return to national unity? Would the people rededicate themselves to the Lord in heart and mind? Would they have enough purpose and courage to resume the battle against those who had inflicted such heavy losses on them at the battle of Aphek?

Here and there among the crowd Samuel saw those whose lives he had touched. He recalled their struggles, their trials, the opposition they faced from family and friends, their temptations, and their eventual triumphs. These personal triumphs were the first evidences that the soft winds of change were beginning to blow across the land.

Dedication to the Lord (7:5-6)

On a solemn day of assembly set apart for fasting[13] and confession of sin[14] the people began by drawing water and pouring it out before the Lord (1 Samuel 7:6; cf. Psalm 22:14; 2 Samuel 14:14; Lamentations 2:19). There was no Biblical precedent for this act, so speculation concerning its meaning has been widespread.[15] Inasmuch as water once poured on the ground cannot be gathered up again, the people seemingly were indicating the irrevocability of their decision to

follow Yahweh and do His will. It was as if they were dedicating themselves to Him with no thought of ever going back on their decision.

Fasting and confession of sin added to the solemnity of the occasion. These acts further attested the desire of the people to renew a
right relationship with the God of their fathers.

"And Samuel judged the sons of Israel" there (1 Samuel 7:6). Dr.
Walter C. Kaiser's comments on Samuel's role as a judge are worth
noting:

> Although some modern versions shy away from using this
> expression [to judge], it is clearly the meaning of the Hebrew.
> Perhaps we do not understand that there is a proper conse-
> quence for all genuine repentance. We thereby miss the fact that
> there must be a work of adjudication to be carried out by God's
> earthly representative.... Samuel was one such representative.
> He was there by God's design for the purpose of directing and
> ordering His people in the administration of justice and
> righteousness. In accordance with the previous acts of
> repentance, the reality of confession must be tested, both [by]
> the amount of restitution and the alacrity with which it was
> carried out. Wherever there had been theft, cheating, or other
> acts of injustice, the sincerity of the nation's confession was
> somewhat in doubt until there were acts of full restoration or
> plans for it. God had placed Samuel in the post of leader of this
> great convocation in order that he might exercise the function
> of "judging."[16]

Defeat of One's Enemies (7:7-11)

We might have expected that with the people rededicating their
lives to the Lord, He would bless and prosper them and in time give
them victory over their enemies. The last thing they expected was a
fresh attack by the Philistines. Once again Dr. Kaiser's comments are
worth noting:

> Mark it well: whenever there are deep stirrings of the Spirit
> of God in the renewing and reviving of lives, there the evil one
> will also be just as active in attempting to counter all the good
> work that has been done. His tricks are too many and varied to
> be listed here, but the people of God would be foolish to overlook
> them or be ignorant of them. Accordingly, just as God was
> stirring the hearts of Israel at Mizpah, the devil was rousing a
> mistaken judgment among the Philistines. [They believed] the

Israelites had assembled at Mizpah in order to launch a national revolt against their rule over them.[17]

It took time for runners to carry messages to the five cities of the Philistine pentapolis and time for the soldiers to be mustered at a place where they could launch an attack. The lords of the Philistines quickly mapped out their strategy. They decided not to wait to be attacked but rather to take the offensive.

Using the valleys and ravines that lead up to Mizpah, the Philistines moved as close as possible before beginning to climb its ravines. Someone saw their vast army ascending the mountain and spread the alarm. Fear quickly spread through the entire assembly. With justified anxiety they implored Samuel to pray[18] for them.

Fear receives its strength when we attribute to a person, place, or thing two qualities that properly belong to God: *almightiness* (the power to take away our autonomy or freedom to function as we see fit) and *impendency* (the power to do us harm). The only antidote to such fear is to place ourselves unreservedly under the sovereignty of God. By committing ourselves unreservedly to Him (1 Peter 5:7) we can trust Him with our well-being. If we do not commit ourselves to God and prefer to face the vicissitudes of life in our own strength, we have to grapple unaided with the crippling effects of anxiety, the defeat of our plans, and the painful reinforcement of our impotency.

When we commit ourselves to the Lord, we are able to employ the resources He has given us. These according to 2 Timothy 1:7 are *power* and *love* and *discipline.* We do not have to rely on our own strength or abilities. Instead as we avail ourselves of the grace God has made available to us, the Holy Spirit empowers us for every good work (2 Timothy 2:1; 3:16-17).

As we contemplate the lives of great men and women whose brief biographies are brought before us in God's Word, we are encouraged by their examples. They drew comfort from God's love for them; knowing that the Lord loves us too, we can commit ourselves to steadfastness of purpose. Then as we persevere in the work the Lord has given us to do, we will be able to overcome the difficulties that otherwise might deter us and cause us to become discouraged.[19]

Samuel's prayer was accompanied by the sacrifice of a seven-day-old lamb (Leviticus 22:27), which was offered as a whole burnt offering (Leviticus 6:22-23)[20] symbolizing the complete dedication of the nation to the Lord. Samuel cried out to God and He answered him (1 Samuel 7:9). The text of 7:10a is parenthetical for the battle was the Lord's. He thundered against the Philistines; Josephus claims that the thunder and lightning were accompanied by an earthquake, which caused the ground under the feet of the invaders to move and open to terrify the Philistines further.[21] William Blaikie stated:

> There is no need for supposing that the thunder was supernatural. It was an instance of what is so common [in Scripture], a natural force adapted to the purpose of an answer to prayer. What seems to have occurred is this: a vehement thunderstorm had gathered a little to the east, and now broke, probably with a violent wind, in the faces of the Philistines. Being superstitious by nature, and acknowledging Baal, god of the storm, as one of their deities, the Philistines are overawed by his supposed opposition to them. The men of Israel, only slightly inconvenienced by the fury of the elements (seeing it came from behind them), rushed on the embarrassed enemy, and drove them before them like smoke before the wind. It was just as in former days—God arose, and His enemies were scattered and they also that hated Him fled before Him.
>
> The thunderstorm, we may be sure, was a natural phenomenon. But its occurrence at the time was part of that great scheme of Providence which God planned at the beginning, and it was planned to fall out then in order that it might serve as an answer to Samuel's prayer. It was an answer to prayer brought about by natural causes.[22]

And the men of Israel, leaving their wives and children behind, ran down the slopes of Mizpah in pursuit of the Philistines and chased them as far as Beth-car (1 Samuel 7:11). (The site of Beth-car is unknown to us.) What is evident from these events is that the victory over the Philistines was the Lord's, not Israel's. He orchestrated events far beyond Israel's power to comprehend and delivered them from those who formerly had oppressed them.

THE REMINDER OF PAST BLESSINGS (7:12-14)

The defeat of Israel's enemies was a thorough one. Not only did the Philistines make no attempt to regroup their forces after the debacle; the "hand of Yahweh was against them all the days of Samuel." Another blessing was that there was peace between Israel and the Amorites. This time of peace gave God's people the opportunity to recover economically as well as morally and socially from the effects of two full decades of hardship and privation (Proverbs 16:7).

Because it is part of human nature to forget those special occasions when God has sovereignly intervened on behalf of His people and blessed them beyond their deserts, Samuel erected a memorial to remind his countrymen of what the Lord had done for them. He called it *'eben hā'ēzer,* Ebenezer, "stone of help," and said, "Until now [thus far, to this point] Yahweh has helped us."

THE REVIEW OF A NOBLE LIFE (7:15-17)

The inspired chronicler concluded his narration of the events by summarizing the remainder of Samuel's life:

> And Samuel judged Israel all the days of his life; and he went from year to year, and traveled a circuit [to] Bethel, and Gilgal, and Mizpah; and he judged Israel in all these places; and he returned to Ramah, for there [was] his house, and there he judged Israel; and he built an altar to Yahweh there (1 Samuel 7:15-17).

There will always be those who try to detract from the greatness of the godly by interjecting questions about the reliability of the record of their deeds. Many modern commentators claim that Samuel could not possibly have judged "*all* Israel" from his circuit of Ramah, Bethel, Gilgal, and Mizpah, for this was too limited a circumference. They forget that while the apostle Paul was in Ephesus "*all* Asia" heard the word of the Lord (Acts 19:10) because (1) from Ephesus Paul sent out people to evangelize other towns and cities (for example, Colossae, Laodicea, Hierapolis) and (2) people from the towns and cities of Asia who heard about Paul came to Ephesus to see and to hear him.

From a careful consideration of 2 Kings 2:3; 4:38; 6:1 and 1 Samuel 19:19-20 we know that Samuel established schools for the training of young prophets in Ramah, Bethel, Gilgal, and Mizpah. It seems natural to assume that he trained young men to go out from these schools to minister throughout the land. Those who had difficult problems to resolve would wait for one of Samuel's visits and then go to him for adjudication.

Dr. Blaikie's assessment of Samuel's life and character puts matters in their correct perspective.

> Samuel stands out as one of the best and purest of the Hebrew worthies. His name became a perpetual symbol of all that was upright, pure and Godlike. The silent influence of his character was a great power in Israel, inspiring many a young heart with holy awe, and silencing the flippant arrogance of the scoffer.[23]

Samuel was a man of vision, courage, fortitude, and great humility. He stood alone against his people's intransigence and desire to practice evil, and through incredible perseverance ultimately restored their national spirit. Following the incidents mentioned in 1 Samuel 7 he continued to minister to his people for perhaps another forty-five years. The Biblical writer, however, concluded this part of Israel's history in his characteristic fashion (cf. 4:18b; 14:47-52) so that he could move forward in the next section to the establishment of the monarchy.

IT'S COMFORTING TO KNOW

As we assess the practical implication of these events, it is comforting to know that *God is sovereign in our disappointments and times of sore trial as well as in our deliverances.* He was with Samuel when he was rejected from the priesthood and He sustained him when his message fell on deaf ears. God also showed His goodwill toward His people when they repented of their sins and gave them the victory over their enemies. A closer examination of the text will show that He is sovereign in all of our circumstances, delights in us when we give Him priority in our lives, and sovereignly restores us to His favor when we repent of our sins.

Sovereign over Our Circumstances

As I think of the different ways in which God shows Himself to be sovereign over all of our circumstances, my mind turns to Amy. After waiting for an appropriate time after marriage, she and her husband Steve decided to start a family. Amy and Steve desperately wanted children, but soon after conception there were the telltale signs of a miscarriage. This scenario would be repeated four times over the next seven years.

Amy was crushed. The more time passed, the more she wanted to be a mother. What made matters worse was that all her married friends had no difficulty bearing children.

In counseling sessions for several months we grappled with the issues of God's providence and His promises on the one hand, and her experience on the other. With much pain and with great reluctance Amy ultimately accepted her childlessness as God's will for her and Steve. She found His grace to be sufficient for her need.

In the course of time Steve felt led of the Lord to prepare for the ministry. After four years of arduous graduate study, he was in his mid-thirties when he and Amy applied to a mission board and were

accepted. Their assignment? To serve as houseparents to missionaries' children in a boarding school.

After long years of wanting a family Amy now had children on whom
she could shower her love and devotion. Her letter from the field
concluded with the well-known quotation from Isaiah 54:1:

> Shout for joy, Oh barren one, you who have borne no child; break
> forth into joyful shouting and cry aloud, you who have not
> travailed, for the sons of the desolate one will be more numerous
> than the sons of the married woman.

God had shown Himself to be sovereign over her circumstances
and had given her the desires of her heart.

Sovereign in Our Priorities

God is honored when we order our priorities in accordance with
His will. Mike had steadily worked his way up the corporate ladder
to the point where he was the vice-president of marketing and enjoyed a lucrative bonus each year as well as many fringe benefits. He
and his wife Debbie had three children and the oldest was rapidly
approaching his thirteenth birthday. They were all active in their
church and Mike felt that "he had it made."

A hostile takeover, however, deprived Mike of his income, and
Debbie and their children of their security. Mike visited with several
firms of "headhunters," but nothing opened up for him. As the shock
to his sense of worth began to wear off, Mike took careful inventory
of their situation. He had prospered in every area of his life—except
one. His friends considered him a great success. He and Debbie drove
fine cars; their children had the best of literally everything. There
was no material benefit they could not afford.

But as Mike reflected on his situation, he realized that he was spiritually bankrupt and that his materialistic way of life was having a
devastating effect on his family. He began studying the Bible for himself and decided on a change. They would sell their fine home and
move to the country. He would take a less stressful job in a small
town so he would have more time with his children.

Several years later when our paths crossed, we reflected on the
trials through which he had passed. He readily acknowledged his
former blindness to spiritual realities. He had a renewed perspective on God's remarkable superintendence of his affairs. He concluded
this part of our conversation by saying, "I being in the way, the Lord
led me" (Genesis 24:27, KJV).

God had sovereignly used a stunning reversal in Mike's life to correct his mistaken sense of values. He needed to reorder his priorities. When he did, the result brought greater happiness to him and also to his family.

Sovereign in Our Restoration

There are some sins that we believe God can and does freely forgive. We are thrilled when we hear someone testify in our churches that he has been saved from a life of drugs or crime. But many believe there are other sins that brand a person as a modern-day incurable leper. These sins are divorce and immorality. But the blessing of the gospel message is that God is sovereign in our restoration as well as in our conversion.

Maddi is a modern-day example of someone who needed restoration. Her story may be hard to understand, but it is true.

She grew up in a dysfunctional family on a farm in Oregon. Maddi was the only girl in the family and had four older brothers. Throughout her formative years she was treated like a thing rather than a person of worth. Her mother was very passive; and the harsh unloving attitude of her father and brothers left her unsure of herself and lacking in personal esteem.

Maddi told me, "As I grew through my teen years I wanted more than anything else to be loved by someone and be made to feel special. As soon as I could, I left home. Being on my own was a new experience. The freedom was exhilarating, but soon the accompanying loneliness and insecurity made me vulnerable.

"Although I had received Christ a few years earlier as a consequence of attending a Bible study in the home of a young couple who were interested in the youth of my school, I lacked a solid faith. It wasn't long before I began sharing an apartment with Joe. I knew inwardly that what I was doing was wrong, but my emotional needs caused me to rationalize the situation. I believed that one day we would be married, and that would make it right. Two years later when Joe and I needed money to pay some debts, we went to California and became involved in the making of pornographic movies.

"In the course of time, Joe dropped me for someone else, and my world fell apart. For several years my conscience had been bothering me, and now I felt inwardly dirty and unclean. In seeking for peace, I turned to the Lord. I wept in contrition, and implored His forgiveness. As a part of my plan for restructuring my life, I decided to go to church. One Sunday evening during a time set apart for testimonies, I tearfully told my story. The instantaneous result was not love and understanding, but rejection and isolation. I felt bewildered and betrayed. And feeling shunned by God's people, I shunned them in return. I know now that this was a foolish and immature thing to do, but I reacted unwisely to the way I was being treated. Naturally, the old feelings of loneliness and insecurity returned.

"How then did the Lord work in my life? Well, I love to read, and one day while browsing through a secondhand bookstore in Long Beach, I came across a book you had written. On the back cover, in the blurb about the author, I found that you lived close to where I was staying. In your book you had treated some of the emotional problems I was struggling with at the time, and I decided to try and contact you."

And that is how we met.

The last three years have been painful ones for Maddi. The process of restoration has been arduous. Suffice it to say that her faith has grown. She has come to understand more fully the grace of God in forgiveness and cleansing, and with this understanding has come a new sense of purpose. She has remained chaste and has begun making new friends. She has also taken courses in a junior college to prepare herself for a career.

At Christmastime she sent me a card. Under her name was a reference to a few Bible verses: "Nahum 1:3,6a,7a." She had learned that while God's way is in the whirlwind and the storm and none can stand before His indignation, He is good to those who trust in Him and is a stronghold in the day of trouble.

As God restored the Israelites, forgiving and cleansing them, so He rebuilds the lives of those who turn to Him in faith confessing their sins. He is sovereign in all of our disappointments as well as in our deliverances. He works all things after the counsel of His will (Ephesians 1:11; Psalm 32:8; 73:24) and makes even the wrath of the ungodly to praise Him (Psalm 76:10). He constantly surrounds us with evidences of His love and grace (Psalm 40:5; 139:17) and after a time of difficulty we find that the experience through which we have passed has yielded the peaceable fruit of righteousness (Hebrews 12:11).

MISPLACED PRIORITIES

1 Samuel 8:1-22

When John Naisbitt's *Megatrends*[1] was published in 1982, we were forcefully reminded of the dramatic changes taking place within our society. The old concerns of the 1960s and 1970s—racism, sexism, and ageism—while still present, were seen to be giving way to concerns over coping with the effects of a radical shift from a reliance on industry to a reliance on information. And as we have all found, change can be both threatening and challenging.

To the person who has not kept pace with recent trends in the area of his specialty, a shift of focus can be very unsettling. When he finds his skills dated, a variety of emotions suddenly surface: anxiety, frustration, anger, disappointment, stress, depression, and eventually despair.

But change also presents a challenge. Now more than ever before, Christians who are knowledgeable of God's Word have the opportunity to apply its teachings to their individual experiences. The result can be a greater impact on those about them than may have been possible in the past.

In dealing with change we can follow the example of Samuel who faced the threats and challenges of radical shifts in his society.

OUTLINE

As we consider 1 Samuel 8 we notice that the winds of change had picked up and were now blowing strongly across the land of Israel. The people wanted a king. Their rationale was simple: "That we also may be like the nations [round about us]" (8:20). We observe:

- The Historic Setting (1 Samuel 8:1-3)
- The Request of the People (1 Samuel 8:4-5)

• The Response of Samuel (1 Samuel 8:6-18)
• The Request Repeated (1 Samuel 8:19-22)

THE HISTORIC SETTING (8:1-3)

Following the defeat of the Philistines by the Israelites, Samuel emerged as the leader of God's people. Throughout the next twenty-five years "the hand of Yahweh was against [upon] the Philistines" (1 Samuel 7:13). As long as Samuel was judging the tribes, their enemies were unable to prevail against them. The advancing Philistine tide was stemmed, and no further expeditions were attempted such as the one that had been so signally defeated following the convocation at Mizpah.

A New Generation

A new generation, however, had arisen. They had only heard from their parents how the Lord delivered them from their enemies. Having been reared in comparative peace and safety, the younger Israelites took for granted the privileges of the theocracy without properly understanding the source of their many benefits. With the passing of time appreciation of the advantages of having God as their King (whom they could not see) began to give way to the desire for a more ostentatious kind of administration. As the memory of the evils from which God had delivered them became fainter and the benefits that God did not bestow (because of their spiritual apathy) became more conspicuous by their absence,[2] the people started to criticize their form of government. They began to talk of the efficiency other nations appeared to enjoy, and they came to despise their own system of administration.

And Samuel was now about sixty-five years of age. He was old by the standards of the day[3] and perhaps his gray hair (1 Samuel 12:2) accentuated their concerns over his continued ability to lead them. Furthermore the weight of his years caused them to question who would succeed him.

In a theocracy, with God ruling His people through an earthly representative, there is no need for people to be anxious about matters of leadership. God is their King, and knowledge of this fact gives stability to those who live under His rule.

The Israelites however lost sight of this important fact and felt that they must act decisively on their own behalf. They exaggerated their fears that Samuel's sons might be designated to follow him. Joel and Abijah were serving as judges[4] in the border town of Tell es-Seba',

Beersheba, the ancient "well of the seven" or "well of the oath,"[5] fifty miles south of Jerusalem on the southern boundary of the tribe of Judah. Because Samuel's circuit was mainly confined to the center of Canaan, he had appointed his sons to serve as judges in Beersheba. From the evidence of 1 Samuel 8:3 we deduce that their duties were chiefly those of civil administrators.

An Old Problem

Preachers have invariably been quick to draw a parallel between Eli and Samuel. They denounce Samuel for being a poor father and for neglecting his familial responsibilities. Dr. Alfred Edersheim corrects this popular though mistaken view. He places the sinfulness of Joel and Abijah in the context of their times.

> Although [they were] not guilty of the wicked practices of Eli's sons, yet among a pastoral and nomadic population there would be alike frequent opportunity for, and abundant temptation to, bribery; nor would any other charge against a judge so quickly spread, or be so keenly resented as this.[6]

We in no way excuse the conduct of these young men. The teaching of Moses clearly forbade any form of dishonest gain or the taking of bribes or the perversion of justice (Exodus 18:21; 23:2,6,8; Deuteronomy 16:19; 24:17; cf. Isaiah 1:23; 5:23; Amos 5:7,12).

Instead of joining in the chorus of condemnation, we as parents can learn from Samuel's experience (Romans 15:4; 1 Corinthians 10:11). While we may rear our children wisely, we have no guarantee that they will be loyal and devoted to the Lord. From what is recorded here and in 1 Chronicles 6:27-28,33 we are given hope in the midst of uncertainty. Let us learn, therefore, from *all* that we are told of Samuel's sons.

While living with their parents, Joel and Abijah benefited from their father's example. He was a man of steadfastness, perseverance, impeccable integrity, and great humility. There can be little doubt that the boys were powerfully impacted by his strong headship. It is also true that Samuel went on an annual circuit to judge the people and minister to students in the schools of the prophets, and while he was away his wife had to care for their sons. But there is no reason to believe that the home of Joel and Abijah was anything but a good one.

In their early years Joel and Abijah endured privation since their father had no sure or steady income, but these financial problems did not prevent them from seeking to follow in his footsteps. They probably studied in and graduated from the school of the prophets at Ramah.

Normally a father will give his sons the advantage of notable positions in his company or organization. Samuel, however, gave his sons a most unattractive assignment. He sent them with no guarantee of financial support to Beersheba. Their remuneration would come solely from those who might contribute a chicken or a lamb to them out of gratitude.

Those who unite to denounce Samuel for appointing his sons to this office believe that he wanted to establish a form of succession to his position as judge. It is more reasonable to assume that Samuel chose his sons for the task of administering justice along Judah's southern border because they were qualified for the task. The difficulties (and perhaps dangers) of their assignment may be better understood when we consider that both of them were sent to the same place, probably so that each could be supportive of the other.

In towns like Beersheba local residents were suspicious of strangers. It was bad enough that Joel and Abijah were outsiders. What made matters even worse was that they came as civil magistrates. Their appointment was far from ideal.

In assessing the failure of Joel and Abijah we need to bear in mind that a very large number of people can function well *under* strong leadership. However, when the restraints of responsibility to a superior are removed, weaknesses not before apparent may be revealed. It may well have been thus with Samuel's sons.[7] They needed time to grow and mature. First Chronicles 6:33 suggests that Joel (and perhaps also Abijah[8]) may have repented of his sins, for he established a godly home and his son is mentioned as officiating in the temple.

From the experiences of Samuel and his sons we can and should learn several important lessons. We all want the best for our children but as they develop their skills we need to remember that *failure is not final.* If they have proper parenting in their formative years, there is no reason why they should not eventually become staunch men and women of God (Proverbs 22:6).

THE REQUEST OF THE PEOPLE (8:4-5)

Sometime during the year 1044 B.C. the elders of Israel gathered to discuss matters of national importance. They agreed on an agenda and then made their way to Ramah. When they had all arrived, they went to Samuel's lowly home (1 Samuel 8:4). The house was unimpressive by their standards, and their meeting with the prophet may have taken place in the courtyard (cf. 9:26) or, depending on the number of men present, in the street.

Standing before Samuel the elders made known their desire for a change in the administration. Their words contained a mixture of (1) unjust criticism, "Look, you have grown old" (implying that Samuel was now incompetent to discharge his duties); (2) condemnation and censure, "Your sons do not follow in your way"; and (3) a consensus of opinion, "So now[9] appoint us a king to judge us like all the nations." Their request, which was in reality a demand, permitted no discussion of the issues (1 Samuel 8:5).

A monarchial form of the theocracy had been foreseen and planned for by God. He had said to Abraham that kings would be among his descendants (Genesis 35:11) and Moses had intimated that the nation would one day be ruled by kings (Deuteronomy 17:14-20). In the plan of God such a leader would be an Israelite, not someone from one of the surrounding nations, and he would be chosen by God.[10]

Latent in the words of the elders, however, was their dissatisfaction with God as their King. To them the deliverance of the nation from Egypt, the greatest empire of that day, happened too long ago to be of contemporary significance. The God-given victories over Sihon and Og were regarded as embellished accounts told and retold around campfires to impress the young. And the triumphant campaign of Joshua as well as the heroic exploits of the judges were looked on as having no lasting importance. Times had changed and the Israelites wanted to be like the other nations.

William Blaikie wisely directs our attention to the prevalence of such a sentiment even among God's people.

> It is too much a characteristic of our human nature that [we are] indifferent to God, and to the advantages which are conferred by His approval and His blessing....Our hearts hanker after the things of the world. Our acquaintances and friends are better off. Our house is bare and [homey], our dress is poor, our simple fare distresses us, and we would fain be in a higher worldly sphere, enjoying more consideration, and participating more freely in worldly enjoyments....To be deprecating the surpassing gifts which God has given, and to be exaggerating those which He has withheld, is far from being in a wholesome condition. Your glory is that you are a chosen generation, an holy nation, a royal priesthood, a peculiar people, your bodies temples of the Holy Ghost, your souls united to the Lord Jesus Christ.[11]

And he is right. But what was Samuel's response to those who demanded that he appoint them a king?

THE RESPONSE OF SAMUEL (8:6-18)

Unjust Dismissal from Office (8:6-9)

First Samuel 8:6 begins with an emphatic *but:* "But the thing was displeasing (literally, bad) in the sight of Samuel when they said, *'Give us a king to judge us.'* And [he] prayed to Yahweh" (emphasis added).

Samuel must have withdrawn into his home or some other secluded place where he poured out his heart to the Lord. He felt his rejection keenly. He was now sixty-five and he had served the people in one capacity or another for more than six decades. His judgeship spanned no less than forty-five years. None had ever had a complaint about him (1 Samuel 12:2-5). He had faithfully discharged his duties and the treatment he was getting now showed the base ingratitude of the Israelites. We can learn some important lessons from the way in which Samuel handled his rejection.

Common Responses to Rejection. People often respond to rejection with aggression or resentment or other negative attitudes. We will be considering common reactions to some situations involving rejection.

The pain of rejection is very personal. It is also persistent and if not handled properly can have far-reaching effects on our lives. Rejection results from a *denial of approval, affection, or recognition* by an emotionally significant person or group. If we are unable to cope with our feelings of rejection adequately, they can undermine our sense of worth, corrode our confidence, and give rise to insecurity, helplessness, and frustration.

A basic form of rejection is *denial of approval.* We are familiar with the reaction of a child when he is reprimanded by his father or mother. His parent's approval means a great deal to him and he is deeply hurt by a reprimand. It is hard for him to live with his father's or mother's disapproval because it makes him feel insecure. His feelings of rejection come from a basic need for security.

The child may respond to his feelings of rejection by asserting himself against some other person or thing (a younger sibling or a dog or a cat). In his mind his assertiveness is equated with strength, and strength with security. Unfortunately this demonstration of assertiveness frequently leads to further reproof and increased feelings of rejection. As a child grows older he may learn not to respond in such an obvious manner, but in repressing his feelings he will more than likely be laying the foundation for an overly sensitive, hyper-critical disposition.

Another form of rejection is *denial of affection*. It occurs most notably in the teenage years but is experienced at other times as well, as the following true story illustrates.

One morning a woman dropped in to see her friend. Since it was really too early for a social call, her friend sensed that something was wrong. As the story unfolded she found that the woman's husband had walked out on her. Their marriage had not been a happy one and that morning he had told her that he was tired of her constant criticism. He felt that nothing he did could ever satisfy her. Just before leaving he announced that some movers would come later in the day and pick up his things.

In leaving his wife this husband was responding to her rejection (her denial of affection). Now it was her turn to experience rejection.

Denial of recognition is equally hard to take. "Sixty Minutes" carried a documentary on the plight of some individuals who were unemployed. The manufacturing plant in which they worked was forced to shut down. Those who were released resented their former employer's failure to recognize their long-term contribution by assigning them to positions in other parts of the country. They responded to their rejection by developing negative attitudes. These attitudes caused invisible barriers as they went in search of other jobs. Their continued attempts to find suitable employment brought the usual empty promise: "We'll let you know if something opens up." Suffering from a lowered sense of worth, they became angry and eventually their days became filled with a lonely brooding over what had happened to them.

Feelings of rejection due to the denial of approval, affection, or recognition are hard to overcome. The inner anguish from which we suffer is acute and if we do not respond appropriately, problems begin to multiply.

Wrong Responses to Rejection. The story of Cain provides examples of wrong responses. Through our study of the Bible we learn not only what happens in a typical rejection syndrome, but also what we can do to avoid it.

Cain felt rejected when God approved Abel's sacrifice but did not accept what he had offered to Him. Cain's facial expression fell, indicating that he was already suffering from feelings of guilt and a lowered sense of esteem. God, however, was not willing to abandon Cain. He gave Cain the opportunity of discussing his feelings.

"Why are you angry?" He asked. "And why has your glance fallen? If you do well, will not [your glance] be lifted up? And if you do not do well, sin is crouching [as a beast] at the door; and its desire is for you, but you must master it" (Genesis 4:6-7).

By inviting Cain to discuss how he felt, God gave him the chance to benefit from talking matters out and setting things right. God said in effect, "Cain, you can deal with your resentment. You can offer the proper sacrifices and enjoy My acceptance as before." But Cain would not admit his error, nor would he offer the proper sacrifices. He wanted acceptance by God on his own terms. He did not ask for forgiveness and as a result he was left in bitterness and disillusionment.

In dealing with his feelings, Cain had three courses of action before him. First, he could have chosen to turn the hurt of rejection inward and inflict punishment for his feelings of guilt on himself. The self-inflicted hurt might have made him feel (temporarily) that he had atoned for the wrong he had done. In reality, however, his relationship with the One whom he felt had rejected him would have remained unchanged. Furthermore, unresolved feelings of guilt would only have led to feelings of unworthiness; and these feelings, if not dealt with, would have led to depression as a result of his sense of loss.

Second, Cain could have attempted to handle his feelings of rejection by projecting his anger outward. He could have blamed his damaged emotions on someone or something else. It is surprising how many grown people resort to this childish way of responding. This kind of response may help us live with ourselves, but in the final analysis it destroys our relationships with others. The eventual result is loneliness and despair.

Third, he could have chosen to see himself as God saw him. Cain could have sought to restore his relationship with the Lord.

Cain chose to project his anger outward. He was in reality angry at God—the authority figure—for rejecting him. Not being prepared to admit his error, he looked for an object on which to vent his animosity and he found Abel. In other words when God would not accept Cain on his own terms, he blamed his brother. The person who is angry is always right in his or her own eyes.

The Hebrew text is most interesting. It reads:

And Cain said to Abel his brother ———— . And it came to pass when they were out in the field, that Cain rose up against Abel his brother and killed him (Genesis 4:8).

How revealing that unfinished sentence is! Cain was unable to give expression to his feelings. His resentment was so great that he became incoherent. He lacked the sophistication with which we mask our emotions today. Our anger, however, is the same—subtle and pervasive.

The final act in the drama took place when God appeared to Cain the second time. "Where is Abel your brother?" He asked.

Cain retorted, "I do not know." His response was a denial of any knowledge of what had happened.

Having first projected blame for his rejection on Abel, Cain now projected blame for Abel's death on God: "I'm not my brother's keeper." Cain's response revealed his anger and implied, "You are wrong even to question me about him."

Cain's improper reaction to his rejection (1) warped his perspective on life, (2) caused him to blame others for what had happened to him, (3) led to a loss of concern for the rights of others, (4) resulted in defiance of God, and (5) ultimately led to loneliness, insecurity, and further rebellion.[12] Cain went out from the presence of the Lord and journeyed as far away as he could.

Right Responses to Rejection. In contrast to Cain, whose rejection was first imagined and then self-inflicted, there is Samuel. Under his leadership the nation had prospered. However, because he was now old and his administration lacked ostentation, the benefits of his superintendence were being ignored. The people had lost sight of the real reason for their success and had begun to compare themselves to those about them. Instead of being thankful for the blessings of Samuel's godly judgeship, they looked askance at his bodily form. The result was the rejection of one of the greatest leaders of all time. As Matthew Henry so clearly pointed out, Samuel "looked mean in the eyes of those who judged by outward appearance; but a king in purple robes with his guards and officers of state would look great."[13]

In learning from Samuel how to handle rejection, it is important for us to notice that he immediately took matters to the Lord (1 Samuel 8:6). The request of the people was displeasing to him but he did not argue with them and pray afterwards. He first retreated inside his home where he laid the whole matter before the One who had commissioned him to lead His people. By praying he was able to let go of the problem, reassure himself of his standing before the Lord, and receive a new perspective on the situation. *This response to his rejection placed him in touch with the Person who was of far more emotional significance to him than the elders of Israel.*

In Samuel's attitude and actions we have the secret of overcoming the debilitating effects of rejection. By means of prayer we are able to discuss everything with the Lord. We are able to tell Him exactly how we feel and why. Through prayer we are given an entirely new perspective that keeps us from harboring resentment and blaming others for the situations we find ourselves in. Furthermore as a result of prayer we are also given new direction.

As Samuel prayed, the Lord was able to encourage him (1 Samuel 8:7).[14] "They have not rejected you," God said, "but they have rejected Me." This new perspective took the sting out of what had happened and kept Samuel from nursing a grievance. God's words reassured him of his standing before Him. The Lord reminded Samuel that the whole history of the Hebrew people had been one of continuous rebellion against God and His authority.[15] They had continuously rejected Him ever since He brought them out of Egypt. And they were now treating Samuel the same way (cf. John 15:18-20).

Samuel also received explicit instructions from the Lord. "Now listen to their voice," God said. "However, you shall solemnly warn them...of the way their king will treat them when he reigns over them."[16]

How different from our own was Samuel's way of handling rejection. All too often we argue first and pray later.

Faithful Discharge of His Duty (8:10-18)

Rising from prayer, Samuel did as the Lord had commanded him. He faithfully related to the people all that God had told him.

The people of Beersheba had every right to be dissatisfied with the administration of Samuel's sons, but the system of government the whole nation was now requesting would be much worse. While all the kings would not act in accordance with each facet of the description of the monarchy in 1 Samuel 8:10-18, Solomon and others would place heavy taxes on the people. We learn from this passage that future events are affected by present decisions!

If the enthronement of a king was to be so detrimental to the people, how can Israel's monarchy prefigure the millennial reign of Christ? How are we to understand the place of the monarchy in God's progressive revelation?

Dr. William Blaikie has again enriched our understanding with an excellent discussion of the kind of king requested by the people and the yet future rule of the Lord Jesus Christ.

[Samuel] now shows them the "manner of the king"—[and] the relation in which he and they will stand to one another.[17] He is not a king that gives, but a king that takes. His exactions will be multifarious. First of all, the most sacred treasures of their homes, their sons and their daughters, will be taken to do hard work in his army, and on his farms, and in his house.[18] Then, their landed property will be taken on some pretext—the vineyards and olive-yards inherited from their fathers—and given to his favourites.[19] The tenth part of their produce, too, of what remains will be claimed by him for his officers and his servants,[20] and a tenth of their flocks. Any servant, or young man, or animal, that is particularly handsome and valuable will be sure to take his fancy, and to be attached for his service. This will ordinarily be the manner of their king. And the oppression and vexation connected with this system of arbitrary spoilation will be so great that they will cry out against him, as indeed they did in the days of Rehoboam, yet the Lord will not hear them. Such is Samuel's picture of what they desire so much, but it makes no impression; the people are still determined to have their king.

What a contrast there is between this exacting king, and the true King, the King that in the fullness of time is to come to His people, meek and having salvation, riding upon the foal of an ass! If there be anything more than another that makes this King glorious, it is His giving nature. "The Son of God," says the Apostle, "loved me, and gave Himself for me." As Prophet He gave Himself to teach, as Priest to atone and intercede, as King to rule and to defend. Even as He hung helpless on the cross, He exercised His royal prerogative by giving to the thief at His side a right to the Kingdom of God. How different the attributes of this King from him whom Samuel delineated! The one exacting all that is ours; the other giving all that is His![21]

THE REQUEST REPEATED (8:19-22)

The people of Israel however were obstinate.[22] They had set their hearts on having a king. Their desire to be "like the other nations" showed their misguided optimism. They were openly courting a despotism whose intolerable yoke future generations would not be able to shake off (1 Samuel 8:18).[23]

The request of 1 Samuel 8:5 became a demand in 8:19. The elders were deaf to reason. They were blinded by self-interest and would not wait for God's appointed time. They rejected the form of theocracy that He had seen fit to establish.

As we analyze the attitude of the people (1 Samuel 8:19-20) we find that they were motivated by a desire for status.[24] Their demand showed their immaturity. They had forgotten that to be different from the other nations was their glory. They believed that they would benefit from the added prestige of having a king judge them.

And then there was fear. They feared the growing strength of the Ammonites (1 Samuel 12:12). In the nearly forty-five years since they were defeated by Jephthah, the Ammonites had greatly increased. They now constituted a distinct threat to Israel's national well-being. The sons of Israel were blind to the testimony of the past: whenever they had walked with and relied on the Lord, He had helped them.

Now their intransigence was evident. They were deaf to Samuel's words—even though he was telling them exactly what God had told him. The people failed to give him the recognition that should crown an honorable career and they turned him out of office to make room for another whose gifts and abilities had not been proven. Such actions invariably lead to a decline in morale and a lessening of momentum. In the final analysis the new administration in Israel proved to be less beneficial to those being led than that which had previously prevailed.

Ingratitude is hard to bear. As Samuel faced his predicament, he knew of only one thing to do. He again took matters to the Lord in prayer. Only through prayer could he find the peace of heart and mind he needed. He repeated all the words of the people in the ears of the Lord, even though God knew perfectly well what had taken place. In this way he was able to give vent to his feelings. And as in the previous instance, God gave him further directions.

It is important for us to observe that Samuel's prayer did not change his circumstances. So often when we pray we expect that God will suddenly and miraculously bring about a reversal of what is unpleasant to us. We are then disappointed when He does not act in accordance with our expectations. The key to Samuel's handling of his emotionally charged situation lay in his submission to the will of God. He allowed the Lord to direct his actions and agreed to the people's demand for a king (cf. Hosea 13:11).

Samuel remained loyal to the people of Israel in spite of their rejection of him. His role was reduced, but his lightened responsibilities gave him the opportunity to spend more time training promising young men in the schools of the prophets.

THE CRUCIBLE

Apart from the obvious points of application already treated at some length, what remains to be learned from this rehearsal of a day's events? Several lessons stand out.

We learn that God allows trials, even the trial of rejection, to come our way in order to refine us. However, He does not abandon us to our fate or watch from the sidelines to see what we will do. With each trial He makes provision for us so that we will not be overwhelmed by adversity (1 Corinthians 10:13).

The way in which God helped Samuel face the ordeal of rejection is most instructive. As is so often the case, there was a definite role Samuel played in the drama and a definite role God undertook. Samuel's part was to bring the whole matter to the Lord and wait upon Him for directions. He is sovereign and the willful plans of capricious people cannot thwart His ultimate goal.

In facing rejection one's primary temptation is to accept the other person's judgment and system of values. One becomes a yo-yo on the other person's string. In the passive individual the result is helpless apathy. He feels that he is of no worth because his value has been determined by another. And having reluctantly but tacitly accepted the other person's estimate, he becomes a sympathy seeker or tries to manipulate others in order to attract attention.

In the aggressive individual the response to rejection is an open display of resentment. A hostile exchange of words may ensue, and there may even be violence.

In the moderate individual—he neither passively accepts nor angrily refuses the judgment of the person who rejects him—the response is a gnawing bitterness. Regardless of how well the bitterness may be concealed, ultimately it shows itself in snide comments and derogatory remarks.

Regardless of whether we are passive, moderate, or aggressive in our handling of rejection, if we accept other people's estimates of us, the outcome is the same: loneliness, bitter recrimination, and self-justifying sorties into the past.

The way to avoid this outcome is conceptually simple. In the case of Samuel he refused to accept the system of values of the elders of Israel. He took the whole matter to the Lord in prayer. He found out how he stood in God's eyes. God's evaluation restored his confidence in himself, preserved his perspective, and helped him maintain his emotional equilibrium. He was still God's servant and would continue to serve the Lord and his own people for another twenty-five or more years. The winds of change had only a temporary effect on him, and in the final analysis God opened up for him an even greater door of opportunity.

The difference between Samuel and many of us is striking. His godward relationship was very real. To him the Lord God was not someone worshiped in a perfunctory sort of way once a week, but a person whom he had come to know intimately. Consequently he felt free to share with his Friend the trials and agonies of his heart. And what Samuel experienced is the same quality of relationship the Lord Jesus offers each one of us (John 15:14-16). Our challenge is to walk before the Lord in humble obedience even as Samuel did, accepting what we cannot change and living to please Him who has called us to be His servants (2 Timothy 2:4).

INTENDED FOR GREATNESS

1 Samuel 9:1–10:27

John Gill, a British theologian of a generation past, has reminded us that God's sovereignty is seen in His control of men and events.[1] Scripture teaches us, "He does according to His will in the host of Heaven and among the inhabitants of earth; and no one can stay His hand or say to Him, 'What have you done?'" (Daniel 4:35)

Illustrations of this principle of the sovereignty of God are to be found throughout history. John Bunyan, for example, was drafted as a soldier in the civil war in England and was sent to take part in the siege of Leicester. As he was about to begin sentry duty one night, another requested that they exchange responsibilities. Bunyan agreed. That night the other soldier was shot in the head and died. Bunyan was spared so that in the providence of God he might minister through the written word to generations to come.

At thirty-two years of age William Cowper faced a great crisis. Tired of the struggle, he decided to take his own life. He took an overdose of laudanum, but this suicide attempt failed. Then he tried to drown himself in the Thames river, but he was prevented from doing so. The next morning he deliberately tried to impale himself on a knife, but the blade broke and he was only slightly injured. Then he tried to hang himself—and almost succeeded. Someone found him unconscious and cut him down. In despair he began reading Paul's letter to the Romans and received strength to believe that God loved him. Later he wrote:

> God moves in a mysterious way
> His wonders to perform;
> He plants His footsteps in the sea
> And rides upon the storm.

Deep in unfathomable mines
Of never-failing skill,
He treasures up His bright designs,
And works His sov'reign will.

Christopher Columbus felt greatly disheartened and discouraged after many attempts to obtain financing for a trip to India. While on his way back to Italy he stopped one day at a convent not far from Granada and asked for a drink of water. The monk who gave him the water and heard his story was the man who intervened on his behalf with Queen Isabella. Out of that request for a glass of water came the money to equip the vessels that ultimately crossed the Atlantic— that request led to the discovery of America.

John Calvin was also on his way to Italy when he experienced God's control of his path. In Italy he hoped to find freedom from Roman Catholic oppression and leisure to continue his writing. The road was closed because of the war between France and Italy, so he decided to make a detour through Geneva. There he met William Farel, who with fiery eloquence demanded that Calvin stay in Switzerland. Impressed with Farel's earnestness, Calvin complied, and the cause of the Reformation owes much to his decision.

One day when Abraham Lincoln was rummaging through a barrel of odds and ends, he came across a copy of Lord Blackstone's *Commentaries* (on British jurisprudence). This "chance" discovery awakened his interest in law and human rights. As a result he ran for political office and eventually played a decisive role in the history of our country.

George Whitefield was employed by his brother in the Bell Inn but could not get along with his brother's wife, so he gave up his job and went to Bristol. Then step by step he went to Oxford, met with the Wesleys, and developed a ministry that touched countless thousands of lives on both sides of the Atlantic. Whitefield was perhaps the greatest preacher of his time.

These seemingly chance contacts and events have literally altered the course of history. They illustrate on a human plane what we see in the Biblical story of Saul and his election to the throne of Israel. We derive encouragement from this story since it underscores God's involvement in the seemingly little things in our lives (cf. Psalm 139; Romans 8:18-39). Far from serving some theological abstraction, this story gives us knowledge that strengthens our faith. As Dr. F. B. Meyer wrote, "All these things, if carefully observed, yield their testimony and assurance that God is in all events permitting, directing, controlling, and causing all things to work out His perfect plan."[2]

THE MAN CHOSEN TO BE KING

Before treating the means God used to bring Saul to the throne of Israel, we need to piece together the background of his life. Saul's father Kish[3] is introduced the way Samuel's father Elkanah was (cf. 1 Samuel 9:1 and 1:1). But whereas Samuel's father had been a Levite, Kish is spoken of as a "mighty man of valor."[4]

Kish's family had at one time lived in Gibeon[5] (1 Chronicles 9:35-36) and had a burial plot at Zela (2 Samuel 21:14). We are not told when or under what circumstances they moved to Gibeah (1 Samuel 10:26).[6] In Gibeah Kish distinguished himself for his courage, and in time he became an affluent and influential man. But there is every indication in the narrative that Kish had no godward aspirations and was authoritarian in his treatment of those in his family.[7]

One of Saul's uncles was named Ner (1 Chronicles 9:36) and he may be the one referred to in 1 Samuel 10:14. Ner had a son named Abner, and in time Abner became his cousin Saul's military commander (1 Samuel 14:50-51; 17:55,57; 2 Samuel 2:8-9).

At the time of our story when Saul[8] was sent to look for certain of his father's donkeys, he was about forty years old. The Biblical writer described him as tall and handsome.[9] He was married to Ahinoam, the daughter of Ahimaaz, and according to 1 Chronicles 8:33 they had four sons: Jonathan, Malchi-shua, Abinadab, and Esh-baal (Ish-baal). Esh-baal (also called Ish-bosheth) had not yet been born. From 1 Samuel 18:19-20 we learn that Saul and Ahinoam also had two daughters: Merab and Michal. Just when Saul took a concubine named Rizpah,[10] daughter of Aiah (2 Samuel 3:7), into his home, we do not know. She bore him two sons: Armoni and Mephibosheth (2 Samuel 21:8).

While Bible critics have been quick to point out real or imagined problems in the text and its structure, they fail to agree among themselves.[11] I concur therefore with the late William Blaikie that in 1 Samuel 9–10 God's sovereignty is evidenced in His remarkable providence. The intertwining of events is like "a web of many threads, woven with marvelous skill; a network composed of all kinds of materials, great and small, but so arranged that the very smallest of them is as essential as the largest to the completeness of the fabric."[12]

OUTLINE

As we analyze the contents of 1 Samuel 9–10, we see clearly:

- God's Sovereignty in the Means He Uses
  (1 Samuel 9:1-14)
- God's Sovereignty in the Choice He Makes
  (1 Samuel 9:15–10:16)
- God's Sovereignty in the Confirmation of His Will
  (1 Samuel 10:17-27)

GOD'S SOVEREIGNTY IN THE MEANS HE USES (9:1-14)

When Kish discovered that his donkeys were missing, his words to Saul were in the form of three commands: "Arise! Go! Search!" And so a series of events were set in motion that would eventually bring Saul to Samuel, who would anoint him as the first king of Israel.

According to tradition the servant who accompanied Saul was Doeg the Edomite (1 Samuel 22:18), but no useful purpose is served by such speculation. The servant is unnamed in Scripture and it is better to leave his identity unknown.

Saul and his servant spent three hot tiring days searching diligently for the missing animals. They traveled northward through the steep hills and valleys of Ephraim and then circled around through the "land of Shalishah" and the "land of Shaalim" without finding a single trace of the donkeys. While it is difficult to identify these locations with certainty, Shalishah may possibly be identified with Baal-shalishah (2 Kings 4:42), situated some fifteen miles north of Lydda at a place where three valleys converge in the Wadi Karawa; Shaalim perhaps lay in the direction of Oprah (Judges 1:35) and the wild country around Tayibeh known as the "haunt of jackals."[13]

After traversing this extensive area Saul and his servant passed through the entire territory of Benjamin, but without success. Frustrated and exhausted, Saul was on the verge of giving up when they came to the "land of Zuph" (1 Samuel 9:5). They were less than three miles from home and Saul, who exhibited many notable traits, was concerned about his father's fears for their safety.

His servant, however, believed that they had one last chance to find Kish's donkeys. He said, "Look now, a man of God [is] in this city, and the man is held in honor; all that he speaks certainly comes to pass; now let us go there; perhaps he will declare to us our way which we [should] go on" (1 Samuel 9:6). The servant did not speak of knowing Samuel by name, but only by reputation. He did imply that Samuel was a true prophet (cf. Deuteronomy 13:1-3; 18:21-22).

Saul had been totally ignorant of Samuel's existence until now. This ignorance cannot but strike us as strange, seeing that Samuel lived so close to Saul's hometown and had been such a blessing to the nation. Saul's lack of awareness indicated that Kish and his family were entirely irreligious and totally immersed in their own pursuits.

On learning of Samuel, Saul still evidenced concern. They had nothing to give[14] him for his services. Their food was gone and so was their money. Giving a prophet some gift in return for his aid or counsel was both customary and expected (Ezekiel 13:19; 1 Corinthians 9:11,13; 1 Timothy 5:18). The messengers who sought the help of Balaam against Israel took the "rewards of divination" in their hands (Numbers 22:7,17); and Jeroboam's wife, who consulted with the prophet Ahijah concerning the sickness of her son, took with her a present of bread and honey (1 Kings 14:3). Saul was therefore rightly concerned about having nothing to give to the man of God. The servant, however, had a quarter of a shekel of silver.[15] He did not offer the money to Saul; the servant said that he would give it to the seer.[16] Being reassured of their acceptance by the prophet, Saul agreed to go.

The sun was dipping in the western sky as the two tired men approached the city gates. Young women were on their way to the well to draw water and Saul inquired of them whether the seer was in the city. They not only told him of Samuel's arrival that day from one of his preaching missions; they also encouraged Saul to hasten into the city, for Samuel was about to leave for the *bāmâ* ("high place")[17] to offer a sacrifice and participate in a meal. Saul and his servant hurried into the city and at the precise time they entered, Samuel was leaving. Had they come to the gate a minute or two later, they would have missed him.

GOD'S SOVEREIGNTY IN THE CHOICE HE MAKES (9:15–10:16)

At Ramah (9:15–10:1)

In a brief flashback we learn that God had taken the initiative in selecting a king for His people. The day before, He had whispered[18] in Samuel's ear, "About [this] time tomorrow I will send to you a man out of the land of Benjamin; and you shall anoint him [to be] the leader of my people Israel" (1 Samuel 9:16).

Samuel's godward relationship was remarkable. His trust in the Lord was implicit. After being rejected by the people (1 Samuel 8) he did not show any resentment when God told him about the man who would replace him as judge of the nation. Instead we note a readiness to further the plan and purpose of God. Such obedience is both noteworthy and praiseworthy. When Samuel saw Saul and his servant, the Lord said to him, "Look, the man of whom I spoke to you; this [one] shall rule[19] over My people" (9:17).

Not recognizing the prophet, Saul asked Samuel for directions to the seer's house. Samuel's response was simple and direct: "I am the seer" (1 Samuel 9:19). And without waiting for Saul to tell him of their errand or for the servant to offer him any money for his services, Samuel invited Saul to dine with him and other hand-selected guests; promised Saul that his return to Gibeah would not be long delayed; assured Saul that he would tell him all that was on his mind; and informed Saul that the donkeys had been found. Then Samuel made a very enigmatic and significant statement: "And to whom [is] the desire of Israel? Is it not to you and to all the house of your father?" (9:20) Samuel's words were designed to arouse Saul's curiosity and lead him into an ever-deepening understanding of himself and God's purpose for him.

Saul's humility was evident in his reply. He claimed he was from one of the least significant families in the smallest of the tribes and asked why he should receive such singular recognition.

Samuel made no direct response. He took advantage of Saul's natural curiosity by giving him time to ponder his words. And in keeping with the seer's instructions Saul and his servant preceded Samuel to the high place where the feast was to be held.

At the feast Saul was seated in the place of honor. The cook brought him the thigh[20] and said to him, "Look! [Here is] that which is left [was reserved for you]! Set it before you; eat, for this set time [it was] kept for you" (1 Samuel 9:24).[21]

A great deal of controversy has arisen over Saul's being given this honor. Some commentators point out that the right thigh was reserved solely for the priests (cf. Exodus 29:27; Leviticus 7:34; 10:14-15; Numbers 6:20) and imply that Samuel was virtually bestowing priestly prerogatives on Saul. These commentators seem to forget that an animal has two hind legs and that the words "that which remains" (1 Samuel 9:24) may well be a reference to the left hind leg that remained after the priests had taken their rightful share. Josephus in his *Antiquities of the Jews* identified this piece of meat as the "royal portion," which would have further indicated to Saul the great events that were soon to fulfill Samuel's words of 9:20.[22]

After dining well, Samuel and Saul returned to the city. They spent time talking on the roof of the house.[23] Of their conversation Dr. William Blaikie wrote:

> Samuel could not but communicate to Saul the treasured thoughts of his lifetime regarding the way to govern Israel. He

must have recalled to him God's purpose regarding His people, beginning with the call of Abraham, dwelling on the deliverance from Egypt, and touching on the history of several judges, and the lessons to be learned from each. We may fancy the fervour with which he would urge on Saul, that the one thing most essential for the prosperity of the nation...was loyalty by the people to their heavenly King, and the faithful obedience to His law and covenant.[24]

Samuel must have gone inside the house, for the next morning he rose early and called to Saul on the roof, "Get up and I will send you on your way" (1 Samuel 9:26).

Samuel showed Saul a significant honor by walking with him down to the gate of the city to see him on his way. As they approached the city limits, Samuel asked Saul to send his servant on ahead of them so that he might "proclaim the word of God" to him. The servant went ahead, and as soon as they were alone, Samuel officially anointed Saul as ruler over God's inheritance.[25] Samuel kissed Saul as a sign of his own loyalty (cf. Psalm 2:12).

Realizing that Saul was probably having difficulty grasping the significance of these events, Samuel gave him three confirmatory signs (1 Samuel 10:2-7). He also told Saul that they must meet again in Gilgal (10:8). The signs would take place in a specified order and at definite places. They would reinforce and establish the word of the Lord to Saul through Samuel.

Dr. Hugh Ross, an astrophysicist from the University of Toronto and now president of Reasons to Believe (an organization dedicated to providing valid rational proof of the Bible's reliability), assured me that at the lowest rate of chance, namely one in ten—thus making allowance for the fact that we do not know the size of the population in the different places through which Saul traveled—the probability of the events mentioned in 1 Samuel 10:2-6 happening in sequence and as Samuel predicted would be one in eight million. As simple as Samuel's signs appear on the printed page, only a sovereign God could orchestrate the necessary events with such precise timing and incredible accuracy.

En Route to Gibeah (10:2-13)

As Saul turned from Samuel, the Lord changed Saul's heart. A herdsman-farmer was given the disposition of a patriot-statesman-warrior. This change caused Saul to think of affairs of state and freed him from the cares of his former manner of life.

En route to Gibeah Saul and his servant met two men close to Rachel's tomb.[26] How these men acquired the knowledge that Kish's donkeys had been found, we are not told. What is significant is that at the precise place mentioned by Samuel the men confirmed the words the prophet had spoken to Saul the night before.

The second sign occurred by the oak of Tabor (probably a large tree that had become a landmark). There Saul and his servant met three men going to worship God at Bethel. This meeting of these two parties previously unknown to each other at the junction of two particular roads was an incident no uninspired man could have foreseen. The supernatural character of Samuel's knowledge of the group of three men was evident because he had predicted not only the number of men, but also their destination, their greeting, their burden, and their gift. Samuel had specifically mentioned that the gift would be two loaves of bread. Originally intended for an offering (Exodus 29:23-25; Leviticus 8:26-29)[27] the loaves were given spontaneously to Saul, who accepted the gift as he had been told he would do.

The third sign took place at the "hill of God,"[28] identified as Tell el-Ful. Some translators add, "where the Philistine garrison is" (1 Samuel 10:5), but this addition appears to be strangely in conflict with the evidence of 7:13-14. If there were a garrison of the Philistines in Saul's hometown, why would he need to be told of their presence? The Septuagint translates the word for *hill* as "height" or "erection," leading some scholars to adopt the idea of a "pillar"—part of a cultic shrine on the summit of the hill. Still others believe the word should be translated "prefect" or "governor." And then there are those who claim that the place had at one time been occupied by a garrison of Philistines but, as there is no verb in the original, there is no necessity for supposing that the place was *then* the residence of a garrison. Finally, certain scholars seek to avoid the problem by changing Gibeah to Geba.[29]

At *Gib'at hā'ĕlōhîm,* "the hill of God," Saul met a group of prophets coming down from a place of worship. As Samuel had predicted, they were playing a variety of musical instruments[30] and singing in praise to God.[31] The Spirit of Yahweh came mightily upon Saul and changed him into another man (1 Samuel 10:6). He now stood in the line of the theocracy and had the power to carry out the desires that had been growing in his heart as a result of his meeting with Samuel. Dr. W. G. Blaikie has rightly shown that "the Spirit of God awakened him to the greatness and responsibilities of his position."[32]

What is most amazing is Saul's behavior when in the company of the prophets. He prophesied among them, possibly singing and praising God as they had been doing. Those who had known Saul previously were amazed by what they saw and heard. From that time onward the expression "Is Saul among the prophets?" became a *māš āl* or proverb for what is most unlikely to occur.[33]

One of the most frequently asked questions is, Was Saul saved when God gave him "another heart"? Was Dr. A. R. S. Kennedy right when he said, "His [Saul's] is the first conversion recorded in sacred literature"?[34] While this issue has been hotly debated, it seems most likely that God gave to Saul that which he lacked by training and heredity. He provided him with the inner disposition to fulfill the tasks of a king. He equipped him, as He had done the judges, so that Saul would be able to deliver His people from those who sought to oppress them. When the transitory enthusiasm of his meeting with the prophets passed, it left Saul with a certain inner sense that could not be satisfied without further communion with the Lord. New powers were at work within him that he did not fully understand. He wanted to be alone to try to sort things out in his mind. Instead of going straight home he probably sent his servant on ahead of him while he ascended the hill to spend time in solitary reflection.

When he arrived at the high place, did Saul use those two loaves of bread for a thank offering? We do not know, but that certainly is a possibility, for he had been given a new disposition.[35]

At Gibeah (10:14-16)

We may well imagine that Saul was received at home with mixed feelings of relief and thankfulness for his safe return. Ironically there is no mention of anything that Kish said to him. Was his father so hardened in his resistance to spiritual realities that he was embarrassed by his son's new association with those who had been worshiping the Lord?

We do read of a discussion with Ner. Having learned from the servant about Saul's interview with Samuel and about the honor paid to Saul by the prophet, and having noted Saul's changed demeanor, Ner asked Saul some leading questions.[36]

Before Saul left Samuel, the aged prophet had told Saul to do whatever seemed appropriate to him. Saul now responded discreetly to his uncle's inquiry. In regard to the matter of the kingdom Saul chose to remain silent. This decision showed his growing maturity. He did not deem it necessary to satisfy his uncle's curiosity. He acted in accordance with his wisdom and modeled for us how we too may keep our own counsel and carefully select those in whom we confide (cf. Galatians 1:16).

GOD'S SOVEREIGNTY IN THE CONFIRMATION
OF HIS WILL (10:17-27)

After the elders of Israel came to Samuel with their demand for a king and God told Samuel to accede to their request, the prophet sent everyone home (1 Samuel 8:22). Now he sent messengers throughout the tribes to summon "the people to [meet before] Yahweh at Mizpah" (10:17). Mizpah had been the site of the national convocation twenty-five years earlier when Israel had renewed their covenant with the Lord. The same site was to be the place where God would lead in the choice of Israel's first king.

While the people were gathering, Samuel met with Saul at Gilgal (1 Samuel 10:8). No one had the slightest intimation of the significance of the sacrifices Samuel offered up on Saul's behalf. The sacrifices were a matter between the two of them and God. The offerings served the purpose of renewing Saul's commitment to the Lord.

Samuel and Saul probably took different routes up to Mizpah. They wanted to avoid as far as possible any charge of collusion. While certain acts may be in God's will, they may cause people to make unwarranted assumptions that may hinder or mar the work of the Lord (Proverbs 16:28; 20:19; Ephesians 4:31; Colossians 3:8; Isaiah 32:7).

Once at Mizpah Samuel reminded all those assembled of what their leaders had determined to do (1 Samuel 8:4-20; 10:18-19). He then went through the process of determining by lot who would be their king (Proverbs 16:33).[37] It is significant that he allowed the personal participation of the different tribes.

The procedure followed is most interesting. Apparently the leader of each of the twelve tribes stepped forward, wrote the name of his tribe on a stone, and placed the stone in a large basin or urn. The container was shaken until all of the stones but one fell out. The remaining stone indicated the tribe from which the new king would come. Imagine the surprise of those present when God indicated not the tribe of Ephraim or Judah or Manasseh, but the tribe of Benjamin.

The heads of the different clans of Benjamin stepped forward and wrote their names on stones. The time-honored procedure was repeated and the clan of Matri was chosen. The heads of the different households of the clan repeated the process and the household of Kish was singled out. And when a selection was made from among his sons, the lot fell on Saul.

Stunned surprise must have been felt throughout the ranks of the nobles, for God had selected not from among the aristocracy but from the smallest tribe, and from a family heretofore unknown in the counsels of the nation. Yet the selection had been conducted in such an open and public manner that no one could refute the means by which God had chosen to reveal His will.

Saul however was not to be found. He already knew the result of the selection process and had concealed himself, revealing his genuine humility and modesty. He was not filled with a consuming ambition that pursued greatness for its own sake; rather he was possessed of the kind of spirit that does not seek great things for itself. And in spite of the fact that the Lord had changed him by giving him a different disposition, he still shrank from the duties that lay before him.

Commentators have taken sides, either praising Saul for his self-abnegation or condemning him for his cowardice. They ignore the fact that other great men have done essentially the same. Athanasius of Alexandria, for example, deliberately avoided meeting with the other clergy when a bishop was to be selected, lest their choice fall on him.

When Dr. V. Raymond Edman knew that God wanted him to teach at Wheaton College, Illinois, he purposely did not attend a meeting in New York City where Dr. J. Oliver Buswell, then president of the college, was scheduled to speak; Dr. Edman was concerned that someone might introduce him to Dr. Buswell, who as a result of the encounter might extend an invitation to join the faculty. Dr. Edman wanted to be sure the invitation came at the prompting of the Lord. A short time later a letter came asking him to accept a position in the political science department. The same spirit animated Saul.

Unable to find their new king, the people apparently appealed to the high priest. He consulted the urim and thummim[38] and Saul's hiding place was revealed (1 Samuel 10:22). Certain representatives of the assembly ran to where the baggage was and found the reluctant monarch. When he was led before the people they were delighted with his appearance. He was taller than all the rest and his size as well as his looks impressed those who were prone to judge by externals.

With a definite allusion to Deuteronomy 17:15 Samuel said, "Do you see him whom Yahweh has chosen?" And the people responded with "Let the king live" (or in the vernacular of western countries, "Long live the king").

Samuel went over the constitution of the monarchy. He may have already written out the "ordinances of the kingdom" and these he placed "before Yahweh" (that is, among the national archives; cf. Deuteronomy 31:26).[39] Samuel then dismissed the people (1 Samuel 10:25) and Saul returned to his home in Gibeah.

With Samuel having made very clear the way in which monarchs are inclined to abuse their power, Saul intended to do what was right.

He had no precedent to follow and did not at once set up an extensive administration. We may be sure that he was grateful that young men whose hearts the Lord had touched accompanied him. Perhaps this group formed his initial bodyguard and carried out errands in the king's name.

As is generally the case when someone is suddenly elevated from among the ranks, there were those who ignored the very evident way in which the Lord had made His will known. They openly opposed Israel's new king. They are described as worthless individuals[40] who may have felt that someone from one of the other tribes (in particular either Ephraim or Judah) would have made a more suitable choice. In their pride they refused to submit to Saul's authority (1 Samuel 10:27). But Saul was not miffed by their arrogant rejection of him. He wisely held his peace[41] and did not regard his opposition as an ominous threat. Instead he rested confidently in the Lord's choice of him to rule over His people.

LOOKING BACK

Looking back we observe God's hand in the events that took place. The probability of so complex a set of circumstances occurring by chance and without God's sovereign control, is impossible to calculate. Consider the intermeshing of events:

- When Kish's donkeys happened to go astray, it was Saul and not one of his brothers who was sent to look for them.
- After three days of fruitlessly searching each canyon and ravine throughout the hill country, Saul and the servant came without premeditation to the place where Samuel lived. A day earlier they would have missed him.
- On approaching the city, Saul and his servant unexpectedly met some young women who had just seen Samuel as they were going to draw water for the needs of their respective households. The exchange of greetings with Samuel had made the women aware of the fact that he was even then on his way to the high place to offer a sacrifice.
- On entering the city, Saul and his servant happened to meet Samuel. Without their telling him of their errand, he set their minds at ease by assuring them that the donkeys had been found.
- Samuel also invited them to dine with him, and they received incidental confirmation of the prophet's prior knowledge of their coming from the cook.

- The next day Samuel gave Saul three signs that would take place in specified places and involve different people (1 Samuel 10:2-5).
- The Spirit of the Lord came upon Saul exactly as Samuel had predicted (10:6,10).
- Confirmation of Saul's selection as king over Israel was conducted in an official manner, proving beyond question God's involvement in the proceedings and His choice of Israel's new king (10:20-21).

Source of Our Confidence

Observing God's hand in all these events is very comforting to us. We see from the experience of Saul how patiently and yet persistently the Lord works behind the scenes to accomplish His purpose in our lives. No incident is insignificant or unimportant. Our most stressful experiences are all a part of His sovereign plan. But lest we allow ourselves to be swayed by an apparent happenstance (Jonah 1:3), let us remember how manifold were God's confirmatory signs to the man of His choosing and how abundant were the proofs of His will.

The truth of God's sovereignty reinforces itself on our minds as we meditate on God's Word and consider how vitally involved He was in the experiences of His people throughout Biblical history. This truth encourages us in times of great blessing when it is easy to rejoice in the Lord and praise Him, and also in times of great depression when we are on the verge of despair and believe ourselves to be forsaken by Him. Then we can remember that as the Lord led Saul even though he was unaware of it, so He has under His control all of the circumstances of our lives. In the final analysis He will accomplish His purposes in and through us (Philippians 1:6).

In light of the teaching of 1 Samuel 9–10, therefore, we can act with confidence and "do as the occasion requires," for God is with us (10:7). The indwelling of the Holy Spirit is given to all believers. There is no partiality with God. He orchestrates the events of our lives even though we may not be aware of His involvement behind the scenes.

With such assurance of the Lord's presence, humility is the only appropriate response. In this respect Saul at this stage of his life serves as a good example. He did not think of himself more highly than was fitting, but instead internalized what was happening in his life and sought to understand the significance of the events that had taken him by surprise. Even those who opposed, ridiculed, and insulted him did not cause him to act unwisely. Rather, he was possessed of the quiet peaceable spirit that seeks for reconciliation instead of retribution.

Greatness of His Power

God's providential intervention is not limited to a single incident in the lives of each of His people. Nor does He reserve these special acts of His providence for a select few.

Consider for example Cyrus the Great (550-530 B.C.). The famous "Cyrus Cylinder"[42] relates how he as king of the Medes and Persians diverted the waters of the Euphrates river and took the city of Babylon in a single night (540 B.C.). He thought that his gods empowered and blessed him in this undertaking. In actual fact the Lord, speaking through Isaiah the prophet, had predicted the event centuries before. God had said: "I am Yahweh and there is no other; beside Me there is no God. I will gird you [for battle] even though you have not known Me" (Isaiah 45:5). Even when Cyrus set about releasing those nations who had been deported to foreign lands either by the Assyrians or the Babylonians, he did so in accordance with the predetermined will of God (Isaiah 45:13; Jeremiah 29:10-14). Yet Cyrus thought he was acting in complete freedom.

From these incidents we take encouragement; we realize how intimately involved the Lord is in all that happens to us. As believers we are exhorted to begin each day by committing ourselves to Him (Psalm 55:22; 1 Peter 5:7). We can trust Him to choreograph the events of our lives, lead us as a shepherd, and show us the way (Isaiah 40:11; Psalm 25:4-5,9). He tenderly cares for us and no circumstance is unimportant to Him.

Of course there are times when we are faced with definite decisions. We are then to conduct ourselves in accordance with God's revealed will (Deuteronomy 29:29). Even the counsel of well-meaning friends is to be shunned if it is not in accordance with the principles taught in Scripture (cf. Nehemiah 6:10-12). The more we know of God's Word the easier it is for us to determine what course of action we should take.

God is honored when we show our reliance on Him, and He pronounces woe on those who carry out plans that are not of His making (Isaiah 30:1-2; Joshua 9:14)—even though they may later ask for His blessing.

Fortunately for us, we have God the Holy Spirit indwelling us, and He leads us into all truth (John 8:32; 16:13; 17:17). As we walk in fellowship with Him, therefore, He is able to guide us not in some mystical or bizarre manner, but in true wisdom (James 3:15-17). Then as we look at the tapestry of our lives we will see that He has divinely chosen the design as well as the colors and worked all things after the counsel of His will.

THE MIGHTY ACTS
OF GOD

1 Samuel 11:1–12:25

In a "Peanuts" comic strip Linus and Lucy are gazing out a window at a thunderstorm. "Look at the rain," Lucy exclaims. "What if it flooded the whole world?"

"It will never do that," Linus affirms. He reminds her of God's promise never again to flood the world (Genesis 9:11-17).

Lucy is visibly relieved. "You've taken a great load off my mind."

Linus responds, "Sound theology has a way of doing that!"

At no time do we need the benefits of sound theology more than when we face the vicissitudes of life. All of us experience setbacks of one sort or another. They are an unfortunate and unhappy part of our earthly existence. Opposition or ridicule, false accusation or injustice, back-room politics or under-the-counter deals—all leave us wondering why the righteous suffer while the ungodly seem to prosper.

None of us can probe the mystery of God's providence and explain why He allowed evil to enter the world. We do know that He has the power to turn the evil intentions of others to work for our good (Romans 8:18-30).[1] We also know that He is not the author of evil and that those who practice sin do so as a result of their own volition (Job 34:10-15; Habakkuk 1:13; James 1:13-15). And yet because He is sovereign we expect Him to exercise His power on our behalf.[2]

Before we consider the teaching of 1 Samuel 11–12 and a situation that appears to lie outside the realm of God's ability to prevent or control, we need to take a brief look at the events that transpired after Saul had been selected as Israel's first king and before Jabesh-gilead was attacked by Nahash.

WISE LEADER OR WEAK KING?

Following the events at Mizpah Saul returned to Gibeah[3] where he apparently made no attempt to set up his kingdom.[4] One reason for the delay may have been his desire not to give those who had opposed his appointment (1 Samuel 10:27) the opportunity to criticize his administration. He needed men and money to establish his throne and these could only be acquired through conscription and taxes. Samuel had warned the people of conscription and taxes when he described the "way of the king" (8:10-18; 10:25) and Saul possibly desired to show that he had no intention of abusing his office.

A second reason for the delay may have been his lack of a unified army. In the absence of military support Saul did not demand his rights. He preferred instead to wait for a more suitable time to consolidate the tribes. In the interim he was content to follow Samuel's instructions and act as each occasion required, knowing that the Lord was with him (1 Samuel 10:7). God in His wisdom had selected a king from the people of Benjamin, the smallest tribe in Israel, and therefore Saul's opponents from the other tribes seem to have contented themselves with expressing their opposition with scornful words.

As we take a closer look at 1 Samuel 11–12, we will notice *God's sovereignty in the events leading up to the establishment of the kingdom.* How long a period of time elapsed between Saul's election and these events cannot be determined with accuracy. Josephus, the Septuagint, and the Latin Vulgate intimate that he may only have had to wait for one month before the messengers arrived from Gilead telling of the invasion by Nahash.[5] This seems unlikely, as I will attempt to prove later in this study.

The Dead Sea scrolls from Cave 4 at Qumran amplify the story for us. Dr. Frank Moore Cross reconstructed the text of the Samuel scroll as follows:

> Now Nahash, the king of the Ammonites, had been oppressing the Gadites and the Reubenites, gouging out the right eye of each of them and allowing Israel no deliverer. No men of the Israelites who were across the Jordan remained whose right eye Nahash, king of the Ammonites, had not gouged out. But seven thousand men had escaped from the Ammonites and entered into Jabesh-gilead.[6]

It appears as if Nahash[7] had launched an ambitious campaign against the tribes of Israel settled on the eastern plateau of the Jordan river. He had probably raised an army by assuring his subjects that Molech,[8] their national deity, had commanded it and would guarantee success. The goal was to take possession of all territory north of the Jabbok river.

The Ammonites had been defeated in battle by Jephthah about forty-four years earlier (Judges 11:1-33). While thoughts of revenge may have spurred them on to conquest, the experience of Balak (Numbers 22:1–24:25; Judges 11:25; cf. Deuteronomy 30:7) should have convinced them that blessing would come to the nations only through Israel (Genesis 12:3; 18:18; 22:18; Zechariah 8:22-23; Isaiah 2:2-4; 14:1-2; 49:6,22-23; 60:14; 61:5). This truth had been confirmed in Ammonite history when they had sought to take away Israel's lands and had been so resoundingly defeated (Judges 11).

Furthermore God had established the boundary of each nation in the ancient Near East (Genesis 10:5,19-20,31-32; Deuteronomy 32:8; Joshua 13:8-10). Nahash and the Ammonites should therefore have been content with their allotted land (Judges 11:24), but they were not.

Communication in Israel during this period of Ammonite aggression was about the same as communication during the early days of the American frontier. News, much of it exaggerated and unreliable, was brought by travelers or those leading caravans. There was no type of postal service; consequently it was easy for people to become isolated. The Jordan river formed a natural barrier between the tribes on the eastern plateau and their kinsmen in the rugged hills to the west. These barriers in communication and geography created a provincial mindset that could only be changed as a result of some crisis that would convince people of their need for help from other tribes. After Saul was chosen to be king he gave no intimation of having set up an information network. And while his fellow countrymen had become alarmed over the way in which the Ammonites had taken over the territory of Reuben and perhaps part of Gad (1 Samuel 12:12), Saul appeared to be waiting for the Israelites who lived to the east of the Jordan river to ask him to help them.

DELIVERANCE FROM AN EVIL OPPRESSOR (11:1-15)

Fear Realized (11:1-3)

In 1043 B.C. at the time of year when kings "go forth to war" (2 Samuel 11:1) Nahash again marshaled his battalions and marched northward.[9] His goal was the subjugation of the tribe of Gad, and in particular Jabesh-gilead, one of its principal cities.[10]

We would have expected the people of God to use the intervening months to repair their relationship with the Lord and do all in their power to fortify their city. Instead the elders appear to have passively accepted Nahash's right to rule over them. They even had their speech ready: "Make a covenant with us and we will serve you" (1 Samuel 11:1).

In place of the repentance, humility, and waiting upon God that had brought results in the past, they proposed an alliance with the enemy. The men of Jabesh readily agreed to become the vassals of the Ammonites. Any recollection of the glorious victory of Jephthah was probably played down (perhaps with emphasis on what Jephthah did not accomplish) and in abject fear and craven cowardice they threw themselves on the mercy of a tyrant.

In a single verse (1 Samuel 11:1) we see the effects of spiritual apathy. Whenever a nation's strong godward commitment begins to slacken, those who rely on political acumen instead of true godliness come to the fore. When they have taken over positions of leadership, those who stand for what is right soon find themselves among the minority. Before long they are outnumbered and outvoted (Proverbs 28:4,12,28; 29:2,7,12). The result is an inevitable deterioration in morale, followed by discouragement, and in time the destruction of the moral fiber of the people. We can see this sequence in the history of the people of Gilead in the years after the time of Jair (Judges 10:3-5) and Jephthah (Judges 12:7). Without godly leadership they were ready to give way to worldly pressures (Proverbs 29:18). Furthermore the elders of Jabesh-gilead were oblivious to the treasonous nature of their enemy's proposal. God was their rightful suzerain and they had no authority delegated to them to make a treaty with the Ammonites.

Nahash's response to the capitulation of the elders of Jabesh-gilead is both arrogant and cruel. "For this [on this condition] I will cut [make] a covenant with you, when the right eye of every one is dug out, and I will make it a reproach upon all Israel" (1 Samuel 11:2). Such mutilation would render the men unfit for war, for it would no longer be convenient for them to hide behind their shields in close hand-to-hand combat.[11]

The news was disquieting. The elders debated the issue and then in desperation, when all alternatives had been discussed and discarded, asked if they could send for help. The request was ludicrous, but it appealed to Nahash's vanity. In a spirit of haughtiness and with supreme confidence in himself, he agreed to give them seven days. He was certain that the tribes to the west were too disunited to be able to raise an army in that brief period of time.[12] In addition he failed to see why he should commit his armies to the field of battle when a few days respite would do them all good and still give him the victory he desired.

Forlorn Request (11:4-5)

Messengers were sent throughout the major cities of Israel. The Biblical writer did not go into details about how each set of runners reached the gates of a city and told of the plight of those in Jabesh-gilead. He was intent on dealing with the way in which the message reached Gibeah in Benjamin, and how the news became the fulcrum on which Saul established his kingdom.

It was probably midafternoon when the messengers from across the Jordan arrived at Gibeah. Ironically they did not make their way to Saul's residence, and we are left to ponder whether or not they were ignorant of their new king. Had their city failed to send a delegation to Mizpah to take part in the selection of the nation's first monarch (cf. Judges 21:8-9)? We do not have the answers to these questions. We do know that early in the period of the judges a spirit of provincialism had resulted in deliberate isolationism on the part of this Gadite town.

It is not hard to picture the scene as the runners—tired, soaked with sweat, and covered with dust—entered Gibeah and told their story to the elders sitting in the shade of the gate. As the news spread, people began to gather around. Questions were asked and confirmation was obtained. It took a few minutes for the truth to sink in and then the people of Gibeah expressed their sorrow in loud weeping, for they were related by blood to the people of Jabesh-gilead (Judges 20:1–21:24).

Fierce Response (11:6-11)

As if by chance, Saul at this very moment was coming from the fields. He inquired about the hubbub and when he was told the facts, the "Spirit of Yahweh" came upon him. God flooded his being with a spirit of courage and enthusiasm. He suddenly became aware of a new ability to size up a situation, determine what needed to be done, and inspire others to follow him with confidence.[13]

In an act of righteous indignation[14] Saul slaughtered two of his father's oxen and sent their dismembered parts throughout the tribes with the message, "Whoever does not come out after Saul and after Samuel, so it shall be done to his oxen" (1 Samuel 11:7).[15] While this strategy may strike us as a barbaric way to raise an army, Saul's method was by no means unique. Other leaders had employed similar tactics. What the people in the other towns and cities saw, communicated the urgency of his message. They had subconsciously been prepared for a call to arms by other runners who had brought similar news of the plight of their brethren on the other side of the Jordan river. Now as they viewed the pieces of the mutilated oxen, the "dread of Yahweh" came upon them and as one man they gathered at Bezek.[16]

This city was only about fifteen miles west of Jabesh-gilead. Since Bezek was situated in a valley surrounded by hills, the Israelites were able to meet there without the Ammonites becoming aware of what was taking place.

At Bezek Saul was busy. It was one thing to summon Israel's fighting men to his side, but it was quite another to develop a workable plan, organize otherwise disorderly volunteers, and motivate them for the task ahead. Furthermore their weapons were conspicuous by their absence (1 Samuel 13:19-23); the Philistines had jealously guarded the secret of the iron-smelting process. The Israelites had farm implements at best: scythes, ox goads, and stakes. Any knives were probably of bronze.

As a strategy took shape in Saul's mind, he sent a message to the anxious elders of Jabesh-gilead, promising them deliverance by the next day. They in turn sent a message to Nahash: "Tomorrow we will come out to you, and you can do with us all that seems good to you" (1 Samuel 11:10).

Nahash of course understood the message to mean that their appeal for help had failed. He believed that the people would surrender themselves to him. And being overconfident he may have recalled his scouts, for no one raised an alarm as Saul and his men made their way down to the Jordan, crossed the river, and converged upon the unsuspecting Ammonite camp while it was still dark.

In Bible times the morning watch lasted from 3:00 a.m. until 6:00 a.m. As the sun began to peek over the hills of Bashan, Saul, who had divided his forces into three groups, launched his attack (1 Samuel 11:11). For six hours they relentlessly slaughtered the enemy. Those who could escape, did. The rout was complete. Israel's victory was decisive. No two Ammonites could be found together. The men of Jabesh-gilead, who had expected to spend that night in humiliation and agony were able instead to rejoice in God's goodness to them.

Formidable Reaction (11:12-13)

The tide of popular opinion suddenly swung in Saul's favor. The people of Israel were now delighted with their new king. Dr. William G. Blaikie wrote:

From the first [Saul] had conducted himself admirably. He had not delayed an hour in taking the proper steps. Though wearied probably with his day's work among the herd, he set about the necessary arrangements with the utmost promptitude. It was a serious undertaking: first, to rouse to the necessary pitch a people who were more disposed to weep and wring their hands, than to keep their heads and devise a way of escape in their hour of danger; second, to gather a sufficient army to his standard; third, to march across the Jordan, attack the foe, confident and well equipped, and deliver a beleaguered city. But dangers and difficulties only roused Saul to higher exertions. And now, when in one short week he has completed an enterprise worthy to rank among the highest in the history of the nation, it is no wonder that the satisfaction of the people reaches an enthusiastic [climax].[17]

Motivated by a new spirit of identification with Saul, the people called to mind those who by their words of criticism and denunciation had sought to detract from his following. This opposition had apparently been felt throughout the tribes because now the people demanded that the traitors be executed (cf. 1 Samuel 10:27). The people addressed Samuel (though not mentioned until now, he had probably crossed the Jordan the night before with the soldiers under Saul's command) and so it is likely that some religious sentiments were intermingled with their newly awakened feeling of national zeal.

Saul did not wait for Samuel to speak, but responded with befitting magnanimity: "Not a man [shall] be put to death on this day, for today Yahweh [has] accomplished deliverance in Israel" (1 Samuel 11:13). Saul perceived the real source of their victory. The Lord was their king; the holy One of Israel was their deliverer. He brought about the same kind of *coup de grâce* that Othniel and Ehud, Deborah and Barak, Gideon and Jephthah had enjoyed. In his words Saul's moral and religious qualities shone forth as conspicuously as his military achievements. The inner satisfaction of the people is not hard to imagine. God had been good to them. It was natural for them to anticipate a bright and successful future.[18]

Formal Renewal (11:14-15)

Samuel saw in these circumstances a favorable time to confirm the kingdom in Saul's hand.[19] He summoned the people to Gilgal where they offered appropriate sacrifices to the Lord (1 Samuel 11:15).

Gilgal was the first place the people had camped after being led into Canaan by Joshua. It was the place where they set up the twelve stones taken from the dry bed of the Jordan river as a testimony to what the Lord had done for them (Joshua 4:1-11). Gilgal had also been the site of the tabernacle during the early conquest of the land (Joshua 4:19; 5:10; 9:6; 10:6,43). In going to Gilgal, Samuel was in effect making it a second Ebenezer, for the people added to their heritage another reminder of the way in which the Lord had helped them.

We err in thinking that this meeting in Gilgal was like our own relatively short Sunday morning or midweek services. It would have taken time for the people to gather, and equally as long for individual families to add their thank offerings and peace offerings to the other offerings made on behalf of the nation. It should not surprise us if the assembly lasted for at least an entire week. God is honored by the praises of His people, and during this time Saul and his subjects "rejoiced greatly" in God's goodness to them.

Because the first election of Saul had been effected without any ceremony, Saul was now officially inducted into his office before the Lord. And so under Samuel's skillful guidance the kingdom was established in Saul's hand.

DEVOTION TO A JUST SOVEREIGN (12:1-25)

Possibly on the last day of the celebrations Samuel, having sensed that the mood of the people had undergone a change, called all the people together. Perhaps he had noted a spirit of presumption beginning to manifest itself. Spiritual leaders need to be constantly on the alert to note those incipient forces that subtly place an emphasis on the energy of the flesh and detract from the praise that is due the Lord. If allowed to continue, such an emphasis will inevitably lead to the kind of humanism that is so prevalent in our day. Samuel took prompt action to curb the change in attitude lest it detract from the worship of the Lord and deprive the nation of His blessing. He assembled the people together and addressed them with a view to confirming them in their loyalty to the Lord as well as in their allegiance to the king whom they had chosen.[20]

Factual Reflection (12:1-5)

Some modern scholars see in 1 Samuel 12:1-5 what they believe to be a legal process whereby the people bear witness to the quality of an official's service before he formerly relinquishes his office to another.[21] Dr. Blaikie is of a different opinion:

The reason why Samuel makes explicit reference to his past life and such a strong appeal to the people as to its blameless character is, that he may establish a powerful claim for the favorable consideration of the advice which he is about to give them. The value of an advice no doubt depends simply on its own intrinsic excellence, but the *effect* of an advice depends partly on other things; it depends, to a great extent, on the disposition of people to think favorably of the person by whom the advice is given.[22]

It fits the context of the passage to see in these verses a resumé of the kind of leadership God blesses. Samuel's years of service had been arduous ones, and yet he had served the Lord and the nation with unswerving fidelity. His example was one that the people, the king, and those of succeeding generations could well emulate.

When compared with the way in which other notable leaders of antiquity spoke of their accomplishments, Samuel's review of his many years of service was clear and concise and without exaggeration. He called on those assembled to testify against him (cf. Apocrypha, Ecclesiasticus 46:19). First Samuel 12:1-3 records his words:

> Look, I listened to your voice in all that you said to me, and I made reign over you a king. And now, look, the king is walking before you, but I am old and am gray; and behold my sons, they [are] with you. And I have walked before you from my youth to this day. Behold, I [am here]; testify against me before Yahweh and before His anointed [Saul]. Whose ox have I taken, and whose ass have I taken, and whom have I offended, whom have I abused, and from whose hand have I taken a bribe, that I might hide my eyes [that I might be blinded] with it? and I will restore it to you.

The response of the people was unanimous. They agreed that throughout his years of service he had neither wronged nor defrauded anyone. His administration had been one of impeccable justice. His life had been marked by unquestioned integrity. He had bowed neither to small nor great. Even in the matter of his sons, he had shown no partiality. They had been removed from office.

A person can preserve his integrity through the various changes and stages of life only if he is inwardly secure. Elkanah and Hannah had laid a solid foundation by giving their son a strong inner sense of his uniqueness as a person, his value to them as their son, and his mission in life. Later as he had grown in his awareness of the Lord and His purpose for him, this feeling of security in his godward relationship, of significance in the plan of God, and of satisfaction in the service of God had been reinforced.

Samuel may well have given his sons the same kind of training he had received, for when it became necessary for him to discipline them, they took the reproof well. Instead of reacting immaturely and either excusing their conduct or rebelling against the system, they showed their commitment to the Lord and His people by continuing to serve the needs of the nation. In all probability they were numbered among those who rallied around Saul at Bezek and fought against the Ammonites. And now they were among those offering sacrifices at Gilgal.

In bearing witness to Samuel's unswerving honesty, the Israelites unwittingly condemned themselves. They had no real reason to be dissatisfied with his leadership. The real reason they wanted a king was that they had grown tired of the restraints of Samuel's godly piety and wanted a more glamorous kind of leader. It has correctly pointed out that

> there was a want of cordiality on the part of the people [of Israel] in acknowledging [Samuel's administration]. They were partly at least blind to its surpassing lustre. The truth is, they did not like all the duties and responsibilities involved. It is the highest honour of a son to have a godly father, upright, earnest, consistent in serving God. Yet many a son does not realize this, and sometimes in his secret heart he wishes that his father were just a little more like men of the world. It is the brightest chapter in the history of a nation that records its struggles for God's honour and man's liberty; yet there are many who have no regard for these struggles, but denounce their champions as [overzealous] fanatics.[23]

These are wise words and well worth noting.

Fearless Rebuke (12:6-15)

Samuel then showed the importance of an accurate understanding of history. He underscored how involved the Lord their God had been in the past. In rehearsing Israel's history Samuel stressed two sets of facts: (1) whenever they had forsaken the Lord, they had been brought into trouble; and (2) whenever they had repented and cried out to God, He had delivered them out of their difficulties.

It is Yahweh who appeared to Moses and Aaron and who brought your fathers up from the land of Egypt....Yahweh set [your fathers] in this place. But [when] they forgot Yahweh their God, He sold them into the hand of Sisera...the Philistines...the king of Moab....Then Yahweh sent Jerubbabel [Gideon] and Bedan [possibly Barak[24]] and Jephthah[25] and Samuel,[26] and delivered you from the hands of your enemies all around, so that you lived in security (1 Samuel 12:6-11).

The Lord had consistently shown His sovereignty by disciplining His people; spiritual apostasy had been punished by physical oppression. Repentance had always brought deliverance (1 Samuel 12:10-11). But the nation had not learned the lessons imbedded in their own history. When Nahash came up against them they capitulated before an external fear-object. Choosing to rely on human wisdom they had demanded a king to save them (12:12). Losing sight of all that God had taught them through Moses and the judges, they blamed their troubles on the form of government under which they lived. They mistakenly thought that with a king to lead them, all their problems would vanish. They also believed that with a king they would enjoy greater unity and continuity of strength than they had ever known before.[27]

In reality Israel's restlessness and discontent evidenced a distrust in the providential care and blessing of the Lord. They ignored the fact that no external form of government could secure for them the spiritual and material blessings they sought. Refusing to consult with Samuel or the priests, they demanded instead a king so that they could be like the other nations.

In spite of their presumption and pride God graciously gave them victory over Nahash. He worked through Saul in the same way He had previously worked through the judges, so there was unmistakable continuity with the past.

Fervent Reminder (12:16-25)

But Samuel believed the lesson of their recent experience needed to be reinforced. It was now the time of harvest (the middle of May to the end of June) when rain was almost unknown. To convince the people of their sin in seeking to set aside the Lord as their rightful sovereign, and to show them that His judgments are always ready to fall on the ungodly, he called on the Lord. A sudden, heavy, and unexpected storm broke upon the assembly. Because it was so evident that this intense storm was the result of Samuel's prayer, the people were filled with fear. Their consciences suddenly convinced them that they had been wrong to persist in their request for a king. They earnestly requested Samuel to intercede for them that God's judgments might not fall on them.[28]

Samuel acceded to their request and admonished them to remain true to the Lord and to His anointed (that is, Saul; 1 Samuel 12:3,5,13-14,25; Romans 11:29). He also promised that he would continue to pray for them and instruct them (1 Samuel 12:23). Finally he encouraged them to continue to walk in reverential awe of the Lord and serve Him wholeheartedly so that they and their king might continue to enjoy His blessings.

LET'S MAKE IT PERSONAL

It is difficult to imagine how a passage of Scripture such as 1 Samuel 11–12 applies to our lives. We are far removed from the events of Jabesh-gilead or Gilgal in both time and culture. However, because human nature is the same regardless of the era of history being considered, principles may validly be drawn from the text that cast light on our trials, difficulties, successes, and acts of worship.

When Help Seems Far Away

The people of Jabesh-gilead faced an external threat. Giving no thought to the Lord and their relationship with Him, they cowered before the army of Nahash. The forces arrayed against them seemed invincible. Relying solely on human wisdom and ingenuity, they sought to cope with their circumstances as well as they could. In reality they capitulated before an improper fear-object. The result was the kind of failure we have all experienced at one time or another.

Jessica, for example, found herself in a position similar to that of the people of Jabesh-gilead. She felt as if hope were gone and believed herself to be trapped.

Jerry, her husband, abused her verbally and physically. He had been on drugs during his teen years and had also helped himself liberally to whatever alcohol was available from his parents' stock. In addition he had stolen money or sold things during this period of time so that he would be able to buy whatever was being pushed on the school campus.

Both Jessica and Jerry had come to know Christ as their Savior after their marriage, but Jerry's abuse did not stop. Yet they were regular in their church attendance and took their two children with them. Everyone thought they were an ideal family. It was no wonder therefore that Jessica felt helpless and alone in her pain. She was also concerned over the effect Jerry's actions might have on their children. Did life hold anything better for them? If so, what? She had come to the end of her own resources. She needed to avail herself of the Lord's provisions of grace and strength in order to cope with life.

When we face situations like Jessica faced—when we face inequities coupled with the excruciating pain of rejection and compounded by feelings of loneliness, fear, doubt, and isolation—we all need the comfort of God's Word. But first we need to avail ourselves of our spiritual resources. As we make the Lord our supreme fear-object, He is able to make all grace abound toward us so that we, always having all sufficiency in everything, may abound to every good work (2 Corinthians 9:8; Jeremiah 32:17; Philippians 4:19).

There are times when help from family or friends is forthcoming. But sometimes the process of recovery from the inequities of life is protracted. God as a rule will not do for us what we can do for ourselves. We may need to commit our troubles to Him as other saints have done (Psalm 55:22; 1 Peter 5:7) and then vigorously confront the difficulties we face, relying (as Saul did when he mustered together the men of Israel) on the Lord for His help (Psalms 18:34; 144). *An active faith honors God, whereas a passive faith fails to energize His omnipotence.*

When God Seems Not to Care

James Hudson Taylor, the founder of the China Inland Mission, faced a situation similar to the one Saul confronted. When the mission compound in Yangchow was attacked and burned by Chinese rebels, certain British politicians in China dispatched gunboats of the Royal Navy to assert Britain's strength in the area. Though shots were never fired, the missionaries were accused of being warmongers. They were also blamed for the incident by the *London Times* and other newspapers. Financial support for the mission plummeted and prospective recruits lost interest. Just as Saul did not give way to fear, Hudson Taylor sought to encourage his dispirited colleagues. He said, "It doesn't matter really how great the pressure is, but only where the pressure lies."[29] The trials he bore pressed him closer to the Lord, and in the process of time he and the mission emerged from the experience stronger than before. Then there was cause for praise and a renewed dedication of themselves to the Lord (cf. 1 Samuel 11:14-15; Matthew 6:33). Praise is honoring to God.

When Special Resources Are Needed

Sandy was unsure of her standing before God. Words like hers are frequently voiced at conferences and retreats: "I grew up in church and accepted Jesus as my Savior at an early age. I cannot remember when I did not go to church with my parents. Then I went away to college. Slowly I lost the 'joy of my salvation.' Now I feel empty inside. My life is barren. I lack fulfillment. What can I do to renew my walk with the Lord?"

In answering this question, 1 Samuel 11–12 comes to our aid once again. Samuel's example shows us how we should walk before the Lord (12:2-5). God does not require us to fulfill some herculean labor in order to gain His favor (Micah 6:8; Romans 12:1-2). Rather He requires that we order our lives in reverential awe of Him (1 Samuel 12:20,24-25). It is as we walk humbly before Him, conscious of His eye upon us, that we are able to please Him and sense inwardly that He is pleased with us.

The teaching of Scripture on the fear of the Lord (reverential awe of God) can be summarized as follows:

- *A positive response to the love of God.* Walking before the Lord in reverential awe of Him does not involve a morbid foreboding in which we reluctantly anticipate the worst at the hands of an angry and sadistic deity. The fear of the Lord is the kind of confidence that David showed in Psalm 56:3-4,11. (Also see Deuteronomy 20:3-4; Apocrypha, Ecclesiasticus 1:11-20.)

- *A proper restoration of our relationship with God.* Reverential awe of God leads to restoration of the proper relationship between the Creator and His creation. The result of this restoration is an awakening of devout respect, which brings all of life into perspective (Proverbs 1:7; 9:10; 1 Corinthians 4:5; Hebrews 4:13; 1 Peter 1:17; 2:17). In our new state we, with Job, "eschew evil" (Job 1:8; Proverbs 8:13; 16:6; 1 Corinthians 3:11-15; 2 Corinthians 5:10,11) and delight in leading godly disciplined lives (cf. Psalm 36:1-4).

- *A present reward from a loving God.* The benefits of a godly lifestyle are many: (1) effective service (Psalm 128:1); (2) the enjoyment of the rewards of righteousness (Proverbs 22:4); (3) a "strong confidence" (Psalm 33:8-11; Proverbs 14:26); and (4) an assurance of our standing before the Lord (Deuteronomy 6:2,5,13; Psalm 33:20-22) that helps us face the rough places of life.

Furthermore Scripture assures us that in the day of judgment special mercy will be shown those who fear the Lord (Revelation 11:18). While we naturally shrink from the thought of judgment, this awesome prospect encourages us to accept Christ now (Romans 8:15; Galatians 4:6). In God's Word true believers are described as those "who fear God" (Malachi 3:16-18; 4:2; Acts 13:26), whereas unbelievers are numbered among those who do not (Luke 18:2-8; Romans 3:18).

Those who fear the Lord have unique privileges. As His children we are accepted by Him (Ephesians 1:6); we have access into His presence (Hebrews 4:16); we are assured of our intrinsic worth (Romans 8:17); and we are instructed and empowered for every task (John 14:12,26).

It is interesting to note the impact of a genuine godly fear in the history of the Christian church. We read of the effect on believers in Acts 5:11-14. Many people came to know the Lord as a result of the reverential lifestyle of those within the early church (Acts 5:14; 2 Corinthians 5:11).

In his address to the people at Gilgal Samuel stressed the importance of maintaining an attitude of reverence before the Lord, for only if they obeyed Him could they continue to enjoy His blessing. He is sovereign. He will not tolerate a rival. To reverence anyone or anything else is a source of entrapment and is looked on as being faithless to God (Isaiah 57:11).

As we serve Him with awe, we are preserved from doing evil (Exodus 20:20; Deuteronomy 13:11; Job 2:3; 28:28; Psalm 119:9,11; Proverbs 8:13). We are also kept from relying on the flesh for success (Psalm 111:10) and restrained from resorting to substitutes to make up for feelings of insufficiency (Psalm 68:35). We remain obedient to His Word (Psalm 119:17; Isaiah 66:2,5) and respond in love to His love for us (Deuteronomy 10:12; 1 John 4:19).

Godly fear also prepares us to receive the truth as it is revealed to us. We become sensitive to spiritual realities (Matthew 17:6; Luke 5:26; 7:16; Acts 5:11); we can face suffering and misfortune without losing our confidence (1 Peter 3:14; Revelation 2:10); and we have the assurance that He is on our side (Hebrews 13:6). An attitude of godly fear is vitally related to worship, for in John's picture of heaven fear and adoration are strangely linked (Revelation 14:7; 15:4).

A proper understanding of sound theology comforts our hearts, provides us with the kind of wisdom that enables us to be appropriately assertive, and helps us face the difficulties of life while also maintaining a vibrant walk with the Lord.

THE INVASION OF GOD'S HERITAGE

PART ONE

1 Samuel 13:1-22

Geologists inform us that far below the earth's crust there are giant plates that undergird its surface and keep it stable (cf. Job 38:4-7; Psalm 104:5). Sometimes, though, these immense geological formations grind against one another. Their movements might be slight, but the plates are so large that along their fault lines even minor shifts can cause volcanic eruptions, earthquakes, or tidal waves.

Living in California has given me the opportunity to experience firsthand some of these tremors. The lesser ones are easily dismissed from our conscious thoughts and receive only passing comment on the evening news. The more severe ones however are scary! Those living closest to the fault lines are most affected by them. People who live at a distance feel only slight reverberations.

Disruptive Tensions

The earth's surface is not the only sphere of our lives to experience such tremors. Social, personal, and economic tensions can be very disruptive. The way we respond to these periods of stress is important. Individuals who receive their cues from power structures within our society survive by adapting to the ever-changing standards and mores of contemporary culture. They will "go with the flow," refrain from "making waves," and become skilled in playing political games.[1] Initially it may appear as if they are coping well with the pressures of the times. In the long run, however, they sacrifice their individuality on the altar of social acceptance and when some severe crisis rocks the fragile framework of their lives, they lack the internal strength of character that could have given them stability in the midst of upheaval.

Early Misconceptions

There were tremors in the life of King Saul. As we study the Bible and note his reactions to stress, let us not be put off by misconceptions we may have picked up. From the time many of us first learned of Saul in Sunday school, we were taught to regard him as a failure. Because our culture has programmed us to model ourselves after those who are successful, most of us have unconsciously placed an emotional distance between ourselves and Saul. We have decided that what is recorded of him in God's Word may apply to others, but certainly not to us.

However, the struggle that Saul experienced in facing the pressures of his life is one we all face. It involves the desires of the flesh versus the leading of the Spirit. As the apostle Paul taught, these are so opposite to one another that if we live after the flesh we cannot do the things that we should (Romans 7:15-25; 8:5-8).

Basic Motivation

At the beginning of his reign Saul was motivated from within. The Spirit of the Lord came upon him and empowered him to do mighty deeds. Later on his old pattern of behavior began to reassert itself. He began to rely more and more on the flesh. His own perception of people and events, his feelings of accomplishment, and his unresolved longings began to control his thoughts and actions.

Whatever the cause, Saul's inner capacity to see things God's way was impaired. His earlier aptitude to evaluate a situation, formulate a plan of action, maintain his own mental/emotional health, and motivate others to follow him with confidence began to wane. He became less and less flexible, more and more defensive, and increasingly unable to cope with the pressures placed upon him. Such traits as a commitment to the revealed will of God, integrity, empathy, likability, humor, adaptability, curiosity, dedication, and courage began to give way.[2] These sociological shifts, like the movement of geological plates undergirding the earth, had a far-reaching effect on Saul personally and on his interpersonal relationships.

STRUCTURE AND OUTLINE OF THE PASSAGE

Before we consider the causes of the changes in Saul, we need to have clearly in mind the structure of 1 Samuel 13–14. This portion of Scripture forms a unit but because of its length the passage will be treated in two parts. (Chapter 8 of this commentary will deal with

1 Samuel 13:1-22 and chapter 9 of this commentary will deal with 1 Samuel 13:23–14:52.) Their oneness of content, however, should constantly be borne in mind.

First Samuel 13:1 begins with a summary statement, which is quite common in Hebrew literature (cf. Genesis 1:1). This statement serves as a caption heading and prepares us for what is to follow.[3]

First Samuel 14 concludes with a resumé of Saul's life and achievements (14:47-52). We certainly would not have expected to find such a digest of his reign so soon in the recounting of the events of his career. As was pointed out in the Introduction, this is the Biblical writer's method of drawing together the contribution of one leader before introducing us to the next (cf. 1 Samuel 7:15-17; 1 Kings 2:10-12). We realize from 1 Samuel 14:47-52, therefore, that God is setting Saul aside as a viable force in his people's history.

Interestingly Saul's wars against the Philistines are mentioned twice in this resumé. Verses 47-48 record his fighting against the people of Moab, Ammon, Edom, Zobah (between the Lebanon ranges), Philistia, and Amalek. Then there is a digression to talk about Saul's family. The concluding statement in verse 52 mentions his wars against the Philistines again.

Having taken a brief look at the beginning and the ending of this portion of the Biblical record, we are now in a position to look more closely at the text to discern the main movements within the narrative.

In between the opening statement and the concluding comment, we take note of three particular verses. The first is 1 Samuel 13:23, which is best seen as a transitional or "hinge" verse; it prepares the reader for the events that are to follow. The second is 14:23, which provides a resumé of one day's activities. The third is 14:46, which presents us with the results of the battle of Michmash Pass.

Subdivisions in the narrative are introduced with the Hebrew *waw* meaning "And" or "Now" or "Then" (1 Samuel 13:2,5,8,16,19; 14:1,16,21, 24,47) and subpoints under these subdivisions may be identified by the writer's use of "Then" (frequently), "So," "When," and "And" (less frequently).

The story is interrupted for an explanatory comment in 1 Samuel 13:19-22. And 14:24-47 comprises a lengthy digression to describe the reasons for and the results of Saul's impulsive vow.

The structure of the entire passage can be outlined as follows:

- Introduction (1 Samuel 13:1)
- The Result of Disobeying the Will of God (1 Samuel 13:2-18)
  Digression: Israel's Predicament (1 Samuel 13:19-22)

- The Result of Neglecting the Provision of God (1 Samuel 13:23–14:23)
  Digression: Saul's Impulsiveness (1 Samuel 14:24-46)
- Concluding Summary (1 Samuel 14:47-52)

INTRODUCTION (13:1)

The opening words of this summary heading bring before us certain problems. The Hebrew text reads, "Saul [was] a son of a year when he became king and he reigned two years over Israel."[4] The numerals have apparently been omitted from the copies of the Masoretic text that have come down to us. As far as we can determine, the original must have read, "Saul [was]———years old when he began to reign, and he reigned———[and] two years over Israel."

Different translations offer varying views on Saul's age at the time he ascended the throne as well as the length of his reign. It seems evident that he must have been about forty years old when he was crowned king, for Jonathan was old enough to assume command of a portion of the army (1 Samuel 13:2).

According to Acts 13:21 King Saul reigned for about forty years. The reign of Ishbosheth in Mahanaim and the interval before the tribes of Israel accepted David as their king were obviously included by the apostle Paul in this forty-year period. King Saul himself therefore could only have reigned for about thirty-two years. In 1 Samuel 13:13-14 Saul was told that his dynasty would not continue and he died in battle in 1011 B.C. The text of 13:1 may be reconstructed as follows: "Saul [was forty] years old when he became king and he reigned [thirty-]two years over Israel."

THE RESULT OF DISOBEYING THE WILL OF GOD (13:2-18)

While Saul and the men of Israel were still at Gilgal he chose three thousand of them to form the basis of his standing army. Two thousand he retained under his own command in Michmash and in the hill country around Bethel, and he placed one thousand under Jonathan's command in Gibeah,[5] Saul's hometown.

Jonathan[6] is *not* introduced to us as Saul's son in 1 Samuel 13:2. Inasmuch as we have not read of him before, the omission of his lineage must have been purposeful. In the mind of the Biblical writer this departure from accepted custom was doubtless designed to prepare the reader for one of those shifts beneath the surface of human relations that has a disrupting effect on the lives of all concerned.

There are many writers who believe that the events of 1 Samuel

13–14 took place in the second year of Saul's reign.[7] The *waw* consecutive, translated "And" in 13:1, does not look at time but at the next event recorded by the author in his selective recounting of Israel's history (see a similar construction in 15:18). The events of 13:5-7, therefore, did not necessarily follow soon after the celebrations at Gilgal, but it was the next important happening as far as God's revelation is concerned.

Several strands of evidence lead us to conclude that a significant number of years must have passed between the events associated with the renewal of the kingdom (1 Samuel 11:15) and Jonathan's attack on the Philistine garrison at Geba.

- The Philistines had infiltrated certain Israelite cities— something they apparently did not do while Samuel was judge (7:13-14)—and they had become strong enough in Geba to establish a garrison there.

- Saul's attitude toward his countrymen had deteriorated to the point where he referred to them as *Hebrews*[8] (13:3)—a pejorative term or expression of contempt used previously only by their enemies.[9] And some from his own tribe had even joined the Philistines against him (14:21).

- Saul's popularity poll was evidently at a low ebb (14:29) for he took credit for Jonathan's victory (13:4). When he defeated Nahash and the army of the Ammonites, his popularity had been at an all-time high.

- Saul's trust in God had given way to an unhealthy reliance on his own resourcefulness and an externalism in matters of faith and practice. He was now motivated by expediency and was easily irked by those who did not appear to share his concerns (13:8-9). He also saw the Almighty as someone who was to be placated before He could be used (13:12).

- Saul had become distanced from Jonathan (14:29) and his relationship with Samuel had become strained. Saul knew that he still needed them but found it easy to project the blame for his failures onto them (13:11-12).

- When Samuel informed Saul that his dynasty would not continue, the prophet added the statement that God had sought for a man "after His heart" (13:14)—implying that Saul had so

far departed from his earlier commitment to the Lord that He
could no longer use him.

• With a strained relationship existing between Saul and Samuel,
  Ahijah had apparently seized the opportunity to move into the
  vacuum and become Saul's "spiritual advisor" (14:3,18,36). In
  this shift we discern another power struggle taking place within
  the structure of Israel's social life.

And so we could go on. Obviously such a decline in leadership
and in interpersonal relationships could not have come about within
the space of a year or even two. Such deterioration would have taken
longer. Thomas Kirk[10] hinted at a possible explanation. After drawing attention to the fact that the Philistines are mentioned twice in
the concluding summary (1 Samuel 14:47,52) he suggested that 14:47
looks at the early years of Saul's reign when he fought against the
Moabites, Ammonites, Edomites, and Zobahites. If a gap of several
years did intervene between the events following the defeat of Nahash
and Jonathan's attack on the garrison in Geba, then it is possible to
place Saul's early wars in this period.

Weight is lent to this theory because 1 Samuel 13 is concerned
with the first Philistine war, which *followed* Saul's wars against the
Moabites, Ammonites, et cetera (14:47). His attack on the Amalekites,
which we read about in chapter 15 (cf. 14:48), came after this first
war against the Philistines. The events of 13:3 therefore may easily
have taken place a decade or more after Saul's coronation at Gilgal
(11:14–13:2).

The Deliverance of the People (13:2-4)

First Samuel 13:2 connects the present events with the past.
While the men of Israel were still at Gilgal commemorating their
victory, Saul took the opportunity to establish a standing army. In
this decision he was appropriately proactive. As William Deane
observed:

> It is in the early part of his reign that Saul begins to form the
> nucleus of an elite corps. He sees that his untrained countrymen
> cannot at once hope to attack with success a powerful enemy
> such as the Philistines. Profiting from the great assembling of
> the tribes, and their unanimous acceptance of him as king, he
> proceeds to select a band of valiant and skillful warriors, who
> not only act as his bodyguard now that he has been inaugurated

as king, but also form the framework of a military system, and train the whole nation to arms.[11]

And what better way for them to gain experience than by defending Israel's borders against lesser enemies?

We are not prepared, however, for the sudden change in the flow of the story. Without prior warning we are made aware of the fact that Philistine infiltration had become so strong in Geba that their presence constituted a threat to Israel's well-being (1 Samuel 13:3). If the Philistines could muster sufficient strength without being challenged (and this they could plainly do; cf. 13:5), it would be a comparatively easy matter for them to drive a wedge between the army under Saul and the contingent of men under Jonathan. And before news of the enemy's actions could be carried to the different tribes, the Philistines could be in a position to decimate Israel's small army, kill the king and any claimants to the throne, and take the land of Israel for themselves.

The Philistines had chosen a most advantageous place to launch their attack. Geba was strategically situated on a low, cone-like rise on the western edge of the ridge that shelved eastward toward the Jordan. Travelers passing from Geba northward and westward came to a steep descent leading into what now is called the Wadi es-Suwenit. On the opposite side of the wadi, on the top of a steep brow, right over against Geba, lay Michmash at a distance of barely three miles in a northwesterly direction.

Two pinnacles (called in the Hebrew *šēn,* "tooth") stood as sentinels, one on either side of the wadi. These pinnacles are important for they have a bearing on the development of our story later on. Side wadis, trending from north to south behind these two rock towers, rendered them quite abrupt and isolated. These two peaks, or "teeth," were respectively called *Bôzēz,* "the shining," and *Sĕneh,* either "thorn" or "the pointed," (1 Samuel 14:4-5).[12]

Jonathan sensed the threat posed by this garrison. He was aware of the fact that the land was the Lord's heritage that He had given to Israel (Psalm 80:8-17; 135:12). Any invasion of it therefore was plainly contrary to His will. The only exception was when He allowed another nation to chasten His wayward people. Such was not necessarily the case at this point in the story or Samuel would have given some intimation of God's displeasure.

Without consulting his father, Jonathan took prompt action. In reality Saul should have been the one to begin the offensive. A change however had apparently come over him, for he lacked decisiveness and had become reactive rather than proactive.

Jonathan attacked the Philistines and completely routed them. Realizing that the gauntlet had been thrown down and that reprisal from their enemies would not be long delayed, Saul summoned the men of Israel to assemble at Gilgal.

On learning that Saul had achieved a victory over the Philistines, the Israelites were concerned about how they now appeared in the eyes of their enemies. They were depressed when they should have been elated (1 Samuel 13:4).

It has often happened in times of spiritual apathy that the bold attitude of some reformer has aroused the enemy to activity and has thus brought God's people into severer difficulty. This is what happened in Egypt when Moses and Aaron, following God's instructions, confronted pharaoh. The temporary result was that the burden of their brethren increased (cf. 1 Samuel 13:4 with Exodus 5). The Israelites saw only the immediate results; they did not realize that the cause of truth was advanced by these confrontations.

Let us remember therefore that while certain external threats may intimidate the majority, such threats should not be allowed to hinder the forward movement of the work of the Lord. Those who are approved of God come to the fore during times of crisis (1 Corinthians 11:19), and so Jonathan was not intimidated by the Philistines. Doubtless many stories told around campfires and authenticated by elders sitting in the gates of the cities of Israel caused the people to dread the Philistines. It is always wise to be cautious, but for the Lord's people to allow the forces of evil to make cowards of them is wrong. The apprehension of the Israelites indicated that they had capitulated before an improper fear-object. They were no longer living consciously under God's sovereignty.

As previously noted, fear is caused by attributing to a person, place, or thing two attributes that properly belong to God: *almightiness* (the power to take away our autonomy) and *impendency* (the power to do us harm). The people of Israel had plainly attributed these powers to the Philistines. The only remedy for such negative emotions would have been for the Israelites to place themselves unreservedly in the hands of the Lord (cf. Daniel 3:13-27). He could then have used them to gain victory or allowed the chastening to continue as He saw fit (Job 13:15). If the Lord had chosen the latter, we could be sure the only reason was to bring more of His people into submission to His authority.

In reality Jonathan's victory at Geba was the beginning of a movement that might have ended Philistine influence within Israel's borders. He was a man of faith who saw the issues clearly. Consequently he acted boldly to repulse the enemy from this important strong-hold. Unhappily too few in Israel shared his faith. Morale among the people was low. They responded to Saul's summons out of duty rather than with eager expectation.

The Reaction of the Enemy (13:5-7)

The Israelites did not have to wait long for the dreaded invasion. The Philistines fielded a formidable force.[13] The battalions that be-gan to converge on Michmash were of such prodigious proportions as to reinforce the negative impressions generated by the timid and fearful in Israel. So panic-stricken were God's people that they hid in caves and thickets, among rocks and ravines, in high places and in pits in the ground. Some even forsook their lands and livestock and crossed the Jordan, seeking refuge in the territory of the tribes of Reuben and Gad.

In obedience to Samuel's instructions, Saul called the men of Is-rael to gather at Gilgal. Above them on the heights overlooking the plain, they could see the Philistine tents. In the still of the night the Israelites could hear the ribaldry of the Philistine soldiers as they drank to their gods and sang the kinds of songs that arouse esprit de corps in the hearts of fighting men.

The camp of Israel, however, was strangely silent. The hearts of Saul's warriors were filled with fear. Here and there among the tents furtive shadows traced the flight of those who believed that safety lay in a hasty retreat across the Jordan into Gilead. Later on Saul would actually see small groups of men defecting from him as he waited for Samuel to come to his encampment.

The sin of Saul's soldiers was the same as that committed by their forefathers when they came out of Egypt (Numbers 13–14). The Lord had promised to give them the land of Canaan as their inheritance. When they came to the border of the land, they sent out spies. Ten of the spies brought back a faithless report. Their description of the difficulties turned the hearts of the people to water. The spies painted vivid mental images of ferocious giants who lived in impenetrable cities ("walled up to heaven") and strode through the land wreaking havoc on its defenseless inhabitants. The Israelites gave way to their fears and concluded that they could never conquer such a mighty people (Numbers 13:25-33; 14:9; cf. 2 Timothy 1:7).

Because the Israelites of the exodus did not submit themselves in obedience to Yahweh, He had to judge their unbelief. The spies who brought the evil report died that day in the presence of the Lord

(Numbers 14:36-37); the rest of the people, who did not hold God as their supreme fear-object, were told that they would not be able to enter the promised land (14:22-35).[14]

As we consider the situation facing Saul and the people, it is evident that they had failed to learn from their own history. It should not surprise us, therefore, that many of them either hid or fled (1 Samuel 13:6-7). They were activated by fear, as were the people in the time of Moses and Aaron. Such fear is always in opposition to true faith.

The renowned Scottish preacher, Dr. William Blaikie, observed:

> On every ground the duty incumbent on Saul at this time was to show the most complete deference to the will of God and the most unreserved desire to enjoy His countenance and guidance. The magnitude of the danger, the utter disproportion between the strength of the defending people and that of the invading host, was fitted to throw them on God. [And] the fact, so solemnly and earnestly urged by Samuel, that, notwithstanding the sin committed by the people in demanding a king, God was willing to defend and rule His people as of old, *if only they had due regard to Him and His covenant,* that should have made Saul doubly careful to act at this crisis in every particular in the most rigid compliance with God's will.... If only Saul had been a true man of faith and prayer, he would have risen to the height of the occasion at this terrible crisis, and a deliverance as glorious as that which Gideon obtained over the Midianites would have signalized his efforts [Judges 7:7]. It was a most testing moment in his history. The whole fortunes of his kingdom seemed to depend on his choice. *There* was God, ready to come to his help if His help had been properly asked. *There* were the Philistines, ready to swallow them up if no sufficient force could be mustered against them. But weighed in the balances, Saul was found wanting. He did not honour God; he did not act as knowing that all depended upon Him.[15]

The Test of Priorities (13:8-14)

As we consider the test of Saul's priorities[16] it becomes apparent that over the past few years he had become conditioned to think in terms of externals. This was not the way he thought at the beginning when the Spirit of God came upon him. His attitude now was typical of a man motivated solely by the flesh (Romans 8:5-8). While he begrudgingly gave deference to Samuel, he was inclined to see everything through the lenses of his own experience.

Saul was instructed to wait, but his obedience was tested daily as he saw the ranks of his army thinned by deserters who fled across the Jordan. It was a severe trial for someone of his disposition. Finally by the seventh day the situation became too much for Saul. He realized that his retreat to the mountains might soon be cut off. He had no guarantee that Samuel had been able to make his way through the enemy lines. If he had been captured or killed, further delay would only make Saul's position more dangerous!

On the seventh day, possibly at the time of the morning sacrifice, Saul's fears gained mastery over him. He yielded to external pressure and instructed the priests to bring to him the burnt offering and the peace offerings.

The majority of Bible scholars suppose that Saul's offense lay in taking on himself the functions of a priest.[17] However, from what follows (2 Samuel 24:25; 1 Kings 3:4; 8:63) it does not appear as if offering the sacrifice was the real reason for the discontinuance of his dynasty. Samuel did not denounce him for intruding into the priesthood, but for disobeying the word of the Lord. Saul's real offense was that he yielded to the prompting of the flesh and did not do as the prophet had commanded.

All of us face testings of different kinds. In and of themselves they may not appear to be very significant. The Lord, however, requires of us obedience to His Word. Small deviations or violations may not appear important at the time, but like a leaf on the surface of a stream, they plainly show the direction of the current.

Saul failed because over the years his view of the Lord had undergone a change. His early godward aspirations had given way to a sense of reality that was limited by his own rational powers and the things that he could see and feel. He no longer viewed his nation's sovereign as the Lord of hosts and the "Strength of Israel" (1 Samuel 15:29), but rather as a mysterious force to be placated before it could be used. He regarded the sacrifices, therefore, as sacraments that had to be performed in order to insure success. And lacking a strong internal God-consciousness to give him stability in the face of a severe crisis, he exercised his prerogatives as king and probably instructed the priests (possibly Ahijah) to offer the sacrifice.

It would appear as if only the burnt offering (symbolizing the dedication of the people to the Lord) had been sacrificed when Saul was told of Samuel's arrival in the camp (1 Samuel 13:9-10). Saul went out to meet the aged prophet and greeted him cordially. The king was ill-prepared, however, for Samuel's stern words of denunciation (13:11-14; cf. Hosea 9:15; 12:11).

William Deane wisely observed that Saul's appointment and continuance in office was conditioned upon his unquestioned obedience to the Lord. Now it was evident that he had failed an important test of his character. The essence of his error was his distrust in the covenant-keeping God of Israel and an overweening confidence in his own prudence and sagacity. True, he offered the first of the sacrifices in order to obtain the Lord's favor, but his motives were anything but devout. He had fallen into that spirit, so often and so strongly denounced by the later prophets, which regards the outward act as everything and believes that the ceremonial observances should be accepted where reverence, faith, and moral obedience are lacking.[18]

Saul's response to Samuel's "What have you done?" provided tacit evidence of his weakness. Saul projected the blame first onto the people and then onto the prophet, and ended by rationalizing his actions: "Because I saw that the people were scattering from me, and you did not come in the appointed days [time], and the Philistines were massing [at] Michmash...and because I had not made sweet [placated] the face of Yahweh, I forced myself..." (1 Samuel 13:11-12).

How like Saul are many today who have a form of godliness but are unaware of its real power; who rationalize their actions in spite of the clear teaching of God's Word; and who spend time in ritualistic observances but know little or nothing of genuine obedience! To them God may be transcendent but He is not immanent. He is the kind of deity who is only resorted to in times of crisis when His power needs to be harnessed on their behalf.

Samuel's response to Saul's vacillation was awesome in its severity. The prophet indicted Saul for his fear of man and told him he should have conducted himself in reverential humility and obedience before God.

> You [have] acted foolishly [in] that you [have] not kept the commandment that Yahweh your God commanded you,[19] for now Yahweh would have set [established] your kingdom over Israel forever. But now your kingdom shall not stand [continue]; for Yahweh has sought for Him[self] a man according to His heart,[20] and Yahweh has appointed him a leader over His people" (1 Samuel 13:13-14).

It seems evident that in the interval between the celebrations at Gilgal following the defeat of Nahash and this unhappy confrontation with Samuel, there had come about a basic, deep-seated shift in the substrata of Saul's life. While outwardly appearing to have all the desirable qualities of a king (1 Samuel 10:23-24) and still giving lip service to the Lord, he was deficient in those traits that are so essential in a leader.[21] Flaws, like geological fault lines in his character, were now becoming apparent. He was inconsistent in his godward relationship; his association with others had begun to lack solidarity; his former confidence (which was God-given) was beginning to wane, and his old doubts about himself were beginning to reassert themselves. These weaknesses were aggravated by the threat posed by the Philistines. Inwardly he sensed his vulnerability and lacking an inner sense of security, he succumbed first to vacillation and then to disobedience.

The Aftermath of Rejection (13:15-18)

Were the peace offerings ever made? Did Ahijah encourage Saul to complete this last remaining rite before going forth to engage the enemy? The text is silent.

We do know that Samuel ascended from the valley to Gibeah. Was this an act of grace on his part? Did he wait there hoping for Saul's arrival? Are we to conclude that Samuel would have been willing to offer the appropriate sin offering on Saul's behalf had the king shown true repentance? Did the old prophet watch the Philistine buildup at Michmash while spending time in prayer for the man whom the Lord had instructed him to anoint as king over His people? All we know is that Saul went to Geba and made that city the base of his operations.

How did Saul handle the rejection of his dynasty?[22] Later events indicate that he felt this loss keenly and became despondent and depressed. And when a roll call was taken, Saul and Jonathan had only six hundred men under their command (1 Samuel 14:2).

While Philistine contingents from their pentapolis were gathering at Michmash, they also sent out raiding parties (Judges 6:4). Saul's puny army was directly to the south, so the first of the Philistine detachments plundered and pillaged on the road toward Ophrah (possibly eṭ-Ṭaiyibeh) east of Bethel; the second headed west toward Beth-horon (Beit 'Ur el-Foqa) ten miles from Michmash; and the third covered the area to the east of the Philistine encampment—a desert area commonly referred to as the valley of jackals or the valley of hyenas.[23]

In these circumstances Saul demonstrated a lack of assertiveness characteristic of an externally oriented person. Until something happened to move him to take action (1 Samuel 14) he was immobilized by fear and an inability to size up the situation and turn it to his advantage. His lack of faith in the Lord further accentuated his indecisiveness.

DIGRESSION: ISRAEL'S PREDICAMENT (13:19-22)

The raiding parties found the Israelites virtually defenseless. No swords or spears were in their possession (1 Samuel 13:19,22). The only exceptions were Saul and Jonathan but they were to the south of Michmash and no resistance was offered from Saul's base camp in Geba. The Philistines had not permitted their own ironsmiths to operate within Israel's borders lest the Israelites learn the science of iron smelting.[24] This made God's people dependent on their neighbors even for repairing their agricultural tools.[25]

Because there is much in the history of this period that has not been told us, the news that the fighting men of Israel lacked suitable weapons comes as a surprise. At the very least we would have expected those who attacked the Ammonites ten or more years earlier to have obtained weapons from them when the army of Nahash fled in disarray (1 Samuel 11:11).

William Deane believes that the Philistines confiscated all arms when they raided the villages. His view, however, does not explain why those of Saul's soldiers who were untouched by the raiding parties had no swords or spears.

Another possible explanation for Israel's lack of arms may be found in the nature of the weapons possessed by those nations that had not mastered the iron smelting process. Their weapons were of bronze, and a bronze sword could easily be shattered by a steel one. Likewise a bronze spearhead could be shivered if it struck something particularly hard. It is possible that many of the weapons possessed by the soldiers in Saul's small army had one by one been broken on different fields of battle (1 Samuel 14:47); only the ones that were of iron remained and these were in the hands of Saul and Jonathan.

Whatever the reason, Saul's soldiers were in a very perilous position. They were poorly equipped, hopelessly outnumbered, and sadly lacking in morale. While the outlook for Israel could not have been worse, the solution was readily available. All Saul needed to do was set matters right with the Lord by submitting to His sovereignty. Then he could have offered the appropriate sacrifices and enjoyed a renewed sense of God's acceptance. With renewed confidence he could have instilled faith and courage in the hearts of his men. As we shall see, the victory that could have been his went to another.

THE INVASION OF GOD'S HERITAGE

PART TWO

1 Samuel 13:23–14:52

The great Bible teacher Dr. Brooke Foss Westcott pointed out that "great occasions do not make heroes or cowards; they simply unveil them to the eyes of men. Silently and imperceptibly, as we wake or sleep, we grow strong or we grow weak, and at last some crisis shows us what we have become."[1] And so it was with Saul.

To grasp the significance of the events described for us in 1 Samuel 14 we need to have a clear understanding of Saul's character. As with all of us, the strengths and weaknesses of his personality were established during his formative years and reinforced as he sought to cope with the different situations and responsibilities he faced.

Because Saul had been deprived in his childhood and youth of inner feelings of security, significance, and the satisfaction that comes from a job well done, he had grown to manhood accustomed to thinking of himself on a par with Kish's servants.[2] As a consequence, even though he was now the king he desperately desired the acceptance, approval, and affirmation of those about him (1 Samuel 15:24; 18:7-8).

To understand Saul's negative attitudes and actions we need to be aware of three important factors: (1) his *knowledge* of himself and others; (2) his ability to *evaluate* a situation and reach a decision based on a comprehensive understanding of the facts; and (3) his *expectations* as these were reflected in his understanding of temporal and spiritual realities.

As we weigh carefully the data contained in the Biblical text, we will gain a better understanding of the workings of Saul's heart. We will also see how much we are like him, for all of us are selfish by nature and apart from God's grace are prone to put first the meeting of our innate needs. Possessed of this information regarding Saul and ourselves, we will be in a better position to avoid Saul's failings and avail ourselves of the resources that God in His lovingkindness has made available to us.

We learn from modern studies of the human personality that there are two primary types of people who have negative assessments of themselves: (1) those who are markedly disorganized and inwardly unstable; and (2) those who are highly organized and inwardly inflexible. As they cope with the realities of life, the former do not know their strengths and weaknesses and are unsure of their beliefs (cf. James 1:8), while the latter are too rigid in their approach to life and expect others to conform to their standards.

In both groups—the disorganized as well as the highly structured—any new information or *knowledge* is received by an individual as a threat to self and a cause of fresh anxiety. As he processes this new information through his mental grid, a vast assortment of impulses, memories, and perceptions come to the fore. If the new data does not mesh with his understanding of himself, the new knowledge creates feelings of insecurity. Such individuals therefore find it easier to adhere to traditional beliefs or values than to broaden their understanding by incorporating fresh truth that would expand their world of reality.

Saul fell into the category of the rigid and inflexible. As a result, when he was not controlled by the Spirit of God his world of reality was limited to the things he could see and touch. Having drifted away from a vital relationship with the Lord, he was no longer motivated by the inner godward orientation that had enabled him to flex when something unexpected happened. He attempted to obey the will of the Lord, but only so long as it did not conflict with his human perceptions and personal goals. His knowledge of himself, as well as his knowledge of God, was limited as well as limiting.

A further indication of Saul's rigidity may be seen in his response to Samuel. In 1 Samuel 13:11-12 Saul was unable to admit his error. The words of the prophet may well have triggered recollections of similar confrontations with Kish or other authority figures. Sensing the need to defend his failings, he tried to project the blame onto others.[3]

So the first step toward an understanding of how people function is to be aware of their knowledge. The second is to be aware of their capacity to *evaluate* their attitudes and actions objectively in the light of temporal and spiritual realities. Those reared in a demanding environment where any form of approval or affirmation is conditional often become highly productive as adults but lack the ability to view their attainments with any degree of satisfaction. Furthermore, as new information about themselves is uncovered they typically react in a rigid conforming manner while inwardly experiencing varying degrees of fear.

Because Saul was no longer controlled by the Holy Spirit, he lapsed back into an earlier pattern of coping with the vicissitudes of life. According to his evaluation, the situation facing Israel was hopeless. The desertion of his men, coupled with the rebuke of Samuel, rendered Saul incapable of being objective and taking appropriate action. Ahijah, we are told, was in the camp "wearing the ephod"[4] (1 Samuel 14:3). Therefore the means for determining the will of God was available to Saul. However, he failed to seek knowledge of God's will during the time when raiding parties were ravaging the land. In a state of mounting anxiety he positioned himself at Migron[5] on the outskirts of Gibeah, presumably ready to jump over the precipice rather than be taken captive by the Philistines. Saul was so despondent that his world of reality became constricted. He made no provision for God's sovereign intervention on behalf of His people (cf. 2 Kings 6:15-18).

The third step toward an understanding of how people function is to be aware of their *expectations*. People who have a negative view of themselves either expect too little or too much of themselves and/ or others. If the goals they set are too low, they spend their lives at the level of mediocrity. If their aspirations are too high, negative people reinforce their low sense of worth each time they fail to achieve an objective. Such failure only serves to aggravate the disorganized person and confirm the rigid individual in his or her inflexible thought processes and routines.

Saul, as we have seen, fell into the category of those who are too rigid. Having failed to live up to his own expectations and sensing that he had lost face with his men at Gilgal, he determined to show everyone how zealous and God-fearing he was. On the day of the battle he imposed a strict oath on his men, forbidding them to eat anything from early morning until sunset (1 Samuel 14:24-44). As subsequent events showed, this decision proved to be counterproductive. It minimized the victory the Lord had given to His people and alienated Saul's men from him (14:45-46).

OUTLINE

First Samuel 14 continues the sequence of events begun in 1 Samuel 13. There we noted *the result of disobeying the will of God.* Here we have *the result of neglecting the provision of God* (13:23–14:23).

In 14:24-46 there is another digression to discuss Saul's impulsive vow, and the chapter ends with a summation of Saul's reign (14:47-52).

THE RESULT OF NEGLECTING THE PROVISION OF GOD (13:23–14:23)

The Setting (13:23)

The Philistines, deciding to keep an eye on the Israelites, set up an outpost overlooking the ravine that separates Michmash from Geba. In light of their superior strength we may well ask why they didn't overrun Saul's camp and destroy Israel's token opposition. Dr. William G. Blaikie wisely observed that the

> two things which probably made the Philistines pause, were the strong position held by Saul, and Saul's repute as a military leader. On account of the narrowness of the Pass, and the steep ascent to Geba, the Philistines could not use their chariots and horsemen... and even their infantry would have to fight at great disadvantage. And as they knew that Saul was a brave and skilled general, they deemed it wisest to delay the attack upon Geba, and pillage in the meantime the country. They sent, however, a portion of their forces to occupy a position to the east of the village of Michmash, nearer to Geba, to watch the movements of Saul's men, and to guard the Pass. It was this outpost that Jonathan ventured to attack.[6]

The Work That Faith Inspires (14:1-15)

As we resume our study of the Biblical narrative we note that Saul set up his spear, the emblem of his authority, under a pomegranate tree facing the precipice. In helpless inactivity he watched the Philistines across the valley. In vain his men looked to him to take some form of action. He, however, felt himself deprived of God's help and too weakened in manpower to launch an attack.

Jonathan, who played a major role in the events of 1 Samuel 14, had all of the noble qualities his father lacked. He assessed the situation and, activated by faith, conceived of a daring plan. Without telling his father, Jonathan left camp early one morning before the Israelites were roused from their troubled sleep. Summoning his armorbearer to his side, he said, "Come, and let us cross over to the outpost of these uncircumcised;[7] perhaps Yahweh will work for us, for Yahweh is not hinder[ed] to save by many or by few" (1 Samuel 14:6; cf. Apocrypha, 1 Maccabees 4:30-33).

Jonathan's armorbearer was activated by the same spirit, and the two of them descended into the valley, crossed the short plain, and positioned themselves below the Philistine sentries. Their actions must have been carried on in the half-light of early dawn, for they were not seen by the Philistines until they chose to reveal themselves.

The Philistine outpost was situated at the end of a promontory, with the tents of the garrison protected by cliffs that formed a natural fortress. According to Claude R. Conder, who personally explored this area, close by the modern village of Mukhmas is a "ridge rising in three rounded knolls above a perpendicular crag, ending in a narrow tongue to the east with cliffs below, and having an open valley behind it, and a saddle towards the west on which Michmash itself is situate."[8] And there, as we have already noted, two pillars of virtually unscalable rock faced each other. The one on the north of the wadi was well lit by the sun and was called *Bôzēz*, "Shining," whereas the one to the south was almost entirely in the shade during the day and was called *Sĕneh*, "Pointed."

Jonathan and his aide did not act recklessly or irresponsibly. They devised a plan whereby they would be able to discern the Lord's will. Their actions sprang from a strong belief that the people of Israel stood in a covenant relationship with the Lord and that He had given them the land. They believed that in endeavoring to fight His battles, they could rightly look to Him for some token of His will to guide their actions.[9]

The sign they chose was as follows: If the Philistines invited them up to the level plateau, they would know that the Lord had given the Philistines into their hand. If the Philistines wanted to descend the steep incline, then Jonathan and his aide would hold their position, knowing that the enemy was exercising due caution.

The Philistine watchmen eventually saw Jonathan and his armorbearer and thinking that they had recently come out of caves and holes in the ground[10] invited them to come up to the plateau. Sensing God's leading the two Israelites climbed the steep and perilous cliff-face, confident that the Lord had given them the victory.[11]

Once on level ground, Jonathan attacked the outpost and with the help of his armorbearer killed about twenty of the enemy. The commotion was enough to arouse the Philistines in their tents. Panic seized those in the camp. Believing that they had been attacked by Saul's entire troop, they hastily grabbed their weapons. Being a heterogeneous group consisting not only of men from the five Philistine cities but of mercenaries and Hebrews as well, they were unsure of who was friend and who was foe. Each soldier therefore struck out at whoever was closest to him.

To the general confusion was added the element of a sudden supernatural terror. The earth trembled beneath their feet, heightening their fear and apprehension.[12]

Before considering the reaction of Saul and the Israelites to this unexpected turn of events, we need to take note of what Jonathan was able to achieve. He exemplified the characteristics of a man of faith. He possessed those inner qualities that might well have caused his name to be enshrined among the heroes of the faith in Hebrews 11. He did not concern himself with who might get the credit for the day's activities but showed that his confidence was in the Lord (1 Samuel 14:12). He gladly subordinated his will to the will of God and by his actions demonstrated that he possessed the kind of commitment to the Biblical principles that results in success.

The Reaction That the Flesh Produces (14:16-23)

The disturbance in the Philistine camp also aroused the watchmen in Gibeah. They were perplexed. They had neither seen Jonathan and his armorbearer leave nor observed the Philistine sentries as they assumed their positions overlooking the gorge. Now, looking across the ravine they saw the Philistines retreating as if before a powerful enemy. There did not appear, however, to be any real cause for the panic.

So perplexed was Saul that he called for Ahijah (1 Samuel 14:3). When the priest came before him, Saul demanded that he determine the cause of the commotion and also ascertain what the Lord would have him do (14:18).[13] But before Ahijah could consult the Lord, Saul changed his mind and decided to attack the Philistine forces.[14]

While it is true that there is a time for prayer and a time for action, Saul's impatient words to Ahijah, "Withdraw your hand" (14:19), caused the priest to lose face before those who were present. He felt as if his rank and position had been reduced. He smarted under the imagined slight and waited for a suitable occasion (14:36) to reassert his authority. When he did so, his reasons were obviously egotistical and his involvement in Saul's decision-making process resulted in a further delay that prevented God's people from capitalizing on the victory He had given them.

In changing his mind about consulting the Lord in 14:19, Saul probably concluded that speed was of the essence. He rallied his men and they pursued the retreating enemy. En route, Israel's meager army was augmented by those Hebrews who had joined the Philistines as well as by their kinsmen from Ephraim who had taken refuge in caves and holes in the ground (14:21-22). These now united to harass the enemy as they took a headlong course down the valley past Beth-aven, skirted the desert to the east of Bethel, and then descended the steep incline toward Beth-horon and the valley of Aijalon.[15]

The route taken by the would-be conquerors covered about twenty miles. Weary, confused, and nursing their wounded pride, they made their way to the nearest Philistine city. Josephus claimed that sixty thousand of them were killed.[16] His figure seems unusually large (cf. 14:30).

The Biblical text does not allude to any success on the part of Israel, but sums up the events of the battle in a single statement: "So Yahweh delivered Israel that day" (14:23).

The Israelites had gone to sleep the night before in feebleness of mind and spirit. They had looked upon their enemy as invincible. The faith of Jonathan showed up his countrymen's timidity and lack of confidence. His brave actions were vindicated in the outcome of his bold and daring assault on the Philistine camp. His courage demonstrated that the Lord does not favor those with the superior weapons, but instead honors those who trust in Him (1 Samuel 14:6; cf. Ecclesiastes 9:11; Zechariah 4:6).

This story reminds us of God's sovereignty and reinforces in our thoughts the fact that the only thing limiting His omnipotence is our unbelief (Matthew 13:58).

DIGRESSION: SAUL'S IMPULSIVENESS (14:24-46)

The Biblical writer next enlarged upon an incident that had taken place earlier in the day. The incident further illustrates the kind of reaction produced by our fleshly impulses.

Soldiers in antiquity had to maintain themselves (provide their own food). Their "remuneration" came from the spoils of war.[17] Apparently, at the time when Saul gave the command to his men to charge he also laid upon them a solemn oath. He demanded that no one take any food from the Philistine camp or eat anything until sunset. The rationale behind his curse was quite clear. He wanted everyone to devote himself unreservedly to the destruction of the enemy. His real motivation however was more personal than national. He wanted to be avenged for the insults he felt had been heaped on him during the period of Philistine occupation. His words to his men revealed (1) his shameful abuse of power and (2) his false system of beliefs (1 Samuel 14:24). He was no longer prompted by the Spirit of God. He ignored the fact that his men had not yet eaten and used his authority to coerce them into abstaining from food for the rest of the day. In this respect Saul has many followers in our day, particularly among those who are task-oriented in their management style and fail to build real humanitarian concern into their administrations.

The essence of Judaism and Christianity—rightly understood and rightly practiced—lies in the power to bless. Only in pagan systems of belief does power reside in the ability to curse.[18] Saul's pronouncing a curse on his men was designed to put them in fear of himself, not God.

Consciously or unconsciously, Saul may have been feeling the effect of Samuel's words (1 Samuel 13:13-14), for in placing his men under a curse he appeared to be determined to show them how zealous he was. He was acting in the power of the flesh, however; and running parallel with his animated though misguided devotion was an imperiousness and stubbornness that further alienated his men from him. Latent in his words was evidence of the kind of rigidity and formalism that are typical of an unhealthy personality.[19]

Just when Saul's men were weary for want of food, just when they were experiencing the faintness and lassitude of exhaustion, their pursuit of the Philistines led them through a forest where honey was so abundant that some of it had fallen to the ground.[20] Jonathan had not been present when his father had exacted an oath from the men, and coming into the wood and seeing a honeycomb at his feet he picked up a piece on the end of his staff. Even this slight amount of nourishment sufficed to renew his energy.[21]

One of the soldiers who saw Jonathan's apparent disregard for his father's directive expressed surprise and informed Jonathan of Saul's vow: "Your father strictly made the people swear, saying, 'Cursed is the man who eats food today'" (1 Samuel 14:28). Jonathan was incensed that his father should have so little regard for the well-being of his men and responded angrily:

> My father has troubled the land;[22] see now, how my eyes have become bright because I tasted a little of this honey. How much more, if only the people had eaten freely today from the spoil of their enemies which they found; for now the slaughter among the Philistines has not been great" (14:29-30).

The weariness of the troops had prevented them from overtaking their enemies and as a consequence Philistine power remained unbroken.

Saul's rash vow produced further unexpected complications. As the sun sank into the ocean, the famished men eagerly slaughtered the sheep, oxen, and calves that had been left behind by the Philistines. Without attending to the requirements of the law, they ravenously satisfied their appetites (cf. Leviticus 3:17; 17:10; Deuteronomy 12:16,23).[23] The Levitical code gave explicit directions concerning the slaughter of animals for food. The blood, symbolic of life, was to be drained away. In their extremity the men did not wait for the process to be completed but may even have eaten the flesh in its raw state. Some actually butchered calves along with the cows (cf. Leviticus 22:28).

Among the warriors of Israel were those who were knowledgeable of the law. They went to Saul and told him what was happening (1 Samuel 14:33). He quickly acknowledged the people's sin, but he did not admit his own culpability. Instead he determined that the letter of the law was to be followed and spoke harshly to his soldiers: "You have acted treacherously [against the command of Yahweh] . . . Each of you bring me his ox or his sheep, and slaughter [it] here and eat" (14:33-34).

The same ends could have been achieved in kinder ways (2 Corinthians 3:6).[24] Saul however maintained an attitude of rigid compliance with the law in an attempt to win the favor of the Lord. His conduct evidenced his unyielding severity.

As soon as the men were sufficiently refreshed from the exertions of the day, Saul proposed that they continue their attack on the Philistines. William Deane is of the opinion that Saul was conscious of the way in which his inconsiderate vow had greatly interfered with the morale of his men, and so he now wished to repair his error by taking further plunder from the Philistines.[25] Perhaps he hoped that the material compensation his men might receive would cause them to forget his treatment of them. He was placing the prospects of personal enrichment ahead of ridding Israel of their enemies.

Saul's soldiers however were dispirited. His capricious attitude had deprived him of an enthusiastic following. They acquiesced: "Do whatever seems good to you" (1 Samuel 14:36).

Ahijah sensed that the men were not really behind the king. The priest also realized that now he had the opportunity to regain his lost prestige while also serving in a mediatorial role between Saul and his troops. Without being consulted Ahijah interjected, "Let us draw near to God."

Ahijah posed as a man of real faith. His words however were tantamount to impeding action. Prayer, like worship and witnessing, has its time and place. In this case God's will was already clear. The Philistines were His enemies. They had invaded His land. Specific guidance was not needed when what He required (confirmed by what He had already done) was well known. Unfortunately for the people of Israel, Ahijah was more interested in himself than in the will of the Lord. He chose to use his office for his own advantage. In effect he counseled delay when it was unwise for the Israelites not to capitalize on the favorable circumstances Jonathan had secured for them.

At Saul's bidding Ahijah apparently donned his ephod and consulted the urim and thummim, but no answer was forthcoming. It was a tense time for both the king and the priest. The people, who were inclined to be superstitious, continued to lose confidence in their leaders—both civil and religious. Instead of gaining the power they sought, Saul and Ahijah eroded the little authority they had left.

When the priest's breastplate did not give any intimation of the Lord's will, Saul tried to salvage something from the day's misdeeds by taking matters into his own hands. He called for his chiefs (*pinnôt*, "corners" in the sense of cornerstones of the people). Then taking upon himself another oath Saul said: "Draw near here…and see how this sin has happened today. For as Yahweh lives…though it is Jonathan my son, he shall surely die" (1 Samuel 14:38-39).

Not having any idea that Jonathan might be guilty of sin, Saul spoke merely as one who desired to give the impression that no favoritism would be shown. His reasoning was very primitive. He believed that sin must be the cause of God's unwillingness to answer him, so he despotically doomed to death whoever might be the unhappy victim of the lot.

If God had chosen not to answer him by means of the urim and thummim, how could Saul presume that the Almighty would now condescend to reveal His will by lot?[26] And how could Saul predetermine the punishment without knowing the offense? He did not pause to consider what penalty (if any) might have been prescribed in God's Word. In an act of presumption and arrogance he decided how the culprit would be exposed and executed. In Saul's new vow we see the outworking of his unyielding personality.

Demanding of God that He "give the perfect lot," Saul proceeded. The lot was cast and Saul and Jonathan were taken. It seemed that God was going along with Saul's plans after all. If He was, His intent was to show Saul how wrong he had been. When a second lot was cast Jonathan was taken.

It is difficult to determine Saul's emotions at this time. We do know that his anger flared up and he demanded, "Tell me what you have done" (14:43). And Jonathan told him. His bravery and true manhood were evident in his words. He was courteous but did not allow himself to be intimidated by his father. Perhaps Jonathan had long since lost respect for the man who had been elevated to the throne of his people.

Though Jonathan's "fault" was one of ignorance, he did not excuse himself; nor did he remind the king that such offenses could be atoned for by a sin offering. Instead he said simply, "Here I am; I must die."

Saul's response showed how he was influenced more by formalism and pride than by true piety and natural affection. He was firmly set on executing his son. He took upon himself another oath:[27] "May God [*'Elōhîm,* one of the names of Yahweh implying power] do this to [me] and more also, for you shall surely die" (14:44).

Saul was unduly zealous in passing judgment on Jonathan. Perhaps the king was projecting his own feelings of guilt (over having imposed an unwise vow on his men) onto Jonathan. It is also possible that Saul's apparent earnestness to vindicate the law of the Lord sprang from Samuel's rankling condemnation of his own disobedience. In attempting to overcompensate for his own weakness, Saul wished all to see how diligent he was in his religious duty (and conversely how undeserving he had been of Samuel's censure).

Saul's threats however were too much for his men. So far they had acquiesced in sullen silence to his tyrannical behavior. Now they voiced their objection. As one man they stood in opposition to his will. Saul might be the anointed of the Lord, but he had exceeded the bounds of his authority. They reminded the king of how the Lord had worked through Jonathan that day and they told Saul that he could not condemn to death one whom God had so singly honored (14:45).

Saul felt humiliated when he heard their words but he could not go against such united opposition. He left the place where he had acceded to Ahijah's counsel, and his men returned to their homes. The enemy had been driven back but Philistine power had not been broken. There would be another time and another battle in which Israel's enemies would be victorious, and Jonathan and Saul would be killed by those they could have beaten earlier.

CONCLUDING SUMMARY (14:47-52)

Saul's great successes over the years,[28] combined with the growing consciousness of his military skill and prowess, had the effect of making him proud and self-reliant. With each accomplishment he became less dependent on God for both counsel and aid. He began to take his victories for granted, as if he had within himself the power to shape his own destiny. The reversals of 1 Samuel 13:5-7 and 9-14, which the Lord permitted to come into his life, were designed to correct the spirit of self-sufficiency and arrogance that had begun to manifest itself in unhealthy ways. Had Saul learned the lesson that the Spirit of God was intent on teaching him, the history of his later years would have been differently written.[29]

As it was, God graciously continued to give him victories over His (and Israel's) enemies. "Wherever [Saul] turns, he prospers" (14:47). None of these triumphs, however, satisfied Saul. He no longer had the capacity to enjoy the outcome of his efforts (cf. 11:15). Instead, what he desired most (to be respected by the people) led him into compromise and away from the path the Lord had set before him.

Was Saul able to draw comfort and satisfaction from his family (14:49)? His relationship with Jonathan, confirmed by subsequent events (20:30-34), would indicate that Saul was not. Apparently he was a driven man—driven by the desire to attain that which was unattainable—and with repeated disappointment and failure there came the reinforcement of discouragement and growing despair instead of comfort and satisfaction.

A STUDY IN CONTRASTS

Having begun our study of 1 Samuel 14 with an assessment of some of the dynamics of Saul's personality, we conclude with a few thoughts about Jonathan.[30] It is difficult for us to escape the fact that in this chapter of the Bible the two men are contrasted with one another.

- In 13:3 and 14:1 Saul is seen to be inactive. It was Jonathan who took prompt action to restore Israel's right to the land the Lord had given them.

- Through his rigid and inflexible policies Saul succeeded in alienating the people. They were sullen and morose. They esteemed Jonathan enough to take issue with the king on his son's behalf (14:45).

- Saul felt acutely God's rejection of his dynasty (13:13-14). He allowed Samuel's rebuke to affect his disposition to such an extent that he became incapable of effective action. Jonathan, who knew that he would never succeed his father, nonetheless continued to serve the nation faithfully (14:12).

- Saul had the means whereby he could have determined the Lord's will (14:3) but he neglected to do so. Jonathan, who did not have access to a priest wearing an ephod, deliberately

sought for a way whereby he could be sure of God's leading
(14:8-10).

• Saul apparently was easily threatened by authority figures or
superior numerical strength. Jonathan, who was a man of faith,
filtered contemporary events through the lens of his godward
relationship and did not give way to fear.

• Saul's disposition led him to become rash and impetuous. He
entered into one vow after another, not learning from past mistakes. Jonathan controlled his feelings even when threatened
with death by his father (14:44).

As Dr. William G. Blaikie noted:

Saul had begun to disregard God's will in his public acts, and
was now beginning to reap the results of that which he had sown.
He felt that he must pay more attention to God's will. If he was
not to lose everything, he must try to be more religious. There
is no sign of his feeling penitent in heart. He is not concerned in
spirit for his unworthy behavior toward God. He feels only that
his own interests as king are imperilled. It is this selfish motive
that makes him determine to be more religious. The fast, and
the consultation of the oracle [via Ahijah], and the altar, and
the oath that Jonathan shall die, have all their origin in this
frightened, selfish feeling. And hence, in their very nature and
circumstances, his religious acts are unsuitable and unseemly.

In place of making such things better by such services, he
makes them worse; no peace of God falls like dew on his soul;
no joy is diffused throughout his army; discontent reaches a
climax when the death of Jonathan is called for; and tranquillity
is restored only by the rebellion of the people, rescuing their
youthful prince [from Saul's hand].

It is a sad truth that terror and selfishness have been at the
foundation of a great deal of that which passes as religion.
Prayers and penances and vows and charities in cases without
number have been little better than premiums of insurance,
designed to save the soul from punishment and pain.[31]

Jonathan stood out as a man who was appropriately autonomous
(1 Samuel 13:3; 14:1). He was not irresponsible but possessed a
healthy independence. As a general in Saul's army he had the right
to make certain decisions. His actions gave evidence of a high degree

of faith in the Lord coupled with confidence in himself. A lesser person could not have acted as he did. He had the capacity to take appropriate action based on an objective evaluation of the situation. His faith was grounded in a belief in the sovereign power of the One whom he worshiped and in his own understanding of the history of his people.

Jonathan's faith was welded to his gifts and calling, for he was also a man of courage. When he saw "uncircumcised Philistines" (pagans) taking possession of that which the Lord had sworn by an oath to give to Israel (Genesis 15:18; Exodus 23:31; Numbers 34:1-15; Deuteronomy 1:8) he took what action he deemed necessary to bring the situation into conformity with God's revealed will (1 Samuel 14:6).

Jonathan was also a man in whom there was a lack of self-consciousness. He did not attack the Philistines to add to his own popularity or prestige but to ensure that his people might be free from oppression (1 Samuel 14:12). In his unselfishness he was animated by the same spirit that motivated the apostle Paul and others whose hearts the Lord has touched. Jonathan did not regard his life as dear to himself but gladly hazarded it for the benefit of his fellow countrymen (cf. Acts 15:26; 20:24).

There is no indication in the text that Jonathan felt inwardly either inferior or insecure. Yet, with all his accomplishments, he was humble. He was resourceful, flexible (he did not feel that the strategy he had used against the Philistines in Geba had to be followed now that Israel's enemies occupied Michmash), and deeply committed to serving the Lord (1 Samuel 14:8-14).

Because of Jonathan's character traits, men were inspired by his leadership. They felt that they could follow him with confidence. They knew that he was honest in his evaluations—of himself, of them, and of situations (cf. 14:29). When events threatened Jonathan's well-being, the people readily showed their allegiance to him (14:44-45).

Dr. F. F. Fuller in some unpublished lecture notes on the stages of educational development[32] has provided a basis whereby we can understand our own growth and compare it to the level of maturity reached by Saul and Jonathan. She has shown that children first learn about themselves. When they are cold or wet or hungry, they want attention. Theirs is essentially a *self-orientation.* Later on they evidence concern about themselves in roles. In play they act out the parts of an engineer or a nurse, a bus driver or a mother. The concern over roles increases through their adolescent years until they are able to function adequately in their chosen professions; they are preoccupied with their *role-orientation.* Only with true maturity do they reach a stage where they are *other-directed* (concerned about helping others, meeting their needs, and developing a servant style of leadership).

Saul's immaturity is seen in his self-orientation; Jonathan's maturity is evidenced in his being other-directed.[33] The goal set before each of us is to become more like Jonathan and less like Saul! Our natural instincts would lead us to an improper or inadequate knowledge of ourselves, an inability to evaluate situations properly, and unrealistic expectations. We see in the life of Saul that such unreadiness for responsibility results in a growing abuse of power (or resentment of authority) or an increasing passivity. In Jonathan we see seasoned responsibility coupled with independence of thought and action, and blended with an accurate assessment of people and events.

RULES OF THE GAME

1 Samuel 15:1-35

Jimmy was hard at work. His Sunday school teacher had just finished a lesson on creation and she had told him and the other children in the class to draw what they had learned. Noticing Jimmy's absorption with the project, she peered over his shoulder to see what he was doing. "What are you drawing?" she asked.

Without looking up from his work, Jimmy answered, "God."

"What is God like?"

"I don't know. I ain't finished Him yet!"

Jimmy has a lot in common with us. Unaided by Biblical revelation we create gods out of our own imaginations. Often, without being aware of what we are doing, we derive our concepts of God from how our parents treated us as children. If they were harsh and austere, distant and demanding, then we think of God as a punitive deity who is far removed from our circumstances and exacts a severe penalty each time someone does something wrong. If, however, our parents were kind and encouraging, then it is easy for us to imagine the Lord as being an all-wise, all-loving parent-figure who will treat us as our earthly parents did, or even better.

As we grow older we realize that God cannot be likened to any living creature (cf. Isaiah 46:5,9; 2:8-22). As we scan intently the pages of the different books of the Bible to learn what He is like, we find a strange complexity. At times He appears tolerant of sin (Acts 17:30) and at other times He punishes an offender with awesome severity (Numbers 15:32-36). There are occasions when He expresses His willingness to answer prayer (Isaiah 58:9; John 16:23-24) and at other times He seems reluctant to do so (Deuteronomy 3:23-26; 2 Corinthians 12:8-9). Certain passages of Scripture intimate that He welcomes His people's worship (John 4:20-24) while other passages imply condemnation of the worshipers and their gifts (Isaiah 1:11-15). We read of the rewards of the righteous (Ruth 2:12; Psalm 58:11), yet note that the righteous are not always rewarded (1 Kings 21:1-13).

These paradoxes touch each area of life. They affect our understanding of the will of God as well as the principles of living in fellowship with Him. These paradoxes reveal how the Lord views the life of the person who walks in his or her integrity and how He views the self-centeredness of those who do not. If we would know more of what God is like, then we need to consider carefully all that is revealed about Him. As we clothe the characters in Scripture with flesh-and-blood reality, we find our knowledge of God as well as our understanding of our relationship with Him enlarged and enhanced. Our study of Samuel and Saul, for example, will help define our concepts of God.

STRUCTURE AND OUTLINE OF THE PASSAGE

Outlining 1 Samuel 15 is made easy for us by another repetitious use of the Hebrew *waw*, "And" or "Then," with which 15:1,4,10,32,34 begin (verses 10-31 form a unit subdivided at verses 16,20,24,30).

As we study the passage section by section, we will see that God's sovereignty lies behind the events that are described for us by the Biblical historian. God is presented as unchangeably and unchallengingly in supreme command of all He does. To disobey Him is an affront to His majesty. He is independent of His creatures, yet vitally involved in all they do. He is compassionate and gracious, slow to anger, abounding in lovingkindness and faithfulness, and merciful toward those who fear Him. He forgives iniquity, transgression, and sin, yet by no means does he leave the guilty unpunished (Numbers 14:18). As we will find in the case of the Amalekites, He visits the iniquity of the fathers on the children and on the children's children to the third and fourth generations (Exodus 34:6-7). In the case of King Saul we will see the awesome reality of how it is possible to oppose and eventually nullify God's will for us by our disobedience (1 Samuel 13:13-14; 15:23).

In 1 Samuel 15 we will observe:

- The Command of the Lord (1 Samuel 15:1-3)
- The Failure of the People (1 Samuel 15:4-9)
- The Result of Disobedience (1 Samuel 15:10-31)
- The Execution of the Ban (1 Samuel 15:32-33)
- The Parting of the Ways (1 Samuel 15:34-35)

THE COMMAND OF THE LORD (15:1-3)

Several years had slipped by since the battle of Michmash Pass. It was now about 1026 B.C. Saul had regained some of his lost prestige among the northern tribes, but the southern tribes paid him only token homage. Whereas the former admired his prudence, energy, and skill as a general, the latter were prone to lay stress on Samuel's prediction of a successor (1 Samuel 13:13-14) and to hope that this "man after the heart of God" would soon appear. The southern tribes were also mindful of Jacob's dying words and looked for a king to arise from the tribe of Judah (Genesis 49:10).

Passing over the events that occurred between 1 Samuel 14 and 15, the narrator, in keeping with his selective recounting of Israel's history, recorded the fulfillment of God's indictment against the Amalekites[1] made approximately four hundred years earlier. These wily nomads of the desert inhabited the Negev[2] or land south of Canaan. They were the descendants of Esau through his son Eliphaz (Genesis 36:12,15-17; 1 Chronicles 1:36).

When the Israelites, as recently emancipated slaves, came out of Egypt, the Amalekites attacked the women and children and the weak and sickly who made up the rear. God viewed this attack as reprehensible and He decreed the absolute overthrow of the Amalekites (Exodus 17:14-16; Numbers 24:20; Deuteronomy 25:17-19).[3] The Amalekites and Israelites also clashed during the wilderness journey (Numbers 14:43-45), and even after Israel had settled in the promised land the Amalekites constantly invaded Judah's border (Judges 3:13; 6:33; 7:12; 10:12). By the time of King Saul the Amalekites' cup of iniquity was full. They had proved themselves to be hopelessly and incorrigibly corrupt. The time of their judgment had come.

How the word of the Lord was communicated to Samuel in Ramah we are not told, but he did receive a message for the king from the Lord. Ever obedient to God's command, Samuel went to Gibeah to see Saul. There is no indication in the text that Saul gave Samuel a cordial greeting (cf. 1 Samuel 13:10) or that Samuel was ushered ceremoniously into the king's presence (cf. 1 Kings 1:22-31). We are left to conclude that a strained relationship existed between these two heads of God's people.

Samuel's words were brief and to the point. If Saul had felt that he could fudge on the previous command (1 Samuel 13:8) because he did not realize that the word of the prophet was indeed the word of the Lord, God's instructions now allowed for no such misunderstanding.

Yahweh sent me to anoint you as [literally, for] king over His people, over Israel; and now listen to the voice of the words of Yahweh.[4] Thus says Yahweh Ṣĕbā'ôt [of hosts],[5] "I will visit [punish] Amalek for [literally, with] what he did to Israel, because he set [himself] against him in the way when they came up from Egypt. Now, go and strike Amalek and utterly destroy[6] all that [is] his; and do not have pity upon him; but slay [everyone and everything], from man even to woman, from child even to suckling, from ox even to lamb, from camel even to ass" (1 Samuel 15:2-3).

There was no breakdown in communication. The Lord had spoken. The supreme commander of the heavenly armies had given His orders. The time of His long-delayed vengeance had come. The destruction of Amalek was to be complete.[7] God desired to make an example of them to show to the nations—present as well as future—how He views those who without provocation make war against His people. No spoils were to be taken from this battle. It was to be a "holy war" and the entire Amalekite nation was to be destroyed.

Many writers in recent years have sought to drive a wedge between the Old Testament and the New by presenting the God of the Old Testament as harsh and despotic and asserting with equal fervor that the message of the New Testament is one of love and forgiveness. These writers show how little they understand of God's nature and what He is like. Dr. William Blaikie's remarks are most judicious. In defending the unity of all of Scripture he wrote:

> The gospel of Jesus Christ does indeed reveal, and reveal very beautifully, the paternal character of God; but it reveals at the same time that judicial character which insists on the execution of His law. That God will execute wrath on the impenitent and unbelieving is just as much a feature of the gospel as that He will bestow all the blessings of salvation and eternal life on them that believe. What the gospel reveals respecting the sterner, the judicial, aspect of God's character is, that there is no bitterness in His anger against sinners; there is nothing in God's breast of that irritation and impatience which men are so apt to show when their fellow-men have offended them; God's anger is just.
>
> The calm, settled opposition of His nature to sin is the feeling that dictates the sentence "The soul that sinneth, it shall die." The gospel is indeed a glorious manifestation of the love and grace of God for sinners, but it is not an indiscriminate assurance of grace for all sinners; it is an offer of grace to all who believe

in God's Son, but it is an essential article of the gospel that without faith in Christ the saving love and grace of God cannot be known. Instead of reducing the character of God to mere good-nature, the gospel brings His righteousness more prominently forward than ever; instead of smoothing the doom of the impenitent, it deepens their guilt, and it magnifies their condemnation.... It is most wholesome for us all to look at times steadily in the face of this solemn attribute of God, as the Avenger of the impenitent [for] it shows us that sin is not a thing to be trifled with. It [also] shows us that God's will is not a thing to be despised.[8]

THE FAILURE OF THE PEOPLE (15:4-9)

Saul's response to Samuel's words was one of obedience. He sent runners throughout the tribes to summon the fighting men of Israel to assemble at Telaim.[9] A very large force from the northern tribes marched south, but only a token contingent from Judah—the tribe most affected by predatory raids from the Amalekites—joined the ranks of those who rallied to Saul's side. We are left to conclude that Judah's poor turnout was indicative of their disaffection for Saul.

Saul must have made it clear to his men that this war was to be a *ḥerem* or "holy war" and some dissatisfaction must have been voiced by the men, for according to 1 Samuel 15:24 Saul capitulated to their demands. The kind of situation Saul faced is not uncommon. Even today opposition tests the courage as well as the resolve of those in positions of responsibility.

As we study the setting we would do well to remember that the voice of reason is always very plausible. It would have been easy for those under Saul's command to rationalize the situation: "The Amalekites have repeatedly plundered us, so why shouldn't we take something back from them?"

Other soldiers, thinking of their families and the many months they had been away from home, would be prone to look on the spoils as just compensation: "We've sacrificed a lot over the years to fight Saul's battles. The spoils of the Amalekites are likely to be the richest we'll ever see. It is unfair to ask us to forego our legitimate compensation."

And then some of the leaders may have reasoned with the king: "Saul, nominally we're a God-fearing nation, but most of the men do not believe the way you do. It's not right for you to impose your beliefs on them."

Finally, the *coup de grâce* may well have been given by one or more of the warrior-priests who so often filled the ranks of Israel's armies.

Being knowledgeable of the law the priests may have argued: "Moses specifically differentiated between cities in Canaan placed under a 'ban' and cities outside the land. And *he* said that the spoils of those cities outside the borders of Canaan are legitimately ours for the taking" (Deuteronomy 20:14-15; if this objection was voiced, then Saul faced the same question the Pharisees put to Christ in John 8:5).

Whom was Saul to listen to—the voice of reason shouting in the clamor of comrades in arms, or the voice of an old prophet who had long since passed his prime and was now regarded by many as a misguided fanatic?

The dissension among the ranks must have increased to the point where Saul feared he would lose not only his men but also the popularity he had fought so hard to regain. He faced a real dilemma. How could he give the people what they wanted, get what he wanted, and also do what God wanted? To accomplish these goals he settled on a compromise. He would allow the people to take the spoils of war, provided they would all go to Gilgal after the battle and present thank offerings to the Lord.

His plan was accepted by the men, and the warriors set off for the central rallying point of the Amalekites. Archaeologists have so far failed to locate any "city of the Amalekites" answering to the description of the text (1 Samuel 15:5). Various theories have been suggested.[10] Apparently the city was near a large wadi, for Saul and his men were able to conceal themselves in it while messengers disguised as Bedouins entered the city and spread word among the Kenites[11] that they should leave (15:6).

The Israelites then attacked the city and completely destroyed it. Because the Amalekites were a nomadic race, the men of Israel even pressed the attack from Havilah[12] toward Shur (meaning "wall" and possibly alluding to the wall of Egypt) a little east of the Nile river (cf. 1 Samuel 27:8). They covered an enormous area and it is fair to conclude that the campaign may have taken several weeks.

When they reassembled (perhaps at Carmel in southern Judah)[13] they concluded that God had indeed blessed their efforts. Their reasoning led them to the erroneous assumption that inasmuch as they had obeyed the law of Moses, they could dispense with the more restrictive words of Samuel.

Saul, perhaps mindful of Samuel's actions following the battle of Ebenezer (1 Samuel 7:12), erected a memorial (literally, hand) to commemorate the victory (15:12). Ostensibly the memorial was to honor the Lord, but in reality its purpose was to remind the people of Judah of Saul's actions on their behalf. The Biblical writer clearly affirmed that Saul set up the monument "for himself." There was probably more selfishness behind Saul's actions than a genuine spirit of thanks-giving.

Saul and his men, with light hearts and joyful spirits, made their way to Gilgal. Among their trophies was Agag, king of the Amalekites.

THE RESULT OF DISOBEDIENCE (15:10-31)

The Indictment (15:10-15)

The full extent of God's judgment against Amalek had not been carried out, and the Lord again spoke to Samuel: "I have repented that I made Saul [to] reign as king, for he has turned [back] from following Me, and My words he has not done" (1 Samuel 15:11).

Samuel was distraught when he heard these words and he prayed to the Lord all night. We do not know the content of his fervent inter-cession. Our concerns, if we found ourselves in a similar situation, would doubtless have differed from his. He accepted the will of the Lord but was distraught over what might happen to the nation. He did not know what might result from the sin of the king and the people. We may well have spent our time questioning how God could change His mind.[14] After all, hadn't He personally led Saul to Samuel, specifi-cally identified him to His prophet (1 Samuel 9:14-17,20-21), confirmed His will with irrefutable signs, even to enduing the king with the Holy Spirit (10:1-10), and confirmed His choice at Mizpah by guiding the casting of the lots (10:19-24; 11:14-15)? How then could He now set aside the man of His choice?

In the morning Samuel began the long walk south to meet Saul. He knew what he had to do. It was a journey of about thirty-seven miles from his home in Ramah to Carmel. When he came to this southern town, someone showed him the monument Saul had erected and told the prophet that Saul and his men had gone to Gilgal. And so the old man had to retrace his steps and then turn eastward across the hot desert sands. After a long tiring walk he at last came to a convenient wadi that led down to the plain of the Jordan where Gilgal was situ-ated.

As Samuel approached the sacred site hallowed by so many blessed memories of God's past involvement with His people, he saw the tents of the soldiers spread out before him and also took note of the sheep and cattle they had taken from the Amalekites. When he ar-rived in the camp the celebrations were well underway and the sac-rifices were being readied.

Saul heard of Samuel's coming and hastily went out to meet him. Saul was in a jubilant mood and for the moment forgot past disagreements.

He said to Samuel, "You [are] blessed of Yahweh. I have performed the word of Yahweh" (1 Samuel 15:13).

But Samuel cut Saul short. The prophet's words were clear and to the point. He said in effect, "If you have kept Yahweh's word, then what is the meaning of the bleating of sheep which I hear, and the lowing of the oxen? The testimony of my senses gives the lie to your words of assurance" (15:14).

Saul did not want the negativism generated by past altercations to dampen the spirits of his men or mar the joy of the occasion. He was too happy to want a repetition of past unpleasantness. Samuel's words, however, rankled him. In Saul's mind were thoughts of the good he had done. In Samuel's thoughts was an echo of the words the Lord had spoken to him. Trying to brush aside the prophet's comment, Saul said:

> They [the people] have brought them from Amalek [because] they had pity on the people and the best of the flock and the herd, [but it was all done with the best of intentions] *to sacrifice to Yahweh your God,* and the rest they have destroyed" (15:15, emphasis added).

The Reminder (15:16-19)

Saul turned to leave. He did not wish to stay and become embroiled in an argument with this feisty old priest, but Samuel said:

> Stop, and let me tell you what Yahweh spoke to me [last] night.... Is it not [true], when you were little in your own eyes, you [were made] head of the tribes of Israel? And Yahweh anointed you as king over Israel, and Yahweh sent you in [the] way, and said, "Go and destroy the sinners, [even] Amalek, and fight against them until they are finish[ed]." Why then did you not listen to Yahweh's voice? Rather you flew on the spoil and did evil [literally, *the* evil] in the eyes of Yahweh" (1 Samuel 15:17-19).

These words cast the king's actions in an entirely new light. His self-seeking and the people's greed had placed him in an invidious position. He had angered the Lord of glory, whose servant he was.

The Defense (15:20-23)

Saul's weakness became even more apparent in the discussion that followed. He continued to project the blame onto the people. But when the nagging voice of conscience pricked him, he admitted to having brought Agag with him (to parade before all the fighting men and any of their family members who had come to join in the celebrations). He excused the people's actions by saying that they intended to sacrifice the animals to the Lord (conveniently omitting to mention what would happen to the numerous animals that would remain after the sacrifices were completed). Finally in a cunning ploy designed to convince Samuel that they were all really on the same side, Saul referred to "your" God. Thomas Kirk's comments on this passage are worth noting:

> There are two things in [Saul's] emphatic declaration of obedience which reveal an uncandid and despicable spirit. One is that he refers to the sparing of Agag as an evidence of his obedience, while in reality it was the very opposite. The other is that Saul persists not only in laying the responsibility of sparing the best of the flocks and herds upon the people, but also in regarding the deed as an act of piety, which was worthy of praise rather than blame.... His pride of heart, which would not allow him to own that he was wrong, involved him in crooked sophistry and base selfishness.[15]

Samuel's response to Saul's sophistry showed that he had not been taken in by the king's pretense of piety. Couching his words in poetic form to add emphasis to what he wanted to say, Samuel pointed out that what the Lord really requires is diligent obedience, not partial acts of compliance.

> Does Yahweh delight in burnt offering[s] and sacrifices
> As [in] obeying the voice of Yahweh? Behold, obeying [His will is]
> better than sacrifice,
> To give attention [to His word is] better than the fat of rams.
> For rebellion is [as] the sin of divination;
> And iniquity and idolatry is [the same as] insubordination.
> Behold you [have] rejected the word of Yahweh,
> He has also rejected you from [being] king[16]
> (1 Samuel 15:22-23; cf. Hosea 13:11).

This sentence struck terror into the heart of Saul. It was unthinkable to him that God could rank him with idolaters and those practicing witchcraft.[17] His error lay in his inability to see things as God sees them. He viewed the externals—a significant victory over the Amalekites, the happiness of the people, and the sacrifices to placate

Yahweh for any possible sin they may have committed—whereas God looked at the attitude of his heart.

As the king whom the Lord through Samuel had anointed, Saul had an obligation to obey God's will. He was not an independent, but a dependent ruler of the people. He was not the master, but the servant. He held the office of king in subjection to Israel's true suzerain. He was subject to the Lord of hosts—a title that denoted God's infinite greatness and might—and his duty was to give strict obedience to His every command.[18]

It must be remembered that as severe as God's words were in 1 Samuel 15:23, He was not rejecting Saul as a person. He was rejecting him from being His representative to His people.

The Petition (15:24-31)

When confronted with such a verdict, Saul's immediate response was to seek to lessen the sentence. "I have sinned," he said, "for I have transgressed the commandment of Yahweh and your words" (1 Samuel 15:24). The confession, however, was not so much the result of inward conviction as it was an evidence of Saul's fear of losing the acclaim of the people. Samuel's unflinching integrity and unwavering earnestness, coupled with the announcement of Saul's rejection as king, placed Saul in a difficult position. He was forced, however briefly, to see his actions as God saw them. But this glimpse only intensified his inner struggle. He desperately wanted to be admired by the people for his military prowess as well as his devotion to Israel's God.

Saul began to realize that instead of maintaining an attitude of reverential awe of the Lord before his men, he had allowed his desire to please the people to dull his sensitivity. As a consequence he had "obeyed their voice" (15:24) instead of holding fast to what the Lord had told him to do (15:1-3). Because of his disobedience he now stood disqualified. He had forfeited the right to rule God's people. As Benjamin Franklin once said, "He that cannot obey, cannot command."[19]

The celebrations, however, were soon to begin and Saul was anxious to save face. He saw Samuel about to leave and asked him to return with him to the place of sacrifice so that he might worship the Lord. Samuel refused and reiterated God's final words to Saul: "You [have] rejected the word of Yahweh, so Yahweh has rejected you from being king over Israel" (15:26).

Samuel again turned to leave. Saul was now desperate. He fell to his knees and grabbed the hem of the prophet's threadbare robe. In the ancient Near East, to grasp the hem of another's garment was an act symbolic of submission.[20] For Saul, however, it was too late. The prophet's cloak tore in his hand. Samuel turned on Saul and, using his torn robe as an object lesson, reinforced the message that the Lord had torn the kingdom from Saul's grasp and given it to one who was more worthy.

This whole confrontation only took a few minutes but it heightened Saul's fears. Once again he appealed to Samuel to accompany him to the festivities. His words showed his abject submission and sorrowful acceptance of his fate. He was anxious about only one thing: how he would appear before the people (15:30). Samuel yielded. Saul's wretchedness seems to have touched him, and the prophet was reluctant to make him grovel. He went with Saul but there is no evidence in the text that Samuel worshiped with them. He no doubt continued firm in his intent not to identify himself with Saul as king.[21]

THE EXECUTION OF THE BAN (15:32-33)

The celebrations over, Samuel demanded that Agag be brought before him. Samuel's orders were carried out. The royal prisoner advanced cautiously. He may have known the reputation of Israel's prophet. Samuel possessed the kind of moral integrity and passionate commitment to the truth that puts fear into the hearts of those whose lives have been spent in corruption, oppression, and gratification of the senses.

"Surely the bitterness of death is passed" (1 Samuel 15:32), Agag said optimistically. He had been spared by King Saul; perhaps he would escape death at the hands of the prophet as well.

Samuel's words, however, came as the harbinger of doom: "As your sword has made women childless, so shall your mother be childless among women" (15:33). And taking a sword from someone standing close by, Samuel cut Agag to pieces before the Lord in Gilgal.

The swift judgment executed upon one who was impenitent was merely a sign of the slower retribution pronounced on all who are unrepentant.[22] God gives evildoers time to acknowledge their utterly lost condition. If they do not respond to His grace, then a time will come when He will by no means acquit the guilty!

THE PARTING OF THE WAYS (15:34-35)

The breach between Samuel and Saul was now final. Saul would continue to rule as king for about another fifteen years, but not as God's representative. He was no longer in the line of the theocracy.

Saul, like most people of his temperament, could not live with a sense of his own failure. In the past he had repeatedly projected blame for his actions onto others and it probably did not take him long to rationalize this new situation and find some way to justify himself. To this defense mechanism he added the strategy of diminishing the authority of the one who condemned him. Saul possibly reasoned from the results of the attack on Amalek that God had blessed his efforts by giving him a notable victory. Samuel therefore must have exceeded his authority in claiming that the Lord had set Saul aside as king. Content with his own rationalization, Saul continued to rule as before.[23]

Some of Samuel's statements, however, stayed in Saul's mind. In the years to follow he would drive all witches and soothsayers from the land (cf. 1 Samuel 15:23 with 28:3); and being mindful of Samuel's indictment of him for his sinfulness and idolatry, Saul would try to demonstrate his zeal for the Lord and his desire to maintain the purity of religion by making war on the Gibeonites (cf. Joshua 9:15-21; 2 Samuel 21:1-9).

However, 1 Samuel 15 closes with the sorrowful words, "Yahweh repented that He had made Saul king over Israel" (15:35).

PERTINENT REMINDERS OF IMPORTANT TRUTHS

The lessons of 1 Samuel 15 are extremely pertinent to our time. As a pastoral counselor I have been constantly amazed at the way in which contemporary predicaments in our lives parallel situations found in the Old Testament.

We Can't Do As We Please

Although God is sovereign, He has given to each of us a will. We can choose either to obey or disobey Him. The Amalekites chose to go against the laws of God and man. Like the people described in Jeremiah 13:23, the Amalekites had "learned to do evil." They were devoid of compassion. They took advantage of the weaknesses and misfortunes of others. The Amalekites have a lot in common with those in business today who exploit their employees for the sake of their own gain or who engage in hostile takeovers that leave loyal hard-working individuals without a means of sustenance.

There is nothing wrong with making money. *It is immoral, however, to treat people as if they were things and things as if they were people.* When our greed or malice adversely affects the lives of others, then we in effect repeat the actions of the marauding Amalekites who took away in a night what others had worked hard over many years to accumulate or develop.

While many will scoff at this kind of teaching, we may be sure that He who sits in the heavens takes note of such attitudes and actions. Though His judgment may be long delayed, it will surely come (Micah 3:8-12).

The defeat of the Amalekites embodies a simple but potent lesson: We cannot do as we please. In time divine retribution will overtake those who practice evil (Romans 1:18; 1 Timothy 5:24-25). As Hosea warned, individuals who sow to the wind will reap the whirlwind (Hosea 8:7). Whatever we do to others will be done to us in return (Matthew 7:2; Galatians 6:7).

The Amalekites chose to disobey God. But what of Saul and his partial obedience to the word of the Lord?

Whenever I think of Saul I am reminded of Donna. We met one Sunday morning when I was preaching in a church whose pastor was ill. After the service she came up to the platform and asked if she might speak with me. I agreed to see her later that afternoon, provided the arrangement met with her husband's approval. There was a coffee shop near the church with booths along one wall. These gave a measure of privacy so we decided to meet there.

Donna was very punctual. After making a few remarks to set her at ease I asked her how I might help her. She began nervously.

"Well, I've served on the missions committee of this church as long as I can remember. I'm active in the youth work—my children, Jeff and Sandra, are involved in just about everything, and I feel this is one way I can take an interest in their activities. Then there's the women's auxiliary (I'm a past president) and the Bible study fellowship (I'm the social chairperson). I sing in the choir and play the piano for our Sunday school class and I also do hospital visitation for the church."

When Donna paused for breath I said, "I'm very impressed with all you are doing, but how may I help you?"

She hesitated for a moment and then said, "It's my husband, Stan. He's not involved in church work. He doesn't study his Bible. He comes home from work and slumps down in his favorite chair to read the newspaper. Then after dinner he watches TV until we go to bed."

"Please continue," I said.

For a moment Donna became silent. Her hands twisted her gloves and she avoided looking in my direction. There was something she wanted to tell me but didn't know how.

"Go on," I coaxed.

The silence could be felt. Then she said quietly, "There's this man. I met him two years ago at a PTA meeting. He's a Christian, a widower. I've seen him a few times and cannot but think how happy I would be if...well, you know...if I were married to him instead of Stan."

I sensed that Donna was still holding something back so I asked very quietly, "Have you been intimate with him?"

A look of surprise came over her face. Suddenly she picked up her purse and for a moment it seemed as if she were going to leave. Then her posture relaxed a little and in a barely audible voice she said, "Yes."

We talked for a long time. It was evident that she was looking for an excuse to divorce Stan and marry Roger. She was thinking, *If I obey God and serve Him devotedly in all these areas of my life, surely He will let me have my way in this one particular.* I tried reasoning with her from the Scriptures, but to no avail.

About fifteen years later I was in the area again and asked my pastor-friend about Donna. It took a while before he remembered who she was. Then he told me what had happened.

"Donna divorced Stan and married Roger. He joined the church and for a time they sang in the choir. This caused Stan and the children to leave and go elsewhere. From what I have heard, both Jeff and Sandra rebelled against the Lord and Stan had a very difficult time with them.

"Donna's marriage to Roger did not last for more than four or five years. After Roger divorced her, she went steadily downhill—drinking, discos, drugs. Finally one night when she was drunk she had an accident and was killed. When no one else claimed the body, Stan and his children buried her in a very private ceremony."

How different their lives might have been had Donna obeyed what she knew to be the will of God. She could have sought forgiveness from the Lord, recommitted her life to Stan, and worked on restoring their lost communication. Stan would have responded to her, and healing could have begun to take place. As it was, at least five lives were adversely affected by her decision. In the eyes of the Lord Donna's partial obedience was not enough; neither was Saul's.

We Can Follow the Will of God

What are we to make of the "changing will of God" for Saul? Why would the Lord go to such lengths to select and confirm him, and then reject him? Surely if God knows the end from the beginning, something went wrong with His plan!

Some Christians use such a line of reasoning to try to explain the conflict between the will of God for their lives and the choices they have made. The following true story illustrates how our choices affect the course of our own lives and the lives of others.

Mel and Irene were part of a Bible class I taught for professional people while my family and I lived in Illinois. Everyone said they made an ideal couple. They both held graduate degrees and had promising careers. They both wanted to know the Lord's will for their lives and this desire was a sign of their spiritual health. Long before they met they had each been praying for a mature Christian who might serve as an able counterpart. Each of them was living alone and, while relatively content, felt a certain lack of completeness. All their friends were married but until now neither of them had thought seriously about marriage. Even after Mel and Irene began dating, they continued to pray earnestly for guidance. Neither of them wanted to make a mistake they both might live to regret. As the months passed they became convinced that the Lord had indeed brought them together, and they began discussing the possibility of marriage.

Irene's parents were not Christians. They were both in their late sixties. Their three older sons were married and Irene, their only daughter, was the baby of the family. They were happy in a way that Irene had not married in her early twenties when all her friends were dating and marrying, for they liked having her around. They also expected that when they became old and too frail to look after themselves, she would take care of them. Mel was perceived as a threat to their plans.

When Irene told her parents about Mel and of their love for each other, her mother and father began to raise objections. Discussions became heated. Irene's mother was particularly adept at controlling people by means of guilt, and she made Irene feel miserable—"After all we've done for you, you now want to turn your back on us and marry that man." (Irene's mother never referred to Mel by name.) On other occasions she would remind Irene, "We've done a lot for you, child, and now it's your turn to do something for us." Once when her mother felt she was losing the argument, she quoted Shakespeare to confirm her belief that there was nothing worse in all the world than a "thankless child."

Irene loved Mel, but her parents' influence proved to be too much for her and she broke up with him. Mel felt rejected and bewildered. For several months he continued to phone Irene and send her flowers, but she steadfastly refused to see him. As Saul "feared the people and listened to their voice," thereby forfeiting the blessing the Lord had planned to give him, so Irene capitulated to her parents' demands.

Mel had to face a difficult theological problem. How could he reconcile Irene's actions with God's unmistakable leading? He loved Irene maturely and with a depth he had never experienced before. He also realized that the kind of mutuality they had enjoyed—a unity of mind and soul—was unlikely to come his way again.

Mel found himself to be in a position similar to Samuel's. Samuel had followed the will of God down to the minutest detail (1 Samuel 8:7,9,22; 9:16; 10:17-21), yet the events of 15:13-14,23 brought about a radical change in his expectations. When faced with things he could not explain, he contented himself with following the will of the Lord as it was revealed progressively to him. He exercised implicit trust in the Lord while remaining flexible. And he continued to serve the Lord faithfully in spite of the things he could not understand. It remained for Mel to do the same. He had to come to the place where he acknowledged Irene's right to make a choice even if it was contrary to the Lord's revealed will. He also needed to own his hurt feelings, grieve the loss of Irene (cf. 1 Samuel 16:1), and then continue to walk reverently before the Lord.

I've kept in touch with several of the men and women from this study group by letter and occasional visits. They tell me Irene is still single and her parents, now in their eighties, are self-sufficient and independent. They take two vacations a year, one within the United States and the other abroad. They are glad to have Irene visit them for dinner on Sunday when they are home. Irene has become more and more materialistic and self-indulgent. Her life now gives every evidence of shallowness and superficiality. She has many acquaintances but no really good friends. Worse still, she has become cold and hardened in her disposition and has lost those beautiful characteristics of femininity that once made her so attractive.

Mel has never married. He has continued to serve the Lord faithfully in his secular occupation as well as in different capacities in the church he joined after he and Irene broke up. He is conscious of a profound void in his life but has not faltered in his devotion to the Lord in spite of the crushing disappointment he has had to bear. For many months he had to grapple with God's clear leading on the one hand and human disobedience on the other. Like Samuel, however, he has persevered in doing what he believes to be right. We too can follow the will of God even when others disobey.

As I think of the possibilities that lay before Mel and Irene, the words of John Greenleaf Whittier come to mind:

> For of all sad words of tongue or pen
> The saddest are these: "It might have been!"[24]

The same can be said of King Saul. God's plans for him and his house exceeded his fondest dreams (1 Samuel 13:13; cf. Proverbs 21:16) but because "he feared the people and listened to their voice" he lost everything!

What We Learn about God

As we reflect on the information brought before us in 1 Samuel 15, we find that the Lord is compassionate and gracious.

God's grace in giving Amalek so long a time in which to repent illustrates the fact that He is slow to anger. He did not punish their sins the moment they transgressed His laws, and *we* may be profoundly thankful that He does not chasten *us* the moment *we* sin (Psalm 103:8). He gives us time to repent and seek His forgiveness.

There came a time, however, when He decided to put an end to Amalek's predatory raids. The cry of the weak and the defenseless in Judah had come before Him. He was moved with pity by their plight. Acting in perfect justice He commissioned Saul to destroy Amalek. It was a case of retribution in kind.

As we continue to meditate on 1 Samuel 15 we also realize that God is sovereign in His power and authority. By giving Israel victory over an enemy far more powerful than themselves He demonstrated the awesomeness of His might.

God is also steadfast in keeping His covenant with those who revere Him (2 Chronicles 7:14). Whenever Israel kept His covenant He gave them victory over their enemies and rewarded them far in excess of what they deserved. In contrast to the Israelites, the Amalekites did not turn from their evil ways, and they were punished. Individuals or nations who spurn God's grace sooner or later find themselves the objects of His wrath.

The more we come to know of God personally, the more we find Him to be compassionate, gracious, patient, longsuffering, and abounding in lovingkindness and truth. He plans to do for us far more than we could ever ask or think (Ephesians 3:20). He reserves His tender mercies for those who fear Him, forgiving their iniquities and rewarding them for their obedience to His will (Exodus 34:6-7).

A MOST UNLIKELY SUCCESSOR

1 Samuel 16:1-23

Painters and musicians, poets and orators have all used the force of contrast to describe what they have seen and felt. The subtle interplay of light and shade on a canvas, the placid notes of a harp set against the cacophony of sounds that come from a city street, the measured cadence of a ballad or a sonnet compared with the powerful polemic of a politician seeking election—these all elicit an emotional response.

Photographers have used contrast to highlight the many moods of nature. Perhaps the most significant example of this form of art in this century is the work of Ansel Adams. His exquisite pictures of Yosemite and the Sierra Nevadas—aptly named the "Range of Light"—have lured travelers to California from all over the United States as well as from other parts of the world. The scenic beauty of Yosemite Valley with its towering mountains and impressive waterfalls never fails to fill sightseers with the same kind of awe they would feel if they were gazing on the snowcapped Andes, the majestic Alps, or the vast Alaskan ranges.

Captured on film by Ansel Adams are the rugged splendor of Half Dome softened at its lower elevations by faint wisps of clouds; the august beauty and enduring permanence of El Capitan set against the fragile elegance of Mirror Lake; and the irresistible power of Yosemite Falls in early spring juxtaposed with the first flowers of the new year pushing their way upward through the melting snow.

Writers also use imagery when they wish to contrast the effects of virtue and villainy, integrity and improbity, altruism and malevolence. This technique was used in the presentation of the material in 1 Samuel 16. Scholars have dubbed this passage "The Rise of David and the Decline of Saul"—and there is some truth to their observation, particularly when attention is focused on verses 13 and 14—but in reality we have been witnessing Saul's decline over several years, while David has already been referred to twice in praiseworthy terms (13:14; 15:28).

The contrast in 1 Samuel 16 is really between a *youth,* the least in his father's house and too insignificant to be invited to the feast with the venerated prophet Samuel, and a *king,* the foremost man of the realm who has become inept in his leadership and has forfeited the right to rule his people. On the one hand we see a lad dedicated to doing well the most menial of tasks, and on the other a monarch who failed to carry out the mandate God gave him. The dissimilarity is further accentuated when we perceive the young shepherd's stability and strong internal God-consciousness, and observe the nation's leader repeatedly faltering because of his pride and self-will.

THE FAMILY OF THE FUTURE KING

David's father Jesse is called an Ephrathite (1 Samuel 17:12)—indicating that he was a descendant of the founders of the small village of Bethlehem and was regarded as a part of the aristocracy.[1] Such distinctions, however, counted for very little in those days. Economically Jesse and his family faced severe struggles, and the expected benefits of having a king had not materialized. There was an uneasy peace between the king and the leaders of the different tribes.

Among the thousands of villages that dotted the landscape of Canaan, Bethlehem was so inconspicuous a hamlet that it had to be specially identified by a prophet as lying in the territory of Judah (Micah 5:2); otherwise people would have thought of other places that had the same name but were more populous and more prominent because of their geographic locations.

Jesse was the grandson of Boaz and Ruth (Ruth 4:18-22). Jesse had been blessed with eight sons of his own: Eliab (1 Samuel 16:6-7, also referred to as Elihu in 1 Chronicles 27:18); Abinadab (1 Samuel 16:8); Shammah (1 Samuel 16:9, also known as Shimeah in 2 Samuel 13:3 and Shimei in 2 Samuel 21:21); Nethaneel; Raddai; Ozem (1 Chronicles 2:13-16); an unnamed son who most commentators believe died early; and last and certainly least in the eyes of his family, David (1 Samuel 16:10-11).

Jesse also had two daughters, Zeruiah and Abigail (1 Chronicles 2:16-17). Some have conjectured on the basis of 2 Samuel 17:25 that Zeruiah was only David's half sister. She was the mother of Joab, Abishai, and Asahel, and seems to have bequeathed to her sons something of her own independent, harsh, and implacable spirit.[2]

OUTLINE

Outlining 1 Samuel 16 is made easy because of another contrast: we read of the Spirit of God coming mightily upon David (16:13) and leaving Saul (16:14). The first division of the chapter, therefore, looks at the anointing of the new king, and the second division looks at how the king-designate became familiar with the activities of the court and commenced fighting the Lord's battles:[3]

- God's Selection of a New Leader (1 Samuel 16:1-13)
- God's Preparation of the New Leader (1 Samuel 16:14-23)

GOD'S SELECTION OF A NEW LEADER (16:1-13)

So far in the Biblical record David has not been referred to by name. He has been described (1) as "a man after [Yahweh's own] heart" whom He has "appointed ruler over His people" (1 Samuel 13:14) and (2) as Saul's "neighbor" to whom Yahweh has given the kingdom (15:28). (The prophetic perfect tense used in 13:14 looks at a future event as if it had already happened.)

When God commanded Samuel to anoint one of Jesse's sons as king in Saul's place, the prophet was still grieving for Saul. Samuel knew how deeply the king was hurting and mourned for him. The prophet was also deeply concerned for his people. They now had a titular head who lacked the power to initiate anything decisive and so they were like sheep without a shepherd. As Samuel cast his eye around the nation, he saw no one who could be compared with Saul for kingly qualifications.[4]

The Man of God's Choice (16:1-3)

God directed Samuel to go to Bethlehem—a little village about six miles south of Jerusalem and approximately eleven or twelve miles south southeast of Ramah—and there anoint one of the sons of Jesse as the next king of Israel. Bethlehem at that time was of no account politically, socially, or economically. The Lord's words, however, were emphatic, and they underscore the theme of this book.

> "Fill your horn with oil and go; *I will send you* to Jesse the Bethlehemite, *for I have selected a king for Myself* from among his sons." But Samuel said, "How can I go? When Saul hears [of it] he will kill me." And Yahweh said, "Take a heifer with you and say, 'I have come to sacrifice to Yahweh.' And you shall

invite Jesse to the sacrifice, and *I will show you what you shall do; and you shall anoint for Me the one whom I designate to you"* (1 Samuel 16:1-3, emphasis added).

To our surprise the intrepid prophet initially objected to the assignment. To go to Bethlehem, Samuel would have to pass by Gibeah, Saul's city. In his objection Samuel revealed his humanity and also gave us some incidental insights into Saul's administration. Samuel looked on Saul as a man of the most passionate and imperious self-will. The people lived in fear of him. The dilemma facing Samuel was real.

When we read that the Lord told Samuel to take a heifer with him, we face an ethical problem. Was God suggesting that His prophet lie or tell a half-truth to conceal his real intentions? Didn't Abraham get into trouble when he did the same thing (Genesis 20:2-12)? To answer this important question we need to remind ourselves that God "desires truth in our inward parts" (Psalm 51:6). He requires that we be open and honest and transparent before Him. He also expects us to be honest in our dealings with others and asserts that liars and those who swear falsely are an abomination in His sight (Proverbs 11:1; 16:11; 12:22). How then are we to explain the Lord's words to Samuel? Are we to do as He says, but not as He does? Dr. Walter C. Kaiser, Jr., summed up God's actions with his usual aplomb:

> There is a vast difference between telling a lie and concealing information that others have forfeited a right to know because of their hostile attitude toward God and his moral standards. King Saul... [had] forfeited his right to know the reasons for the prophet Samuel's visit [to Bethlehem].[5]

Part of our growth toward maturity involves our learning to discern the realities of life. We are not obliged to divulge to everyone who asks us all we know on a particular subject. Some cannot be trusted with the information, and others might turn it around and use it against us. We are expected to be as wise as serpents and as inoffensive as doves (Matthew 10:16); gullibility has no place in the life of a maturing believer. In matters of ethics our primary relationship must be a vertical one.[6]

Where our horizontal relationships are concerned we need to use appropriate discernment. Some people are adept at asking questions when they have neither the right to the information nor the ability to use the data wisely. We are under no obligation to give them the information they seek; instead we need to turn away their questions with polite but evasive comments. And when people do have a right to certain information, even then circumstances may dictate that they be told only what is germane to the situation.[7]

We should also remember that if a person has entered into a hostile or adversarial relationship with us and by his or her attitude evidences a desire to harm us, we are under no obligation to respond to any inquiry. Nowhere in God's Word is a person obliged to witness against himself or tell truth that will result in harm to himself or another.

Some writers are fond of posing improbable cases and using them to establish their theories of ethical norms.[8] They befuddle issues and fail to establish viable ethical standards.

Thomas Kirk pointed out that

> Samuel was under no obligation publicly to proclaim the whole truth about his mission to Bethlehem. He injured no one by concealing the main purpose of his journey. And by his silence on the point, he not only did no one any wrong, but he prevented wrong [being done] to others. To conceal the truth with the truth for an injurious and nefarious end, is base; but to conceal the truth with the truth in order to outwit malice and ensure self-preservation is permissible and wise. To suppose that Samuel was under an obligation to tell every one or any one who asked him about the object of his visit, that he had come to anoint one of the sons of Jesse to be king, and thereby endanger [that person's] life, is to suppose that Samuel was under an obligation to become a fool and be devoid of discretion.[9]

True maturity shows itself in wise, responsible action that is independent of the influence of one's peers—action that is based on knowledge of the issues. A truly mature person seeks the highest good in the lives of others. We have much to learn, therefore, from God's words to Samuel.

The Leaders of God's People (16:4-5)

Reassured by what the Lord told him, Samuel went to the little hamlet of Bethlehem. As he approached the gates, the elders came out to meet him. They did not offer him a friendly greeting, but asked, "Do you come in peace?" The question indicated their fear that someone in the village was guilty of an offense and Samuel had come to hold court and judge the offender.

They were reassured by Samuel's response (1 Samuel 16:4-5) and willingly set about consecrating themselves in preparation for the coming feast. Their preparations probably involved washing their clothes, bathing, anointing themselves with oil, and readying themselves in heart and mind to worship the Lord. Before they began these preparations, they possibly witnessed the ritual sacrifice of the heifer and the separation of the parts of the animal that belonged to the Lord from the parts that would be eaten by the people invited to the feast.

If Jesse was not numbered among the elders of the city, then Samuel no doubt asked for directions to his home. There he made known to him the fact that one of his sons was to be set apart for special service to the Lord. No one seemed to have the slightest idea of the significance of the special anointing that was to take place. No one seemed to understand that it would designate Israel's next king.

The Process of Determining God's Will (16:6-10)

At the time of the feast Jesse's sons were shown one by one into the room where Samuel was waiting. The first was Eliab, the eldest. He was handsome and robust, and Samuel thought to himself, "Surely Yahweh's anointed is before Him." The Lord knew Samuel's thoughts and said to him,

> Do not look at his appearance or at the height of his stature, because I have rejected him; for God [sees] not as man sees, for man looks at the [outward] appearance, but Yahweh looks at the heart (1 Samuel 16:7).

In this verse we have the key to one of the subordinate themes of the book of 1 Samuel: the difference between an external locus of control and the kind of internal God-consciousness that the Holy Spirit desires to develop in us. The Biblical writer had been building toward this point with hints and suggestions. Here he made explicit what he had previously illustrated. Dr. Blaikie applied the teaching of this verse with his usual keen discernment:

> It is not merely in the choice of kings [or mates or careers] that men are apt to show their readiness to rest in the outward appearance. To what an infinite extent has this tendency been carried in the worship of God! Let everything be outwardly correct, the church beautiful, the music excellent, the sermon able, the congregation numerous and respectable—what a

pattern such a church is often regarded! Alas! how little satisfactory it may be to God. The eye that searches and knows us penetrates to the heart—it is there only that God finds the genuine elements of worship.

The lowly sense of personal unworthiness, the wondering contemplation of the divine love, the eager longing for mercy to pardon and grace to help, the faith that grasps the promises, the hope that is anchored within the veil, the kindness that breathes benediction all round, the love that beareth all things, believeth all things, hopeth all things, endureth all things—it is these things, breathing forth from the hearts of a congregation, that give pleasure to God.[10]

The prophet learned his lesson well. As each of Jesse's sons was brought before him, he was compelled to say to Jesse, "Neither has Yahweh chosen this one." None was qualified for the work of the Lord.

The Basis of God's Selection (16:11-13a)

Samuel was mystified. The Lord had told him to anoint one of Jesse's sons, yet He had shown His disapproval of all seven. So Samuel asked, "Are these all the children?" And Jesse replied apologetically, "No, there's one more. He's the youngest, his mother's darling.[11] We don't have much use for him either in the city or working on the farm, so we've given him the task of looking after our small flock of sheep. If none of my other sons is acceptable, Samuel, I doubt if you will find him suitable."

Tacit evidence that the heifer sacrificed earlier in the day must have been roasting for some time comes from verse 1 Samuel 16:11. The meat was ready to be carved and served, but Samuel instructed Jesse to send a runner for David and said that they would not sit down to eat until he arrived.

When David reached Bethlehem, he may well have run several miles. He was shown in to the place where his father and brothers and Samuel were waiting. He had not gone through the ritual consecration, yet when he came before the man of God, the Lord said to Samuel, "Arise, anoint him; for this is he" (16:12).

No one was told the significance of the anointing. All David felt was the Spirit of God coming mightily upon him. Thus endued with power from on high he stood in the line of the theocracy. Josephus conjectured that at the time Samuel anointed David with oil he whispered in the young shepherd's ear that he was to be Israel's future king.[12] No verification of this theory can be gleaned from the text, but it is quite probable that Jesse and his family understood that from now on some of David's time was to be spent with Samuel in Ramah. There, in company with the other young men in training in the schools of the prophets, he would have the opportunity to improve his skill as a musician, learn to write, and receive instruction from Samuel in the law of the Lord.

These unique schools apparently enjoyed to an eminent degree the gracious power of the Holy Spirit. The hearts of the students burned with a holy zeal. They were animated by a joy that could not be restrained, but poured forth from them in song and ascriptions of praise to God. At times the students' effusive spirits affected even the coldness of Saul's heart. It seems probable therefore that when David was attending Saul at Gibeah, he also spent time with Samuel at Ramah. If so, we can easily see how his devotion to the Lord was powerfully impacted and reliably challenged by the prophet's teaching, and why at a later time his Psalms would breathe such inimitable trust and confidence in the Lord.

> In the mysterious exercise of that mysterious sovereignty which we are unable to fathom, He made [David's] youthful heart a plot of good soil, into which when the seed fell it bore fruit an hundredfold. In strong contrast to Saul, whose early sympathies were against the ways and will of God, those of David were warmly with them.[13]

The training received by the students in the schools of the prophets was intermittent, so David still had time to be responsible for keeping his father's sheep. In the leisurely evenings the young shepherd played the harp or flute and meditated on the different portions of God's Word taught him by the aged prophet.

William Deane draws the threads of 1 Samuel 16:11-13a together for us. Thinking of the events that took place in a room in or near Jesse's home Deane said:

> What the spectators thought of the transaction we are not told. Certainly neither David nor they saw in it any immediate delegation to the kingdom; the high destiny to which [David had been] called was not mentioned, and he returned to his usual occupations afterwards as if nothing uncommon had happened. The anointing seemed to his brethren to be merely a mode of designating the boy as assistant at the sacrificial ceremony, or enrolling him in the prophetic school. But it had

an inward effect upon David himself; the Spirit of the Lord came mightily upon him; his character developed itself in many ways, and the divine influence was shown in the high and noble qualities which he exhibited.[14]

The Conclusion of God's Assignment (16:13b)

With the anointing of David, Samuel's mission had been completed, and he returned to Ramah. He did not wait around to discuss affairs of state or the events of the previous night with the elders at the gate of the city. He was not antisocial, but wisely recognized that little is to be gained by idle conversation.

GOD'S PREPARATION OF THE NEW LEADER (16:14-23)

While the remainder of 1 Samuel 16 seems to be concerned primarily with King Saul and his afflictions, it is really a means of showing us how David was brought to court and given the opportunity to learn how to administer the realm.

The inspired historian began with a flashback: "Now the Spirit of Yahweh departed from Saul, and an evil spirit from Yahweh terrified him." Saul may have suffered the effects of the evil spirit for several years before some of his trusted counselors (*'abādîm,* "ranking members of the court") summoned up enough courage to confront him and propose a solution (1 Samuel 16:15-17).

During this period David killed both a lion and a bear (1 Samuel 17:34-35) and for his bravery received from the people of his village the coveted title of *gibbôr ḥayil,* "a mighty [man] of valor." He joined the local militia and distinguished himself in battle against marauding Bedouins who frequently raided the villages and drove off the livestock, for Saul's servant referred to David as *'îš milḥāmā,* "a man of war" (16:18).

Also during this time, and in the providence of God, even his experiences as a shepherd were preparing David for his future service. His duties—to watch over his flock, to feed and protect them, to heal the sick, to bind up the broken, and to bring back those that wandered away—corresponded to the responsibilities of a faithful and godly ruler. It is from the time of David that shepherd phraseology began to be applied to rulers and their people. We hardly carry away the full lesson the prophets intended to teach us in their denunciations of shepherds who fed themselves and not their flocks (Ezekiel 34:2,8,10; Isaiah 56:11; Jeremiah 10:21; 12:10; 23:1-2; 50:6) when we apply these prophecies exclusively to the shepherds of our souls. So appropriate was the emblem of the faithful shepherd for denoting the right spirit and character of rulers, that the figure of speech was ultimately appropriated in a very high and peculiar sense to the person and office of the Lord Jesus Christ[15] (cf. Psalm 78:70-72 with Isaiah 40:11).

A Grave Problem (16:14)

First Samuel 16:14 begins a section of Biblical history in which the rise of David is in contrast to the decline of Saul.[16] Scholars show little agreement when it comes to explaining the cause of Saul's affliction. Everything from epilepsy to meningitis to schizophrenia has been proposed.[17]

In the Bible the "evil spirit from Yahweh" is looked upon as a divine judgment on Saul. Everything in the Old Testament is seen as being under God's sovereign control (Deuteronomy 13:2-4; 2 Samuel 24:1; Amos 3:6); He rules over all. When He withdraws His hand from someone, such an act can also be the means whereby Satanic forces are allowed to do their malevolent work. That is why the Lord is portrayed as sending an evil spirit to cause dissension between Abimelech and the men of Shechem (Judges 9:23) and commissioning a lying spirit to cause the false prophets to disagree with the testimony of Micaiah (1 Kings 22:19-22).

It seems probable that Saul's anguish was caused by feelings of severe depression (cf. the usage of the word *bāʿath*, "overwhelmed, terrified," in 1 Samuel 16:14 to its usage in 2 Samuel 22:5; Job 7:14; Psalm 18:4). Depression occurs whenever we suffer the loss of something of intrinsic value to us. In Saul's case his sense of loss was aggravated and accentuated because, in judgment, the Spirit of the Lord had departed from him, leaving him vulnerable to attacks from the nether world. The evil spirit that afflicted Saul took advantage of the situation and increased his natural suffering.[18]

Not all depression however is the result of demonic activity. Psychological depression may range from mild to severe, depending on the nature of the loss.[19] We know that Saul had suffered some significant emotional losses: he was alienated from Samuel; he forfeited his dynasty by his impatience and lack of trust in the Lord; and finally, as a consequence of his disobedience and fear of the people, he was rejected by God as His theocratic representative. In addition, while Saul had always been victorious in battle (1 Samuel 14:52), the wars had been hard fought and Saul may have felt that he had not received sufficient positive reinforcement from his subjects. Coupled with these reasons for being depressed was the fact that his early home life had predisposed him to dysphoria, making him vulnerable to the kind of suffering he now had to endure.

A Plausible Solution (16:15-23)

Suggestion of Servants. When matters at court became unbearable, Saul's servants urged him to find someone skillful in playing on a harp. It was widely believed that music quieted the spirit and that if uplifting words accompanied certain tranquil refrains, the mind could be stimulated as well and brought into harmony with the emotions.[20]

The practical ramifications of this kind of therapy should not be ignored. Charlene, a woman I know, looked after her mother during a long and painful illness. One day Charlene asked, "What can I do to help her? I feel so powerless." I suggested that she make tapes of soft music and play them for her mother by the hour. I also recommended that during her mother's more lucid moments she could play devout hymns set to quiet music to remind her mother of a believer's hope and the blessings of the gospel. Charlene followed my suggestions and found that "music has charms to soothe the troubled soul." When music was played, her mother became calmer and appeared to be more at peace as she approached death.

Saul heeded his servants' suggestion and commanded, "Look now for a man [for] me who is good at playing, and bring [him] to me" (1 Samuel 16:17).

Preparation of David. As we have noted, following his anointing by Samuel, David returned to his work among the sheep. We may suppose that the prophet, having begun a new work in the life of this young man, would periodically summon him to Ramah in order to continue his training and prepare him to fulfill the will of God. Support for this supposition is gleaned from 1 Samuel 19:18-19. When trouble arose between David and Saul, it was to Samuel that David fled, and there is every indication from what took place that the two men were close friends.

Whether David derived his views of government from Samuel cannot be determined with accuracy. There is much in David's later approach to the administration of the kingdom to suggest the prophet's influence. For example David readily acknowledged God's absolute sovereignty and the earthly king's subordination to Him; the unique position of the people of Israel as God's elect; and the shameful nature of idolatry and the dishonor done to the Lord when His people succumbed to the worship of pagan deities.[21]

Invitation from Saul. One of the subtle evidences of God's involvement in our lives is found in 1 Samuel 16:18. There just happened to be a man at Saul's court who knew of Jesse's youngest son. The man responded to Saul's request for a musician by saying, "Look, I have seen a son of Jesse the Bethlehemite who knows [how to] play, and [is] a mighty warrior, and a man of battle, and skillful in speech, and a man of form [handsome], and Yahweh is with him." From the courtier's description of David we realize that the young shepherd's gifts, courage, mental acuity, and personal winsomeness, had become quite widely known. Most important of all was the acknowledgment that the Lord was with him.

Saul was pleased with the report and sent a message to Jesse, "Send to me your son David who [is] with [looking after] the flock" (16:19). Jesse could not disobey such an order. And because a king must be approached with a present, he sent some produce from his farm with David.[22]

In this seemingly incidental manner the Lord brought David to court and at the same time provided the means whereby Saul's troubled spirit might find a measure of peace. After playing for Saul, David returned to Bethlehem until he was needed again (17:15).

As time passed, Saul came to appreciate David more and more.[23] The king promoted his musician to the position of armorbearer. This promotion did not mean that David remained at court indefinitely, but from this time onward, during the summer months when wars were fought, he accompanied Saul to the field of battle. And when David's services were found to be indispensable, Saul sent another message to Jesse stating that he wanted David to be permanently assigned to the court (18:2).

In these court experiences David was growing in his knowledge of people and how to lead them wisely. He also had the opportunity to learn firsthand about Israel's friends, the best way to maintain unity among the tribes, and the nature of his country's enemies. The Lord also uses *our* experiences to prepare *us* for service.

The last verse of 1 Samuel 16 summarizes the events of the next few years. David's playing on a harp and perhaps his singing of some comforting songs soothed Saul's troubled spirit.

A STUDY IN CONTRASTS

The story is interesting but what does it have to do with us? We can find encouragement in the account of David's success and warning in the account of Saul's failure.

David is so revered by humble students of God's Word that it is difficult for us to think back to a time when he was lightly esteemed by the members of his father's household—and even despised by his brothers (1 Samuel 17:28). His rise to fame was slow and steady, reminding us of another man: he was born to James and Eunice Simpson and they named him Orenthal James. He also rose from an obscure background to become a national hero and a leader of men.

Like many other young boys, O. J. desperately wanted to play football. He was thought to show so little promise, however, that he was dropped from the youth football league team called the Power Gliders.

When O. J. became a teenager he joined a street gang named the Superiors. Times were hard but somehow he learned to survive. Because of poor grades in school he could not go to one of the better colleges, so attended City College in San Francisco for two years. There his years of practicing different plays paid off and he began to excel as a running back. He also showed promise as a sprinter and could run 100 yards in 9.4 seconds. His sports abilities helped him win a scholarship to attend the University of Southern California.

In his first year at USC he ran for 1,543 yards and 13 touchdowns and earned USC a place in the Rose Bowl. There they defeated number-one-ranked UCLA. O. J.'s second year was even better, and that was the year he was awarded the Heisman trophy. Since then Simpson's accolades have multiplied and he is today highly esteemed by all who know him.[24] His growth through the difficult obscure years serves to remind us that we should never look down on someone from a poor or deprived background, for in such individuals there may well be a David or a Lincoln or an Einstein just waiting to be discovered.

David's success may be attributed to his faithfulness and loyalty in doing little things well. In the course of time he was entrusted with greater things (cf. Matthew 25:21-23).

As our thoughts turn to King Saul, we strike a somber note. We are reminded of another American, a man of great potential who allowed bitterness and the opposition of a colleague to corrode his spirit. His name was Aaron Burr.

When he could no longer tolerate Alexander Hamilton's attacks, Burr challenged him to a duel he felt sure he could win. After killing Hamilton, however, Burr found that people no longer trusted him. He decided to move west and crossed the mountains to Pittsburgh. From there he floated down the Ohio river. Everything he attempted withered at his touch. He traveled abroad but could find no acceptance in England or France. At length he returned to New York in disguise, landing at night so that no one might recognize him. His wife had left him several years before, and he was alone. He rented a small room in the basement of a boarding house from which he planned to resume his practice of law, but only a few people sought his services. He remained there until death relieved him of his loneliness.[25]

Aaron Burr is thought to be the most brilliant person ever to have received a degree from Princeton University. Like Saul, however, Burr turned his back on God. When a mighty movement of the Spirit swept the campus and hundreds of students surrendered their lives to Christ, Burr shut himself in his room to wrestle with the issues involving his eternal salvation. He decided that the claims of Christianity were too costly and would stand in the way of his personal ambitions. According to tradition, late one night Burr threw the shutters of his windows open and yelled to the heavens, "Goodbye, God!" From that time onward Aaron Burr opposed Christianity. He charted his own course and forfeited the only possibility of peace ever afforded him, just as Saul forfeited his kingdom.

Viewed from a human perspective Saul had all the outward attributes of a king (1 Samuel 10:23-24) and David was a most unlikely successor. In the course of time, however, Saul was set aside and David proved to be an able shepherd of the Lord's people.

THE BIGGER THEY ARE,
THE HARDER THEY FALL

1 Samuel 17:1–18:5

One of the most widely watched television series was "Star Trek." Its spinoff "Star Trek: The Next Generation" is also popular. Today's young adults grew up hearing Captain James T. Kirk say: "Space... the final frontier. These are the voyages of the Starship *Enterprise*. Its five-year mission: To explore strange new worlds; to seek out new life and new civilizations; to boldly go where no man has gone before."

In each episode the crew of the *Enterprise* faces some new threat to their safety and their mission. These dangers take many forms: a clash with their archenemies, the Klingons; a painful confrontation with a cloud formation concealing a malignant intelligence; an electronic force field that holds the crew motionless in an implacable grasp; an insidious virus the landing party contracts when they beam down to an unfamiliar planet; an unsuspected time warp that propels the Starship into another dimension; or a deceptively alluring civilization that promises all one's heart could desire, but whose real intentions are far from benign.

The fictitious and futuristic adventures of those on board the Starship can be interpreted as allegories of our own encounters with external threats.[1] When we face outer challenges to our autonomy, we have at our disposal the resources and strategies that are illustrated in the well-known story of David and Goliath.[2]

OUTLINE

The following outline indicates the thrust of the passage of Scripture we will now consider:

- The Occasion of the Opposition (1 Samuel 17:1-3)
- The Nature of the Opposition (1 Samuel 17:4-11)
- The Defeat of the Opposition (1 Samuel 17:12–18:5)

THE OCCASION OF THE OPPOSITION (17:1-3)

Before the battle of the valley of Elah began, the leaders of the Philistines held a secret meeting. The five lords may well have converged on Ashkelon as the most central of their cities. It was also close to the ocean and offered certain recreational advantages. The purpose of the meeting was to discuss the ever-present problem of overpopulation. This was not the first time they had debated the issue. They needed land and revenue, and their previous attempts to subjugate the Israelites had not been entirely successful. Recent inroads however had been made into the territory of Judah, and the Philistines realized that if prompt action were taken, their problems might be resolved.

A new kind of warfare was gaining popularity throughout the Near East.[3] To prevent unnecessary loss of life, each of the contending armies would choose its most able warrior. These champions would be matched and the winner of the contest would gain victory for his people; the vanquished would become the vassals of the victors. The Philistines had an invincible champion: Goliath, the giant from Gath.[4]

A plan of attack was agreed upon by the lords of the Philistines and a place of battle was carefully chosen. The five lords were to muster their armies near Socoh, where they would effectively cut off Israel's supply route to the interior. Saul would then be forced to a show of arms at a place favorable to the Philistines. If the Israelites failed to accommodate themselves to the new style of warfare, the Philistines would quickly get reinforcements from the fortress city of Azekah (modern Tell es-Zakariyeh; 1 Samuel 17:1).

With his usual meticulous attention to detail, Dr. Alfred Edersheim described the place of the battle:

> Outside of Socoh was a broad wadi, or valley, marking a watercourse which began near Hebron and, running in a northerly direction for about eight miles passes Keilah and the forest of Hareth on the right and the cave of Adullam on the left. Finally it reaches the Mediterranean Sea a little north of Ashdod. At its center is a curious ravine worn by winter torrents. It is about twenty feet across and has steep banks about ten or twelve feet high.

This gorge is known today as the Wadi es-Sant, or "the valley of the acacias." Dr. Edersheim continued:

> At the modern village of Sakarieh (ancient Shaarim), the wadi divides, turning westward towards Gath, and northwards by the Wadi es-Surar towards Ekron. Socoh and Ephes-Dammin (modern Damum) lie on the southern slope of the wadi, and that is where the Philistine camp is pitched. When the host of Israel arrives they camp on the northern slope. The two then face each other across the deep part of the wadi of Elah.[5]

When Saul was informed of the buildup of Philistine forces within Judah's border at a point about ten to twelve miles southwest of Bethlehem, he quickly marshaled the fighting men of Israel.

THE NATURE OF THE OPPOSITION (17:4-11)

Having noted the events that occasioned the second Philistine war[6] we are now able to focus our attention on the nature of the opposition.

The Challenge (17:4-10)

On the first morning the men of each army ran down to the edge of the small gorge, uttering their battle cries. The purpose of this exercise was to reinforce their own spirits and also to provoke the opposing army into attacking them. The attackers would have to descend into the wadi, cross its width in plain view of any archers, and then scale the opposing bank before they could commence fighting. The defenders would have an unparalleled advantage.

The Philistines had not fared well in their battles for the possession of Israel's border towns, so they were reluctant to place themselves at such a disadvantage. The Israelites were just as anxious to avoid an open clash with the Philistines. The Spirit of the Lord, having departed from Israel's leader, had left the men without the courage to fight. The battle therefore became a war of words and a contest to see who could hold out the longest.

While the armies faced each other across the valley, the followers of Saul saw two men descend the far side of the wadi. One was of average build and was plainly the armorbearer because he was carrying a shield—the largest any Israelite had ever seen. The other was a man of immense proportions. His scale armor clanked ominously as he walked with ponderous steps toward the middle of the gorge. He was so tall that his head almost reached the rim of the wadi on which the men of Israel were standing.[7] He had on a bronze helmet and his armor[8] weighed about 125 pounds. His legs were protected by bronze greaves or shin guards, and his spear[9] was a massive weapon with an iron head[10] weighing 15 or 16 pounds. It could easily pierce through any ordinary shield or coat of mail.

The giant's name was Goliath. Having taken his stand in the middle of the ravine, he bellowed out the conditions of the contest: "Choose [a man] for yourselves and let him come [down] to me. If he is able to fight with me and kill [literally, strike] me, then we will become your slaves; but if I am able to prevail against him and kill [literally, strike] him, then you shall become our slaves and serve us" (1 Samuel 17:8-9).

Understandably the men of Israel were not eager to take a one-way step into the next world, so Goliath's challenge was not accepted. Goliath began goading them, "I defy the ranks of Israel this day; give to me a man and let us fight together" (17:10).

The Response (17:11)

Neither King Saul (now in his early fifties) nor any of the men of Israel was willing to pick up the gauntlet Goliath had thrown down. They were filled with dread. They ascribed to the giant the attributes of almightiness and impendency, and as a result were incapacitated by their fear.

But what of Jonathan? Why didn't he take on the giant from Gath? No one should ever doubt Jonathan's courage or confidence in the Lord. It is possible that Saul had expressly forbidden him to accept the challenge. We know from what is revealed later on (1 Samuel 20:13) that Saul was determined to establish his dynasty regardless of the words of one whom he had come to regard as a cantankerous old man. Perhaps Jonathan did not feel compelled on this occasion to do what he had done at the battle of Michmash Pass. Thomas Kirk is of the opinion that Jonathan still believed, probably stronger than ever, that the Lord was able to save by many or by few, but he lacked the assurance that on this occasion the Lord was willing to deliver Israel through him. Without that conviction, to take on Goliath would have been an act of presumption.[11]

It is harder to follow the leading of the Holy Spirit when He does not lead us forth to action than when He does lead us to volunteer for a difficult or dangerous assignment. As we learn from 1 Samuel 17:12, God was about to use the challenge of Goliath to bring David to public attention. The forty days of monotonous repetition of Goliath's challenge showed the completeness of Israel's weakness and prepared the people to receive the one on whom God's hand now rested.

David is not introduced to us in 1 Samuel 17 as a man but as a lad in his early to midteens, the youngest son of one who was now too old to fight alongside the other leaders of his people. It should be remembered that in a society that followed carefully the laws of primogenitor, to be the eighth of eight sons[12] meant that one had a very low standing in the community. No one was expecting anything significant from Jesse's youngest son. It is true that he had distinguished himself for his prowess in protecting his father's sheep; but Israel was now facing the Philistines and they were a far cry from ewes and their lambs.

During the six weeks Goliath had uttered his challenge both in the morning and again toward dusk, he had become bolder and more arrogant. At times he must have walked up to the very edge of the wadi, for we read of the men of Israel fleeing from him in disarray.

As the days passed, Saul became increasingly dismayed that none of his fellow countrymen would accept the challenge, and so (perhaps progressively) he began to offer certain inducements: great riches, his elder daughter in marriage, and freedom from taxation (1 Samuel 17:25). Still no one was prepared to step forward and take on Goliath.

THE DEFEAT OF THE OPPOSITION (17:12–18:5)

The Family (17:12-16)

Meanwhile David had returned to Bethlehem (1 Samuel 17:15). His rank as Saul's armorbearer seems to have been an honorary one. Back on his father's homestead he resumed the menial task of looking after the sheep.

We know how the story develops, but the Biblical historian thus far kept his readers in suspense by not mentioning who Israel's champion would be. In 1 Samuel 17:12 the opening words, "Now David," gave a faint clue to what was to follow. The writer also reiterated David's background, for it would later become the subject of the king's inquiry (17:12,55-58). The mention of David not only gave clues but also raised questions. How could a young lad in his midteens take on a man of war such as Goliath? What set of circumstances could ever bring the two of them together?

The Visit (17:17-19)

Jesse's three oldest sons were with Saul in the valley of Elah and their father naturally wanted to know how they were doing. Since soldiers at that time had to maintain themselves while fighting the enemy, he decided to send David to the camp with provisions:

> Take now for your brothers an ephah of this roasted [grain] and these ten loaves, and run to the camp to your brothers. And you shall take these ten cuts of cheese to the captain of the[ir] thousand; and you shall look into the welfare of your brothers and bring back their token [evidence of their welfare]" (1 Samuel 17:17-18).

David lost no time in traveling the twelve miles to the camp and arrived by midmorning just in time to hear the verbal salvos as the different tribes took up their positions on the edge of the wadi. He hastily handed the provisions to the baggage keeper and ran down to the ravine to see what was going on (17:22). He also looked around for his brothers and found them just as Goliath was coming toward the Israelites.

The Battle (17:20–18:5)

Preparations for the Battle (17:20-23). Dr. William G. Blaikie drew an interesting parallel between David's arrival in the camp and Saul's meeting with Samuel.

> The coming of David upon the scene corresponded in its accidental character to the coming of Saul into contact with Samuel. Everything seemed to be casual, yet those things which seemed most casual were really links in a providential chain leading to the gravest issues. It seemed to be by chance that David had three brothers serving in Saul's army; it seemed also to be by chance that their father sent his youthful shepherd son to inquire after their welfare; it was not by design that as he saluted his brethren Goliath came up and David heard his words of defiance; still less was it on purpose to wait for David that Saul had sent no one out as yet to encounter the Philistine; and nothing could have appeared more ridiculous than that the challenge should wait to be answered by a stripling shepherd, who, with his sling and shepherd's bag thrown over his shoulder, had so little of the appearance of a man of war.

It seemed very accidental, too, that the only part of the giant's person that was not thoroughly defended by his armour, his eyes and a morsel of his forehead above them, was the only part of him that a small stone from a sling could have inflicted a fatal injury. But obviously all these were parts of the providential plan by which David was at once to confer on his country a signal boon, and to raise his name to the pinnacle of fame. And, as usual, all the parts of this pre-arranged plan fell out without constraint or interference; a new proof that divine pre-ordination does not impair the liberty of man.[13]

After uttering his same challenge Goliath must have approached the edge of the embankment where the Israelites were standing, for to a man they fled from him and were greatly afraid.[14]

Inducements of the King (17:24-25). The Spirit of God rested mightily on David and he was conscious of God's presence with him. The Lord enabled him to see the issues clearly. He was distraught at the craven cowardice shown by his countrymen. In contrast to them he felt no fear. He was not overawed by the size of the Philistine and kept the reality of the situation in perspective. He knew that Goliath in defying the armies of Israel had in reality defied the Lord (1 Samuel 17:10,36). Israel was a theocracy whose head was none other than Yahweh, their covenant-keeping God. Goliath had in effect been taunting the Almighty. He had issued his challenge to the Lord of hosts. Pharaoh, king of Egypt, had done the same thing (Exodus 5:2) and the death of the firstborn throughout the land and the destruction of his army was the result (Exodus 12:29; 14:26-28).

As David expressed his disdain for Goliath in the hearing of some of the soldiers, one of their number asked, "Have you seen this man? Why, he's bigger than anyone I have ever seen. He is even bigger than Saul by a good three feet." The soldier went on to enumerate the inducements by which Saul had sought to encourage his men—the king promised "fame, fortune, and a fair maiden" to the man who killed Goliath (1 Samuel 17:25). Seeking to rekindle the morale of the men, David added a further motive: "taking away the reproach from Israel" (17:26).

Clarification of the Issues (17:26-30). Eliab, the eldest of David's brothers, was angered by David's words and responded with a stinging retort:

Why have you come down? And with whom have you left those few sheep in the wilderness? [You imply that we are derelict in our duty, when your actions show greater irresponsibility.] I know your insolence and the evil of your heart; for you have come down in order to see the battle" (17:28).

Eliab had probably regarded David with a jaundiced eye ever since he had been passed over by Samuel. His response to his youngest brother was designed to belittle him in the eyes of the soldiers. Eliab implied that great things could not be expected from a shepherd, particularly when men twice his age and experienced in fighting Saul's battles could do nothing to change the situation.

David's answer was calm and showed that Eliab's fierce and insulting words had not ruffled his spirit (Proverbs 16:32). Instead of taking the put-down personally, David revealed his inner strength of character by responding graciously to Eliab's blustering rage. Turning away from Eliab, David said, "What have I done now? Was it not a question?" (1 Samuel 17:29).[15]

David's bold confident assurance caused a stir among the demoralized troops and word of his actions reached the ears of King Saul.

Acceptance of the Challenge (17:31-54). When the young shepherd was brought before Israel's monarch, Saul first questioned him and then tried to dissuade him from what appeared to be a foolish course of action. David's reply was indicative of the faith that activated him:

> Let no man's heart fail on account of him [Goliath]; your servant will go and fight this Philistine.... [When] your servant was tending his father's sheep [and] when a lion and a bear came and took away a sheep out of the flock, I went out after him and struck him, and delivered [it] from his mouth; and [when] he rose [up] against me, I took hold of [him] by his beard and struck him and killed him. Your servant has struck [killed] both a lion and a bear; and this uncircumcised Philistine shall be as one of them, for he has taunted the armies of the living God (17:32-36).

Realizing that David could not be dissuaded from taking on Goliath, Saul offered the young shepherd the use of his armor (17:38). Outwardly this gesture appeared to be magnanimous. A coat of mail had to be carefully forged. It was also very costly and few in Israel possessed one. Apparently Saul believed that the young champion should not be armed less adequately than his opponent.[16] David, however, was smaller than Saul and could not move with ease with the added weight of his armor. David realized he must have superior maneuverability to be successful against Goliath. So declining Saul's offer,

David took with him only those weapons with which he was familiar—his sling and his club.

In picking up the gauntlet Goliath had thrown down, David was not foolhardy. He was activated by a strong inner principle. In his eyes it was inconceivable for a nation that believed in the Lord to cower before pagans, no matter how strong they were. Human logic might have implied that he was embarking on a fool's errand, but his confidence in the God of his fathers was so strong it assured him of victory.

Putting aside Saul's armor, David descended the hillside and as he crossed the small stream he chose five smooth stones, which he put into his shepherd's pouch. As Saul and his men watched with bated breath, David made his way toward the Philistine champion.

Because of the heat of the day (summer was the only time kings went forth to war) and the heaviness of his armor, Goliath had been sitting down. The stir in the ranks of his countrymen caused him to look up. He was surprised to see that a boy was coming out against him. His first words were ones of disdain. He had expected a tall muscular man who might prove to be a worthy opponent. "Am I a dog," he asked, "that you come to me with sticks?" Goliath showed further his contempt for the shepherd by hurling curses at him. The giant's boastful attitude was typical of the speeches we read about in Homer's *Iliad* and other works of antiquity.[17]

David was undismayed by the profane and vainglorious attitude of the giant. His answer was calm and poignant:

> You are coming to me with a sword, a spear, and a javelin, but I am coming to you in the name of *Yahweh Ṣăbā'ôt,* the God of the armies of Israel, whom you have reproached. *This day Yahweh shall deliver you up* [literally, shut you up] *into my hands* and I will strike you down and remove your head from you. And I will give the dead bodies of the army of the Philistines this day to the birds of the sky and the beasts of the earth *that all the earth may know that there is a God in* [literally, for] *Israel, and that this assembly may know that Yahweh does not deliver by sword or spear; for the battle is* [belongs to] *Yahweh's and He will give you into my hand* (1 Samuel 17:45-47, emphasis added).

On hearing David's words Goliath became indignant. Believing that David had insulted him before the armies of the Philistines, Goliath rose to his feet and advanced to meet David. Instead of retreating as Goliath had expected, David ran forward. He was remarkably calm under pressure. The excitement of the moment did not unnerve him.

As he hastened toward the giant David took from his shepherd's bag one of the stones, put it into the pouch of his sling, whirled it three times about his head, and released one end.

The stone flew unerringly toward its mark. Too late the armorbearer tried to raise the shield to ward off the stone. It struck Goliath on that small part of his head left unguarded by his helmet[18] and stopped him in his tracks. For a moment he tottered back and forth. The soldiers on both banks held their breath. Then, ever so slowly, he began to fall forward gathering momentum as he fell.[19] There was a loud clanging of armor as Goliath's huge frame crashed to the ground.

David did not lose any time in running toward the prostrate form of the Philistine champion. Drawing Goliath's long sword from its sheath David hacked off the head of his enemy.

When the Philistines saw that their leading warrior was dead, they forgot the conditions of battle and leaving everything behind them ran as fast as they could toward their nearest towns. And the Israelites, uttering their battle cries, pursued their enemies as far as Gath (Goliath's hometown) and Ekron (1 Samuel 17:51-52). Then Saul's soldiers returned to plunder the Philistine camp.

At this point in the story many commentators raise a series of objections. Why did David take Goliath's head to Jerusalem? How could David place Goliath's armor in his tent when he didn't have one? These commentators believe that an editor (or redactor) was careless in piecing different accounts together into a more or less uniform narrative.

We do not know why or when David took Goliath's head to Jerusalem. We may confidently assume that he was prompted by the Spirit of God to do so. He may well have wanted to let the Jebusites know that the same Lord who had delivered the Philistine champion into his hands would one day do the same with them.

The pursuit of the enemy and the looting of the Philistine camp may have taken a couple of days. Because the Israelites desired to honor David for his courage, we may safely presume that they asked him to remain in the camp of the Israelites until everyone returned home and they gave him a tent to use in the meantime. It was in this tent that he stored his trophies as explained in 1 Samuel 17:54.[20]

Inquiry of the King (17:55-58). When we read Saul's question to Abner, we are confronted with another problem that has led some expositors to claim that our Bible is errant and contains conflicting accounts that cannot be harmonized. They claim that if David had played the harp before Saul, and Saul had come to love the young shepherd (1 Samuel 16:21), Saul would have recognized David.

The rebuttal to this argument is really very simple. First Samuel 17:55-56 takes us back to the time when David, declining the use of Saul's armor, descended into the valley. Having promised his daughter to whoever defeated Goliath, Saul would naturally be interested in David's family. That is why he asked, "Whose son is this young man?"

And when David returned from defeating Goliath, and Abner brought him before the king, the question was the same. David's answer, "I [am] the son of your servant Jesse the Bethlehemite" (17:58), was perfectly consistent with all that had gone before. He did not have to give his name or explain the things Saul already knew. He only needed to remind the king of who his father was.

Results of the Victory (18:1-5). Saul had promised that whoever killed Goliath would be handsomely rewarded, but his promise was not fulfilled. Instead, something that had not been promised was gained. David never married Merab, but his soul was knit[21] to the soul of Jonathan. As Dr. Alfred Edersheim explained, this "is the one point of light in a history which [from now on] grows darker and darker as it proceeds."[22]

As we reflect on what took place after David was presented to Saul, it is not difficult for us to imagine Jonathan's generous spirit being drawn toward the unaffected brave youth who had just killed Goliath. David seemed to be the very embodiment of Israelitish valor and piety. And David found in Jonathan a kindred spirit. The bond that united them, however, was not mere admiration for one another's courage and skill (for Jonathan's exploits were by now legendary, whereas David was only beginning to come to public notice) but their common faith and their love for the Lord God of Israel.

We see the greatness of Jonathan's love for David in (1) the covenant he made with him and (2) the tokens of affection he lavished upon him. In our familiarity with their friendship, let us not overlook certain basic truths. Jonathan was by this time in his mid- to late thirties and nearly two and a half times David's age. Jonathan was also a prince and heir apparent to the throne. David was but a shepherd, the least in his father's house. Their differences in background and social standing might well have caused them to feel unsuited to each other had it not been for that deeper spiritual commitment they shared.

Having received princely gifts from Jonathan, David possibly reciprocated by giving him his staff and sling. While the cost of the tokens Jonathan gave David showed how greatly he prized his relationship with the young Bethlehemite, the gifts David gave to Jonathan possessed intrinsic value and were treasured for different reasons. More important than the exchange of meaningful gifts was the fact that the friendship of Jonathan and David, begun under auspicious circumstances, remained undimmed in spite of the difficulties that soon overtook the young shepherd.[23]

After the events in the valley of Elah, Saul permanently attached David to his staff and during the course of the next few years sent him out on different missions against the Philistines (1 Samuel 18:5). In time Saul also made David commander of a thousand men (18:13) and David continued to distinguish himself as a brave and skillful soldier.

FIVE PRINCIPLES OF SUCCESS

Several important principles emerge from 1 Samuel 17 about how to deal with the inevitable trials of life (Job 5:7; 14:1; John 16:33; cf. Matthew 18:7). Throughout our sojourn on earth we face numerous and sometimes unexpected threats to our safety and well-being. To confront these difficulties we need adequate preparation, proper discernment, inner confidence, spiritual resources, and unselfish involvement.

The Need for Adequate Preparation

We are all familiar with the way athletes train for the Olympic games or any other meet. They diligently prepare themselves over many years for these events. Surgeons spend years in medical school to develop their skills so that they will be able to perform delicate operations. And those commissioned with the task of teaching our children should be well-educated in theoretical truths as well as practical skills; a teacher needs to be able to communicate the content of a course in ways that motivate students to learn. We are all convinced that preparation is necessary in such fields as sports, medicine, and education. When it comes to spiritual matters, however, some people think that acquiring a knowledge of God's Word and developing a Biblical philosophy of life are unnecessary. They are making a false assumption.

As we take a look behind the events of 1 Samuel 17, we need to remind ourselves that David did not suddenly acquire skill in using a sling. While caring for his father's sheep he had plenty of time to become adept in its use (cf. Psalm 144:1). At first he possibly practiced hitting large boulders or tree trunks, but later on he had to use his skill to drive off wolves that threatened the flock. Years of diligence made him proficient in the use of this weapon.

In addition to his prowess with a sling, David had also developed a remarkable sensitivity to the presence of God. Evidence of this awareness comes from his many Psalms. While sitting in the shade of a tree on hot sultry afternoons he had time to meditate on the events that had happened since Samuel's visit to his home. While looking up into the azure sky or watching the stars appear at night and seeing the moon rise over the hills of Moab, he gained insights into God's power and majesty; the greatness of His works developed in him a sense of awe (Psalm 8:3-9; 19:1-6; we may see something of Samuel's influence in Psalm 19:7-14 and Psalm 29). All of these preparations culminated in a devout spirit that led him to identify himself with Yahweh and His plans for His people.

David was prepared experientially and spiritually to meet the threat posed by the Philistine invasion. Saul and the men of Israel were not. The forty days during which they endured Goliath's taunts showed the bankruptcy of their faith.

The life of Robert G. LeTourneau illustrates the way the Lord uses the experiences of the past to aid us in times of crisis. He was an entrepreneur who became a millionaire and gave 90 percent of his earnings to the work of the Lord. But he had not always been rich. In fact when he received a contract from the General Construction Company to build a highway from Boulder City to the site of the proposed Boulder Dam, he "lost his shirt" on the project because of misleading reports. As he confronted each new calamity he was surprised to find how the Lord in a remarkable way had prepared him through past experience to handle each difficulty.

Trust in the Lord is essential to success, but so is adequate preparation for the work He would have us do. A passive faith achieves little or nothing. Active dependence upon the One whom we worship and serve is essential if victory is to be ours.

The experience of Nicholas Herman, better known as Brother Lawrence, illustrates how we may develop a sense of the Lord's presence even as David did. Nicholas had been badly injured in a war and as a result of a pronounced limp could not find suitable employment. Not knowing what else to do, he began washing pots and pans in a monastery in Paris. As he cleaned endless grease and grime off cooking utensils, he began to meditate on Christ's presence. The knowledge that the Lord was with him in that hot, smelly, humid, and poorly ventilated kitchen transformed his entire outlook. Christ's presence became so real to him that he began doing each task as unto the Lord (Colossians 3:17). In time he wrote a book about his experiences entitled *The Practice of the Presence of God.*

We need adequate preparation for our careers and a thorough

knowledge of the Bible and its application to life. In facing the different crises of life we will then find that we have been prepared spiritually and experientially for our tasks.

The Need for Proper Discernment

When Goliath defied and taunted God's people, they cowered on the bank of the wadi because they lacked discernment. They attributed to Goliath the power to do them harm and take away their ability to be self-determining. Never once did they think of praying to the Lord for His aid and no mention is made of any priests in the camp. The Israelites gave no thought to the Lord and as a result they were powerless before their enemies.[24] Their lack of faith brought the whole nation into reproach.

The possibility of being deprived of one's freedom or of being harmed in some way is not the only danger people face. Throughout history external threats have taken on different forms—persecution for one's beliefs; pressure to compromise with a superior power for the sake of some temporal advantage; temptations accompanying the increase of the power, wealth, and political influence of the clergy; false ideologies (both political and religious). All these threats have in some way or another adversely affected God's people.

In our day some of the most dangerous threats are not physical but philosophical. The news media with its commitment to secularism subtly seeks to bias our minds by presenting a well-packaged but misleading view of life. The entertainment industry with its adherence to hedonism daily erodes our moral values. In our schools and universities educators who are thoroughly committed to the tenets of humanism and existentialism mislead our young people. Even in the "helping professions" (sociology, psychology, medicine) counsel is all too often based on behaviorism, relativism, and expediency. In commerce and industry those who wish to rise to the top sometimes adopt a credo of pragmatism in which the end frequently justifies the means.

These philosophical dangers are every bit as ominous as the giant David confronted in the valley of Elah. Just as he needed discernment in his evaluation of Goliath's threats, so we need the kind of wisdom that comes only from prolonged meditation on God's Word.

The Need for Inner Confidence

The inner confidence we need when facing the crises of life is different from a macho attitude or a bragging spirit. From 1 Samuel

17:32,36-37 we realize that David felt confident in himself and in his relationship with the Lord. His inner sense of security came from the assurance that God had chosen him. As a result of this assurance he enjoyed all of the blessings of his acceptance by God as well as access into His presence.

In much the same way the ground of our confidence comes from our godward relationship. We know that we have been chosen in Christ from before the foundation of the world (Ephesians 1:4). We have been given the adoption of sons and are members of His family (Galatians 4:5; Ephesians 1:5). Consequently we call Him Father and are encouraged to come boldly before Him (Romans 8:15; Galatians 4:6; Hebrews 4:16).

David possessed an intrinsic sense of his worth. The Holy Spirit had clothed Himself with him. Whatever gifts David had formerly possessed were now enhanced and perhaps new abilities were given to him. He had an increased sense of being special and a new perspective on his life and mission.

David's privileges parallel our own. As we study the Bible we come to a fuller understanding of our worth and of the gifts the Holy Spirit has given us. We gain a new appreciation of our value to the Father as we contemplate the price the Lord Jesus paid for our redemption (1 Peter 1:18-19). Our union with Christ has made us joint heirs with Him of all the riches and benefits of His Kingdom (Romans 8:17; Galatians 3:9). While what we will be is now only dimly discerned, we know that one day we will be like Him, for we shall see Him as He is (1 John 3:2). In our present state it is our privilege to use our gifts in ways that please Him.

When David went out to face Goliath, he felt competent. The Spirit of God controlled, motivated, and guided David. He scorned the armor of Saul and relied entirely on the Lord for success. With this inner confidence David faced Goliath unafraid. In like manner the Holy Spirit can bring every facet of our lives under His control, empowering us for service and giving us the confidence that we too can achieve victories for Christ and begin to remove the reproach that rests on His people.

The Need to Use Our Resources

In facing crises we need to use the resources listed in Ephesians 6:11-18. After we have diligently prepared ourselves for whatever work the Lord would have us do, and after we have subordinated our wills to His will for our lives, we need to avail ourselves of the resources which He has made available to us.

David alluded to this need when he said to Goliath, "I come to you in the *name* of the Lord of hosts" (1 Samuel 17:45, emphasis added). The "name" of God implies the totality of all that He is (cf. Psalm 22:22; John 17:6,26). As we live our lives in accordance with His Word and come progressively to know more about His power, we will enjoy the same assurance David had (cf. Matthew 28:17-20). Such confidence is more than pious theory; it is a practical reality.

Several years ago I was reminded in an unusual way of the reality of the resources available to Christians. I was visiting my good friends Jack and Jean Gamble in Ireland. Jack is an antiquarian and is also one of Ireland's leading historians. He showed me many places of historic importance and I could not have had a better guide! While passing through County Down one day he pointed out some of the settings used by Charlotte and Emily Brontë in their books. Charlotte of course is known for her masterful *Jane Eyre* and Emily for *Wuthering Heights.* Emily brought to fruition in her life what we have been learning from 1 Samuel 17. When she died her family found among her unpublished materials a poem that read in part,

No coward soul is mine,
No trembler in the world's storm-troubled sphere.
I see Heaven's glories shine,
And faith shines equal, arming me from fear.

Oh God within my breast,
Almighty, ever-present Deity!
Life—that in me has rest,
As I—undying Life—have power in Thee!

Emily had an unshakable confidence in the Lord and throughout her life availed herself of her spiritual resources.

The Need to Become Involved

David became involved when he tried to encourage Saul's dispirited soldiers and when he volunteered to take on Goliath. David overcame Eliab's attempt to intimidate him and Saul's attempt to dissuade him from doing combat with the Philistine. Neither his brother's belittling nor Saul's well-meant counsel could turn him from the course of action he believed he should take.

David's motives for becoming involved were pure (1 Samuel 17:26,37,45-47). The honors promised by Saul were never claimed. His victory over Goliath was the direct outcome of his desire to see

God's name once more honored and held in esteem. His desire was "that all the earth may know that there is a God in [literally, for] Israel. And [that] all this assembly may know that Yahweh does not deliver by sword or spear; for to Yahweh [belongs] the battle" (17:46-47).

Do we still have men and women like David—people who recognize the need to get involved and take action when they are confronted with difficulties? Bruce Larson would answer the question with his story of Frank Loesch, an unimposing leader in the Chicago church that Bruce attended during the time when Al Capone's rule was absolute. The local and state police were powerless to stop the crime boss's well-oiled machinery, and the FBI was afraid to oppose him. In the face of this moral interregnum Frank Loesch single-handedly organized the Chicago Crime Commission. During the time the Commission met, Loesch's life was in constant danger. There were also threats on his family and friends. Loesch, however, never wavered. Because he was prepared to become involved, ultimately he won the case against Capone. The Lord worked through Loesch to remove the reproach that had for so long rested on the city of Chicago and indeed the whole United States![25]

HOW TO HANDLE UNJUST AUTHORITY

1 Samuel 18:5–20:42

This chapter of commentary was written while the XXIV Olympiad was being held in Seoul, Korea. Throughout the games the Koreans showed themselves to be the epitome of gracious hospitality, and the contestants and spectators tried their best to reciprocate by behaving like grateful guests. For the most part the sixteen days of the Olympiad passed uneventfully. Only on the last night of the televised broadcasts did the commentators make any mention of the perceived injustice in the low scores given Americans in boxing, diving, gymnastics, and wrestling.

At least three of the five judges for each of these events came from communist countries, and it was evident to those of us who could benefit from television's instant replays that the United States was being discriminated against. It is to the credit of our athletes that they bore these inequities with fortitude and appropriate decorum.

All of us at one time or another have experienced unfair treatment, biased judgments, and other injustices. (For example, parents whom we tried to please may never have been satisfied with what we did. Teachers may have graded us unfairly. Bosses may have given promotions to colleagues of demonstrably lesser abilities. Superior officers in the armed forces may have been prejudiced against us. People may have victimized us because of our faith). Therefore we need to understand both the reasons for unjust authority and our responses to it.

The root of injustice lies in the *insecurity* of those who use their positions of authority to serve their own ends. Inwardly they sense their inferiority. This perception of inferiority causes them to focus on external temporal variables or issues in order to direct attention away from themselves. In contrast to those who are insecure, confident people look within for their strength.

Three evidences of insecurity are illustrated in 1 Samuel 18:5–20:42: pride, hostility, and paranoia. All three can be found in a close study of the disposition and actions of King Saul.

Pride is an evidence of insecurity because the outwardly arrogant or haughty person is actually seeking to cover his feelings of inadequacy by making reference to his ancestry (contrast the apostle Paul in Philippians 3:4-7), accomplishments (Daniel 4:30), or acquaintances (Esther 5:12). Pharaoh, king of Egypt, fell because of his pride (Exodus 5:2; Proverbs 16:18; Matthew 23:12; 1 Peter 5:5; James 4:6). An attitude like his is offensive to God for it elevates the self, seeks recognition by others, and is blind to its own faults.

Another evidence of insecurity is *hostility.* Hostility is an intense emotional reaction often arising from frustration, humiliation, and/or rejection. When feelings of anger are repressed or suppressed for a period of time, they are sometimes expressed later in some form of overt hostile behavior.

A third sign of insecurity is *paranoia.* In people with paranoid dispositions the pendulum often swings from feelings of persecution to illusions of grandeur. In the former instance paranoid people tend to withdraw from society and become loners; or they are hypersensitive, guarded, and suspicious and use projection of blame as a defense. In the latter they indulge in fantasies of what they would like to be. (See James Thurber's insightful story "The Secret Life of Walter Mitty."[1]) A person suffering from paranoia may not initially appear to be different from his friends or colleagues (the effect on the mind of course differs in severity according to the extent that the individual distorts reality). Noteworthy symptoms, however, can be detected in the individual's defenses against anxiety, aggression, masochism, and inferiority and in his proneness to depression.

As we will see, King Saul evidenced pride, hostile anger directed toward (that is, projected onto) David, and paranoia over his fear of losing his kingdom. Saul's insecurity led him to abuse his authority and persecute the one he blamed for his misfortunes (namely, David).

STRUCTURE AND OUTLINE OF THE PASSAGE

First Samuel 18:5–20:42 is an extensive section and my commentary on the passage is relatively brief. Its theme is Saul's attempt to get rid of his rival David. The action oscillates from the friction between Saul and David to the help given David by others. The outline is at once simple and complex (the more complex elements being the "seams" within the narrative):

- The Introduction (1 Samuel 18:5)
- The Nature of Unjust Authority (1 Samuel 18:6-29)
- The Growth of Unjust Authority (1 Samuel 18:30–20:42)

First Samuel 18:5 is a hinge verse. It properly belongs to the events of 17:1–18:4, for it carries forward the thought of 18:2. At the same time the verse is vitally connected with 18:6-29, for 18:5 covers the period between Goliath's death and David's flight from Saul (about five to seven years).

The Biblical writers used many devices to indicate the trend of their thoughts. Sometimes they used a repetitious statement or phrase; at other times they used words like "Now," "Then," and "After" to show the progression of their thoughts. In 1 Samuel 18–20 the device the writer used was a *summary* in each section (18:9,14,29b, 30b; 19:7b,10b,12; 20:1,23b,42). Understanding these summaries is essential, for they reveal what was going on in the heart of Saul and at the same time show how the Lord protected and helped David; they demonstrate once again the Lord's absolute sovereignty in the use of different means to accomplish His ends.

THE INTRODUCTION (18:5)

We have no means of knowing how long the war with the Philistines lasted. Most of the older commentators believed it continued for many months.[2] First Samuel 17:52-53, however, seems to contradict this view. What is indicated in 18:5 is David's obedience to Saul as well as the success that attended the young man's efforts. In every respect David showed himself to be loyal and resourceful. Over the next few years he was involved in several more wars with the Philistines and, as a result of his developing military prowess, he won the favor of all the people as well as the noblemen (that is, Saul's "servants") who were a part of the king's court.

Through these years the Lord was preparing David for the throne. We may presume that in his contacts with Samuel, David was being led slowly yet surely to understand his role in the plan and purpose of God. To the patience and vigilance he had developed as a shepherd—enduring the heat of summer as well as the cold of winter—he now added the experience gained from living in the palace and leading a company of soldiers.

Dr. William Blaikie drew the diverse threads of the tapestry of David's training together when he wrote:

> How often do we find, in the biography of the men who have been an honour to their race, that their early life was spent amid struggles and acts of self-denial that seem hardly credible, but out of which came their resolute character and grand conquering power?...In the case of David, [the Lord's] purpose manifestly was to exercise and strengthen such qualities as trust in God, prayerfulness, self-command, serenity of temper, [and] consideration for others.[3]

William Deane added:

> Thus early [David] showed his power over the hearts of men, no one disputing his claim to advancement, all agreeing that his rapid promotion was entirely well deserved, so that he was "accepted in the sight of all the people," and "all Israel and Judah" (for the distinction between the two already existed) "loved him."[4]

THE NATURE OF UNJUST AUTHORITY (18:6-29)

Examples of social, economic, or domestic injustice are not hard to find. They are seen on virtually every page of the newspaper. While injustice wears many masks, the strength of its attack always lies in our vulnerability. Injustice may be directed against either our identity—our sense of belonging, worth, or ability—or our personal freedom, and if we do not deal with our emotional responses properly, we will become bitter and resentful. Ultimately any unresolved feelings will grind cinders into our souls.

How then are we to handle unfair treatment and/or infringements on our liberty? Is our experience to be the same as that which Claudian described? He wrote, "When I observe [in] the affairs of men...the guilty flourishing in continuous happiness, and the righteous tormented, my religion, tottering, begins once more to fall."[5] How did David handle the unfair treatment that resulted from Saul's jealousy?

The Fruit of Jealousy (18:6-9)

Before the defeat of Goliath the people of Israel languished as a result of the dark cloud that hovered over the valley of Elah. Scarcely a home was unaffected by the Philistine invasion. Husbands and sons had answered Saul's call and when victory was not forthcoming and the conditions of the contest became public knowledge, hope died in the hearts of wives and mothers. No satisfactory answers could be given to the questions of little children.

Then all of a sudden the news spread that God had remembered His people. He had given them a champion. Goliath was dead and the Philistines were running pell-mell to their nearest fortified cities. The sun broke through the ominous bank of clouds. The happiness of relief was reflected in the faces of old and young alike.

In one of the villages to which the word of Israel's victory was carried, the nation's "poet laureate" hastily composed a ballad so that the women could welcome back their loved ones with joyful enthusiasm. With more zeal than common sense he included a chorus,

> Saul has struck [killed] his thousands,
> But David his myriads [ten thousands].
> (1 Samuel 18:7)

At that time in Israel's history no one knew who David was. His name however was on everyone's lips.

After plundering the Philistine camp the relieved warriors took the road from Azekah to Gibeah en route to their own homes. In traditional fashion the women came out of their villages with singing, dancing, laughter, and happiness.[6] They played their musical instruments and sang for sheer gladness of heart. But when Saul heard their antiphonal song, his feelings of jealousy were aroused and he became very angry.[7]

All the people knew who King Saul was, for he was taller than any of the other men in his army and handsome in spite of the advance of the years. No one knew who David was (there must have been a lot of speculation on the part of the people as they tried to point him out) but this fact was lost on Saul as deep within his heart a fire burned and feelings of paranoia welled up within him. His jealousy was evident from the muttered verbalization of his thoughts: "They have ascribed to David myriads, but to me they have ascribed [only] thousands. Now [what] more [can he have] except the kingdom?"(18:8) The Biblical writer added one of his summary statements, "And Saul eyed David [looked at him with suspicion] from that day on" (18:9).

David unwittingly captivated the imagination of the populace and was given what Saul wanted most—the praise and affirmation of the people. Saul, having no internal resources to draw on, projected the blame onto David. As thoughts began to come together in Saul's mind, he concluded that the young shepherd might well be the one of whom Samuel had spoken (1 Samuel 13:14; 15:23,28-29).

Paranoid personalities are characteristically astute in assessing the potential danger of a situation, and Saul was particularly keen and accurate in his perception. For him a day of jubilation had turned into one of brooding suspicion. He deliberately set himself against the one who had been the source of much blessing to his people.

The Favor of the Lord (18:10-16)

Saul, having allowed anger to take root in his heart and having made no attempt to handle this powerful emotion in an appropriate manner (Ephesians 4:26), left himself open to an attack from the adversary (Ephesians 4:27). On the very next day an evil spirit came mightily upon him, and he raved in the midst of his house (1 Samuel 18:10).

David, quite unaffected by his newly acquired popularity,[8] played his harp in hopes of quieting the tormented spirit of the king. David's music, however, had lost its power to soothe Saul's troubled soul. Saul, who had cut himself off from helpful, wholesome, godly influences, was left to sink into the mire of his own willfulness and disobedience (cf. Proverbs 1:20-33). Evil had undisputed control of his mind, emotions, and will, and in a fit of pent-up rage he hurled his spear at his minstrel.

Whether the men of Saul's guard sought to restrain him, we do not know. It does appear as if David was reassured that no further attempt would be made on his life, for he resumed his position and took up his song as before. Within a relatively short period of time, however, he again had to evade Saul's javelin.

We are not told of the effect of Saul's aggressive and hostile actions on David. In all probability he attributed the king's sudden animosity toward him as evidence of Saul's unbalanced and deeply disturbed state of mind. We are given a glimpse into the workings of Saul's heart, however, for we are told that he became even more fearful because he perceived that the Lord was with David.[9] This perception should have served to warn Saul, but he was so set on attaining his own ends that he ignored the voice of his conscience.

No longer able to tolerate the presence of the one on whom the Spirit of God rested, Saul made the farmboy-turned-soldier a commander of part of the Israelite army (1 Samuel 18:13). This appointment was a high honor (cf. 13:2). The people doubtless believed that David had earned such a promotion. Saul however hoped the new inexperienced general would be killed by the Philistines. In the providence of God the wrath of man was turned to His praise (Psalm 76:10) and David gained valuable experience in leadership.

Another of the writer's summary statements appears in 1 Samuel 18:14: David prospered "for Yahweh was with him." Success did not go to his head. Instead he continued to behave himself with maturity far beyond his years. Verses 15 and 16 give the reaction of the king and the people to David's success. Saul's fears were aggravated to the point of dread, while the people of Israel came to love their new hero.[10]

The Fulminations of the Proud (18:17-29)

After he killed Goliath, David should have been given Saul's daughter as his wife. But time passed and because David did not claim his prize, the matter was conveniently forgotten. Here we see the injustice of broken promises—something to which the affluent and the influential are often particularly prone!

Now, with David gaining in popularity, Saul devised a diabolical plan. He determined to offer David his elder daughter Merab as his wife[11] provided he would continue to distinguish himself and act valiantly on the king's behalf (1 Samuel 18:17). Saul acted under the pretext of giving David the opportunity to demonstrate his patriotism, but Saul hoped that a reckless daring would characterize David's activities so that he would be even more likely to fall before a Philistine spear or carefully laid ambush (cf. Psalm 140).

But when Merab should have been given to David in marriage, Saul with deliberate malice gave her to Adriel—a man who heretofore has not been named in the Biblical record. Perhaps Adriel could pay the king a suitable dowry. Perhaps Saul was prepared to barter away his daughter to secure some personal advantage on the eastern bank of the Jordan river.

How did Saul expect David to respond to such a cold calculated insult? Not only was Saul guilty of a breach of faith; his actions had humiliated David before all who knew of the king's offer. Saul felt he had David where he wanted him. If David gave way to anger and led his one thousand men against the king, he would be guilty of treason and discredited before the people for wanting to take the throne by force. The king's personal bodyguard, who must have been alerted to such a possibility, would then be perfectly within their rights in killing David. If David repressed his anger and turned it inward, he could be expected to act with reckless disregard for his own welfare in fighting the Philistines.

The Psalms that may have had their origin during this period of

David's life show his implicit faith and trust in the Lord (Psalm 7; 9:1-10,13,16; 11).[12] No indiscretion marked his conduct. His inner trust in God kept him from falling into Saul's trap. His eyes were on the Lord (Psalm 16:8) and his internal motivation preserved him from unwise actions. Had he been eager for a position of honor or prestige (contrast 1 Samuel 18:18) or motivated by fleshly concerns, the story might very well have had a different ending. As it was, Saul was the one who was faced with the failure of yet another of his carefully laid plans.

As we look back over the narrative, we notice that after the Spirit of God left Saul he became more and more tyrannical in his ways. In such administrations, tyrants nearly always gather about them those who are skilled in observing the moods of their leaders as well as the trends of the times. Lacking scruples, these counselors aid and abet the oppression of the just and favor those who lack commitment to principles of right and wrong. Such men now comprised Saul's court. They sensed the king's desire to be rid of David, and without acknowledging what they had surmised they assisted the king in his evil plans by telling him of his younger daughter's love for David (1 Samuel 18:20).

We have tacit proof of the breakdown of Saul's relationships in the fact that he was quite unaware of Michal's attachment to the young general. But he was quick to turn this news to his own advantage; he instructed his noblemen to let the word slip to David that the king would like to have him as his son-in-law. David however declined by stating that he was a poor man with no aspirations to become a part of the king's family (18:23).[13]

Saul's lackeys took the message back to the king and in turn were told to convey a message to David: "The king does not desire any dowry[14] except one hundred foreskins of the Philistines" (18:25). Saul's real intent was to make David fall by the hand of the Philistines.

On hearing these words from Saul's servants, David was pleased. He perhaps hoped that by becoming the king's son-in-law their former relationship would be restored. He was aware of the king's duplicity, yet to show his loyalty to the crown David delivered twice the requested quota. The mention of "today" in 18:21 and "the days were not expired" in 18:26 seems to indicate that Saul had set a short specific time limit for the feat of bravery to be performed. David more than satisfied the king's wish for a "dowry" and Saul, realizing that he could not sidestep the issue, gave Michal to David in marriage (18:27-28).

With renewed evidence of God's blessing of David, Saul became even more afraid of him than before.[15] David had hoped his marriage to Michal would heal the breach, but instead Saul became David's enemy continually (18:29). And with this summary statement the inspired chronicler drew to a close this account of Saul's attempts to have David killed by the Philistines.

Through all of the difficulties David faced after killing Goliath, he conducted himself wisely. Although he was the object of the king's unmerited hatred, the victim of his unrelenting plots, and the one on whom the king projected his unbridled fears and ungoverned fury, David continued to remain steadfast in his allegiance to the crown. He exerted every effort to demonstrate his faithfulness to Saul and the principles of the theocracy.[16]

THE GROWTH OF UNJUST AUTHORITY (18:30–20:42)

Opposition from Without (18:30)

Some writers are inclined to think that the battle mentioned in this verse is a reprisal for the two hundred Philistines whom David and his men killed in order to supply Saul with the "dowry" he demanded.[17] The summary in 18:29, "Thus Saul was David's enemy continually," and the statement in 18:30, "And it happened as often as they [the Philistines] went out," do not support such a view. Both verses look at an extensive period of time during which David continued to lead Saul's army. On each occasion when war broke out the young commander was ready. Success attended all his efforts and his popularity increased.

Opposition from Within (19:1—20:42)

As we survey the last days of David's life at Saul's court, we notice four things: (1) the importance of friends, (2) the value of loyalty, (3) the need to depend entirely on the Lord, and (4) the results of jealousy.

The Faithfulness of a Friend (19:1-7). No longer attempting to disguise his evil designs, Saul spoke openly to Jonathan and the noblemen of his court. David, he said, must be put to death. In the machinations of his mind Saul fabricated some reason he hoped would justify his actions before the people.[18]

Jonathan was not bound by misplaced ties of loyalty to his father.[19] He sought out David and warned him of danger. Then he waited for a suitable opportunity to intercede on David's behalf. He successfully argued the case before the king and Saul was persuaded of his son-in-law's integrity. Saul promised with an oath that David would not be harmed. Thoroughly reassured, Jonathan told David the good news. The summary in 19:7 indicates that Jonathan brought David to Saul, and David was in the king's presence as formerly.

The Importance of Loyalty (19:8-17). The reconciliation between the king and his loyal servant lasted for some time. The terms of intimacy and confidence for which David had longed were restored. Then the Philistines again invaded the land, David achieved another notable victory, and Saul's envy and jealousy were reawakened, making him susceptible to another of Satan's attacks. His slumbering suspicions erupted one evening in another demonstration of anger. He seized his spear, the emblem of his authority, and hurled it at David.[20] David, who had learned to read Saul's moods, was able to evade the weapon and it struck the wall behind him.

The summary at the end of 1 Samuel 19:8-10 is repeated like a refrain throughout the remainder of chapters 19–20: "And David fled and escaped that night." These words or ones similar to them occur at the end of each subdivision (19:12,18; 20:1; reaching a climax in 20:42).

Psalm 59 provides a graphic description of David's experience after he went home to Michal (19:11-17). She too showed her loyalty to David. Somehow she became aware of the presence of soldiers surrounding the house. Perhaps her knowledge of her father's malicious nature made her suspicious. As soon as her fears were confirmed, she thought not of herself but of her husband. "If you do not save your life tonight," she warned, "tomorrow you will be put to death" (19:11).[21]

Drawing on her ingenuity, Michal let David down through a window. If their house was one of those that had been built in the city wall, David would have been able to make his escape without risking detection. Their parting of course was hasty. Neither of them knew when they would meet again. Ironically, for the second time David's life was saved by a member of Saul's household.

To give her husband time to make good his escape, Michal devised a subtle plan. She put a lifelike representation of him on his pallet and when Saul's soldiers inquired the next morning why David had not come out of the house to go about his duties, she told them that he was sick. When Saul heard this report he demanded that David be brought to him on his pallet. Imagine the consternation of the soldiers when they found a teraphim (idol) made to look like David, covered with a blanket, and lying on his bed.[22]

Saul was incensed at his daughter's deception and asked why she had connived with his enemy and made possible his escape. Michal knew what would carry weight with her father and told him that she had only complied with David's demand because he had threatened her life.[23] Saul was angered by her duplicity, but nonetheless he took her back into his home.

The story presents us with an ethical dilemma. What was God-fearing David doing with a pagan idol in his house? Several explanations have been offered.

- David was familiar with statues in the mansions of the rich and never regarded the one he possessed as offensive.

- The teraphim belonged to Michal, and David—as with Jacob before him (Genesis 31:32)—was ignorant of its existence.

- It was an ornate piece of workmanship that David had acquired as a part of the spoils of war (cf. 2 Samuel 5:21). No religious overtones, therefore, were connected with his possession of it.

The Protection of the Lord (19:18-24). David escaped to Samuel at Ramah, about three miles away. The prophet was probably in bed when David knocked on his door. The story was quickly told, and Samuel believed that they would be safer in Naioth—the buildings that comprised the schools of the prophets. He took David to this compound on the adjoining hill and there the prophet's young protégé enjoyed a most stimulating time of fellowship with the men of the seminary. This brief period of refreshment was designed by God to strengthen him for the trials that were soon to be thrust upon him.

David remained with Samuel until someone wishing to ingratiate himself with the king reported David's whereabouts. Saul immediately sent a body of men to apprehend David and bring him back to Gibeah dead or alive. When the soldiers came to Naioth, however, they were overpowered by the Holy Spirit. Thus constrained, they joined the young men from the schools of the prophets in praising God.[24]

Saul waited with growing impatience for the return of his men. When word was brought to him of what had happened, he sent a second contingent, and then a third.[25] Instead of being warned by this divine intervention and the threefold failure of his plans, he decided to go himself. He was so hardened to the will of God that he did not shrink back from following through with his murderous plot in spite of God's evident protection of David.

When Saul arrived at Ramah he inquired of the whereabouts of Samuel and David and was directed to Naioth. With David almost within his hands, Saul was likewise overpowered by the Holy Spirit and he continued on up the hill telling forth the praises of God. When he reached the summit he stripped off his armor and fell to the ground. Saul remained there all that day and the entire night, and David had ample time to make good his escape (1 Samuel 19:24).

Some commentators have seen a contradiction between 19:23-24 and 15:35, which says that Samuel did not see Saul again until the day of his death. Obviously Saul saw Samuel, but there is no indication that Samuel saw Saul, even though Samuel must have been told of Saul's arrival. Saul was not standing upright, but lying face down on the ground, and no mention is made of the king's entering the circle of men and standing before the prophet. Rather the implication is that Saul was overcome by the Holy Spirit as he approached the gathering. In all probability he never got beyond the outer circle of buildings.

Somewhat chastened by what had happened, Saul returned to Gibeah in the morning. His servants may have been aware of David's return to the city, and Saul no doubt presumed that David would take up his normal duties.

An Exposure of Evil (20:1-42). In this section we have (1) the strategy used to expose evil (20:1-23) and (2) the results obtained (20:24-42).

Once within Gibeah, David sought out his friend Jonathan. David was aware of the fickleness of the king and had good reason to believe that any good intentions that may have come over Saul in Naioth would soon pass away.

At first Jonathan did not believe David. Saul had entered into a solemn oath not to do David any harm. It was only as David earnestly reasoned with Jonathan that he, guileless as always, came to believe that his father might not have taken him into his confidence. Jonathan agreed to do whatever David asked and the two friends renewed their covenant with each other.[26] Now however there was a difference. Over the years Jonathan had come to believe that David, not he, was destined to sit on the throne of Israel. The pact they now made, therefore, included their children.

The feast of the new moon was only a day or two away. At this time each month Saul invited his special council members to a time of banqueting. Jonathan, Abner, and David were included. David, however, determined to remain in hiding, and he and Jonathan developed a strategy to determine Saul's true attitude toward his son-in-law.[27] Their plan (which involved some duplicity) was that when Saul inquired why David had not come to the feast, Jonathan would tell Saul that David's older brother required his presence at a special family feast in Bethlehem.

The first evening Saul said nothing about David's absence. The king presumed that David had contracted some ceremonial defilement (Leviticus 15). The second evening, however, Saul questioned Jonathan and referred to David in a most derogatory manner. Jonathan, with masterful control of his emotions, told Saul the story David had devised as a means of discerning Saul's true feelings toward him (1 Samuel 20:28-29).[28] Saul was not deluded by Jonathan's explanation. The king's anger burned against his son and Saul spoke words calculated to inflict deep hurt:

> You son of perverse rebelliousness! Do I not know that you are choosing the son of Jesse to your own shame and to the shame of your mother's nakedness? For all the days that the son of Jesse lives on the earth, neither you nor your kingdom will be established; and now, send and bring him to me, for he [is] the son of death [must surely die] (20:30-31).

This insulting remark revealed a great deal about Saul. He betrayed his own awareness of David's destiny. Saul also insulted his wife Ahinoam (cf. Apocrypha, Judith 16:12). Apparently Jonathan and his mother were of similar temperament. Her piety had been duplicated in him and Saul, who could no longer tolerate righteousness in his presence, rejected both his dutiful wife and her firstborn son.

When Jonathan asked, "Why should [David] be put to death? What evil has he done?" (1 Samuel 20:32) Saul flew into a rage. He hastily seized his spear and probably without rising flung it at Jonathan. Saul's aim was poor and he missed. And Jonathan, angered by his father's insult, left the room.

The next morning Jonathan went out into the field for target practice. As previously arranged, he shot the arrows in a way that signaled Saul's continued animosity toward David. Jonathan told the young lad who had accompanied him to retrieve the arrows and take the weapons into the city, and the two friends met in secret. It was a heart-wrenching parting. Not only was David tearing himself away from all that he held dear; he was also facing the future as a fugitive with a price on his head. And as David made his way over the hills, Jonathan returned with leaden steps to Gibeah. For both men the light of the noonday sun had been darkened by Saul's unbridled jealousy and unrestrained anger.

SOME TRUTHS WORTH NOTING

Targets of Injustice

We note first the fact that a person is most vulnerable to unjust authority when it is directed against his identity or imposes a limitation on his freedom. The following two stories are about people who were vulnerable but overcame difficulties associated with injustice. Stories such as these could be multiplied ad infinitum.

Soon after Greg Louganis was born he was placed in an orphanage. The color of Greg's skin differed from that of the other children (his father was Samoan), so he was less likely than they to be adopted. However, when he was six years old a couple took him into their home.

The youngsters in the school he attended picked on him because he was different and they ostracized him from their company, so Greg spent a good deal of time on his own. He liked swimming and began to excel in this sport. Then he practiced diving. He worked hard to perfect his form while conducting himself wisely so as not to give offense to those who thought of him as inferior to themselves.

Greg became one of the heroes of the XXIV Olympiad and today he is admired and honored by all who have seen him in action. Having overcome the injustices of his early years, he is every inch a champion.[29]

Marcia was blessed with good looks and a shapely body. After high school she enrolled in a modeling school and became the envy of her peers. Job offers seemed to fall into her lap, and her agent made sure she met all the right people.

One day, however, he asked her to "entertain" one of his biggest clients in return for a major advertising job. She refused. Apart from the obviously immoral nature of the request, her agent was imposing a limitation on her freedom. He was depriving her of the liberty of determining when and with whom she would have sex. And as a Christian, Marcia was offended by his suggestion. She did not believe in intercourse outside of marriage. In the year that followed, Marcia received only seven invitations to do commercials. Her six-figure salary plummeted to twelve thousand dollars for the entire year. When she tried other agencies she found that word had spread; she was now persona non grata. The other agents were polite, but none offered her any work.

Marcia had to turn her back on a lucrative livelihood, move out of her expensive apartment, trade down her foreign car to a domestic model, and at twenty-five years of age use her dwindling savings to support herself while she attended a state college to prepare for a different career. She overcame unjust opposition, however, by refusing to compromise or let others control her life.[30]

The Sin of Jealousy

Another truth worth noting is that jealousy can lead to an abuse of authority. Saul gave way before his jealousy over David's popularity. Saul allowed his anger to control his thoughts and actions. Fuel was added to the fire because he feared that someone would arise to take his throne from him. This fear made him suspicious of others. The devil took advantage of Saul's weakness and attacked him at his most vulnerable point.

Injustices caused by jealousy abound. Bigotry, favoritism, racism, envy, pride, physical and emotional abuse, and various forms of inequity and discrimination all bring pressure to bear on our "churning" place (Proverbs 30:33). Christ's words in Matthew 5:10-12,44 remind us that the insecure person is unsure of his or her own worth. Our task when we face unjust authority is to emulate David's example and relate positively to those who misuse us. We do not need to insist on our rights or compromise our standards (Psalm 37:1-4; 73:21-28). David showed us how to be wise in the Biblical sense (Proverbs 1:20-33; 3:13-26; 4:1-13). He was aware of the dangers that faced him, yet never slacked off doing all that was required of him.

The Help of Friends

There is a modern heresy abroad that sounds very spiritual, but in reality is unbiblical and does great harm to those who find themselves battered and broken as a result of the injustice of others. The heresy takes different forms but basically affirms, "Since you are a child of God and have the limitless resources of the godhead at your disposal, you do not need the help of others. To seek another's help is to say in effect that God and His salvation are insufficient for your needs." Such teaching implies that one who seeks the help of a friend when facing a crisis is sinning because he is not casting himself unreservedly on the Lord.

David was often helped by others. Sometimes he sought their aid and at other times they offered it to him. The truth is that friendships are important. Even the apostle Paul needed his many friends, and when he was alone this bold champion of Christianity felt very weak and insecure (1 Corinthians 2:3; 2 Corinthians 2:12-13; Romans 16:3-16). The Lord Jesus Himself on the night of His betrayal took His eleven disciples with Him and asked them to pray with Him (Matthew 26:38).

Good friends are God's gifts to us and only pride and a false understanding of God's Word will cause us to rely on our own resources alone when we face the trials and testings of life.[31]

The Grace of God

What happened at Naioth may well have been the final act in the extension of God's grace to Saul. The Lord, who had so evidently protected David from the Philistines, came upon Saul and subdued his malevolent spirit. Saul however was only temporarily halted. He deliberately set out to destroy David; Saul's hatred had no bounds. He knew that it was the Lord who was constantly frustrating his plans, yet he persisted in them. Little did he realize that all his evil designs were working toward preparing his successor for the throne.[32]

David's ups and downs, therefore, lead us to place our trust confidently in the lovingkindness of the Lord when we experience injustice (Psalm 37:7-40; Romans 8:18-39). And having experienced the pain inflicted by unjust authority, we are better prepared to enter into the sufferings of others (2 Corinthians 1:3-7; 4:7-10). We are encouraged by the truth that all things do work together for the good of those who love the Lord!

WHERE'S THE HAPPY ENDING?

1 Samuel 21:1–23:14

My sons are firmly convinced that I received my schooling in that unenlightened era when people still believed that the earth was flat. Their reasons are threefold: (1) I was compelled to study Latin; (2) computers had not yet been invented; and (3) World War II had just broken out and the Allied forces were fighting what was then a losing battle in Europe.

As was common in that era, each day of first and second grade my teacher read to the class tales of the daring adventures of those whose resilience helped them survive the adversities of life. We listened in rapt delight to stories such as J. R. Wyss's *Swiss Family Robinson* and Homer's *Odyssey.* During third and fourth grade we read of the exciting events recorded in Daniel Defoe's *Robinson Crusoe* and R. M. Ballantine's *The Coral Island.*

From Odysseus adrift on a raft in the Mediterranean to the people shipwrecked in the South Seas, all the characters were suddenly deprived of the comforts they had known and the relative security of the ships in which they had been sailing. The imperiled heroes were forced to face the demands of survival as well as they could. In the course of time, however, other needs besides survival began to be felt, and these had to be met as realistically as circumstances would allow.

Like these fictional characters, David—wrenched from the loving embrace of his wife and compelled to turn sorrowfully from his dearest friend—experienced aloneness, isolation, and fear. From the way David conducted himself we can learn many important truths about human nature in general and ourselves in particular.

We are aided in our understanding of David's experiences by the research of Dr. Abraham Maslow. In the mid-1950s he structured a hierarchy of needs that he believed were felt by all people—

"species-wide, apparently unchanging, genetic or instinctual"—and represented the physiological and psychological components necessary to good mental and emotional health.[1] While we are not obliged to accept his findings uncritically, we do observe that the most basic of our instinctual drives is for survival. Depending on the circumstances, we need food or water, oxygen or sleep, shelter or companionship. When these essentials are removed, our behavior changes. We begin to think and act in uncharacteristic ways. This observation is borne out in 1 Samuel 21.

The second set of needs is also illustrated in the story of David's outlaw years. These needs have to do with our safety. We desire to feel secure within a given environment. When we sense our insecurity or vulnerability, we become anxious and fearful. The focus of our attention is on ourselves; we concentrate on avoiding any catastrophe (real or imagined) that we believe threatens our well-being.

When our physiological and safety needs have been met, we next crave love and a sense of belonging. As Dr. Maslow noted, "Now the person will hunger for affectionate relations with people in general, namely, for a place in [the] group. He will want to attain such a place more than anything else in the world."[2] This need too is illustrated in the Scripture we are studying.

Demonstrations of the need for love and belonging are particularly noticeable during the teen years. The need is also experienced by those who would like to be married but so far have not found suitable mates. If our jobs compel us to move from one place to another and we try to become an integral part of a new assembly of believers, we may have a similar need for acceptance and a sense of belonging. Many elderly people show a strong desire for assurances of love and belonging from their family and friends.

Next in the hierarchy of needs in the mentally and emotionally healthy individual is esteem. Esteem is found *personally* when one gains confidence in himself, shows mastery in some skill, achieves certain set goals or objectives, and becomes more autonomous (enjoying his freedom but maintaining well-balanced relationships with others). Esteem is found *socially* when one merits respect from others, receives recognition for his accomplishments, is granted a new sense of acceptance because of his contribution to society, and is accorded status befitting his service.

As we grow older our desire is to live up to the full measure of our abilities (cf. Philippians 4:12-15; 1 Timothy 4:10); to come to know and understand ourselves, however incomplete that knowledge may be (1 Corinthians 13:11-12); and to enjoy the things that are truly beautiful and of lasting worth (Philippians 4:8).

As simplistic as these basic stages seem to us, their importance becomes apparent when we are deprived of one or more of our needs. *We cannot begin to understand the experiences of David in 1 Samuel 21–23 without realizing how deeply he was affected by Saul's malicious rejection of him, by the loss of all that he held dear, and by the unjust persecution that became a part of his life for about the next ten years.*

OUTLINE

While most writers have denounced David for his actions after fleeing Saul, I believe we need to grasp the essentials of his experience. The following outline will help. (You will notice another digression—this time explaining the extent to which Saul abandoned the principles of righteousness he was obliged to uphold.)

- The Actions of a Desperate Man (1 Samuel 21:1-9)
- The Conduct of a Fearful Man (1 Samuel 21:10-15)
- The Concerns of a Good Man (1 Samuel 22:1-5)
    Digression: The Caprice of an Evil Man (1 Samuel 22:6-23)
- The Benevolence of a Courageous Man (1 Samuel 23:1-5)
- The Response of a Righteous Man (1 Samuel 23:6-14)

Studying the Psalms David wrote during this period of his life (Psalm 34; 56; 57; 59; 142; and possibly 7[3]) will also help us understand him.

THE ACTIONS OF A DESPERATE MAN (21:1-9)

After leaving Naioth, David met with Jonathan. David could not go home to Michal for fear that one of Saul's informers might see him. The plan Jonathan and David had agreed on necessitated his spending at least three days in hiding (1 Samuel 20:5,35). He could not take any chances on being discovered. It is unlikely that those at Naioth had given him any food, and it is certain that Jonathan could not have sent any to him without arousing suspicion.[4] The success of their plan to test Saul's intentions toward David depended on Saul's being totally unaware of his son-in-law's whereabouts. When the two friends parted (20:42) David was hungry and alone. All human comforts had been taken from him. Furthermore he was in imminent danger. Anyone finding him was free to kill him.

While it is easy to criticize David's actions and claim that "he was not living so near to God as before, and in consequence his course became more and more carnal and more crooked,"[5] we must not overlook the desperate straits in which he found himself. His fear of Saul, however, did show that he was no longer consciously abiding under God's sovereignty.[6] William Blaikie observed:

> It is God's purpose now to allow David to feel his own weakness; he is to pass through that terrible ordeal when, tossed on a sea of trials, he will feel like Noah's dove, unable to find rest for the sole of his foot, and seem on the very eve of dropping helpless into the billows, till the ark presents itself, and a gracious hand is put forth to rescue him. Left to himself, tempted to make use of carnal expedients, and taught the wretchedness of such expedients; learning also, through this discipline, to anchor his soul more firmly on the promise of the living God, David is now undergoing a most essential part of his training, gaining the experience that is to qualify him to say with earnestness to others, "O taste and see that the Lord is good: blessed is the man that trusteth in Him."[7]

Wondering where to go, David decided to ask the priests at Nob for help.[8] He realized, however, that his arrival without an escort might raise questions, so he devised a story to put to rest any fears the priests may have had.

Nob has been identified as el-'Isawiyeh,[9] just north of the old city of Jerusalem and about six miles south of Gibeah. Ahimelech, the brother of Ahijah (1 Samuel 14:3,18) and the great-grandson of Eli, was serving as priest. He was not spoken of as the high priest and it may well be that his brother was either too ill to continue in office or had recently died. In either event Ahimelech appears to have been serving in an interim period when although much was required of him, he had little power to function effectively.

When Ahimelech heard that David had entered the gates of the city, he came trembling toward David.[10] The times were troublesome and Ahimelech's chief concern seems to have been the survival of Eli's dynasty and the sanctuary at Nob. His question was most apropos (1 Samuel 21:1). David lied to cover the fact that he was fleeing from Saul. In response to David's requests Ahimelech gave him five loaves from the twelve placed in the sanctuary[11] and the sword of Goliath (21:3,6,8-9). The priest also inquired of the Lord on David's behalf[12] (22:9-10,13,15).

While in Nob, David saw Doeg, an Edomite, the chief of Saul's shepherds. Doeg was "detained before Yahweh" (21:7) but no further explanation is given. Dr. John Kitto conjectures that Doeg was returning to Gibeah but with the sabbath approaching he could not complete his journey.[13] Other writers believe he was there because of some ceremonial defilement. David knew instinctively that Doeg's presence would lead to trouble, and as soon as possible David left. First Samuel 21:10 provides us with another of the Biblical writer's summary statements, "David arose, and fled that day for fear of Saul." But where was David to go? He was a homeless helpless wanderer who had to beg for food; all who showed him kindness put themselves in danger.

THE CONDUCT OF A FEARFUL MAN (21:10-15)

With his need for food met, David's next desire was for security. Yet we are surprised that he chose to flee to Philistia, and in particular to Gath—twenty-three miles southwest of Nob—the city in which Goliath had once lived. Perhaps as he made his way there, passing Azekah and crossing the valley of Elah, he determined to rely on a precedent quite widely honored in the ancient Near East whereby warriors dishonored in their homeland were welcomed by those who had formerly been their enemies.[14] Such sanctuary, however, was often provided only if the fugitive entered the service of his protector and was ready to fight against his own people (1 Samuel 28:1).

The servants of Achish recognized David and even attributed to him the title "king of the land" of Israel (1 Samuel 21:11). Their reaction showed the prominence given David by his enemies. They also reminded Achish of the antiphonal song—possibly it had become traditional—the Israeli women sang as they danced in the streets after each successful battle against the Philistines:

Saul has struck [slain] his thousands,
But David his myriads.

According to Psalms 56 and 34 (their chronological order) David was not given a warm welcome; he may even have been imprisoned. Eventually he was brought before the king, and to obtain his freedom David pretended to be insane since in those days people believed that epileptic and deranged individuals were under the protection of the gods. He scribbled on the doors of the gate as if writing some momentous message and even allowed his saliva to run down onto his beard.

The king's advisors in Gath who had either seen or heard of David's military prowess may have been inclined to disbelieve that he had been driven from Saul's presence because of insanity; but when David let his spittle run down his beard, they were convinced. Dr. John Kitto asked rhetorically, "Considering the regard in which the beard is held, the care taken of it, and the solicitude of the owner to protect it from insult and pollution, who could possibly doubt the abject and absolute madness of the man who thus defiled his own beard?"[15]

Psalm 34 records David's release from Gath.[16] It enlarges upon 22:1a, "So David departed from there and escaped to the cave of Adullam." This is another of the Biblical writer's summary statements. Whatever happened to David in Gath caused him to acknowledge the inadequacies of his own wisdom and brought him to a place in his experience where he again placed his confidence in the Lord.

THE CONCERNS OF A GOOD MAN (22:1-5)

On leaving Gath, David sought safety and security in the cave of Adullam. This place is usually identified today with Tell esh-Sheikh Madhkûr, about ten miles southeast of Gath.[17] A hillside honeycombed with caves, it took its name from a town given by Joshua to the tribe of Judah (Joshua 15:35). Adullam lay so near Philistine territory that on occasion it was regarded as a part of their land (cf. Joshua 12:15). It is questionable that this border town was under Saul's direct control at the time of David's residence there.

Loneliness weighs heavily on a person of David's temperament, and now that his physiological and safety needs had been met, it was only natural that his desires for love and affection and a sense of belonging would emerge. Only those deprived of being able to share their lives with a significant other know the pain of being isolated and companionless, destitute of sympathetic understanding and friendly conviviality.

Word of where David was hiding began to spread and we are glad to read that his family from Bethlehem joined him (1 Samuel 22:1). They had probably found themselves in an unenviable position after Saul's hostility toward David became public knowledge.

From 2 Samuel 23:8-39 and 1 Chronicles 11:10-47 we know that in addition to those in distress, those in debt, and those discontented with Saul's reign, many renowned warriors left the ranks of Saul's army and joined David in Adullam. Among them were Jashobeam, Shammah, Benaiah, and the sons of Zeruiah—Joab, Abishai, and Asahel.

David must have stayed for a fairly lengthy period of time in southern Judah near the Philistine border, for a total of four hundred men (and their families) threw in their lot with him. It was to David's credit that he won their love and loyalty and welded them into a powerful unit.

While they were living in the caves near the city of Adullam, the Philistines again made inroads into Judah and succeeded in bringing under their control all the land up to and including Bethlehem. Their presence in the area placed certain restraints on the people who had joined David. They could not go freely to draw water from the nearby stream, but had to wait for the cover of darkness. At the end of a long hot day David was overheard to mutter, "Who shall give me a drink [of] water from the well of Bethlehem, which [is] by the gate!" (1 Chronicles 11:17). That night three of his friends journeyed up the wadi, broke through the Philistine lines, filled a goatskin with water, fought their way out of the city, and retreated into the darkness. They brought the water to David, thus demonstrating their love for him (1 Chronicles 11:18).

But the love of one's comrades is insufficient. God built into us a need for a counterpart—a wife or husband who brings to the relationship what we lack (Genesis 2:18). In the reciprocal giving that follows there is the potential for the greatest human happiness known to mankind. Like many who long for the nearness of someone dear to them, David may well have spent untold lonely hours scheming how Michal might be brought to him. Unhappily, while confined to the barrenness of this border district, he heard that Saul had given Michal to Palti (1 Samuel 25:44). It must have taken David some time to recover from the grief of this loss.

Because those who joined David came with their families, the size of the young outlaw's following was quite large. From 1 Samuel 25:43 we know that among their number was a young woman named Ahinoam. Her parents originally lived in Jezreel. David took her as his wife[18] and she met his need for tender affection while also giving him someone to love and cherish.

In the course of time when David's band became too large for the natural resources of the area or else aroused the suspicions of Saul or the Philistines or both, he decided to move. But where could he go? And what would he do with his aged parents?

Realizing the great dangers of moving but probably feeling that they would all be safer elsewhere, David and his following made their way around the southern tip of the Dead Sea to Moab. There he entrusted his father and mother to the care of the king of Moab. David's great-grandmother had been a Moabitess and perhaps on this account he felt that his parents would be safe outside Saul's kingdom. Saul's victory over the Moabites (1 Samuel 14:47) had ill-disposed the people toward Israel's king, but it predisposed them toward anyone suffering at Saul's hand.

David had no means of knowing what would happen to him but in his words to the king of Moab—"Please let my father and mother come out [and stay] with you until I know what God[19] will do to me" (1 Samuel 22:3)—we see evidence of David's confidence in the Lord. He and his men went to a place called *Mizpah* ("Watchtower") in Moab.

Dr. Alfred Edersheim, who shares the concern of many over David's apparent willingness to live outside the borders of Israel (the promised land), wrote:

> It is impossible that such a movement on the part of David could long remain unknown.... It seems highly probable that tidings reach Naioth, and that it is from there that Gad (afterwards David's "seer" and spiritual adviser, 2 Sam. xxiv, 11-19; 1 Chron. xxi, 9, and the chronicler of his reign, 1 Chron. xxix, 29) goes to David [possibly at Samuel's suggestion]. But the stay in the land of Moab is not in accordance with the purpose of God. David must not flee from discipline and suffering, and God has some special work for him to do in the land of Israel.[20]

In obedience to God's revealed will David and his men sought shelter in the forest of Hareth.[21]

DIGRESSION: THE CAPRICE OF AN EVIL MAN (22:6-23)

Saul heard of David's return to Judah and this news brought on a hostile paranoid reaction. Saul summoned his officers of state to a hilltop in Gibeah.[22] Among them was Doeg, who had to all intents and purposes become a Benjamite (1 Samuel 22:7). From Saul's berating of his senior staff we learn that all are from Benjamin. Apparently he did not feel that any of the leaders of the other tribes were trustworthy. Even Jonathan was looked upon as an enemy. The king's words revealed the awful results of his departure from the Lord. Saul said to his servants (that is, his high ranking officials) who stood around him,

> Hear now, [you] Benjamites! Will the son of Jesse also give to any of you fields and vineyards? Will he make each of you commanders of thousands and commanders of hundreds? Yet all of you have conspired against me, and none is there who reveals [literally, uncovers my ear as if passing along a secret] to me when my son makes [cuts a covenant] with the son of Jesse; and none of you is sorry for me or reveals to me [speaks in my ear] that my son has aroused up my servant against me, to lie in ambush, as it is this day (22:7-8).

Before we proceed with our consideration of the events that took place in Gibeah, we need to bring into sharper focus Saul's persistent persecutory delusions and delusionary jealousy. Such mistaken impulses may be simple or complex in nature, and they usually involve a single theme or a series of connected themes. It is not uncommon for people suffering from this kind of mental/emotional disorder to imagine that they are being conspired against, cheated, spied on, or followed, or that they are in danger of being poisoned or drugged or killed in some way. The root of such feelings is insecurity. Any threat (perceived or real) intensifies the sufferers' sense of vulnerability. They become fearful of all whom they see as rivals; isolate themselves from those who they do not believe can be trusted; and filter all information through a preconceived grid that ends in confirming their worst fears or suspicions.

In Saul's condition we also see the outworking of evil (Psalm 81:12). He had refused to walk in the Spirit and as a consequence came more and more under the control of the flesh (Galatians 5:16). Saul reminds us of the words of Erich Fromm: "Our capacity to choose changes constantly with our practice of life. The longer we continue to make the wrong decisions, the more our heart hardens; the more often we make the right decision, the more our heart softens—or better perhaps, comes alive."[23]

Saul permitted self-will—almost imperceptibly at first—to turn his steps away from the Lord. In the process his heart became hardened and now it was relatively unmoved by spiritual considerations and questions of right and wrong.

Because Saul had walked away from the Lord with ever-increasing deliberation, he was now the victim of his own destructive thought processes. He became suspicious of those who were the most loyal to him and accused his followers of concealing Jonathan's deep affection for David (1 Samuel 22:8). Saul's unbalanced mind imagined that people were scheming to kill him when no such schemes existed; even as he spoke he imagined that David and his men were lying in ambush somewhere.

While Saul's men were silent, perhaps intimating their disagreement with the king in his perception of the situation,[24] Doeg the Edomite stepped forward. He detected in Saul's words the means whereby he might further ingratiate himself to the king. Using Saul's own contemptuous phrase for David, "son of Jesse," Doeg launched into a form of confession that seemed to confirm the king's suspicions: "I saw the son of Jesse coming to Nob, to Ahimelech the son of Ahitub. And he inquired of Yahweh for him, and gave him provisions, and [also] gave to him the sword of Goliath the Philistine" (22:9-10).

The facts of Doeg's charge were true, but the implication was that Ahimelech was guilty of treason. Because of the ease with which some malign others, the words of William Blaikie should constantly be borne in mind: "It can never be too earnestly insisted on that to be just to a man you must not merely ascertain the real facts of his case, but you must put the facts in their true light, and not colour them with prejudices of your own or with suppositions which the man repudiates."[25]

Doeg did not put the facts in their true light. And Saul, the supreme judge in the land, failed to uphold the law. In anger he demanded that Ahimelech and all his house be brought to Gibeah. A runner quickly carried the message to Nob and the priests hastened to respond to the king's unprecedented command.

When the servants of the Lord, all clothed in their sacral vestments, stood before the king, Saul commenced the proceedings. So far there was only one witness and his testimony had not been corroborated, nor had there been any cross-examination (cf. Deuteronomy 17:6; 19:15-21). Showing his anger as well as his disdain for the priesthood (evidenced by his referral to Ahimelech as the "son of Ahitub") Saul stated the charge in the form of an accusation: "Why have you conspired against me, you and the son of Jesse, by giving him bread and a sword, and have inquired of God for him, that he should rise up against me, to lie in wait [for me] as [it is] this day?" (1 Samuel 22:13)

Ahimelech, who before had been timid (21:1), now conducted himself with manliness. He was also supported by the other priests. His defense was straightforward but indiscreet. He was not obliged by Biblical law to witness against himself and yet he did. He admitted the facts and then attempted to vindicate the honorable character and services of David. Ahimelech also stated categorically his lack of any knowledge of a conspiracy (22:14-15). His lack of discretion was further evident in the fact that he left no way for the king to save face before the ranking officials of his court.

Without introducing the witness or permitting any cross-examination of Doeg by Ahimelech, Saul in a fit of rage pronounced sentence: "You shall surely die, Ahimelech, you and all your father's house" (22:16). Then turning to his soldiers, Saul demanded that they put the priests to death. The soldiers were awed by Saul's imperious spirit but refused to obey his command. Sensing that he was losing control of the situation, Saul demanded that Doeg kill the priests of the Lord (cf. Deuteronomy 17:7). He obeyed and eighty-five innocent men were soon lying in their own blood around the king.

The city of Nob was then placed under a *ḥerem,* or ban, and utterly destroyed (cf. Deuteronomy 13:15). Only Abiathar escaped the massacre (1 Samuel 22:20). He had apparently been left at Nob to attend the sanctuary, and when he saw Doeg and his men coming up the hill he hid from them.

Ironically the Lord used the treachery and the capricious nature of Saul to fulfill the judgment placed upon the house of Eli. Not one of the priests reached old age (1 Samuel 2:31). But the majority of commentators are not prepared to accept this massacre as a valid fulfillment of God's word to Eli. They have difficulty believing that God's sovereignty extends to and includes the actions of the wicked (cf. Habakkuk 1).[26] Instead most commentators look for a scapegoat, someone to blame for the massacre, and they find David (cf. 1 Samuel 22:20-23). Then to justify themselves, they become moralistic and discourse on the evils of lying.

I have no intention of excusing David's lie to Ahimelech, but I do wish to point out that David's admission to Abiathar only expressed regret for going to Nob. And Doeg knew nothing of the conversation between the priest and the king's son-in-law, so Saul was solely responsible for the slaughter of the servants of the Lord. The king acted precipitously in flagrant violation of the law and Doeg was his willing accomplice.[27]

THE BENEVOLENCE OF A COURAGEOUS MAN (23:1-5)

The atrocity perpetrated by Saul on the priests, coupled with the total destruction of the city of Nob, further alienated the pious among the people from him. At least two hundred more fighting men of Israel defected to David, increasing his force to six hundred (1 Samuel 23:13).

An opportunity for David's army to test their military skill soon presented itself. The Philistines had been eyeing the ripening fields of wheat and barley outside of Keilah,[28] a fortified city eight miles northwest of Hebron and close to Adullam (Joshua 15:44). As soon as the Israelites completed the harvest, the Philistines swept over the adjoining hills and took possession of the threshing floors.

Under normal circumstances Saul would have been the one to notify of the attack, for it was his responsibility to protect his subjects. The people however sent the message to David. A young lad, fleet of foot and able to take advantage of natural concealment, made his way to Hareth. There he told David what had happened and indicated he was the people's only hope.

On being informed of the Philistines' attack, David immediately sought the Lord's will. The Lord told him to attack the invaders and deliver Keilah. David's followers however held back. They feared the Philistines more than they feared Saul (1 Samuel 23:3). David inquired of the Lord again and this time He assured him of victory over the Philistines (23:4). Thus encouraged, David's army undertook the difficult and dangerous mission.

On reaching Keilah, David and his men began by taking away the Philistines' livestock so that the invaders could not remove any of the wheat and barley the people had gathered. Then David defeated Israel's archenemies with a great slaughter.

Naturally the people of Keilah were delighted. They had been spared the total collapse of their economy. They welcomed David and his men into their city with every evidence of delight. Keilah became the home of David's army, and each man sent for his wife and children to join him.

Inside the city David and his troop were treated like conquering heroes. The victory—their first—gave them a new sense of competence. Their success also increased their confidence in themselves and in David as their leader. Living inside a walled city seemed to offer them a degree of security and autonomy not known before. Furthermore they had the respect of the people. David and his men gained acceptance because of what they had done, were accorded status befitting their service, and enjoyed recognition for their accomplishments. What more could they ask for? Their basic needs had been met above and beyond their expectations. They were content.

THE RESPONSE OF A RIGHTEOUS MAN (23:6-14)

While in Keilah, David was joined by Abiathar, who came with an ephod in his hand (1 Samuel 23:6). Now in addition to the godly counsel of Gad the seer, David had the services of a priest. And the ephod was a further means of discerning the will of the Lord. How remarkably God provided for His servant!

Meanwhile back in Gibeah, Saul was delighted to learn that David was living in a fortified city. Saul believed that David had made a tactical blunder by relying on the protection of a city with double walls and double gates. In the twisted workings of Saul's mind, he thought he had God's blessing. Saul expressed his pleasure in words of praise to the Lord: "God[29] has delivered him into my hand" (23:7). And he made plans to march on the city.

When news of Saul's activities reached David, he faced a new dilemma. Should he remain in the city and withstand a siege? Or would the people, to save themselves, give him up to Saul? He inquired of the Lord (probably through Abiathar who used the ephod) and was told that the people of Keilah would give him into Saul's hand (23:12).

Without any harsh words or inner feelings of recrimination, David led his men out of the city and into the wilderness of Ziph. They were outcasts once again. But they were being sovereignly protected according to the summary in 23:14: "And Saul sought him every day [literally, all the day], but God did not give him into his hand."

DRAWING THE THREADS TOGETHER

In my counseling I continually exhort those facing various difficulties to spend time each day meditating on some portion of Scripture. In particular I recommend the book of Psalms. Tucked away between the leaves of this portion of God's Word are comfort, encouragement, direction, and instruction.

David and the great men and women of the Bible were not perfect. They shared our human nature (cf. James 5:17). That is why their experiences and examples can be so beneficial to us (Romans 15:4; 1 Corinthians 10:11). From David's Psalms written during this period of his life when he was fleeing Saul, we learn some very valuable truths.

Physical Needs

First Samuel 21 begins with David in despair. The passage concludes in 23:14 with David able to handle bitter disappointment because of his confidence in the Lord. Earlier, lover and friend had been removed from him, and his acquaintances maintained a discreet distance (cf. Psalm 25:16-21; 88:18). He knew what it was like to be alone and afflicted, deprived of the necessities of life and overwhelmed by anxiety. In his extremity he took refuge in the Lord and trusted Him to bring him out of his distresses (cf. Psalm 18:4-6; 43:5; 56:3,8-13; 69:1-4).[30] Trusting God, he regained his stability, but it was only afterward that he was able to rejoice in God's goodness to him (cf. Psalm 23).

The Need for Safety

David also knew what it was like to be in danger. In Gath there were those who spoke against him, and in Israel certain groups of people would quickly run to Saul and inform him of his son-in-law's whereabouts. David longed for safety—he longed to be "set on high" out of the reach of his enemies, or to have the wings of a dove so that he might fly away and find a place in which he might live in peace. In his suffering he called out to the Lord. And "his cry for help came into His ears" and he was helped (cf. Psalm 18:16-19,48; 31:7-8; 34:4,8-10; 55:1-16; 59:1-10; 61:1-4; 69:14-18,29-33). David could then conclude his plea for the meeting of his safety needs with the following words of encouragement to those who suffer: "Many are the afflictions of the righteous; but Yahweh[31] delivers him out of them all" (Psalm 34:19).

The Need to Be Loved

All of us need love and affection. To feel secure in a meaningful relationship is very important. David knew the pain of losing those who were dearest to him. He experienced firsthand what it was like to be in constant distress, to spend his life in sorrow and his years in sighing, to look for sympathy and find none, and to feel all over again the aching void that could only be filled by the companionship of a loving wife (cf. Psalm 31:9-13; 69:20). In his extremity he cast himself on the Lord (Psalm 55:22) and as he sought the Lord above all else (cf. Psalm 18:1-3; 25:4-5,9-10; 27:4-8; 31:19-22; 35:9; 62:1-2,5-7,11-12) he found Him to be sufficient for his every need. In time he could say,

> [I would have despaired] unless I had believed that [I would] see the goodness of Yahweh in the land of the living. Wait for [hope in] Yahweh; be strong and He will strengthen your heart; yes, wait for [hope in] Yahweh" (Psalm 27:13-14).

The Need for Esteem

As our basic needs are met, we desire to use the gifts God has given us, to live up to our potential, and to experience the blessing of God on our lives. Psalm 18:20-24 speaks eloquently of David's stead-fastness; he thanked the Lord for rewarding him according to his righteousness.

When the people of Keilah showed their lack of gratitude to David, it would have been natural for him to express his disappointment over their shallowness and lack of true loyalty. Instead he rejoiced in God's goodness and said, "Yahweh preserves the faithful" (Psalm 31:23). David's confidence in the Lord had been fully restored. As a consequence he could turn to those who were listening to his song and offer them hope in the midst of their struggles:

> Be strong and He will strengthen your heart,
> All you who wait for [hope in] Yahweh.
>   (Psalm 31:24)

Spiritual Needs

As we desire to come to a fuller knowledge of the truth, enjoy the good things the Lord has provided for us, and become more complete in ourselves, we find that our godward relationship becomes increasingly important to us (cf. Psalm 18:1; 25:5,9-15; 26:8-12; 27:4-8; 62:1-2,5-6,11-12; 63:1-11). Our horizontal relationships do not become less significant. Rather they are enhanced by what we are before the One whom we worship and serve. He it is who enables us to live up to the full measure of our abilities. We are then led step by step to praise Him as long as we have breath.

The Purpose of Suffering

None of us likes to suffer, but suffering is a part of life and in the providence of God it can serve a useful purpose.

The late Clarence Edward Macartney, one of the great preachers of this century, illustrated for us the value of adversity. Several years before Dr. Macartney died, a friend of his returned from Austria with a beautiful mother-of-pearl carving of the Lord's supper. Dr. Macartney took the gift to a jeweler and asked him to suspend it next to a light so that all of the carving's beautiful colors would be revealed. The jeweler looked at the carving with his practiced eye and said, "No, this must be mounted against something dark."

Likewise it is in the dark valley of grief and sorrow that we begin to reflect the beauty of the image of Christ. It is through the reminder of our weakness, when we suffer from the calloused betrayal of a spouse or the fickleness of a trusted friend, that we are refined in character. It is when the ominous cloud of undeserved criticism or the unjust opposition of an employer casts a gloomy shadow over us that we evidence the reality of the work of the Holy Spirit in producing fruit in our lives.

But some will ask, "Is there no happy ending? Are we to be continually deprived of the sources of happiness and blessing we so desperately seek?" There is a happy ending indeed. David's needs were met. Our needs are met as we are able to put the Lord first in our lives (Matthew 6:33; Philippians 4:19). The blessings of God are reserved for those who fear Him (that is, live in reverential awe before Him). On them He lavishes the promises of His grace.

UNCERTAIN FUTURE

1 Samuel 23:15–24:22

With their day's work done a group of men were sitting around an open-air fire. Above them the dark canopy of the sky formed a perfect backdrop for the innumerable stars that cast their faint light on those below. Around them was the night, and the only sound that disturbed the crackling of the logs on the fire and their own conversation was the lonely whine of a jackal in the distance.

After a couple of hours of leisurely conversation one of the men got up and threw some additional logs on the fire. Immediately sparks from the burning embers wafted upward. Possessing an oriental turn of mind that looks for truth in natural phenomena, the sage of the group pondered what he and the others had seen. Then gesturing toward the fire he said, "Man is born to trouble as [naturally as] the sparks fly upward" (Job 5:7).

Although we are many centuries removed from Job's time, his words are a truism. We all experience numerous trials, disappointments, frustrations, and injustices. Sometimes we bring problems on ourselves; other times they drop in on us like unwelcome guests. But the difficulties of life need not be decisive. We determine how we will respond to adversity.

Consider the lives of some of the great men and women of history who overcame a wide variety of setbacks. Walter Scott, the great novelist and lawyer, was disabled. John Bunyan, described by some as the "immortal dreamer," spent much of his life in jail. George Washington, in fighting for America's freedom at Valley Forge, had to endure perpetual hardship. The problems of war were compounded by improperly trained soldiers and inadequate supplies, and aggravated by one of the worst winters in many years. Abraham Lincoln was raised in poverty yet became one of our country's most beloved presidents. Franklin D. Roosevelt was stricken with poliomyelitis yet proved to be a tower of strength during World War II. Ludwig van Beethoven, whose concertos, sonatas, and symphonies have captivated the spirits of millions of people, was deaf. Albert Einstein's teachers thought he was retarded. Booker T. Washington, Harriet Tubman, Marian Anderson, and George Washington Carver had to cope with racial prejudice. All of these great men and women succeeded because they persevered in spite of difficulties.

As we consider the events in 1 Samuel 23–24 we are reminded of the words of the Lord Jesus in Matthew 18:7: "It must needs be that offenses come, but woe to that man by whom they come." The people of Ziph were the means whereby trials and difficulties were heaped on David and his followers. The Ziphites' malicious slander and willing betrayal were unconscionable. In those dark days it seemed as if Jonathan were the only one whom David could trust; his lack of confidence in others made his friendship with the king's son all the more precious and meaningful.[1]

OUTLINE

First Samuel 23:15–24:22 is linked to 23:14 in a vital way. There we were given a *general* statement of the persecution David had to endure. Here we have *specific* examples of Saul's malignant persecution of his son-in-law and David's magnanimous actions toward the king.

As we consider this passage, we should not allow the events before us to obscure the hand of God in David's affairs. Whether using direct means to prevent David's capture (23:27-28), or giving David warning so that he could escape from Saul of his own accord, or prevailing upon the remnants of Saul's better nature to rest from his persecution of one whom he formerly loved, the Lord was sovereignly orchestrating the events of David's life.

In this passage we will note the Biblical writer's purposeful use of contrasts. He juxtaposes

- Human Willfulness and Divine Protection (1 Samuel 23:15-29)
- Human Opportunity and Divine Restraint (1 Samuel 24:1-22)

HUMAN WILLFULNESS AND DIVINE PROTECTION (23:15-29)

After leaving Keilah, David and his men together with their families moved southward and passing Hebron took up residence in the wilderness of Ziph.[2] The town in the region is now a ruin and is identified as Tell Zîp (cf. Joshua 15:55). It had originally been built by

Caleb's son Mesha (1 Chronicles 2:42) on the crest of a hill, for it commanded a good view of the surrounding area. Two roads passed beneath ancient Ziph—one leading to Carmel, Maon, and Beersheba, and the other northwest to the central mountain range of Canaan. Because of the strategic military importance of Ziph, it was later fortified by Rehoboam when he feared an attack by the Egyptians (2 Chronicles 11:8).

The region in which David and his followers sought refuge was situated nearly 2,900 feet above sea level. It was a hot, dry, rocky area with valleys running off to the gulf of Aqaba and affording good opportunities for concealment.

While the area was suited to the grazing of sheep and goats, we may well ask by what means David and his troop were able to sustain themselves in this parched and sequestered region. They would be able to find pastureland for their flocks, but a large group such as David had would need to find alternate means of livelihood.

A wood (which is no longer in existence[3]) near Ziph may have made possible the shooting of game and it is probable that David's men became experts in tracking wild goats, capturing coneys, and snaring partridges. The women may well have cultivated small parcels of soil and grown corn and barley for their families. Furthermore, information gleaned from the Psalms indicates that on occasion David or his men entered the city to buy goods or trade for the things they needed (Psalm 54 including superscription).

In addition to the problem of finding food, there were enemies to contend with. Israel's enemies would also have been David's enemies. He and his men may well have fought against Amalekite tribesmen who had escaped the edge of Saul's sword or against marauding bands of Bedouin. David's men would have fought these battles while also acting as guardian to the shepherds in the neighborhood (1 Samuel 25:15-16). Now Saul sought David's life from the north and the desert tribes to the south were equally eager to separate David's head from the rest of his body (cf. Psalm 86:14-17). It is not hard to sense his fears or understand his reason for praying, "Consider my enemies, for they are many, and they hate me with a cruel hatred" (Psalm 25:19) and "My enemies would daily swallow me up, for there be many that fight against me, O Thou Most High" (Psalm 56:2; cf. 59:1).

The Renewed Opposition of a Determined Enemy (23:19-24)

During this time of daily hardship David became aware of Saul's activities in the area. David was even more alarmed to learn that the king was being led by Ziphite scouts!

Possibly out of some misguided sense of loyalty the Ziphites had sent a message to Saul in Gibeah: "Is David not hiding with us in the strongholds at Horesh, on the hill of Hachilah, which is on the south of Jeshimon?[4] Now then, O king, come down according to all the desire of your soul to do so; and our part [shall be] to surrender him into the king's hand" (1 Samuel 23:19-20; cf. 26:1-3).

The people of Ziph may have felt indebted to Saul for his attack on the Amalekites who had consistently raided the southland, raped their women, and driven off their livestock (1 Samuel 15:1-8). And perhaps the Ziphites also felt guilty for not having supported Saul more wholeheartedly (for only ten thousand from all of Judah accompanied Saul into battle). Becoming aware of the presence of David and his men in the area, they decided in one diplomatic move to show their gratitude to the king as well as demonstrate their loyalty to the crown. Their actions showed how fallible human perceptions can be. They judged David a traitor solely on hearsay and became guilty of raising their hand against the one who was innocent of all wrongdoing.

Saul's response to the message from the Ziphites was revealing. His heart was no longer set on serving Israel's suzerain (Yahweh), yet he did not hesitate to use the name of the Lord as he pronounced a blessing on the misdirected and misinformed people of Ziph. In his message, as Thomas Kirk pointed out, we have a "singular illustration of [Saul's] hypocrisy and blind infatuation [with his own plans and goals]."[5]

> May you be blessed of Yahweh, for you have had compassion on me. Go now, make more sure, and investigate and see his place where his haunt is, [and] who has seen him there; for I am told that he is very cunning. So look, and learn all the hiding places where he hides himself, and return to me with certainty, and I will go with you; and it shall come about if he is in the land that I will search him out among the thousands of Judah (1 Samuel 23:21-23).

The Welcome Faithfulness of a Devoted Friend (23:16-18)

In marked contrast to the perfidy and perversity of the people of Ziph is the love and loyalty of Jonathan. One night while David and his men were still hiding in the forest on the hill of Hachilah, Jonathan visited him. Although left in Gibeah by Saul, Jonathan sensed David's anxieties and frustrations, so he journeyed to the land of Ziph for the sole purpose of reassuring his friend of God's protection and blessing. "Do not fear," Jonathan said when he found David, "for the hand of Saul my father shall not find you; and you shall reign over Israel, and I shall be to you [your] second [-in-command]; and my father Saul also knows [that this is] so" (1 Samuel 23:17).

Who can tell how much Jonathan's words meant to David? The affirmation and encouragement that Jonathan imparted made the burdens David carried lighter. His eyes were taken off himself and fixed on the Lord.[6] It is no wonder that David could write after meeting with Jonathan,

> O God, save me by Your name and judge me by Your might. O God, hear my prayer; give ear to the words of my mouth. For strangers have risen against me, and cruel men seek after my soul; they have not set God before them. Behold, God [is] my helper. The Lord [is] with those who uphold my soul. He shall return evil to [my enemies] (Psalm 54:1-5).

It is tragic indeed that in our day men and women set aside the benefits of long-term friendships for shallow temporary relationships. Instead of building their attachments on internalized principles, they adhere to externalized and ever-changing social norms. People feel that they must respond with appropriate behavior to the "group" if they are to remain "in" with them and continue to be accepted by them. As a result many have missed the benefits of a relationship such as David and Jonathan enjoyed. *It is through the absence of competition, the presence of mutual esteem, the sharing of experiences, and real empathy that we are strengthened and helped over the rough places of life.* No wonder the Bible lays emphasis on the role of Jonathan in the crises David was called on to face.

God the Holy Spirit has given to each of us certain gifts, and these are to be used to strengthen and build up one another. All believers possess the gift of faith, but not all in the same measure. Happy are those men and women whose friends are strong in faith and able to encourage them in the Lord when all about them seems to be tottering and ready to crash to the ground.[7] All believers possess the gifts of giving, of helps, and of showing mercy, though not all to the same extent. We are without excuse if we turn our backs on those who need our encouragement because we are more concerned with what others may think than we are with the opportunity for service that the Lord has given to us.

When ministering to others we should remember that Jonathan did *not* give David advice. All Jonathan did was help David turn his eyes away from the hazards posed by Saul and renew his confidence in the Lord (cf. Psalm 55:22; 1 Peter 5:7).

When Jonathan and David parted, these friends renewed their covenant, and they were conscious of the Lord's presence.[8] Their covenant did not have to be confirmed, but to these godly men the renewal was an expression of their highest and most spiritual commitment to each other. Neither doubted the goodwill of the other; each desired what was best for the other. Their mutual promise was much the same as two friends today praying as they part and asking the Lord to watch over each other until they meet again.

When Jonathan left, he returned to his house.[9] Like all great men, he is not without his critics. There are those who reason, "If Jonathan was convinced of the rightness of David's cause, why didn't he throw in his lot with him?" They then go on to state, "For God's king [David], suffering must precede glory.... Jonathan fails in the path of discipleship because he does not break with the city and go out with David....and because he refused to suffer with David he did not reign with him."[10]

By remaining at court, however, Jonathan was able to be faithful in his duty to both the king and his country while also adhering unalterably in his loyalty to David. His decision to return home required real discernment and true spiritual maturity.

Thinking of Jonathan's situation some are sure to ask, "Do situations ever arise that necessitate our taking a stand that we know will result in the severing of relationships with those (perhaps even family members) with whom we disagree?" The obvious answer is yes. But we should not sever relationships simply because we cannot get along. Only some far more abiding reason would justify breaking ties—some behavior that is a direct affront to the Lord, some belief that robs Him of His glory, or some decision that implicates one in compromise and causes him to become a stumbling block to others. In such instances it is essential that a parting of the ways occur (cf. 2 Corinthians 6:14-18). Separations should be the result of doctrinal or ethical problems, not personality clashes. Until doctrinal or ethical problems arise, quiet perseverance in well-doing is the best course of action to follow.[11]

Let us not forget the principle teaching of this passage about friendship: In times of adversity when we are hard pressed by difficulties too numerous to mention, we too need the uplifting presence of a true friend. His or her cheering words and warm embrace will most assuredly encourage us.[12] And may the Lord have mercy on those who withhold such encouragement and affection for fear of what others may say or think. Such neglect may cause a faithful follower of the Lord to have to tread a cheerless path when a word of comfort might have strengthened his or her hand in the Lord.[13]

Timely Intervention of a Sovereign God (23:25-29)

Since Jonathan had been able to find the hiding place of David and his men, David presumed that Saul would be able to do the same. Believing that they would be safer elsewhere, David with his men and their wives and families left the hill of Hachilah and went out into the barren wilderness of Maon[14] south of Ziph.

A city occupied the crest of the conical hill of Maon. About one and a half miles south of Carmel in Judah and about eight and a half miles south of Hebron, it is known today as Tell Ma'in. The hill is filled with limestone caves and it is possible that David and his followers took shelter in them for a time while they looked about for a more secure place in which to live.

A few miles to the northeast of Maon is the great rocky gorge of Malaky. There are competent Bible scholars who believe that this is the place David chose as a retreat for his men and their families. Here they would be most secure. In spite of the strategic advantages of this new location, David and his men kept a sharp lookout for Saul. From the hill of Maon they would be able to see if Saul entered the area known as the wilderness of Maon.

One day soon after venturing forth into the vast expanse of the desert, David and his men saw a column of dust rising to the north and the glint of the sun's rays on the spear tips and shields of Saul's soldiers. David and his men descended the hill and hastened to join their families.

The Ziphites informed Saul of David's movements, and the king decided to take advantage of the terrain and catch David in a pincers movement. Thomas Kirk described the scene:

> On learning from the Ziphites, who have doubtless their spies about, that David had fled thither [to Malaky], Saul follows with his men. On coming to the great gorge, he finds himself on its northern side, while David is on its southern side; and as the gorge is a narrow, deep, and impassable chasm for some miles, Saul can not at once get at David. This explains the statement in the sacred narrative, "And Saul went on this side of the mountain, and David and his men on that side of the mountain." But Saul, instructed probably by the Ziphites, sends a strong force to march around the gorge at both ends, so as to surround [David and those who are with him].[15]

Saul's plan almost succeeded. But just as the noose was about to be drawn tight, a runner arrived. Tired and breathless he blurted out his message: "Hurry and come, for the Philistines have made a raid on the land" (1 Samuel 23:27). And Saul was compelled to give up his pursuit.

The summary statement in 23:29 says, "And David went up from there [out of the gorge] and stayed in the strongholds [at] Engedi."[16] Engedi nudges up against the limestone hills to the west of the Dead Sea and a little north of Masada. It is bounded by two perennial streams, between which the stretch of land forms a beautiful oasis that has been described as a little paradise. The plain is dotted with palm trees and the slopes of the mountains are covered with the choicest vineyards in Judah. The scent of henna blossoms hangs in the air (cf. Song of Solomon 1:14).

But above this oasis is a wilderness as barren as anyone might find. The hilltops have been rounded by the wind and their summits lie exposed to the withering heat of the sun. These hills are from two hundred to four hundred feet above the valley and contain numerous caves. Some of them are virtually inaccessible, but it is reported by the local tribespeople that at one time one of the larger caves sheltered thirty thousand men. It is possible that this was the cave in which David and his followers concealed themselves from Saul.[17]

HUMAN OPPORTUNITY AND DIVINE RESTRAINT (24:1-22)

Opportunity for Vengeance (24:1-7)

Once the Philistines had been repulsed from the land, Saul again turned his attention to David. The king learned from those in either Ziph or Maon that the outlaw and his men were now at Engedi, called the "rocks of the wild goats."

Taking an elite corps with him, Saul marched in a northwesterly direction across a formidable arid waste and in six or seven hours arrived at the place where water coming out of a rock fell in a thin cascade to pools below. The slope from the uplands to the plain below was about a mile and a half long. At the foot of this decline was a sheltered canyon where the city of Engedi once stood (cf. 2 Chronicles 20:2). All about was desert; the Dead Sea was in easy view and the mountains of Moab formed a buttress against the horizon.

It was to this area that Saul pursued David. The king came to the sheep pens but found no one there. Then, answering the call of nature,[18] he went into one of the caves to relieve himself. The interior was so dark that he was unable to see inside beyond the circle of light cast by the rays of the sun. He had no means of knowing that in the pitch black interior David and his men lay concealed. Saul however was silhouetted against the opening and in full view of those in the inner recesses of the cavern.

Seeing Saul in such a defenseless position, one of David's men verbalized the thoughts of the rest. He urged David to take advantage of the situation and rid himself of his implacable enemy. "Look, [this is] the day of which Yahweh said to you, 'Lo, I will deliver your enemy into your hand'" (1 Samuel 24:4). This supposed prophecy is nowhere to be found in Scripture. In all probability the saying had had its origin one evening when the men were gathered around a campfire and one of their number, purporting to speak for the Lord, predicted that the day would come when David would kill Saul. His "prophecy" must have captured the imagination of the others, for in the ensuing months and years its origin was forgotten. But those with David came to believe that the prediction was indeed from God.

David however was guided by inner principles and declined to take Saul's life. David showed us how important it is to guard what we hear and believe. Instead of listening to his men, he rose and inched forward until he was standing directly behind the king. It would have been easy for David to plunge his drawn sword through Saul's back so that the point would come out just below his breastbone. Instead David cut off the hem of the king's cloak.

The men were angered, wishing to be avenged for all that they had suffered. David restrained them by explaining, "Far be it from [literally, to] me, from Yahweh that I should do this thing to my lord [the king], to Yahweh's anointed, to put forth my hand against him" (24:6).

Saul, oblivious to all that had transpired, arose and went his way.

Confrontation with the Enemy (24:8-15)

After Saul left the cave and descended the hill, David experienced a sense of guilt. He had always respected Saul's right to rule the people of Israel. He had always submitted to his authority. So why should he now experience pangs of conscience over cutting off a portion of the hem of Saul's outer garment? The answer is found in the customs of the times. Often vassals, to show their submission to a suzerain, would compare their attitude to bowing before him in lowly submission. To lend weight to their words they would use the figure of speech, "holding the hem of [their sovereign's] garment,"[19] to signify their loyalty. It was this hem cut from Saul's garment that David now held in his hand!

After Saul left the cave, David suddenly realized that he had in effect defied the king and shown his contempt for the crown. David chose to make amends. It was a risky course of action. Going outside the cave he called after Saul, "My lord the king!"

As Saul turned, David bowed with his face to the ground and then prostrated himself as a sign of his subservience. Then rising he explained what he had done and how his actions disproved the accusations of others.

> Why do you listen to the words of man, saying, "Look, David is seeking to do you evil"? Look, this day your eyes have seen how Yahweh has delivered you this day into my hand in the cave; and [one] said [that I should] kill you, but [I] had pity on you; and I said, "I shall not put forth my hand against my lord, for he [is] the anointed of Yahweh. And my father, see; yes, see the skirt of your robe in my hand; for in that I cut off the skirt of your robe and did not slay you, know and see that there is neither evil nor transgression in my hand, and I have not sinned against you; yet you are lying in wait for my soul to take it! Yahweh shall judge between me and you, and Yahweh shall avenge me on you; but my hand shall not be against you (1 Samuel 24:9-12).

David was respectful of Saul's position. David's defense of his actions was eloquent in its simplicity. He took advantage of what had happened to prove his innocence. Others had maligned and misrepresented him to the king, but David was innocent of their charges. When he had the opportunity to avenge himself for the wrongs heaped on him, he refrained from taking advantage of what his men thought was a fortuitous situation.

David's confidence was firmly placed in the Lord. Without vacillating or entertaining any false hope of being restored to Saul's favor or showing any signs of weakness, David concluded by saying: "Therefore Yahweh shall be judge and shall judge between me and you; and He shall see and plead my cause and will vindicate me [deliver me] out of your hand" (24:15).

Temporary Truce (24:16-22)

The effect of David's positive and respectful confrontation of Saul is striking. While the king's eyesight had perhaps begun to fail, he nonetheless recognized David's voice. Saul was touched by the singular generosity of his son-in-law. Inwardly Saul felt reproved. He was overwhelmed by David's magnanimity and in loud lamentation expressed his grief over what he had done. He admitted that David had dealt with him far better than he deserved. Saul also acknowledged that David would reign after him and asked David to enter into an oath not to kill off his family when he became king.[20]

First Samuel 24:22 contains another of the Biblical writer's summaries. Saul returned to Gibeah but David and his men, their retreat now known to Saul, sought safety in "the stronghold." The use of the article has led some Bible scholars to conclude that this was the cave of Adullam. Others believe it was Masada, which is the greater probability.

One important fact made obvious in the summary is that David knew Saul's character. David realized from past experience that the king's good intentions would vanish as rapidly as they had been manifested. Being prudent, David took good care to place a suitable distance between himself and the king.

THE NATURE OF TRUE FAITHFULNESS

As we look back over 1 Samuel 23:15–24:22 we observe (1) the misguided loyalty of the people of Ziph, (2) the devotion of Jonathan, and (3) the utter reliability of God.

The Ziphites were not guided by the truth. Their thoughts were solely of themselves and the benefits that a grateful king might lavish upon them. Jonathan, on the other hand, was motivated by his integrity. He perceived the issues clearly and could therefore deal in faithfulness with David even though he had nothing to gain and a great deal to lose by his actions. Throughout the passage the Lord is seen using different means to protect those who placed their trust in Him.

Self-serving Zeal

We all hold in high esteem patriots whose loyalty to their country leads them to protect their families by taking up arms in the defense of freedom; or families whose ties bind them together so tightly that their members can be counted on to help each other regardless of the cost; or missionaries whose commitment to the Lord leads them to labor unrelentingly to bring the good news of salvation in and through Jesus Christ to people who have never even heard His name. Loyalty, however, if not regulated by the truth, can deteriorate into an unwise fanaticism or subservience to some tradition or the kind of bigotry that embodies ideas and/or ideals that are contrary to the teaching of God's Word.

The people of Ziph were intent on demonstrating their loyalty to Saul. They were fully persuaded that by betraying David's whereabouts, they would be doing themselves a favor. They tried again and again to trap him. David had done them no harm, but their sense of right and wrong was so warped that truth was excluded from their thoughts. In time, and guided by the Holy Spirit, David would describe their malicious slander in Psalm 54:3-5,7b.

It would please us if we could conclude that human nature has changed over the centuries and that the Ziphites stand alone in their perfidy. Unfortunately in all eras of history there have been those whose malicious tongues have been quick to carry gossip or spread slander. They perhaps hope that they will profit by someone else's downfall (Nehemiah 6:1-9, for example).

Nicole knew the heartache caused by gossip. She phoned me at home one day just before Thanksgiving and told me about a problem that was tearing her family apart. It was a tradition for the grown daughters to take turns inviting the extended family for Thanksgiving dinner. However, since some of her relatives who made much of their devotion to the Lord had the habit of gossiping and slandering others in the family, she questioned whether she in good conscience could include the gossips in her invitation. Nicole's primary reason for calling me was to find out what the Bible taught and how she should order her conduct in light of God's Word.

In responding to her question I stressed the importance of reaching a decision in concert with her husband so that unity might be preserved in their relationship. Then we spent about an hour talking about the Bible's teaching. Nicole and I discussed passages of Scripture like Leviticus 19:16; Proverbs 6:16-19; 22:24-27; 24:1-2; Romans 16:17; James 3:5-6; 2 Timothy 3:1-5; Titus 3:10; and 1 Peter 2:1. Slander, we found, is certainly one of the most common and most destructive of sins. It is often linked in Scripture with the sins of immorality and murder (Matthew 15:19). Sometimes those who would never think of committing adultery or murder, seem to see nothing wrong with one-line put-downs and constant criticism of others. The root of their unkind words is a heart filled with malice, deceit, hypocrisy, jealousy, and envy.

Nicole decided to discuss her concerns with her husband. He sided with her and spoke to the relatives about their habit of gossiping. They did not take his reproof well and chose not to come for Thanksgiving dinner.

The sin of the Ziphites—the sin of those who seek to discredit others—should not be allowed to gain a foothold in our assemblies, for gossip and slander and destructive innuendoes destroy fellowship among believers. These sins should be denounced by those who fear God and seek to do what is pleasing in His sight.

Trusted Friends

The sin of the Ziphites is set in contrast to the faithfulness and devotion of Jonathan. Friendships such as the one Jonathan and David enjoyed are not very common, though here and there one still reads of a person who loyally supports a friend even though such a course of action is unpopular and brings the helper into disfavor with others.

Jonathan's friendship with David was based on truth and character. And the evidence of God's hand in bringing them together was confirmed in numerous ways. Each was loyal to the other, though Jonathan as the king's son had much to give and little to gain by befriending David. In Scripture we see Jonathan interceding (1 Samuel 19:1-7) and intervening (20:1-11,27-34) on David's behalf with no thought of ever having David return the favor. David trusted Jonathan implicitly and as a result was transparently honest and totally unafraid in his presence (20:1). And Jonathan never betrayed his trust! In our last glimpse of Jonathan before the fateful events on the slopes of mount Gilboa, he was meeting with David secretly in the wood near Ziph. To encourage his friend Jonathan had to travel many miles from his home, perhaps at great risk to himself. His sole purpose was to encourage his friend and strengthen his hand in the Lord (23:16-18).

It is no wonder that among the great friendships of history the friendship of Jonathan and David still ranks highest. It is held up as the model against which all other friendships are measured.

It is much easier for us to stay in contact with our friends. We can cross intervening miles much more quickly than Jonathan could journey from Gibeah to the forest of Hereth. We have the convenience of jet planes, telephones, the postal service, and fax transmissions. It is tragic how often we fail to use these facilities to bring a word of encouragement and cheer to someone who needs to be uplifted by a kindly voice and fortified by a reminder of God's faithfulness.

Jeremy felt very much alone when he came to southern California. He came from a small town in Wisconsin and was overwhelmed by the largeness of our cities and the fast pace of our lives. He tried attending church but found himself ill at ease with those of his age who were more sophisticated in their ways and more skillful in the art of repartee. Jeremy withdrew more and more until he was spending his weekends alone in his apartment. No one was sufficiently concerned to take an interest in him.

Finally, however, a wise young woman named Ruth began to try to break down the barriers he had erected about himself. It took about two years for her to get him to come to her home and meet with some of her friends. Later Ruth encouraged him to accompany her to church and stayed by his side so that he would not feel alone and out of place. With Ruth's help Jeremy began to develop some lasting relationships; in the course of time he gained confidence and began making friends on his own.

Because of Ruth's perception of his situation and kindly interest, Jeremy is now living a happy, contented, and fulfilled Christian life. The change in Jeremy would not have occurred if someone had not reached out to him and sought to meet a deeply felt need.

Strong Confidence

Having considered the slander and misrepresentation of the Ziphites and the uplifting counsel and encouragement of Jonathan, we can now focus our attention on the ways in which the Lord works in our lives. He does not take away our trials or carry us over them, but strengthens us so that we can persevere through them.

Dr. William Blaikie has drawn together the different ways in which the Lord helped and preserved David.[21] Dr. Blaikie reminds us that when Saul first told his servants and Jonathan to kill David, it was the wise and judicious counsel of Jonathan that turned the king from his murderous purpose (1 Samuel 19:1,4-5). Later when Saul tried to pin David to the wall with a spear, it was the harpist's watchful eye and nimble ability that enabled him to escape (19:9-10). Then when Saul gave his servants instructions to kill David, it was Michal's keen mind and knowledge of her father that led her to detect the danger. It was also her ready wit that devised a plan so that Saul's soldiers searched her house in vain for her husband (19:11-17). When Saul sent emissaries to Naioth to capture David, none could carry out the king's command, for the Spirit of the Lord overpowered them. And when Saul attempted to succeed where his men had failed, the same happened to him (19:18-24).

After several years during which David and his men endured the hardships of nomadic life, God led them to deliver the city of Keilah from the Philistines. David's men were received into the city as conquering heroes. They believed that at last they could live in peace and enjoy the comforts of a home. When Saul learned of their whereabouts, however, he marched on the city. He was sure that he could either bribe or intimidate the citizens into handing David over to him. Saul was foiled in his plans, however, for the Lord saw to it that David learned of the king's movements in time to escape (23:9-14).

At Maon when the king's soldiers had almost surrounded David and his capture was sure, a messenger arrived with news that the Philistines had invaded the land (23:24-28) and Saul was forced to give up the pursuit.

All of these incidents should bring us great encouragement. The Lord has a thousand ways of protecting us. He allows trials to enter our lives to test us and also to deepen our trust in Him. His *ḥēsed* (that is, His lovingkindness, faithfulness, tender mercies) never fails. Through our trials we learn to call on Him, even as David did, and to say, "Save me, O God, by Your name and judge me by Your strength" (Psalm 54:1). And the God who heard him and answered his prayer hears and answers us as well.

To be saved by God's *name* is to be delivered by all that God is— the totality of His nature. To be judged by God's *strength* is to be vindicated by His power. How marvelous it is to have One such as our God to intervene on our behalf and accomplish for us that which we could never do for ourselves!

David learned through the things that he suffered to place his confidence in the Lord. Our trials likewise help us focus our attention on Him so that we can trust Him more fully.

THE POWER OF INFLUENCE
1 Samuel 25:1-44

Influence has been defined as "1. capacity or power of persons or things to produce effects on others by intangible or indirect means. 2. action or process of producing effects on others by intangible or indirect means."[1]

One's influence can either be positive or negative, of lasting benefit or a blight upon people's lives. When Mark Antony delivered his famous funeral oration over the body of his friend Julius Caesar, he commented on the apparent longevity of evil when compared to the seeming short duration of those acts done for the benefit of others.

> The evil that men do, lives after them;
> The good is oft interred with their bones.[2]

As we look back over this century (including two world wars, the spread of the Mafia, alcoholism and drug abuse, sexual promiscuity and divorce) few of its evils can rival the oppression and violence of communism. But where did communism have its origin? Not in the Bolshevik Revolution of 1917. It began, according to Robert K. Massie in his book *Nicholas and Alexandra,* when the czar and empress of Russia began to place their confidence in a priest named Grigorii Rasputin.

The son of Nicholas and Alexandra suffered from hemophilia and was often at death's door. Rasputin would pray for the lad who would miraculously recover. In the course of time the royal family placed more and more trust in Rasputin and his influence over them increased. Eventually he could ask for the dismissal of any high-ranking Russian official who dared to oppose him and his request would be granted. Rasputin could also have those who favored him and his policies appointed to office. Graft and corruption permeated every level of the bureaucracy and for many years the whole Russian government reeled under the sway of this unscrupulous monk. The seeds of revolution were planted and then watered with the discontent of citizens forced to live with injustice, oppression, and perpetual poverty. Finally when the people could stand it no longer, they revolted and the royal family was murdered.

Alexander Kerensky, a key government official during those trying times, stated emphatically, "Without Rasputin, there could have been no Lenin!"[3] Rasputin's avarice and ambition paved the way for the emergence of the antisupernaturalistic ideology we today call communism, and people in many parts of the world are still paying the price of Rasputin's pathological desire for power.

Good influences, on the other hand, benefit those who receive them. For example, Elizabeth Barrett Browning shared the thoughts of her heart as she reminisced about her daughter Kate.

> She never found fault with you, never implied
> Your wrong by her right; and yet men at her side
> Grew nobler, girls purer, as through the whole town
> The children were gladder that pull'd at her gown—
> My Kate.
>
> . . . .
>
> The weak and the gentle, the ribald and rude,
> She took as she found them, and did them all good.[4]

Kate's life lifted people to a higher level. She touched the chords of love and compassion in those whom she met so that they reverberated with new hope.

The same can be true of us. Our outlook, words, and deeds have an effect on others. Perhaps our influence is nowhere more evident than in the home. What happens when we get out of bed in the morning? We are either positive or negative in our attitudes, understanding or demanding, patient or intolerant, affirming or discouraging in the things we say to our spouses and children. What we say or do sets the tone of the day for those whom we love. If this principle is true in little things, think how influential one person's example is on the many people whose lives intersect his during the course of a lifetime!

STRUCTURE AND OUTLINE OF THE PASSAGE

As we begin our study of 1 Samuel 25 we are confronted with a verse that seems out of place (25:1). We find ourselves compelled to ask, What possible connection does it have with David's triumph over his natural desire to avenge himself by killing King Saul (1 Samuel 24) and with the events that transpired between David and Nabal (1 Samuel 25)? In dealing with this verse we can follow the precedent set by other commentators and treat it as nothing more than a historical note. Or we can do as still others have done and ignore it. Or we can sift the passage to see if this verse contains a clue to understanding what follows. In actual fact this verse provides an important transition between the old order and the new; it contains the key to unlocking the truths that lie latent in 1 Samuel 25.

Samuel had been David's mentor, the one to whom he had been accountable and on whom he had constantly relied for counsel and encouragement. With the prophet's death that stabilizing force was removed. And, like all who suffer loss, David entered a predictable period of mourning, which is often accompanied by a sense of vulnerability, feelings of depression, and a possible change in behavior. First Samuel 25:1 strikes the keynote, providing us with a backdrop so that we can better comprehend David's reaction to the treatment given his men by Nabal.

The theme of 1 Samuel 25 is *the power people have to produce an effect in the lives of others.* Those to whom prominence is given in the sacred record (namely, Nabal and his wife Abigail) should be studied in light of this central concept.

The outline of the chapter revolves around the different personalities mentioned by the Biblical writer. Verse 1, as we have noted, describes the removal of Samuel's godly influence; verses 2-13 contain an account of David's reasonable request and Nabal's graceless refusal; verses 14-31 concern Abigail, her wisdom and understanding, and her gracious intervention; verses 32-35 give us David's prompt response; verses 36-38 record God's righteous judgment of Nabal; verses 39-42 contain David's proposal of marriage to Abigail; and verses 43-44 conclude the chapter with a postscript about David's wives.

REMOVAL OF A GODLY INFLUENCE (25:1)

The Statement of Fact (25:1a)

From the Biblical writer's record of the events as they transpired, we conclude that Samuel passed to his eternal rest soon after David had spared Saul's life at Engedi. Thomas Kirk calculated the prophet's age to be ninety-six.[5] It seems more likely that he was about ninety-two, but even this age implies that he had served his people faithfully for nearly nine decades. Now his work was done. His death appears to have been a peaceful one. He had spent his last years training his successors—small groups of students in the schools of the prophets—and he was now ready to lay aside the labors of his lifetime.

The Public Response (25:1b)

As news of Samuel's death spread throughout the land, people from Dan in the north to Beersheba in the south came to Ramah to pay homage to him. They had seldom supported him wholeheartedly during his lifetime, but now that he was gone from them they realized something of the magnitude of their loss. Josephus, writing in the first century A.D., recalled Samuel's influence on the people:

> His moral excellence and the esteem with which he was regarded are proved by the continued mourning that was made for him and the concern that was universally shown to conduct the funeral rites with becoming splendour and solemnity. He was buried in his own native place, and they wept for him very many days, not regarding [his passing] as the death of another man or a stranger, but as that in which each individual was concerned. He was a righteous man, and of a kindly nature, and, on that account, very dear to God.[6]

Samuel was too poor to afford a burial lot (cf. Genesis 23; 2 Samuel 21:14) so he was interred in the garden of his home in Ramah. His wife may have predeceased him and perhaps his body was laid in a grave next to hers. In his passing he left behind him an enduring legacy. Throughout his life he had influenced others to live on a higher level of spiritual awareness; he had modeled for them the difference between an external conformity to the will of God and the internal dynamic of a truly spiritual life.

If eulogies were given at his funeral, perhaps Samuel was remembered by his countrymen for organizing the courses of the Levites (1 Chronicles 9:22). When he reinstituted their service (possibly while he was still living in Shiloh) he ensured that all of the Levites could once again participate in the work of the Lord.

Others who spoke on Samuel's behalf may have remembered him as a man of vision. Historians later recorded that he began to accumulate treasures for the temple that Solomon would one day build (1 Chronicles 26:27-28).

There would have been many present who remembered him as a

man of great devotion to the Lord, who zealously adhered to His Word. During a time of crisis when the worship of the sanctuary had fallen into disuse (and perhaps before it was re-established at Nob), he organized a special nationwide Passover feast (2 Chronicles 35:18).

There may have been those who with prophetic foresight realized that the one who had so recently gone from their midst had stood at the crossroads of history and inaugurated a new era. We know from Acts 3:24 and 13:20 that in the economy of God Samuel served during a transitional period of his people's history. He brought into being the prophetic movement that lasted until John the Baptist (Matthew 11:13), and he was instrumental in anointing the first two kings of Israel.

Certain men within the group would also have reminisced about the events that had transpired at Mizpah many years earlier. They would have testified that Samuel was a man of great faith and courage who succeeded in bringing about a remarkable awakening that resulted in a victory over the Philistines (1 Samuel 7).

For his deeds his name rightly appears with other great men and women of the faith in the Bible's "hall of fame" (Hebrews 11:32-33). But above all, Samuel would have been remembered as a man of prayer (Psalm 99:6; Jeremiah 15:1). As Dr. F. B. Meyer remarked, "It has yet to be seen, and probably we shall never know until the veil of eternity is lifted, whether the world has benefitted most by our prayers or labours."[7]

It is no wonder that David, who probably could not attend Samuel's funeral, would nonetheless lament the passing of the mentor whose influence had made such an impact on his life. While Psalm 12 was probably composed at a later period, verse 1 in particular looks back on the godly men whom he had known.

The Removal of Restraint (25:1c)

Samuel's death did more than cause David to grieve the loss of an old and dear friend. David experienced a new sense of fear. Although the prophet had not been able to oppose Saul directly, he had exerted an influence for good upon the people. The Ziphites were the only ones mentioned by name as having taken upon themselves the betrayal of David's whereabouts to the king. Now that Samuel's restraining influence was removed, David felt it expedient to move as far from Saul's reach as possible. He and his men with their wives and children journeyed south to the wilderness of Paran (cf. Numbers 10:12; 12:16; 13:3,26).[8] There they became an effective deterrent to raids by the Amalekites and Bedouin tribesmen (cf. 1 Samuel 25:14-16,21). The service they rendered is looked upon by their countrymen as "fighting the battles of Yahweh" (25:28).

RESPONSE OF A GRACELESS MAN (25:2-13)

At this point in the narrative we are introduced to Nabal.[9] His influence was of a different sort. He was wealthy and the Biblical historian placed an account of his possessions ahead of a description of him. His three thousand sheep and one thousand goats must have required a considerable grazing range, so it is likely that Nabal's shepherds and goatherds were compelled to go far to the south in search of adequate pasture. The size of his flocks must also have given him a virtual monopoly in the area. Smaller farmers must have had a difficult time contending for water and range rights in this barren and desolate southland.

Nabal is described as "harsh and evil in his dealings" with others (1 Samuel 25:3). This description leads us to believe that he was cruel and unscrupulous and abused the power created by his wealth. His wife's name was Abigail[10] and she is portrayed as being as wise and gracious as her husband was coarse and insensitive. She may have been much younger than Nabal. Since marriages in their culture were arranged by one's parents (or if they were dead, by the oldest brother) Abigail may have been given to Nabal because he demanded her as his wife, or in payment of a debt, or to secure some favor for the family.

At the annual shearing of the sheep Nabal hired shearers. They were drifters whose rough uncouth ways had become notorious.[11] They were also clannish (much like some unions today) and this solidarity gave them considerable influence. Notwithstanding these elements, Dr. Alfred Edersheim pointed out:

> The shearing season was one of those occasions being proverbially given to open-hearted hospitality, and David, who had protected Nabal's shepherds and flocks in the wilderness, sent ten of his young men to salute Nabal, and say to him: "Peace be to you, and peace to your house, and peace to all that you have.... Wherefore let the young men find favor in your eyes...[and] give, I pray you, whatsoever comes to your hand to your servants, and to your son David."
>
> Every part of this courteous address is in admirable keeping with Oriental etiquette, and perfect in all its detail in this very region to the present day.[12]

The ten-person delegation carried out David's instructions. The evidence of the text shows that David sought neither harm nor inconvenience to Nabal. His request was legitimate in light of the favors done by him and his men. Furthermore, his reference to himself as Nabal's "son" displayed his respect for a man who was from his own tribe and had attained a position of influence in the community (cf. 2 Kings 8:9; 16:7).

In contrast to the studied courtesy and modesty of David's request, Nabal's reply was arrogant and uncouth. He refused to acknowledge any benefit from David. Instead, with words calculated to add insult to injury, Nabal heaped scorn on the one who had done him such notable service. Nabal stated that he had never heard of David and yet tacitly indicated he knew that David was the son of Jesse and that he had to flee from the service of Saul (1 Samuel 25:10-11).

David's young men had no option but to return empty-handed. So infuriated was David by Nabal's hostile reply and vaunted independence that he determined to teach Nabal a lesson in humility by exterminating every male in his household.[13] David's attitude now was in marked contrast to what it had been when he spared Saul's life. Then he had been controlled by spiritual principles; now he was intent on personal revenge. In all probability (and quite unconsciously) his grief over the death of his dear friend and confidant, compounded by the depression resulting from his loss and the fear that Saul might again seek his life, caused him to react in an uncharacteristic manner. Arming four hundred of his men, David set out for Carmel.

INTERVENTION OF A GRACIOUS WOMAN (25:14-31)

God understood David's feelings and intervened to keep him from committing a presumptuous sin (cf. Psalm 19:13).

A servant who had overheard Nabal's coarse and offensive refusal and naturally dreaded the consequences hurried to Maon where Abigail was staying and informed her of what had transpired. His words to her give us some indication of Nabal's loss of respect from his staff. Maon was only half an hour's walk from Carmel, but David and his troop were evidently living south of Maon. Therefore it took his men longer to return to him than it took Nabal's servant to reach Abigail.

Abigail quickly devised a plan and her servants responded with alacrity to carry out her instructions. Sending on ahead of her a munificent gift of food (cf. 1 Samuel 25:18 with what Barzillai brought to King David when he fled from Jerusalem, 2 Samuel 17:27-29) she hastily followed. It appears, however, that she took a different route

to intercept David, for she met him before the heavily laden donkeys
bearing her gifts arrived. Neither David nor Abigail was aware the
other was approaching until they rounded the covert of a hill. Then
suddenly they were face-to-face (1 Samuel 25:20-23).

With the humblest Near Eastern courtesy, Abigail dismounted from
her donkey and prostrated herself before David. Then with words of
great modesty and sincerity she took upon herself the guilt of Nabal's
actions (25:24,28). Then she went on to imply that one such as Nabal
was not a fit object for David's vengeance. To insist on retribution
would require that David descend to her husband's level. She stated
that Nabal had perpetually conducted himself as one devoid of sense
and his insults were not worthy of David's attention.[14]

But Abigail had far weightier arguments to convince David to ignore Nabal's picayune spirit. She entreated David on the basis of
their common faith in *Yahweh,* the covenant-keeping God of Israel,
to live up to the high and holy purpose for which he had been
called (25:26-31). She believed with unshakable confidence that
David would be Israel's next king. It was for this reason (Abigail
used the past tense as if the matter had already been settled) that
the Lord (not her) had restrained him from avenging himself by
his own hand.

Abigail added, "Now then, let the enemies and those who seek evil
against my lord [David] be as Nabal" (25:26). This statement has given
critics of the Bible an opportunity to postulate either the work of a
later editor who added in these words as if spoken by Abigail after
Nabal had died, or who included the information from a different
manuscript. In the latter case, the information is believed to have
been incorporated into the text in a clumsy fashion. Either of these
views tacitly denies the doctrine of inspiration, and in reality neither
explanation is needed. Abigail had just gotten through describing
Nabal as a fool—one devoid of understanding and fatally wayward—
and she expressed her wish that all of David's enemies be as inept
and ineffective as her husband.

Having said that she desired all of David's enemies to be as Nabal
in their inability to harm him, Abigail next urged David to let *Yahweh*
Himself avenge His servant of the wrongs done to him. Then returning to her prayer for forgiveness, she pointed to the bright future
that awaited David, particularly as he would not be haunted by the
memory of any private vendettas. Abigail was reminding David that
when God fulfilled all of His gracious promises to make him king, his
forbearance in not avenging himself on Nabal would become a source
of blessing to him (25:31). Finally, and perhaps thinking of King Saul,
she said: "And though a man is risen to pursue you and seek your

soul, nonetheless the soul of my lord [David] is bound up in the bundle of life with Yahweh your God; and the soul of your enemies He will sling out from the hollow of [His] sling" (25:29).

Then, realizing that the lesser is blessed by the greater, Abigail asked David to remember her when he is king (25:31).[15] Her words again placed her in a subordinate role. They remind us of Joseph's request of the king's cupbearer when they were in the central dungeon of the prison in Egypt (Genesis 40:14).

Dr. Alfred Edersheim summarized Abigail's intercession for her worthless husband.

> Three things in [her] speech chiefly impress themselves on our minds…. The fact that David was God's anointed, on whom the kingdom would devolve, seems to have been the conviction of all who were godly in Israel…. Equally strong was their belief that David's present [duty], as [well as] his future mission, was simply to contend for God and for His people. But most important of all was the deep feeling prevalent, that David must not try to right himself, nor work his own deliverance. This was a thoroughly spiritual principle, which had its foundation in absolute, almost childlike trust in Jehovah the living God.[16]

Like Jonathan, who had on an earlier occasion turned his friend's eyes away from his predicament and fixed them on the Lord, Abigail strengthened David's hand in the sure mercies of God. Her faith was similar to his. They were in a very real sense kindred spirits (cf. Philippians 2:20).

RESPONSE OF A GODLY MAN (25:32-35)

The disaster that seemed to be inevitable was averted. David was kept from sullying his reputation by not responding with violence to the provocation of a fool (Proverbs 26:4). Nabal had returned evil for good, but David was now content to leave the matter of restitution in God's hands.

In contrast to Abigail's entreaty, which was unusually long, David's response was short and to the point. He began with an exclamation in which he acknowledged how the Lord had used her to turn him from an evil course. "Blessed be Yahweh," he said (1 Samuel 25:32). Then he went on to praise both the Lord and Abigail for their goodness to him. He saw Abigail's actions as part of a much broader plan whereby God had sovereignly intervened in his life to keep him from evil. He had failed to seek the Lord's will before setting out for Carmel and now he realized his error. He expressed his thanks to Abigail who, discerning what he was about to do, had courage enough to restrain him (25:32-33). With these words of blessing, David received the food from Abigail and sent her back to her home in peace (25:35).

JUDGMENT OF A RIGHTEOUS GOD (25:36-38)

God does not always intervene swiftly to right the wrongs done to His servants. In this instance He did.

When Abigail returned to Maon, Nabal was there. A lavish banquet was in progress and Nabal was already very drunk. The honored guests were presumably the migrant shearers (1 Samuel 25:11) whom Nabal had employed and with whom he seemed to have a great deal in common. Their coarse stories and vulgar anecdotes kept everyone laughing. If people are to be judged by the company they keep, it is significant that Nabal had established rapport with the least desirable members of Hebrew society.

Abigail was wise enough not to interrupt her husband while he was in a state of intoxication or do anything that might cause him to lose face in front of his guests. She waited until morning to tell him what she had done (cf. 25:19 and 25:37). Whether it was the effect of years of overindulgence or a sudden rush of fear that brought on a paralyzing stroke, we do not know. The Biblical historian merely recorded, "And [Nabal's] heart died within him so that he became [as] stone" (25:37).He lingered for ten days during which time God gave him the opportunity to think on eternal realities. At the end of that period he died. His death was attributed to an act of divine judgment (cf. Psalm 37).

SECURITY FOR A DEVOUT WOMAN (25:39-42)

At Nabal's death his estate (according to the Mosaic law) would devolve upon his sons. If he had no sons, his estate would go to his brothers. If none of his brothers survived him, his estate would go to his next of kin. A woman was entirely dependent on her children for support after her husband died (Numbers 27:9-11).

Abigail was childless. Her future was bleak. The only options open to her were to return to her family (if any of them were still living and could afford to take her in) or become a Levirate wife of one of Nabal's brothers. In the latter case, their first child would inherit Nabal's property. It is most unlikely that a brother, having recently inherited Nabal's fortune, would be willing to give it away to his firstborn by Abigail. It would be much easier to allow her to stay on in the house during the period of mourning and then let her go wherever she wished.

From Abigail's point of view neither of these options was really viable. She was alone with her uncertainties.[17] Her position was similar to that of Ruth the Moabitess. When Ruth as a young widow accompanied her mother-in-law to Judah and Boaz saw her gathering grain in one of his fields, his question to his supervisor was, "Whose young woman is this?" For a woman to *belong* to someone and benefit from his care and be safeguarded from harm was part of their culture. Like Ruth, Abigail now belonged to no one. Apparently her parents had died and she did not have a home to which she could return.

When David heard of Nabal's death, he realized that the Lord had intervened on his behalf. He also sensed that Abigail was a person whose beliefs, values, and goals answered to his own, so he sent her a proposal of marriage (1 Samuel 25:39-40).

In her reception of David's messengers, Abigail's courtesy and meekness were once again evident. Treating the men with the greatest respect she bowed in acquiescence and said, "Behold, your maidservant is a maid to wash the feet of my lord's servants" (25:41). While such words of deference might be out of place today, they revealed a healthy attitude. Abigail did not betray feelings of insecurity by demanding respect from others. Rather she showed the strength of her character by willingly offering herself to David (cf. 1 Peter 3:1-6).

Taking only five maids to wait on her, she followed David's men to the place where he was waiting for her "and [she] became his wife" (1 Samuel 25:42). There was no ritual; no exchanging of vows; no elaborate ceremony. We are surprised for we are accustomed to a far more detailed commitment before a couple can call themselves husband and wife. Dr. Ralph W. Klein assures us, however, that the marriage of David and Abigail was perfectly legal.[18] They both recognized that they were entering into a relationship that would last for the rest of their lives. David took her as his wife, and Abigail accepted him as her husband. It was as simple as that.

David assured Nabal's widow of protection and security, and Abigail was happy to become the wife of the one whom she regarded as the servant of Yahweh. They enjoyed each other's companionship and found in each other reflections of their own spiritual commitments. In the course of time Abigail bore David a son Chileab (2 Samuel 3:3; also called Daniel in 1 Chronicles 3:1). *Chileab* meant "whom [God] has perfected." Whether other children were born to their union we do not know.

POSTSCRIPT (25:43-44)

The conclusion to 1 Samuel 25 indicates that David was gaining in influence and importance even though he was still forced to live as an outlaw. The acquisition of wives points to his gradual rise in affluence and status. Saul may have sought to weaken David's claim to the throne by giving Michal in marriage to Palti (called Paltiel in 2 Samuel 3:15), but Saul could not prevent David's rise to fame.

Certain modern writers see in David's marriages the means whereby he was seeking to strengthen his relationship with different tribes so that at a convenient time they would support his appointment as their king.[19] Such a view is not only distasteful; it also demeans David's marriage to Abigail and is the outgrowth of a humanistic spirit that completely ignores God's hand in David's affairs. David, whose heart was moved by the good and noble qualities he found in Jonathan, also felt drawn to Abigail for the same reasons. She was the feminine counterpart of David; with her intelligent godly wisdom she was someone who mirrored his own quest for spiritual growth.

THIS THING CALLED INFLUENCE

As we summarize the thoughts of this chapter of commentary, it is important for us to note the different ways in which people or circumstances influence our lives. In our review we remember:

- The influence of Samuel on the nation. When the old prophet died, the people sensed the loss of his godly presence.

- The influence of Samuel's death on David. At the prophet's death an element of righteous restraint was removed and David feared Saul's renewed pursuit of him.

- The influence of Nabal on those about him. He was unscrupulous and overbearing. Not even his servants could speak well of him.

- The influence of Abigail on David. Her wise counsel and winsome attitude turned him from his plans for revenge.

People who exert an influence on others for good or ill generally possess *stature, position,* and the power to confer some *benefit.*

General Principles

People who possess *stature* have acquired status, authority, and significance. They receive the recognition of others. That which keeps their influence from becoming evil is their integrity. If integrity is lacking, all sorts of demagoguery is possible.

People who influence others have often attained a *position* that confers on them the respect of their peers. They have incorporated the principles of truth and justice into their lives and in time have become known for their sagacity. In the military, position is signified by one's rank; in business and industry by one's title; in academia by one's degrees; in research by one's knowledge and skills. That which prevents people from misusing their position is their commitment to honesty coupled with practical wisdom.

People who have power to confer some *benefit* need compassion if they are to exert a positive influence on others. Compassion is what prevents the abuse of such power. A compassionate person has an understanding of human nature coupled with the ability to empathize with others in their struggles; he is regulated by his commitment to the truth and his wisdom (or discernment) in dealing with different situations.

Specific Issues

From the "wisdom literature" of the Bible (the books of Job through Ecclesiastes) we realize that "the fear of the Lord is the beginning of wisdom" (Proverbs 9:10; 1:7). It is from our godward relationship— our standing in reverential awe of Him—that we gain integrity. The basic disposition of those who have integrity finds its outworking in doing justice, loving kindness, and walking humbly with God (Micah 6:8; cf. 3:8. Contrast Micah 2:1-2; 3:1-4,9-12). Those who exert a negative influence do so because they have status, position, and the power to confer some benefit on those whom they choose to favor, but their lives are not regulated by the truth. As a result people like King Saul or Nabal are frequently overbearing in their treatment of others.

When Saul was confronted with David's integrity and compassion in sparing his life, his power to act dissipated as readily as water disappears when poured on desert sand. When Nabal learned how Abigail's wise intervention had saved his life, he suffered from a stroke and was powerless to answer her. Integrity causes a person to think clearly (cf. Matthew 6:22) and act positively. Such an individual can maintain a balanced perspective, make decisions, and be appropriately proactive. Abigail's integrity enabled her to make the decision to send a gift of food to David and his men; to exercise restraint, not confronting her husband while he was entertaining the shearers; and to be open in disclosing her actions the next morning.

Her spirit also prevailed over David for, as Dr. F. B. Meyer pointed out, hers was "a cool hand upon a hot head."[20] She persuaded David to exercise forgiveness out of compassion instead of avenging himself for the insults heaped on him. Confirmation of Abigail's influence on David is found in 1 Samuel 25:32-33. His perspective was restored. He saw God's hand in her actions. His first words were ones of praise to the Lord and then he went on to praise her for her discernment (that is, practical wisdom). All thought of performing an unrighteous vow was dismissed from his mind (25:21-22). He gladly received her gift of food, thus recognizing her as his benefactor. Those believers who daily put into practice the teaching of God's Word gain in influence even when they, like Abigail, are not placed in positions of authority.

Just as Samuel faced the opposition (that is, negative influence) of those in positions of power in his day and David faced persecution from Saul and the insults of Nabal, we face injustice, prejudice, discrimination, and even oppression. It may help us to retain a positive outlook if we take one last look at what constitutes negative influence. Those who exert a negative influence often manifest the characteristics found so prominently in Saul and Nabal. Such people reveal their *pride, arrogance,* and *impoverished personalities* by the things they say and do. They are self-centered and very likely were denied adequate love and affirmation during their formative years. As they progressed through adulthood they were subject to feelings of fear and guilt and became highly defensive whenever their failings were drawn to their attention. The result is a lack of the ability to be open, tolerant, compassionate, and loving; and this lack impairs their interpersonal relationships.

In contrast to the impoverished personality, the enriched personality is able to cope socially and give freely to others. David Livingstone was one such individual. Henry Stanley, who went in search of Dr. Livingstone and eventually found him, was profoundly influenced by the medical missionary's quiet unassuming ways. Stanley later wrote:

> For four months and four days I lived with him in the same hut, or the same boat, or the same tent, and I never found a fault in him. I went to Africa as prejudiced against religion as the worst infidel in London. To a reporter like myself, who had only to deal with wars, mass meetings, and political gatherings,

sentimental matters were quite out of my province. But there came to me a long time for reflection. I was out there away from a worldly world. I saw this solitary man there, and I asked myself, "Why does he stop here? What is it that inspires him?" For months after we met I found myself listening to him, wondering at the old man carrying out the words [of Christ], "leave all and follow me." But little by little, seeing his piety, his gentleness, his zeal, his earnestness, and how he went quietly about his business, I was converted by him, although he had not tried to do it.[21]

David Livingstone lived for a little more than a year after Stanley left him. One morning his African servants found him (as someone may have found Samuel) kneeling beside his bed. He was dead. Their love for him was so great and their sense of loss at his death so profound that before delivering his body and papers to his former associates on the East African coast, they buried his heart under a Mpundu tree. They did not want the influence of his godly life to be forgotten, for in his enriched personality they found one whom they loved and respected and whose example lifted them out of their paganism to a life lived according to the spirit of Christ.

PROBLEMS AND OPPORTUNITIES

1 Samuel 26:1–27:12

Monday morning quarterbacking is a well-established part of American life. We all know with perfect hindsight what play should have been called, who was open and could have received the ball, and how a different decision on the part of the referee would have affected the outcome of a game.

The same is true when we study the historical portions of God's Word. We know who the main characters were and how the story progressed and ended. Consequently we are inclined to judge the participants from our viewpoint. We would give David the "most valuable player" award for his conduct in 1 Samuel 24 and 26, but only our unbridled criticism for a dismal performance in 1 Samuel 27.

We need to remember that pressures, whether on a playing field or in real life, come from without as well as from within. Continuing the football analogy, we may fear the strength of the opposing team—their formidable offense and powerful defense. Then we have to contend with the expectations of our coach, family, and friends—all of whom are watching the game. These are external pressures. Internally there may be areas of weakness brought on by stress, injury, and poor morale. All these pressures have a bearing on our concentration and how well we play the game.

In pondering David's situation in 1 Samuel 26–27 I was reminded of the pressures on General Douglas MacArthur in World War II. Following the bombing of Pearl Harbor on December 7, 1941, the Japanese proceeded to take command of the Pacific. Their well-laid plans—that had been a full year in the making—enabled them to move with lightning speed so that one island after another fell before their methodical advance.

The American agenda had called for the navy to keep open the sea lanes so that supplies could be sent to United States ground forces in the East. These ground forces were to hold their positions for between four to six months. The Pacific fleet would then move in with a massive invasion force...and the war would soon be over. "Home for Christmas" was a slogan all believed in.

With the destruction of the fleet at Pearl Harbor, however, supply lines were cut and the way was opened for the Japanese to invade the Philippines. Within two weeks after the bombing of Pearl Harbor they launched their attack. Their strategy was to confuse General MacArthur by launching two almost simultaneous assaults from different sides. It was a brilliant move designed to catch the American, Australian, and Filipino forces in a pincers movement and force them to defend Manila on the central plain. In such an exposed position the entire Allied army could then be destroyed within a few days.

The army under General MacArthur was hopelessly outnumbered. They had inadequate medical supplies, minimal air power, poor equipment and transportation, and were running low on ammunition. To add to the difficulties the Japanese (strictly in accordance with their preset plans) herded tens of thousands of fleeing Filipinos toward the Allied lines. The Japanese knew that the Americans would feed the Filipinos, thus drastically reducing their own food supplies.

As soon as General MacArthur saw what the Japanese planned to do, he developed a strategy of his own. While delaying the advance of the imperial army on his flanks, he performed a series of lateral movements toward the Bataan peninsula. His plan was to hold Bataan until the relief promised by President Roosevelt arrived.[1] If it became evident that he would have to withdraw from Bataan, then he could retreat to the Marivales mountains. And as a last resort there was Corregidor.

The promised aid never arrived and historians have subsequently learned that all the president intended to do was keep up the morale of the men for as long as possible. When it became evident that help would not be forthcoming, MacArthur had to contend with a drop in the esprit de corps of his men.[2] Their courage and perseverance are now well known, as are the decisions made by our leaders. Those were difficult times and we who were not vitally involved find it hard to understand some of the issues facing our commander-in-chief.

General MacArthur's situation, however, helps us understand some of the pressures David faced. Saul's suddenly renewed pursuit constituted an external threat that had to be taken seriously. David handled this external pressure quickly and efficiently. Of a vastly different nature was the internal pressure he had to bear: he was ultimately responsible for the support of his men and their families. He faced a dilemma for which there was no easy answer. Looming large on the horizon was the fact that Saul now knew of all his hideouts. Israel was only about 150 miles long and an average of about 45 miles wide, and because of the general loyalty of the northern tribes to Saul, David (who was from the south) had to confine himself to an even more restricted area. He felt himself to be in a very vulnerable position.

STRUCTURE AND OUTLINE OF THE PASSAGE

The contents of 1 Samuel 26–27 revolve around two focuses: Saul's pursuit of David and David's flight to Philistia. We notice again the repetitious use of the Hebrew *waw*, "then," signifying the major divisions in 26:1,6,13,17,21; 27:1,5. (*Waw* can also be translated "now" or "and" at the discretion of the translator.) Minor divisions in the narrative occur at 26:8,25; 27:8.

Continued Persecution

In the continuing saga of Saul and David, the king again sought David's life. On this occasion, however, David did not flee from Saul as before. Several possible reasons for David's change in tactics suggest themselves: (1) Most probably the needs of the women and children now compelled David to adopt a different approach to Saul's harassment. Their slower pace might result in the entire force being overtaken by Saul's soldiers. (2) After being a homeless fugitive for about eight and a half years, David had more than likely grown weary of running from Saul. He was tired of constantly looking over his shoulder and wondering who among the people he had helped would be the next to betray him. (3) David sensed that with his growing strength he could defend himself if such a decision was forced upon him. Whatever the reason, he decided on one last confrontation.

Changed Attitude

Adversity had molded and changed David. He still had a shepherd's heart, but he was now tougher when it came to making hard decisions. He was also wiser and more experienced than before. The outline reflects these changes.

- Renewed Opposition and a Change in Tactics (1 Samuel 26)
- Political Refuge and a Change in Strategy (1 Samuel 27)

Comparing 1 Samuel 26 and 24[3] we are reminded of the fact that previously when David spared Saul's life, Samuel was alive. In a very real sense David had been accountable to the prophet. Now Samuel was dead. David had a second opportunity to kill Saul and had to decide whether to spare his life. We need to keep in mind the subtlety of this and other tests David faced.

Calculated Move

When Saul's malicious intentions were confirmed, David realized that he would have to seek refuge as a political exile in Philistia. We observe in the text that his decision was not sudden; he had counted the cost, as his words to Saul indicated (1 Samuel 26:19-20). David was acutely conscious of the slander and betrayal of those who had no cause to malign him to the king (cf. Psalm 7; 109). David also knew that in leaving the land he would be separating himself for a time from the places of worship that were so dear to his heart. But he hoped that once he was in Philistia, Saul would give up his pursuit (1 Samuel 27:1,4).

1 Samuel 26 and 27, so different in content and yet so intimately related to one another, possess a cause-and-effect relationship. They demonstrate David's leadership ability as he changed his tactics and adopted a different strategy when in a strange land.

RENEWED OPPOSITION AND A CHANGE IN TACTICS (26:1-25)

A Further Act of Betrayal (26:1-12)

Once again it was the people of Ziph who sent a message to King Saul to advise him of David's presence in their area. Whereas on the earlier occasion they may have wanted to show their gratitude to Saul for waging a successful war against the Amalekites, now they were probably motivated by fear of David's growing strength.

Suspicious minds often sow the seeds of mistrust, and Saul's soul was fertile soil in which such seeds could grow.[4] The Ziphites' message, "Is not David hiding in the hill of Hachilah on the edge of Jeshimon?" (1 Samuel 26:1) was sufficient to arouse Saul's old animosity. We may be sure that Cush, a member of Saul's court (Psalm 7 inscription), used the information to further his own plans for David's speedy demise. The negative in "is not David hiding" was a Hebraic idiom for stating something certain. Without delay Saul took his personal guard of three thousand picked men and marched southward to the wilderness of Ziph.

While David had not placed his confidence in Saul's show of repentance following the events at Engedi (even though the king had
taken an oath not to harm him), he must have hoped that now at last
he would be able to enjoy some respite from the relentless harassment of the past several years. However, the news of David's marriage to Abigail possibly strengthened Saul's belief that David was
working to turn the people of Judah against him, and his fears were
rekindled. Even though Samuel was dead, it was as if Saul could still
hear the old prophet saying, "Yahweh has torn the kingdom from
you and given it to your neighbor who is better than you" (1 Samuel
15:28).

Within a day's forced march, or two at the most, Saul and his men
reached the hill of Hachilah. They were very tired but believed that
the element of surprise was on their side. They planned to begin
their search for the fugitive the next day at first light.

In God's sovereign protection of His anointed, He caused one of
David's men to see some dust rising in the distance to the north. It
was too large a cloud to be dismissed lightly. The news was reported
to David and he sent spies to determine the cause.[5] When he was
told that Saul had indeed come to search for him, he and Ahimelech
and Abishai circled around behind the hill of Hachilah and climbing
to its summit took note of the layout of Saul's camp. Then they waited
for darkness.

The moon was high in its orbit when David, leaving Ahimelech to
stand guard and taking only Abishai with him, descended into the
valley below. A shimmering whiteness illumined the landscape. One
loose rock dislodged from its place would arouse the recumbent sentries and perhaps awaken others in the camp as well, so very cautiously the two men made their way to the camp and tiptoed around
the sleeping bodies that circled the place where the king himself had
bedded down for the night. Saul was nearly seventy years old and
the long hard march had left him exhausted.

As the two outlaws looked down on the form of their unsuspecting adversary, Abishai remembered the former occasion at Engedi
when David could have killed Saul. Abishai did not share David's
scruples and did not want David's beliefs to stand in the way of this
new opportunity. He whispered:

> Today God ['Ĕlōhîm, not Yahweh] [has given] your enemy into
> your hand; and now let me strike him, I beg you, with the [the
> Hebrew contains the article and may refer to Saul's own] spear
> even to the earth [at] one time [with a single blow] and I will
> not [have to] repeat it a second time (1 Samuel 26:8).

David restrained his impetuous nephew. David knew that he would be guilty even if another performed the act (26:9).[6] Instead of consenting, he expressed his belief that one day Saul would be summoned to meet his Maker. When and under what circumstances this would happen, David did not know. He was sure, however, that Saul would be punished and removed from office (cf. Psalm 109:6-9) and that the Lord would perform all that He had promised (Psalm 109:21-29).

Then taking Saul's spear and waterskin, the two men silently left the camp and rejoined Ahimelech on the top of the hill. The Biblical writer, wishing to underscore God's dealings with His people, stated that David and Abishai were able to accomplish their mission because a deep sleep[7] from the Lord had fallen on Saul and his men. Even the body's need for rest after exertion is seen to be under God's direct control.

A Rude Awakening (26:13-16)

David, Ahimelech, and Abishai placed a suitable distance between themselves and Saul's force before David deemed it safe to rouse his enemies. Then he called out loudly to Abner, Saul's second-in-command. David's voice carried clearly in the still night air: "Do you not answer, Abner?"

There is scarcely anything more unnerving than suddenly waking from a sound sleep to be questioned about something of which one is entirely ignorant. Abner's dilemma was heightened because Saul also awakened and wanted to know what was going on. With little elegance and less grace Abner responded, "Who [are] you [who] is calling to the king?"

David was enjoying the mental and emotional discomfort of Abner and the men, most of whom at one time or another may have been his friends. Without answering Abner's question, David returned to his former accusation and he challenged Abner by saying:

> Are you not a man [can't you take responsibility]? And who [is] like you in Israel [brave, resourceful, and entrusted with the life of the king]? But why have you not guarded over your lord the king? [You are derelict in your duty.] For one of the people came to destroy the king, your lord. This [negligence of yours] is not good. [As] Yahweh lives, you [are] all sons of death [you all deserve to die] in that you have not guarded over your lord, over the anointed of Yahweh; and now [do

you want proof of what I am saying?] see where the king's spear [is] and the skin of water which [was] at his head (1 Samuel 26:15-16).

A Superficial Show of Repentance (26:17-25)

Before Abner could think of an answer, Saul replied. He recognized David's voice. And David, aware now that the king was listening, earnestly pleaded his cause. He showed the folly of constant persecution of him, for his loyalty was evident by his actions. If he were disloyal, he would have killed the king in his sleep.

David went on to reason with Saul. There were only two possible causes for the king's actions: (1) the Lord had stirred him up against David, in which case Saul should let him know so that he could offer an appropriate sacrifice and be restored to favor with God and the king; or (2) the slanderous and malevolent words of evil and unprincipled men had inflamed the heart of the king against him. If the latter was true, God would punish them for their calumnies, for their actions had brought David to the point where he knew that there was no longer a safe refuge for him in the land of Canaan. Then with great eloquence David pleaded that he not be compelled to go into exile far from the places where God was worshiped.

In brief broken sentences Saul expressed his remorse for his inglorious conduct. But he was no longer moved to tears as he was at Engedi. His heart was even harder now than it had been then and his cry, "I have sinned; return, my son David, for I shall not do evil to you any more because my soul was precious in your eyes today," lacked the full weight of conviction.

As a token of his good faith David returned to Saul his spear (and probably the skin of water as well) and concluded his confrontation of the king by declaring his unalterable belief in God as the One who judges uprightly and rewards the righteous. Saul, touched by the sincerity of his son-in-law, stated that he was sure David would do mightily and surely prevail.

Then the two men parted, never again to meet in this life. The king, pursuing a course that continued to harden his heart, returned to Gibeah. David, the maligned and misused servant of the Lord, rejoined his men.[8]

Saul's repentance was short-lived. We do not know in what manner he continued to seek for David, but the inspired historian told us that he only abandoned his search when he was told that David had become a vassal of the Philistines (1 Samuel 27:4).

POLITICAL REFUGE AND A CHANGE IN STRATEGY (27:1-12)

Encouraged by a Favorable Reception (27:1-4)

David has been severely criticized for going to Gath. Most Bible commentators concur with the opinion expressed by the great Scottish preacher Dr. William Blaikie:

> We are not prepared for the sad decline in the spirit of trust which is recorded in the beginning of the twenty-seventh chapter. The victory gained by David over the carnal spirit of revenge, shown so signally in his sparing of the life of Saul a second time, would have led us to expect that he would never again fall under the influence of carnal fear. But there are strange ebbs and flows in the spiritual life, and sometimes victory brings its dangers, as well as its glory. Perhaps this very conquest excited in David the spirit of self-confidence; he may have had less sense of his need of daily strength from above; and he may have fallen into the state of mind against which the Apostle warns us, "Let him that thinketh he standeth take heed lest he fall."
>
> In his collision with Nabal we saw him fail in what seemed one of his strong points—the very spirit of self-control which he had exercised so remarkably toward Saul; and now we see him fail in another of his strong points—the spirit of trust toward God. Could anything show more clearly that even the most eminent graces of the saints spring from no native fountain of goodness within them, but depend on the continuance of their vital fellowship with Him of whom the Psalmist said, "All my springs are in Thee" (Psalm lxxxvii. 7).[9]

In our consideration of David's actions we should not overlook the fact that Saul and his men had not only become familiar with all of David's hiding places; in all probability they had also stationed troops in various parts of the southland. Their presence hampered his movements and made continuation in the land impossible. We must understand as well the cunning and relentless opposition of Cush the Benjamite (cf. Psalm 7) as well as others who may have sought to arouse the king's suspicions against David.

William Deane offered a second explanation for David's journey to Gath. Deane believed that it was becoming more and more difficult for David to restrain his men from making reprisals on the Ziphites and any others who were favorable to the crown. Being loyal to Saul and feeling his movements constricted (a form of external pressure), David knew of no other way to prevent his men from taking the law into their own hands and avenging themselves on those who had betrayed them (an internal form of pressure that had to be handled daily). The only option open to him was to remove his men from the source of their antagonism[10] and seek political asylum in either Moab or Philistia.

David chose Philistia so that he could continue to look after the interests of the people of Israel and protect their borders. Arriving in Gath, he and his men presented themselves at the court of the king where they were given a favorable reception (1 Samuel 27:2-3).

William Deane corrected some false assumptions that are current in the church. He wrote:

> What such a [decision to live in Philistia] cost [David] we can ill understand unless we put ourselves in his position, and see what this banishment involved. To a devout Hebrew the land of Canaan was the Lord's sanctuary; here only could He be duly served and acceptably worshipped. Where the Ark and Tabernacle rested there was the presence of Jehovah, and there were His covenant graces outpoured. Outside the limits of the promised land...there was no possibility of joining in public services so inexpressibly dear to the heart of a true Israelite. We learn how precious was this privilege considered from the Psalmist's words on another occasion (Psa. xlii):
>
> > As the hart panteth after the water brooks,
> > So panteth my soul after Thee, O God.
> > My soul thirsteth for God, for the living God;
> > When shall I come and appear before God?
> > My tears have been my meat day and night,
> > While they continually say to me, "Where is thy God?"
>
> It was an act of human prudence [and one which neither Gad the prophet nor Abiathar the priest appear to have protested], overruled indeed by Divine Providence, but fraught with grave dangers and temptations [for David's men might easily succumb to the temptations of heathen forms of worship].[11]

How David explained to Achish his recovery from his (supposed) former insanity is not told us. We do know that David and his followers lived in the royal city long enough to establish their credibility.

If Israel and Philistia had been at war, then David's actions would have been treasonous. The fact that the two countries were now in a period of uneasy peace made David's consorting with Israel's traditional enemies possible.

David and his followers spent only a short time in Gath. While there the "sweet singer of Israel" learned the music of the Gittite, for one of his later Psalms is "set to the Gittith" (Psalm 8). A Psalm by Asaph (Psalm 81) and one compiled by the sons of Korah (Psalm 84) follow the precedent set by David. "The Gittith" was either a unique style or cadence peculiar to the people of Gath or an instrument made only by craftsmen of that city.

David's friendship with the brave and loyal Ittai—one of the lesser known but significant personalities of the Bible (2 Samuel 15:18-22; 18:1-2)—may well have dated from this period. So once again we see how God sovereignly overruled the wrath of men (Saul, Cush, the Ziphites) and turned it to His praise.

Given Opportunity for Further Service (27:5-12)

David's entire following possibly numbered close to 2500 people. A group this size must have caused Achish a severe housing shortage in his already populous city. And then they all had to be fed.

During the time the Israelites were in Gath, Achish and David must each have sought to know how far the other could be trusted. When David sensed that he had gained the king's confidence, he made a suggestion to him. Phrasing his request with the utmost tact, David began by pointing to the obvious inconvenience he and his men were to the king and the people of Gath. David expressed his desire not to be a burden to his host or his people and then suggested that Achish assign him a city where he and his followers could live.

Achish acceded to David's request and gave Ziklag[12] to him (1 Samuel 27:5-6). Ziklag at that time may have been uninhabited. It was situated in a sparsely populated section of the Negev (that is, southland) and was an ideal residence for these exiles from Israel.

From Joshua 15:31; 19:5; 1 Chronicles 4:30 we learn that Ziklag had originally been given to the people of Judah as a part of their inheritance. Later it appears to have been transferred to the tribe of Simeon. Living in Ziklag, David and his followers were once again within the borders of the promised land.[13] And though a vassal of Achish, David was virtually able to act as a petty king.

Under his leadership the city became a center of military operations. It was also a refuge for the oppressed (1 Chronicles 12:1-22). A valuable contingent of archers and slingers who were completely ambidextrous came from Saul's own tribe. David had reservations about some who defected to him, so he inquired, "Do you come peaceably?" His fears were quickly laid to rest when they responded, "To you, David, and with you, son of Jesse, peace! Peace to you, and peace to your helper, for your God has helped you" (1 Chronicles 12:18). Others from the district of Manasseh and still others from beyond the Jordan river also joined David. Before long his troop of six hundred swelled to a great throng "like the army of God" (1 Chronicles 12:22).

Having appointed captains over his army, David infused into his men a spirit of discipline. Then he proceeded to protect his countrymen by checking the predatory raids of the Amalekites. The Geshurites and Gezrites had already taken up residence in portions of the territory assigned to the tribe of Judah. They were occupying land given by God to His covenant people and David led his forces against them and took their sheep, oxen, asses, and camels as the spoils of war. Because of the tenuous nature of his position as a vassal of Achish, David could not risk word of his actions getting back to Gath; consequently David and his men took no prisoners.

We should not overlook the fact that Israel was designed to be a warrior nation that would bring the heathen nations under the sway of the Lord of glory. Individuals from among these southern nations were not left without a choice. At any time prior to the engagement they could have embraced the worship of Yahweh and joined themselves to Israel. Many of David's men had made the choice, for there were numbered within his ranks several foreigners including Uriah the Hittite, Ittai the Gittite, and Ithmah the Moabite (2 Samuel 23:8-39; 1 Chronicles 11:26-47).[14]

As David's patron, Achish was entitled to some of the spoils of war, and these David dutifully paid. When David brought the spoils to Gath, Achish asked, "Where have you made your raids today?"[15] David responded, "Against the south of Judah, and against the south of the Jerahmeelites, and to the south of the Kenites" (1 Samuel 27:10). In this way he led Achish to believe that he had been attacking his own countrymen. Actually David had been operating in these areas, but in defense of his people. Achish, receiving no contrary report, believed David, even concluding that David and his successors would remain in his employ for the rest of their lives.

David and his men stayed in the land of the Philistines for only sixteen months. They were comforted by the knowledge that Ziklag was in reality a Hebrew city even though it was now under the control of the Philistines. In that city the outlaws established their families while also enjoying freedom from King Saul's unpredictable forays against David.

THE FACE OF EVIL

As we apply certain of the principles found in 1 Samuel 26–27 to our own experiences, we notice that David responded in a righteous manner to pressures from without and within. From without was Saul's unjust persecution; from within was his sense of responsibility for the safety and security of those who looked to him for protection and the provision of their temporal needs.

Some of David's actions, if judged by western standards of morality, appear questionable. But let us not forget that we have spent all of our lives in safety and have never known the heel of a tyrant. We have been spared the undeserved trials that were thrust upon David.

While we are commanded to walk in reverential awe of God, there may be times when the evil that men do pushes us into uncharacteristic roles. At such times, others may criticize us or impugn our motives. When we are criticized we can draw comfort from the experiences of David. He was at heart a righteous man (cf. Psalm 7:8; 18:20-24; see also 15:2-4; 35:27) and to the best of his ability he walked in his integrity. Instead of criticizing David, we should probe the origin of David's difficulties.

Deceit in High Places

After reading 1 Samuel 24 we are surprised to find Saul in search of David again. At Engedi there seemed to be a complete and harmonious reconciliation between the two men. Saul even acknowledged that David was the more righteous. Yet after a short time Saul was again hunting David as one would stalk a partridge on a hillside.[16]

At Saul's court Cush had apparently gained the confidence of the king. In much the same way that Iago in Shakespeare's *Othello*[17] sowed the seeds of discord between Othello and Casio, Cush stirred up Saul's anger toward David (cf. Psalm 35:15). Dr. Alexander Maclaren was emphatic in assigning Psalm 7 to this period of David's life.[18] Dr. Maclaren was probably right (though we should not overlook the fact that Cush had probably been maligning David to the king for many years) and his view helps us understand the rapid vacillations in Saul's behavior (cf. Proverbs 13:2-3).

When Saul was away from Cush, it was easy for him to come under the good and godly influence of David (1 Samuel 24:16; 26:17,21). But after Saul returned to Gibeah, little by little Cush influenced him again until the king became convinced that David was plotting insurrection and the nation would soon be plunged into a civil war.

Graft among the People

Let us not forget the treachery of the men of Ziph. Not once, but twice they offered to betray David's whereabouts to the king. Their calumny and persistent slander must not be allowed to pass unnoticed.

David (possibly repeating what he had heard others say) asked King Saul if it was indeed true that men had stirred up his wrath by saying, "David seeks your life." If the report was true, David reasoned, the Ziphites deserved punishment from the Lord because they had accused him falsely. Saul had not punished them in accordance with the law (Deuteronomy 19:15-19; Leviticus 19:16; Psalm 101:5); had he done so, David would not now be forced to seek refuge outside the promised land.

The Sins We Tolerate

Slander, gossip, malicious innuendoes, defamation of character, and unjust criticism are rife in our lives, in our communities, and in our churches.[19] The *Wall Street Journal* once devoted an entire page in bold type to expose the harm caused by the tongue. The article read:

> It topples governments, wrecks marriages, ruins careers, busts reputations, causes heartaches, nightmares, indigestion, spawns suspicion, generates grief, dispatches innocent people to cry in their pillows. Even its name hisses. It's called gossip. Office gossip. Shop gossip. Party gossip. It makes headlines and headaches. Before you repeat a story, ask yourself: Is it true? Is it fair? Is it necessary? If not, shut up.[20]

More people go to their pastors for help as a result of hurtful criticisms by others than for any other reason. Because few of these injustices are rectified, the sufferers become disillusioned. In time they may leave their own churches and try to find other assemblies in which these vices are not so prominent. Ultimately many of the victims stop attending places of worship altogether.

Unexpected confirmation of this phenomenon came from a Gallup Poll. The pollsters found that 60 percent of those who call themselves Christians and claim to have had a "born again experience" do not attend church. Various reasons were given, but most non-attendees reported an inability to relate meaningfully to other Christians and a feeling of rejection after being around those who profess to love the Lord (cf. Galatians 5:15; James 1:26; 3:6,10).

In time, estrangement takes its toll on one's human resources, and depression and loneliness then take the joy out of living. Some estranged people seek the services of a Christian psychologist or counselor because they feel they are alone, unable to cope with the pressures of life, and on the verge of despair. When the counselor questions them about their support groups or friends who can give them the emotional stability they need, many of these lonely people confess to not having been to church in years.

While the sins of the tongue inflict greater harm on the body of Christ than any other transgressions (cf. Psalm 15:1-4; 34:12-14; Proverbs 11:9; 16:28; 18:8,21) the majority of preachers are inclined to play it safe; not wanting to offend their congregations, they do not denounce the sins of the tongue. As a consequence the innocent suffer and the guilty go unpunished.

David was compelled to leave his homeland because of the slander of Cush and the unscrupulous conduct of the people of Ziph. They did not fear God or consider that on the day of judgment the Lord will require of each of them an account of every careless word spoken (Matthew 12:36-37).

Scripture is replete with admonitions about the wholesome use of the tongue. Accordingly, David's defense of his conduct before Saul was discreet as well as appropriately assertive. David's son Solomon would one day write:

> The words of a wise man's mouth are gracious (Ecclesiastes 10:12).
> A wholesome tongue is a tree of life (Proverbs 15:4).
> The lips of the wise disperse knowledge (Proverbs 15:7).
> He who keeps his mouth and his tongue keeps his soul from trouble (Proverbs 21:23).

These Scriptural admonitions about controlling our tongues remind me of a story told by the late V. Raymond Edman, for many years the president of Wheaton College in Illinois.[21] After returning from the missionfield he spent some time with friends in Simi Valley, California. They were pruning their orchards and he volunteered to help. The brush was placed in small piles and burned. Just before lunch Dr. Edman lit a pile of brush and then went to get cleaned up for the noon meal.

Mrs. Harrington, his friend's wife, noticed some smoke down in the valley and asked what it might be. They investigated and found that the fire from the pile of brush had moved toward a eucalyptus grove and ignited the eucalyptus trees. Of course everyone dropped everything and worked long and hard to bring the fire under control. The incident reminded Dr. Edman of the words of James, our Lord's brother:

> The tongue is a little member and boasts great things. Behold how a little fire kindles [sets aflame] a great wood [forest]; and the tongue [is] a fire, the world of iniquity among the members of the body spotting [corrupting, defiling] the whole body and inflaming the course of nature and being inflamed [itself] by hell (James 3:5-6).

Let us remember that the Lord hates the sowing of seeds of discord among the brethren; we should pray with the psalmist that the Lord would set a watch before our mouths and keep the door of our lips so that we will not sin with our tongues (Psalm 141:3)!

DIFFERING ORDEALS

1 Samuel 28:1–29:11

As the Lord Jesus concluded His famous sermon delivered on a hill-side that overlooked the sea of Galilee, He told a story to those who had gathered to listen to His teaching. Actually the story was a par-able about life. He contrasted two men, the one wise and the other foolish. Each built a house. The wise man ensured that the home he and his loved ones would live in was erected on a solid foundation. The foolish man leveled some sand, laid wooden planks to which he attached uprights, and succeeded in completing his house in record time.

Christ then drew a parallel between the fate of these houses and the destinies of the two men. The building of their houses was lik-ened to the choices each man made throughout his life. In the course of time the houses were subjected to the fury of the elements. The man who had quarried rock to build a secure foundation found that what he had built could withstand the onslaught of wind and flood. When the other man faced the vicissitudes of life, he saw his house collapse around him. The key to this parable is to be found in the words of the Lord Jesus:

> Everyone, therefore, who *hears* these words of mine and *does* them shall be likened to the prudent man who built his house upon the rock.... But everyone who *hears* these words of mine and *does not do them* shall be likened to the foolish man who built his house on the sand (Matthew 7:24,26, emphasis added).

We are all responsible for the choices we make. God has revealed His desires and purposes for us in Scripture, and we can choose either to obey or disobey His will. Adversity tests our resolve and shows us what kind of people we are.

We can only speculate about the thoughts that crisscrossed the foolish man's mind as he was building his house and living in it. He knew of the strength of the siroccos that periodically blew in off the desert and he knew the danger of flash floods that might suddenly sweep down on his house as a result of heavy rains up in the hills. Yet he built his house with complete disregard for the adverse elements that might threaten his well-being and the safety of those whom he professed to love.

Perhaps in no other single passage of the Bible is the contrast between a wise man and a foolish one brought before us more clearly than in 1 Samuel 26:1–31:13. David and Saul are set opposite one another. Although David's life was not immune from difficulty, he was able to stand firm in spite of the changing winds of fortune. Saul likewise faced adversity, but in the end the whole structure of his life collapsed. Whatever rationalizations Saul had made over the years to limit his culpability or excuse his conduct were in vain. The day of reckoning came. His weaknesses were exposed.

HISTORICAL BACKGROUND AND OUTLINE OF
1 SAMUEL 28:1–29:11

A Matter of Interpretation

Many earnest believers are convinced that David erred when he went to Philistia. They condemn him for what he did and then state in simplistic terms what they feel he should have done. In effect they reduce God's guidance to a series of elementary principles and ignore the fact that life becomes more complex with the addition of different responsibilities. Their view also tends to detract from human accountability; they forget that a godly person who walks in his or her integrity can make certain decisions that might appear to others to be questionable but that are in reality within God's will for him or her (cf. 1 John 3:20-21).

It is true that David is not said to have inquired of the Lord about whether or not to go to Philistia. However he did not reach his decision without much introspection. External pressures apparently left him no other choice. Neither Gad (who may well have written this part of the record) nor Abiathar raised any objections (cf. 1 Samuel 22:5). It seems evident that they concurred with him in believing that Saul's harassment allowed for no other course of action.

In Philistia God blessed David. Ittai of Gath came to believe in Yahweh, and in time six hundred Gittites were also won to David's side by the qualities of character they saw in him (2 Samuel 15:18-22).

Even Achish may have come to a knowledge of the truth, for in 1 Samuel 29:6 he used the covenant name for God, *Yahweh,* when taking an oath. No pagan would ever take the name of another person's god upon his lips for fear of offending the deity he worshiped and relied on for prosperity. The names of Daniel and his three friends were changed (Daniel 1:7) because their Hebrew names honored Yahweh; their Babylonian names honored the gods of the Chaldeans. Even if Achish was not a true believer, his use of *Yahweh* showed at the very least both his knowledge of and respect for David's beliefs.

The months David spent in Philistia may be seen as God-given, for he had the opportunity to train the increasing number of men who gathered about him. It is apparent that the Lord was giving him the time he needed to raise the army that would soon be needed to defend Judah's borders from invasion (cf. 2 Samuel 5:17-25). The Lord knew by what means He would later uproot David from Ziklag. There was much for David and his followers to do, and the peace afforded them in Ziklag gave them the freedom to perfect their skills and develop the esprit de corps that is so necessary if an army is to be successful.

Some devout believers will still hold a contrary point of view, and their analysis of 1 Samuel 28–29 will naturally differ from what follows.

An Analysis of the Structure

The events around which the narrative revolves are as follows:

- An Act of Aggression (1 Samuel 28:1-2)
- An Important Digression (1 Samuel 28:3-25)
- An Unexpected Dismissal (1 Samuel 29:1-11)

The repetitious use of "Now" and "Then" indicates the divisions within the narrative.

AN ACT OF AGGRESSION (28:1-2)

The Setting (28:1a)

We are not told what precipitated the third Philistine war. We do know that the invasion from the west placed Saul in an unenviable position. The tribes to the east of the Jordan river had been alienated from him. Those to the south (except for the people of Ziph) had long since shown their disaffection for him. Much of their territory already lay in the hands of the enemy. And the king's heavy-handed policies and favoritism shown to a select few (1 Samuel 22:7) caused many from his own tribe of Benjamin, as well as some from the adjoining tribe of Manasseh, to desert Saul and join the ranks of David's growing army (1 Chronicles 12:1-22).

Whether Saul was aware of it or not, the Philistines had been developing a strong military force. Camps for the training of soldiers had been established throughout the coastal plain and in the low foothills of the Shephelah.[1] Now these contingents began to assemble at Shunem[2] (1 Samuel 28:1,4). It took time for the Philistines to advance northward along their own maritime plain and beyond it along the plain of Sharon. They assembled first at Aphek and then turned eastward to the great plain of the Esdraelon before proceeding to occupy the valley of Jezreel. The site that had been chosen definitely favored the Philistines. Saul was forced to encamp on the southern side and occupy the northern slope of mount Gilboa. And so the two armies faced each other across the valley.[3]

The Summons (28:1b-2)

These verses take us back in time to the events that preceded the gathering of the Philistines for battle. Achish, king of Gath, ruled over one of the most powerful cities of the Philistine pentapolis. His prestige in the eyes of the other kings (sometimes referred to as "lords") would be greatly enhanced by a large following. Therefore he said to David, "Surely you know that you shall go out with me [as a part of my] army, you and your men" (1 Samuel 28:1).

While David may have been surprised by Achish's words, he could not back out, for to do so would be to insult his benefactor. He was caught in a difficult situation and was left with no alternative but to reply ambiguously: "Therefore [by this, by my actions] you shall know what your servant will do" (28:2a).

Achish was moved by David's words and responded by honoring him with a significant promotion. He elevated him to one of the highest and most responsible posts in his realm: "keeper of his head [chief of his bodyguard] for life" (28:2b).

We may well imagine that David received this news with mixed feelings. His patriotic zeal had always kept him from fighting against his own people. Under these circumstances, however, he was compelled to go along with Achish's plan.[4]

AN IMPORTANT DIGRESSION (28:3-25)

Opposition Which Gave Rise to Fear (28:3-7)

The scene now shifts to the slopes of mount Gilboa. Before discussing Saul's reaction to the Philistine invasion, the Biblical historian reminded us of certain facts: (1) Samuel was dead and (2) Saul had expelled all mediums and spiritists from the land (1 Samuel 28:3; cf. Leviticus 19:31; 20:27; Deuteronomy 18:10; Isaiah 8:19; 19:3).

Power of the Opposition (28:4-5). As King Saul watched the buildup of the Philistine forces he was filled with dismay. He had belatedly been made aware of the new threat posed by his archenemies and had summoned *all* Israel to his side. How many fighting men actually answered his call is not told us. The focus of attention is the king.

Never before had Saul seen such well-disciplined troops. He could see the banners of Ekron; the soldiers from this city had arrived the day before. Their tents were erected in straight lines, making for easy access to the field of battle. In the distance coming down the broad expanse of the valley, the pennants of Ashdod were visible. The glistening helmets and pointed spears reflected all too readily their numerical strength. It perhaps took a day for them to billet themselves. On succeeding days Saul watched the armies of Ashkelon, Gaza, and Gath arrive. By the end of the week the whole valley opposite him was filled with Philistine soldiers. Nothing like this had happened since the Midianites' invasion when they filled the valley like a swarm of locusts.

Why had the Philistines chosen to make the scene of battle so far to the north? (Brief consultation with a map of the area shows that the site of the battle was far from both the cities of Philistia and the residence of Saul.) It seems that the Philistines, who already had control of much of the south all the way to Bethlehem (cf. 1 Chronicles 11:16-18), now wished to obtain unchallenged supremacy in the north. A decisive victory would divide the land in two. They would then be able to subdue all opposition on the part of the scattered and disunited tribes.

The Philistines' selection of this portion of the great plain of the Esdraelon was most appropriate for achieving their goal. The valley itself shelved down to the Jordan river and was obstructed in the east by two mountain ranges. On the southern side of the valley, which was about three miles wide, were the mountains of Gilboa. At their foot and on a slightly elevated spur was the city of Jezreel, where a spring gushed down into a pool of considerable size. On the northern side of the valley was Little Hermon, and at its base the village of

Shunem. Behind and to the north of Little Hermon was another narrow valley where Endor was situated—a small collection of huts with most of the people living in the limestone caves that permeated the hillside.[5]

The Means of Obtaining Guidance (28:6-7). The visual evidence of the overwhelming superiority of the Philistine forces left Saul in a quandary. He had fought many battles with them before, but this one was entirely different. He must have asked himself, "What shall I do? Where now is the God who gave victories to Barak and Gideon?" (Judges 4:14-16; 7:1,19-25)[6] Then perhaps Saul mused wishfully, "If only Samuel were alive, I would speak to him. The old prophet seldom had anything good to say about me, but if he were still living at least he would reveal the will of God to me."

In the ancient Near East there were several different ways by which people discerned the will of the gods. One way was by the teraphim; these household idols were a sign of authority, land ownership, and fertility, and were used for divination purposes. Another means was hepatoscopy or seeing omens and portents of the future in the entrails or liver of an animal (cf. Ezekiel 21:21; Zechariah 10:2). A third method was hydromancy—the use of water for the purpose of supposedly discovering the will of the gods. Among the Greeks and Romans great store was placed on the flight of birds, rhabdomancy (the use of a divining rod), and the flight of arrows (cf. Hosea 4:12). Astrology was also popular. Consulting the stars presupposed that the heavenly constellations were in fact deities or else were controlled by deities; such a practice was very common in ancient Babylonia (cf. Isaiah 47:13; Jeremiah 10:2). Finally there was necromancy—consultation with the dead.

All of these methods were forbidden to the Hebrews. God's will was readily made known to all who sought Him in sincerity and truth.[7] Therefore 1 Samuel 28:6 poses a problem for all who believe in the efficacy of prayer.

Saul, experiencing fear such as he had never known before, inquired of the Lord (Yahweh) what he should do. His inquiry was progressive. It began with dreams, moved on to urim (a priest wearing an ephod), and climaxed with consulting different prophets.[8] Each time God refused to answer him. Saul stands out as an example of those whose many years of self-will have left them bereft of any viable relationship with the Lord. The heavens were closed to Saul's pleas and no answer was given. With each successive failure to obtain the information he sought, Saul's fears increased and he became desperate.

His apparent willingness to know the will of God and the Lord's refusal to answer him appear to be in conflict with passages of Scripture like 2 Chronicles 7:13-16. In reality, as 1 Chronicles 10:14 indicates, it was as if Saul did not pray at all. In his heart there was no real commitment to doing the will of God, so he inquired in vain.

William Blaikie's comments on 1 Samuel 28:6-7 are most apropos.

> Among other effects of sin and rebellion, one of the worst is a stiffening of the soul, making it hard and rigid, so that it cannot bend, it cannot melt, it cannot change its course. The long career of wilfulness that Saul had followed had produced in him this stiffening effect; his spirit was hardened in its own ways, and incapable of all exercise of contrition or humiliation, or anything essentially different from the course he had been following....
>
> Saul was incapable of that exercise of soul which would have saved him and his people. Most terrible effect of cherished sin! It dries up the fountains of contrition and they will not flow. It stiffens the knees and they will not bend. It paralyses the voice and it will not cry. It blinds the eyes and they cannot see. It closes the ears and the voice of mercy is not heard. It drives the distressed one to wells without water, to refuges of lies, to trees twice dead, to physicians who have no medicines, to gods who have no salvation; all he feels is that his case is desperate, and yet somewhere or other he must have help!...
>
> [Saul] tried every authorized way he could think of for getting guidance from above. But God took no notice of him. He answered him neither by dreams, nor by Urim, nor by prophets. Men, though in heart rebellious against God's will, will go through a great deal of mechanical service in the hope of securing His favour. What a strange conception they must have of God when they fancy that mere external services will please Him! How little Saul knew of God when he supposed that, overlooking all the rebellion of his heart, God would respond to a mechanical effort or efforts to communicate with Him![9]

Little did Saul realize that his iniquities had separated him from God and his sins had hidden the Lord's face from him. With each failure to ascertain the will of the Lord his feelings of apprehension increased. He became desperate. He wished that Samuel were still alive. Ultimately, driven by anxiety that had deprived him of his appetite during the day and would not allow him to sleep at night, he conceived of a daring plan that he would never have entertained earlier in his life. He would seek Samuel's counsel via the services of a medium who could commune with the dead. Acting on this slender thread of hope, he sent his servants to find a necromancer. In Endor, north of the Philistine camp, they located a medium, an *'ēšat ba'alat 'ôb,* a woman who readily consorted with an evil or "familiar" spirit.[10]

Actions Produced by Fear (28:8-14)

Taking two of his trusted servants with him, Saul, in disguise, circled the Philistine camp and made his way with determined steps toward Endor. Some scholars have estimated that the distance between Gilboa and the home of the medium was about ten miles, but with the detour the king had to make, the trip would be more like nineteen miles.

The medium of Endor, who is nowhere called a "witch" in Scripture, had apparently escaped Saul's purge of the land. Either she had retired from the occupation of spiritist or else had become very selective in her choice of clients.

On being shown into her single-room dwelling, Saul said to her, "Please divine for me through necromancy and bring up [from Hades, the abode of the dead] whomsoever I tell you" (1 Samuel 28:8; cf. 1 Chronicles 10:13).The woman was very cautious and accused the men of laying a trap for her. Only when Saul vowed to her in the name of Yahweh that no harm would come to her did she accede to his request.

"Whom shall I call up for you?" she asked. Saul replied, "Bring up Samuel for me" (1 Samuel 28:11). The woman no doubt expected her "familiar spirit" to appear.[11] When she saw a different figure who was radiant in appearance arising from out of the earth, she shrieked in alarm. It was not her "familiar spirit" who would imitate the voice of the departed, but the real appearance of the old prophet. God had evidently intervened by setting aside the normal approach of the medium. In allowing Samuel to come in person He was demonstrating His sovereignty even over the realm of the dead.

All at once the woman realized who it was who had asked her to use her nefarious gifts. Turning on Saul, she denounced him for his deception. Saul reassured her that no punitive action would be taken and asked her to describe what she had seen. "I saw a god [*'ĕlōhîm,* 'a divine being'] coming up out of the earth," she said (28:13). Saul inquired further and was given a description of an old man wrapped in a robe. Saul realized the man was Samuel and bowed in homage (28:14).

Information That Reinforced Fear (28:15-19)

Samuel reproved Saul for his actions. "Why have you disturbed me?" the prophet asked. Saul answered, "I am greatly distressed; for the Philistines are waging war against me, and God has departed from me and answers me no more...therefore I have called you, that you may make known to me what I should do" (1 Samuel 28:15). Samuel stated what should have been obvious to the king: "Why do you ask me, since Yahweh has departed from you and has become your adversary?" Samuel's words were designed to show Saul the folly of his actions. Then to remind the king of the deeds of the past that had brought him to his present state, Samuel continued:

> Yahweh has done according as He spoke through me; for Yahweh has torn your kingdom out of your hand and given it to your neighbor, [even] to David. As you did not obey Yahweh and did not execute His fierce wrath on Amalek, so Yahweh has done this thing to you this day. Moreover Yahweh will also give over Israel along with you into the hands of the Philistines; therefore, tomorrow you and your sons will be with me. Indeed, Yahweh will give over the army of Israel into the hands of the Philistines!" (28:17-19)

As Samuel spoke it seemed to Saul as if the hammer blows of the misfortunes that awaited him became heavier and heavier. He fell on his face before Samuel. Saul was so terrified that he could not get up. His weakness was aggravated by the fact that he had not been able to eat all day because of his fears.

Before considering the events that followed, we need to spend a few moments clarifying some thoughts that seem to be in conflict with the teaching of the New Testament. The Gospels affirm that following His resurrection Christ ascended into Heaven (John 6:62; 20:17). Paul's letters state that when a believer dies he or she goes immediately into the presence of the Lord (2 Corinthians 5:6-8; Philippians 1:23). How then could Samuel arise up out of the earth? Wouldn't he have been in Heaven with all of the other righteous men and women who had believed in the Lord? And why did Samuel say that the next day Saul and his sons (some of whom may not have been God-fearing men) would be with him? And finally, does 1 Samuel 28 teach in a tangential way the doctrine of universal salvation?

To answer the last question first, this passage does *not* give unsaved people any hope that they will one day enjoy the peace and rest promised to believers; see Hebrews 9:27.

To answer the other questions, we need to refer to the teaching of the Lord Jesus in Luke 16:19-31 and the assurance He gave to the thief on the cross (Luke 23:32,39-43). Apparently Hades—the nether world or abode of the dead—is divided into two sections with an impassable chasm separating them. One section is called paradise and is a place of peace, tranquility, happiness, and freedom from the cares of this world. This is the place to which all the righteous dead of Old Testament times went—the place where they waited for Christ to complete their redemption by dying on the cross (Hebrews 10:4; cf. Romans 4:24-25). When the Lord Jesus died He "descended into the lower parts of the earth [paradise]" (see Ephesians 4:9-10). After He arose from the grave, the righteous dead ascended from paradise into Heaven. The part of Hades that is called paradise is now empty. The other section of the underworld is a place of torment and is referred to in the Bible as *she'ōl* and *gehenna*. There the unrighteous dead of all ages await the final judgment.[12] Whether saved or unsaved, therefore, Saul and his sons would be in one of the two sections of Hades before another twenty-four hours had run their course.

Conditions Produced by Fear (28:20-25)

How tragic was Saul's condition. It reminds us of others who spend their lives in rejection of the Lord and refuse to own His claim on them. Some imagine that they can have the best of this world and the next. They plan to live for the present, satisfy the desires of the flesh, and then just before they die confess their sins and be saved for all eternity. How little such people understand the course of sin. It hardens the heart until repentance becomes impossible. Their end is like Saul's: joyless, helpless, and hopeless.

On hearing Samuel's words, Saul was not moved to repentance. He was overcome by dread of what lay before him. While he had not expected the interview with Samuel to be a pleasant one, he never imagined that it would sound his death knell.

The medium and Saul's retainers probably had not heard the words spoken by Samuel. While he was speaking the woman had time to recover from her initial shock. Seeing Saul lying prostrate on the floor, she was moved with compassion. She asked if she might prepare some food for him. At first Saul refused, but she prevailed upon him.

After eating the meal, Saul and his servants retraced their steps through the darkness back to the camp on the slopes of mount Gilboa. They probably arrived just before sunrise.

AN UNEXPECTED DISMISSAL (29:1-11)

In 1 Samuel 29 our thoughts are turned from King Saul back to David. He was en route to Aphek with the Philistines, and we may be sure he prayed often and in earnest to be spared from entering the field of battle against his countrymen. But how could David extricate himself from this dilemma?

Fear of a Fifth Column (29:1-5)

A few days prior to Saul's visit to Endor and after the different divisions of the Philistine army had reached Aphek, the entire army passed in review before the lords of the pentapolis. When they saw David and his men among their own troops, they questioned the wisdom of having Hebrews in the midst of their own forces. The lords challenged Achish:

> "What [are] these [men within your ranks] Hebrews?"... And the lords [literally, captains] of the Philistines said, "Send the man back, that he may return to his place where you have appointed him, [for] he may not go down with us into the battle, and not become to us an adversary in the battle. And how should this [man be] reconciled to his master, if not with the heads of these men [that is, our own soldiers]?" (1 Samuel 29:3-4)

In vain the king of Gath urged upon the other feudal lords David's past faithfulness. The reasons Achish gave for his implicit trust in Saul's former son-in-law fell on deaf ears. The kings of Ekron, Ashkelon, Ashdod, and Gaza argued vehemently that including David would present him with an excellent opportunity to be reinstated in the good graces of King Saul. The risk was too great. Why hazard all of their plans on the questionable loyalty of someone who in the past had earned fame as the killer of myriads of Philistines?

We see how God in His great mercy was using the jealousy and distrust of the Philistine leaders to extricate David from his dilemma. In David's dismissal from active service in the Philistine army, we glimpse His sovereignty even over those who do not know Him.

Release of the Reluctant Warriors (29:6-11)

With great reluctance Achish acceded to the pressure brought to bear upon him. He confronted David in a most gracious manner. Achish knew David to be a godly man and did not hesitate to use the name of David's God in his oath. Since a pagan would have been most unlikely to use the name of God[13] perhaps the Philistine king came to trust in Israel's God during the sixteen months David and his men resided in Philistia. Note the words of Achish carefully:

[As] Yahweh lives surely you [are] upright and good in my eyes [in] your going out and your coming in with me in the camp. For I have not found evil in you from the day of your coming to me until this day; but in the eyes of the lords you [are] not good. And now, return and go in peace, and you shall do no evil in the eyes of the lords of the Philistines (1 Samuel 29:6-7).

Although David was greatly relieved, he could not allow Achish to know his true feelings. His remonstrance was wisely framed in the form of a question: "But what have I done? And what have you found in your servant from the day that I have been before you until this day that I may not go in and fight against the enemies of my lord the king?" (29:8)[14] David's words drew further praise from Achish:

I know that you [are] good in my eyes, like an angel of God; yet the captains of the Philistines have said, "He shall not go up with us into the battle." And now, rise early in the morning, and [your] servants that have come with you, you [all] rise early in the morning, when [there is sufficient] light, and go" (29:9-10).

Early the next morning before the camp was astir, with a sense of intense relief David and his men took their leave and set out for Ziklag. The Philistines, as we have seen, moved out by divisions and began to occupy essentially the same section of the valley that the Midianites had chosen approximately 180 years before.

THE IMPORTANCE OF OUR DECISIONS

Throughout their lives both Saul and David made important decisions. Saul's took him farther and farther from the will of God. David's brought him closer to the Lord. Saul's choices were motivated by self-will and his desire for self-aggrandizement. He was like the man who built his house on the sand: what he had sought to establish was swept away before his eyes. In contrast to Saul, David "set Yahweh always before his face" (Psalm 16:8); in times of difficulty the Lord sustained him and helped him. With God-given stability, David was able to withstand the harsh winds of misfortune and the rising tide of slander and false accusation that encircled him.

William Shakespeare illustrated the importance of the criteria by which we make our choices in *The Merchant of Venice*. Both the prince of Morocco and the prince of Aragon wanted to marry the beautiful Portia. Each sought to add the fortune she had inherited to his own. Bassanio was in love with Portia, but could not rival her other suitors in influence or affluence.

Portia's father had been a wise man. Before his death he realized what might happen so he devised a scheme by which the true nature of each suitor could be tested. He commissioned a craftsman to make three identical caskets. The only differences were to be in the metals out of which they were made and in the inscriptions engraved on them. The first was to be made of fine gold, the second of pure silver, and the third of base lead. The plan was that Portia would place a gold locket bearing her image in one of the caskets. The suitor who selected the box with the locket would become her husband and the unsuccessful rivals would have to promise to remain unmarried for life.

Portia inherited her fortune and the prince of Morocco was the first to vie for the prize. He carefully read the engravings on the boxes and then chose the gold casket. Its inscription read, "Who chooseth me shall gain what many men desire." He presumed that to be Portia's hand in marriage. And gold, he believed, was certainly befitting a person of his rank and importance. When he opened the box, however, he found in it a scroll containing a poem denouncing him for having made his decision based on selfishness and pride.

It wasn't long before the prince of Aragon arrived. He carefully read all the engravings. Suspecting a trick he chose the silver casket. Its inscription read, "Who chooseth me shall have as much as he deserves." His greed blinded his eyes and warped his judgment. He concluded that he deserved Portia's ample fortune. On opening the casket, however, he found a scroll exposing the folly of his avarice.

Finally Bassanio visited Portia. His love for her was genuine and self-effacing. She tried to dissuade him from entering the contest, but to no avail. After he had read the engravings on all of the caskets, he chose the lead one. Its inscription read, "Who chooseth me must give and hazard all he hath."[15] Inside he found Portia's locket. His attitude was not one of arrogance or greed, but of true self-sacrifice.

We all must make important choices. And some choices that seem to be insignificant now may have far-reaching consequences that will only become apparent later on. We need to seek the Lord's will in all situations and remember that pride, selfishness, arrogance, and greed place us outside the realm of God's guidance; it is the humble whom He leads in His way (Psalm 25:9; also see Psalm 32:8; Jeremiah 42:2).

Saul erred greatly in some of his decisions. His final years as well as his final hours only served to reinforce the tragedy of the choices he made. How much better for us to:

- Be sincere in asking God to guide us (Jeremiah 42:3,6)
- Be willing to wait on Him for direction (Jeremiah 42:7; Isaiah 30:18; 49:23)
- Be ready to obey His will regardless of the cost (Jeremiah 42:10-12; Isaiah 1:19)

If we heed these admonitions our experience will be different from Saul's when we face our final curtain call and our departure from this world.[16]

UPROOTED
1 Samuel 30:1-31

Times of deep trial or misfortune often precede eras of new opportunity. Throughout the book of Acts we find that persecution almost always came before the spread of the Word of God in a new area (see Acts 4:29,31; cf. 5:17-18 with 6:7; see 11:19-21; 12:1-3,24; 13:44-50; 19:9,18-20). In ways that we cannot fathom, God in His sovereign wisdom often uses the seeming misfortunes of life to prepare us for greater and sometimes different spheres of usefulness (2 Corinthians 1:4).

Carolyn Koons was abused as a child. The emotional wounds she sustained took years to heal, but when she finally was able to write of her experiences in *Beyond Betrayal*[1] she brought hope and help to thousands of people whose childhood experiences paralleled her own.

Howard Ruff was a wealthy and highly respected entrepreneur, but a change in a franchise he held forced him into bankruptcy. His spectacular collapse made headline news in the San Francisco newspapers. To add insult to injury, civic organizations with which he had been associated asked for his resignation because he had become an embarrassment to them. Feeling much as Job must have felt when he sat on an ash heap of poverty and humiliation outside of the city, Ruff and his wife tabulated their assets: $11.38; a commitment to the Puritan work ethic; a strong religious heritage; the ability to speak well before crowds; and excellent training in economics. With determination and persistence they set about rebuilding their shattered world. They repaid their creditors (something they were not obliged to do) and today Howard is president of a financial consulting firm that gives counsel to millions of people who otherwise would be ignorant of investment opportunities.[2] He is the author of several best-selling books and has his own television program.

Sharalee Aspenleiter was widowed in her mid-forties. In the years that followed her bereavement Sharee (as she is known to her friends) went through the grieving process and in time incorporated her own experiences as well as the experiences of others in her book *Through the Valley of Tears,*[3] which has been instrumental in helping countless people deal realistically with the trauma that follows the loss of a loved one.

Charles Colson was former President Nixon's "hatchet man" and participated in the Watergate coverup, which ultimately led to Richard Nixon's resignation and Colson's incarceration. While in prison Chuck Colson turned to the Lord and accepted Jesus Christ as his Savior. His life was changed and during the months he spent in jail he began to experience a real concern for his fellow inmates. Once released, he founded Prison Fellowship, Inc., an organization that is devoted to providing practical help to prisoners as well as their families.[4]

Stories such as these could be multiplied ad infinitum. Each one illustrates how the Lord can use apparent misfortune to prepare a person for a wider, more influential kind of ministry.

In 1 Samuel 30 we see David facing an unexpected crisis. He had always zealously safeguarded the well-being of those who looked to him for protection, but when he and his men returned to Ziklag, they found that their families had been taken captive by the archetypal bandits of the ancient Near East—the ruthless and cunning Amalekites. The houses of Ziklag had been destroyed and the city lay in ruins.

Beneath the surface issues of the story we see how God in His sovereignty was preparing the men to accompany David to Hebron[5] (2 Samuel 2). The destruction of Ziklag served to shake them loose from the comforts and permanence offered them by Achish, king of Gath.

STRUCTURE AND OUTLINE OF THE PASSAGE

In much the same way that 1 Samuel 28:3-25 formed an important digression in the recounting of the events of 27:1–31:13, so 1 Samuel 30 digresses from the story of the war with the Philistines to describe the way in which God was preparing Israel's future king for his ascension to the throne.

The outline is again made easy for us by the repetitious use of the Hebrew *waw,* which may be translated "then," "now," or "and" (30:1,7,11,16,21,26). First Samuel 30:1-6 highlights the disappointed hopes of David and his men when they returned to Ziklag; 30:7-10 provides the backdrop for David's seeking to know the will of God;

30:11-15 explains the unexpected help the Lord gave David and his men; 30:16-20 describes their notable victory; 30:21-25 describes the equitable distribution of the spoils of war; and in closing, 30:26-31 mentions the gifts sent by David to those who had helped him and his men during their outlaw years. Interpreting these events in light of the theme of 1 Samuel, we can group our thoughts under the following headings:

- Removal of Earthly Comforts (1 Samuel 30:1-6)
- Reliance upon Spiritual Resources (1 Samuel 30:7-10)
- Recovery of Personal Possessions (1 Samuel 30:11-25)
  —Help from an Unexpected Source (30:11-15)
  —Attack upon an Unsuspecting Enemy (30:16-20)
  —Rebuke of Unconscionable Conduct (30:21-25)
- Recognition of Past Favors (1 Samuel 30:26-31)

REMOVAL OF EARTHLY COMFORTS (30:1-6)

First Samuel 30 begins with the return of David and his men to Ziklag and the anguish each one felt as he discovered that his wife and children had been captured to be sold as slaves or kept to serve the needs and sensual desires of those who had suddenly become their masters.

Anyone who has spent any length of time away from the comforts of home can readily empathize with David and his men. They had not wanted to accompany Achish and the Philistines to the valley of Esdraelon, but having accepted the king of Gath's protection they had no option but to join the ranks of his soldiers. If David had demurred and asked Achish for permission to leave a couple of hundred men behind to safeguard Ziklag, the king may well have assured him that no desert tribe would dare to attack Ziklag while it was under his protection.

The march along the maritime road to Aphek, the rallying point of the Philistine armies, took three days. None of the Israelites had enjoyed inhaling the dust raised by the feet of the Gittites who were in front of them. Once at Aphek, David's men joined the forces of Ekron, Ashdod, Ashkelon, and Gaza. When this mighty army marched in review before the kings of the Philistine pentapolis, David and his men were quickly identified and dismissed, and breathing sighs of relief they wearily retraced their steps toward home.

On the first day after their departure from Aphek there was probably lighthearted joking among different groups and the kind of robust humor that is found among men of war. But as they neared

Ziklag a change may have come over them. More than likely each began to think of his wife and family—of warm embraces and his children's innumerable questions, of the happy sparkle in his wife's eyes and a hearty meal, of quiet conversation beside the glowing fireside and a comfortable bed. The troop made good time, for the Biblical text implies that they reached Ziklag early enough on the third day to take off after the Amalekites and arrive at the brook Besor well before nightfall.

As the men reached the plateau that ascended gradually toward Beersheba, they expected someone within the walled city to notice their approach. Instead there was a strange silence. An eerie stillness hung over the place. Quickening their pace they hurried toward the gate. They were ill-prepared for the scene of desolation that awaited them. Passing through the gate they saw the charred ruins of what used to be their homes. A few unimportant playthings or items of clothing lay scattered about—probably dropped as the owners were being dragged to a place where the women and children were cruelly bound with rawhide cords or ropes of camel's hair and linked together to form a human chain.

At first the soldiers were numb with shock. Then as the reality of what had taken place began to penetrate their conscious thoughts, each man gave way to agonizing groans and tears of grief. David was likewise overwhelmed with anguish, for his two wives—Ahinoam and Abigail—had also been taken captive (1 Samuel 30:5). There is therapy in tears, and while it is more common for those in the Near East to show such emotion, there is nothing unmanly in weeping (John 11:35). Those in Ziklag had no means of knowing what fate had overtaken their loved ones, and each man suspected the worst.

David has been severely criticized by some commentators for leaving Ziklag unprotected. Certainly it is hard for us to imagine him carelessly disregarding the safety of those who looked to him for protection. As we have pointed out, however, Achish may not have given him a choice. As always, the wise words of Dr. William G. Blaikie bring to the fore God's hand in the events that transpired.

> It appears from the chapter now before us that, in the absence of David and his troop, severe reprisals had been taken by the Amalekites for the defeat and destruction which had lately been inflicted on a portion of their tribe. We must remember that the Amalekites were a widely dispersed people, consisting of many tribes, each living separately from the rest, but so related that in any emergency they would readily come to one another's help. News of the extermination of the tribes whom David had

attacked, and whom he had utterly destroyed lest any of them should bring word to Achish...had been brought to these neighbours; and these neighbours were determined to take revenge for the slaughter of their kinsmen.

The opportunity of David's absence was taken for invading Ziklag, for which purpose a large and well-equipped expedition had been got together; and as they met with no opposition, they carried everything before them. Happily, however, as they found no enemies they did not draw sword; they counted it a better policy to carry off all that could be transported, so as to make use of the goods, and sell the women and children into slavery. As they had a great number of beasts of burden with them (ver. 17) there could be no difficulty in carrying out their plan.

It seems very strange that David should have left Ziklag apparently without the protection of a single soldier; but what seems to us folly had all the effect of consummate wisdom in the end; the passions of the Amalekites were not excited by opposition or by bloodshed; their destructive propensities were satisfied with destroying the town of Ziklag, and every person and thing that could be removed was carried away unhurt. But for days to come David could not know that their expedition had been conducted in this unusually peaceful way; his imagination and fears would picture far darker scenes.[6]

All leaders have dissidents within their ranks. Such individuals may oppose their leader's policies, criticize his decisions, or try to detract from his authority. David was no exception. Malcontents, described in the text as *mārâ nepeš* ("bitter of soul"), projected the blame for their calamity onto David.

We can well imagine the scene. One man surveying the ruins of the city grumbles, "He should never have brought us to Philistia. We were more than a match for Saul's elite troop." Another argues, "If he had only left a detachment of men to guard the city, at least our wives and children would have had a fighting chance." And a third complains, "If his policies hadn't antagonized the Amalekites, they would not have staged this reprisal. And now who knows what has happened to our women and children?"

In their inflamed frame of mind the men looked for a scapegoat (1 Samuel 30:6) and David became the object of their passion for revenge.

William Deane reminds us that the circumstances David faced on this occasion were very similar to those with which Moses had to contend at Rephidim. The people were ready to kill him (Exodus 17:4) and he acted then as David did now. David was greatly dismayed by the dissidents' threats and he laid everything before the Lord. As he strengthened himself (*hithazzēq*, literally "made himself strong," cf. Psalm 27:14) in Yahweh his God, he reassured himself of the Lord's plans for his future. Inwardly encouraged, he was able to commit the whole matter to the Lord (Psalm 18:2-3; 55:22).[7]

RELIANCE UPON SPIRITUAL RESOURCES (30:7-10)

By not giving in to his feelings David was able to be proactive. He took prompt action and called for Abiathar the priest. Remember that when Abiathar came to David in Keilah (1 Samuel 23:6) he brought with him the ephod. David now inquired (possibly by means of the urim and thummim) of the Lord, "Shall I pursue after this troop? Will I overtake [them]?" God answered, "Pursue, for you will certainly overtake [them], and you will certainly recover [all that they took from you]" (30:8). Such assurance was sufficient to appease those who had threatened to stone David.

Taking six hundred of his loyal veterans with him, David set out to follow the tracks of the Amalekites across the ever-changing desert sands. On reaching the brook Besor,[8] generally identified with the Wadi esh-Sharī'āh which was about fifteen miles south of Ziklag, one third of David's men were too exhausted to go any farther. The remaining four hundred discarded anything that might impede their progress and, leaving their belongings in the care of those who remained behind, set out once more. Speed was of the essence. If they were to "recover all" as God had said, they would have to overtake the Amalekites before they reached a city or some desert rendezvous where tribesmen gathered to barter goods or buy and sell slaves.

RECOVERY OF PERSONAL POSSESSIONS (30:11-25)

Help from an Unexpected Source (30:11-15)

At this point we see how the Lord had anticipated the needs of David and his men. En route, some of David's men came across a young Egyptian who had been left to die in the desert. "No events could have fallen out more favourably," wrote William Blaikie. "The special providence of God, so clearly and frequently displayed... provided a guide for David in the person of an Egyptian slave, who, having...been abandoned, had spent three days and nights without meat or drink."[9]

With food and water from their own meager supply David's men revived the Egyptian. David then asked him, "To whom [do] you [belong]?" In the young man's reply there was tacit confirmation of the facts David and his men had begun to piece together.

> I [am] a young Egyptian, servant to a man, an Amalekite; and my lord abandoned me, for I had been sick [for] three days. We raided the Negev [southland] of the Cherithites,[10] even to that which [belongs] to Judah, even to the Negev of Caleb; and Ziklag we burned with fire (1 Samuel 30:13-14).

Realizing that the raiders had a considerable start on them, David then asked the young man if he would guide him and his men to the Amalekites' camp. The young man's answer was most revealing. Apparently he feared death and his master in equal proportions. He said, "Swear to me by God [*'Elōhîm,* possibly 'your gods'] that you will neither kill me nor close me up [give me] into the hand of my lord, and I will bring you down to the troop" (30:15). Reassurance was given and the Egyptian, perhaps taking a shortcut, brought David and his men to the place where the Amalekites were celebrating their victory.

Attack upon an Unsuspecting Enemy (30:16-20)

From a place of safe concealment on the top of a sand dune, David and the leaders of his small army surveyed the Amalekites' camp. Confident that no one would pursue them, these sons of the desert had spread themselves out over a considerable area. They were in a festive mood[11] because of the extensive spoil they had taken from Philistia and Judah. David and his men took note of where their wives and children were being kept and pondered how best to divide the Amalekite force.

They launched their attack at twilight.[12] Perhaps burning torches outside each tent and a full moon helped them see the enemy. In spite of their long march and general fatigue, they battled on until the evening of the next day. God was gracious to David and his men. Compared to the vast hordes of Amalekites, David's group was only a handful in number, but they completely routed their enemy (1 Samuel 30:17). Only four hundred Amalekites were able to escape on camels. In accordance with God's promise, David's troop recovered all that had been taken from them. Nothing was missing. As wives and children were cut free from their bonds, there were tender reunions. Those who formerly were frightened and apprehensive now joyously embraced their strong husbands and fathers.

As David led the enlarged group of tired but happy people back to Ziklag, they drove before them the sheep and cattle the Amalekites had stolen from the villages and hamlets of the Negev. Surveying the numerous sheep and cattle, one of David's men said, "This [is] David's spoil" (30:20).[13] This expression, with its kingly overtones, was quickly picked up by the others. While some may have thought it presumptuous to use such an expression before David was actually crowned, it does show us the esteem in which God's anointed was held by his people. Unknown to David and his men, Saul and his sons were already dead.

Rebuke of Unconscionable Conduct (30:21-25)

As the people with David arrived at the wadi Besor, they were met with cheers and shouts of adulation. The men who had remained behind eagerly searched the faces of the women and children to pick out their loved ones. And those who had so recently been released from captivity searched the faces of the men. Tears of pure joy coursed down tired dusty faces as each embraced those who were more precious than life itself.

In the midst of this glad reunion a discordant note was struck. It is introduced by the word "Then."

> Then every evil and worthless man of the men who had gone with David answered; and they said, "Because they did not go with me [us] we will not give them [any of] the spoil which we have captured, except [that each man may] take his wife and sons, and let them take [them] and go" (1 Samuel 30:22).

David rebuked this selfish spirit. Acting on information probably gained from Samuel (Numbers 31:25-31; Deuteronomy 20:4,14; Joshua 22:8) David established a policy that all would share equally in the spoils of war (1 Samuel 30:23-24). Dr. Ralph W. Klein sees in David's actions the exercise of judicial authority belonging to a king.[14] Having shown kinglike leadership in war (1 Samuel 18:7; 21:11) and in the defense of his people, he now established a custom that would endure for generations (1 Samuel 30:25).

RECOGNITION OF PAST FAVORS (30:26-31)

Ziklag was in ruins. Instead of thinking of himself and launching a massive rebuilding project, David was motivated by feelings of gratitude. He recognized God's goodness in granting him the spoils of the

Amalekites and, in royal style, desired to bestow gifts on those who had helped him during the past decade.

Many commentators are prone to see in David's actions an ulterior motive. They believe that he was reminding the people of his presence so that they would be inclined to choose him as their new king. But David did not yet know of Saul's death (2 Samuel 1:1-4). Such commentators ignore completely David's generosity and godliness.[15] Their criticism tends to draw our thoughts away from the theme of 1 Samuel 30. The Biblical historian was placing due stress on David's *godward relationship, endurance, heroism, equity, and generosity.*

David sent all his gifts to places in the southern part of Judah. They were in part compensation to those people in the villages and hamlets of the Negev who had helped him during his outlaw years.[16] We may be sure that those to whom the gifts were sent were glad to receive them.

We should not ignore the hand of the Lord in His servant's affairs. God proved Himself faithful by causing David and his men to be honorably dismissed from the field of battle. The Lord also overruled the usual Amalekite animosity so that they did not kill any of the captives. He protected David when some of his men talked openly of killing him. God gave assurance and guidance through the use of the ephod and led someone in David's troop to find an Egyptian who was willing to lead them to the rendezvous point of the tribespeople. The Lord enabled David to defeat a well-armed, rested, and highly mobile force many times larger than his group of four hundred tired men. And it was He who prompted David to send gifts to the inhabitants of the southland who had been ravaged by the Amalekite attack. Reviewing these scenes, we gain a glimpse of God's behind-the-scenes involvement in the lives of His people.

PRACTICAL CONSIDERATIONS

We are all familiar with Murphy's famous maxim, "If anything can go wrong, you can be sure it will."[17] To the extent that we believe in a sovereign God who orders our steps, we can confidently face each new day knowing that from life's varying reverses we will learn important truths about ourselves as well as others.

The Significance of Proper Values

The events of 1 Samuel 30 show the importance of a right set of values. Since our society has lost its appreciation of the worth of the individual, people are often treated as if they were things, and things are often invested with the worth that rightly belongs to people. The prevailing sense of values may be seen in the way a husband treats his wife and vice versa; it is also observable in the attitude of employers to their employees, of government officials to those whom they are supposed to serve, and of men and women in public office toward their constituencies.

David and his men had a proper sense of values restored very quickly when they returned to Ziklag and found that their wives and children had been taken captive. Suddenly each remembered how intrinsically precious his family was to him. No thought was given to the material loss they had sustained. Instead every man was overcome with grief over the loss of loving relationships.

A good friend of mine, Dr. Charles Piepgrass of the Unevangelized Fields Mission, realized life's true values. He spent many years as a missionary in Haiti, and he and his wife Arlene reared their children there.

Charles is a man of many talents. In addition to being a skilled linguist and evangelist, he is a gifted artist and carpenter. When everyone else was looking for some shade in which to rest on hot sultry afternoons, he showed his love for his family by using the time to make furniture and paint pictures to adorn their home. Home was a very special place to them.

The missionary families remained relatively unaffected by the frequent coup-attempts in Port-au-Prince a few miles away, but on one occasion the political situation became so bad that it was decided the women and children should be flown to the United States. Only the men would remain to continue the work. As each man bade farewell to his loved ones, watched them board the vintage aircraft, and then saw it take off, he realized as never before how dramatically his life would be altered if the plane were to crash or be shot down.

Life's true values lie in our relationships with one another, not in our possessions (Luke 12:15).[18]

The Importance of Divine Guidance

First Samuel 30 also shows the importance of knowing and doing the will of God. Those who have walked closely with the Lord for many years will readily admit that God not only orders our steps, but He also orders our stops (Proverbs 16:9). This truth was illustrated in David's life. When he and his men returned to Ziklag they found their homes destroyed. After giving full expression to his grief, David called for the priest to come to him with the ephod. David inquired of the Lord and was assured that he should by all means pursue the Amalekites. An additional incentive to do the Lord's will was the promise that he would recover everything. As David sought the Lord's will, so should we.

We have God's Word and the illuminating ministry of the Holy Spirit to guide us. In spite of these advantages there are times when we still have difficulty discerning His will. Oswald Chambers, author of the popular devotional *My Utmost for His Highest,* was aware of this difficulty. As Mr. Chambers preached and taught in the Bible Training School in London, he found that people did not know what God expected of them. As many do today, they were relying on a subjective experience for guidance—a supposed voice of prophecy or a dream or an ecstatic utterance or a vision or some other strange occurrence or sign. God was supposed to communicate His will to them through one of these phenomena instead of through personal Bible study and fellowship with the Lord. In seeking to help earnest inquirers Mr. Chambers said:

> The words of Scripture [taken out of context], the advice of the saints, strong impressions during prayer, may or may not be an indication of the will of God. The one test given in the Bible is *discernment of a personal God and a personal relationship with Him....* God's eternal purposes will be fulfilled, but His permissive will allows Satan, sin and strife to produce all kinds of misconceptions and false confidences until we all, individually as well as corporately, realise that His order is best.[19]

We are guided by the Lord when we are in fellowship with Him (Psalm 32:8). The Holy Spirit leads us as we obey His Word and do those things that are pleasing in His sight (1 John 3:22). As we habitually submit ourselves to Him at the beginning of each day, He is able to direct our steps.

The Necessity of Human Effort

It is fine for us to have a clear understanding of Biblical principles that in turn form the basis of our values and to walk with the Lord so that we understand His will, but little will be accomplished if we do not also become personally involved in the circumstances of our lives. Far too many people today take a passive approach to the Christian life.

David and his men would not have recovered their wives and children if they had sat disconsolately among the ashes and charred timbers of what had been their homes. As tired as they were, they needed a firm resolve and the determination to pursue their enemy and engage them in hand-to-hand combat in order to take back those who had been torn from their grasp.

First Samuel 30 shows the importance of human effort. The sense of fulfillment that many seek comes only from the realization of a job well done (Ecclesiastes 2:24-26; 5:18-20; Colossians 3:17). Alexander Miller was right when he said,

> Our self-centered and subjective-minded generation tends to think that work is justified only if it "assists in the development of personality."... The ready acceptance and faithful performance of work because it is socially necessary will develop the only kind of personality worth developing.[20]

Unless we are prepared to become involved in a task so that God can accomplish His purposes through us, much that needs to be done will remain undone. To "claim the promises" may sound pious, but to do so passively will only lead to an ever-deepening feeling of disillusionment and disappointment. Positive action is needed if we are to accomplish great things for God.

The Demonstration of Sincere Gratitude

As we reflect upon the closing scene of 1 Samuel 30 we find that David gladly acknowledged the help he had received from his friends. His practical approach is seen in the way he willingly contributed to their needs as they in earlier days had contributed to his.

David taught us the importance of demonstrating gratitude. Though often conspicuous by its absence, gratitude is essential. Dr. John Baillie wrote:

> Gratitude is not only the dominant note in Christian piety but equally the dominant motive of Christian action in the world. Such gratitude is for the grace that has been shown us by God.... A true Christian is a man who never for a moment forgets what God has done for him in Christ, and whose whole comportment and whole activity have their root in the sentiment of gratitude.[21]

Applying the truths of 1 Samuel 30 to ourselves, we conclude that the Christian life does not exempt us from trial or misfortune. Christians often appear to suffer more than their unsaved neighbors. But difficulties highlight the dynamic quality of Christianity. It restores a sense of reality to our values, places us in touch with a God who makes His will known to us, energizes us for service, and helps us exercise the grace of giving to those in need. When we experience times of uprooting and sense that we are being shaken loose from a place where we had begun to establish ourselves, we can be sure that the Lord in His all-wise providence is leading us to a new place of service (cf. 2 Samuel 2).

THE END OF AN ERA

1 Samuel 31:1-13

Toward the end of Alan Jay Lerner's musical *Camelot* there is a very touching scene in which King Arthur, unable to sleep, is seen warming himself by the side of a dying fire. The gray light of early dawn reveals heavy mists that swirl about the tents of his soldiers. Then a gentle breeze blows the mists into the forest. Suddenly Arthur hears a noise in the bushes and demands to know who is there. For a moment there is silence and Arthur, fearing an assassin, takes his sword Excalibur from its sheath. Again he demands to know who has entered his camp unannounced. This time a young boy steps forward and comes slowly into the faint glow cast by the fire.

"Who are you?" asks the king.

"Tom, sir," is the reply.

"And why have you come here?" asks Arthur.

"To see the fight, sir."

Arthur detests war and the goal of his reign has been to put an end to the senseless shedding of blood. He calls Tom to him and, kneeling on one knee, places his mailed arm around the lad's shoulder. There is so much he wishes to share with Tom about the inequities of battle and the destruction it causes, but time is short.

When Arthur was much younger he had united all of England under his banner and instituted a form of democracy unheard of in England up to that time. For a while he had succeeded in bringing peace and honor to his realm. His people had been happy. Then jealousy and selfishness, spurred on by slander and innuendo, began to circulate through the palace. These evil influences quickly spread to the castles of the different earls and barons. One by one the knights of his famous Round Table became restive and left. Now he faces the prospect of a battle with Lancelot to preserve the laws of the kingdom.

As the soldiers begin to stir in their tents, King Arthur commissions young Tom to write the story of his reign.

> Don't let it be forgot
> That there once was a spot
> For one brief shining moment
> Called Camelot.[1]

Arthur realizes with deep sadness that he has failed to achieve his goal. He loves Lancelot as much as Lancelot loves him, but justice must be carried out.

Fortunately Lancelot decides to go into voluntary exile rather than fight his king. And Queen Guinevere, whose love for Lancelot caused much of Arthur's misfortune, enters a nunnery.

But evil still follows Arthur. The wily and unscrupulous Mordred stirs up the chieftains against him. Mordred lacks all of the fine qualities Lancelot possessed and a battle cannot be avoided. In it Arthur is mortally wounded. He lingers for a time and then dies. With his passing the peace and prosperity his people had known comes to an end.

A similar kind of pathos confronts us as we turn to 1 Samuel 31. The Biblical historian picked up his story from where he had left it in 28:4.

Like Arthur, Saul felt that his kingdom was crumbling about him. He had been chosen by God as Israel's king. Arthur, according to legend, was chosen by pulling a sword from a stone; but according to Scripture the Lord had directed His prophet as well as His people in their selection of Saul. In the early years of his reign he had sought to unite the scattered and disunited tribes and for a time he had succeeded. In the end, however, his fate was even more terrible than Arthur's. Whereas Arthur had been deserted by his knights, Saul had been forsaken by his God. Arthur's last words were a prayer to the Lord to receive him mercifully.[2] Saul could only demonstrate a stolid fortitude as he went to meet his end, for repentance had been denied him. Knowing that within an hour or two he would look on the rising sun for the last time, he summoned his men to prepare for battle.

OUTLINE

The description given by the Biblical historian of the third Philistine war is very brief. First Samuel 31:1-10 presents the perspective of the Philistines. Verses 11-13 form a postscript and describe the actions of the brave men of Jabesh-gilead. The contents of the chapter may be divided as follows:

- The Account of a Significant Victory (1 Samuel 31:1-7)
- The Actions of the Proud Victors (1 Samuel 31:8-10)
- The Remembrance of a Past Kindness (1 Samuel 31:11-13)

THE ACCOUNT OF A SIGNIFICANT VICTORY (31:1-7)

After reading of David's military success in the Negev, we are presented with a contrasting situation in 1 Samuel 31:1. (The Biblical writer gave only the barest description of the battle. Instead he focused attention on the concluding events on the slopes of mount Gilboa. We are left therefore to piece the details together.) Apparently the Israelites met the Philistines on the open plain of Jezreel. Israel's footsoldiers were no match for Philistine chariots; after an initial clash the ranks of Saul's army were broken and the men fled from the field.

In vain Saul and his elite corps tried to rally their forces and make a stand. Outmaneuvered and outnumbered, many were killed. Saul and his sons and his bodyguard made a valiant attempt to hold their position on one of the five knolls that rose toward the summit of the mountain.[3] Philistine archers took up strategic positions and one by one Saul's men fell before the merciless barrage.

Saul likewise became the target of the bowmen. His height, the gold crown encircling his helmet, and the royal bracelet on his forearm were easy to see. Time and again the archers found their mark[4] and Saul was badly wounded.

Undaunted by the opposition he continued fighting long after success had become a practical impossibility. Finally, realizing that the Philistines were getting ready to charge his position and fearing that if captured alive he would be cruelly tortured to death, he asked his armorbearer to kill him.

But Saul's armorbearer was afraid to comply with the request, for he had taken an oath to protect the king's life even if doing so meant losing his own.[5] When he refused, Saul positioned his sword firmly between some rocks and then threw himself on the upturned blade. His armorbearer then impaled himself on his own weapon.

There is some doubt as to whether Saul actually died by his own hand, for in 2 Samuel 1:2-10 (which continues the narrative) an Amalekite claimed credit for killing him. If the Amalekite was telling the truth, the armorbearer must have thought that Saul was dead when in reality he may only have fainted. The words of the Amalekite certainly can be correlated to Saul's request in 1 Samuel 31:4.[6]

The result of the Philistine victory was the wholesale retreat of God's people (31:7). They dispersed in all directions and even crossed the Jordan river into the territory of Gad. Delighted with this move, the Philistines took possession of the Israelites' homes and everything they had not been able to carry away with them.

THE ACTIONS OF THE PROUD VICTORS (31:8-10)

The Biblical writer then turned his attention from the occupation of the cities of Israel by the Philistines to what happened on the day after the battle. Early in the morning the proud conquerors began to strip all valuables off the corpses of the slain Israelites. In the course of going from one body to another they came across Saul's sons. Realizing that they may have been near the king when they died, the Philistines engaged in an excited search for Saul's corpse.

We know that an Amalekite had taken Saul's crown and bracelet from his body, so the king could only have been identified by the Philistines by his size and armor. When they found Saul, they showed their contempt for him by cutting off his head. In all probability it was placed on top of a spear and runners took it through the cities and villages of Philistia to give their people conclusive proof of Saul's death.

Then Saul's armor was stripped off his headless form and placed in the temple of Ashtaroth (possibly in nearby Beth-shan or Ashdod). Finally the naked bodies of the king and his sons were fastened to the wall of the city of Beth-shan.[7] There, as people went in and out through the gate of the city, they saw the bloodstained corpses of those who had dared to stand against the united power of the Philistine armies.

THE REMEMBRANCE OF A PAST KINDNESS (31:11-13)

The gloating of the Philistines was short-lived. Without consulting any committees or asking for the permission of the elders of their city, certain valiant men of Jabesh-gilead crossed the Jordan river at night. They avoided the Philistines guarding the ford of the river and, moving stealthily through the darkness, made their way to Beth-shan. Then as quietly as possible they took down the bodies of Saul, Jonathan, Abinadab, and Malchi-shua.[8] The men of Jabesh-gilead had not forgotten Saul's act of kindness toward them when he became king about thirty-two years earlier (1 Samuel 11:1-11).

The distance from Jabesh-gilead to Beth-shan was about fourteen miles. If it had been dangerous to traverse the Philistine-occupied territory from the Jordan to Beth-shan, the return journey was even more so, for now they were carrying the stiffened bodies of their late king and his sons. The men from Jabesh-gilead finally reached their hometown on the eastern side of the Jordan, and to avoid any further desecration of the bodies of the royal family, they burned the remains and then buried the bones under a tamarisk tree. Then they fasted for seven days as a sign of their respect for the dead.

THE LIGHT OF HISTORY

George Frideric Handel in his famous oratorio *King Saul* gives us a glimpse of the greatness of Israel's first monarch. While Handel passes over the fateful scene that took place on the foothills beneath the city of Jezreel, his treatment helps us focus on Saul's good qualities.[9]

Like many young people today, Saul did begin well. The gates of a noble destiny opened before him. The Lord was with him and to the best of our knowledge (and prior to the events of 1 Samuel 31) his armies were never defeated in battle.[10] His physical form and personal presence won the hearts of his subjects, and his magnanimity toward those who had at first opposed his rule showed the greatness of his character. He was a popular king (11:15).

Just how and when the first wedges of discord were driven between him and his people, we do not know. By the time of Jonathan's victory at Geba (13:3) the "honeymoon" was over. Neither the king nor his subjects could rely on the other's goodwill.

When the Philistines gathered at Michmash, Saul assembled a token force at Gilgal. There he waited for Samuel's arrival. The Lord however tested Saul by delaying His prophet. This test revealed the flaws in Saul's character. As the pressure mounted, his impatience and fear revealed the inadequacies of his godward relationship. Finally he chose to offer the first of the sacrifices himself and as a result he was told that his dynasty would not continue.

Saul had reverted to viewing reality solely in terms of externals and thus to him God's chastisement appeared unusually severe. Not being able to accept the prophet's indictment of his conduct, Saul used (1) denial of the facts and (2) the projection of blame onto others to quiet his conscience and dismiss the judgment for his disobedience.

Perhaps in no other way could Saul's weaknesses have been as dramatically demonstrated as in his response to God's command to destroy Amalek. He and his men fought bravely and for several days (perhaps weeks) pursued their enemy. Saul however feared the people and this fear led him to compromise with God's explicit directive (15:10-23). Although he gained a significant military victory, in God's eyes he failed miserably and no amount of sacrifices could remove the guilt of his impenitent heart.

Samuel was told of the king's disobedience and sought him out. The confrontation took place at Gilgal. There Samuel had the painful duty of telling Saul that God had removed him from the line of the theocracy. The Spirit of God then left Saul and although he continued to reign, he did so in the energy of the flesh.

Throughout Saul's reign the Philistines were Israel's relentless enemies. They were constantly invading Israel's borders. Frequently these incursions were limited to specific areas. On three occasions, however, Israel faced the combined forces of the enemy. The first time was at the battle of Michmash pass; Jonathan was the instrument God used to accomplish the defeat of the Philistines there. The second was at the valley of Elah.

Now on this third occasion the Philistines invaded the land and cut off the supply route to the interior. Saul was compelled to face his adversaries in territory favorable to them. Instead of the usual kind of battle, however, the Philistines proposed a duel. The victor would win the victory for his country. On seeing Goliath, Saul's confidence in himself waned and his impotence was decisively demonstrated. For forty days the Israelites were exposed to the ridicule of the pagan from Gath. But even this threat did not drive Saul to his knees. Finally David arrived and by God's good grace gave Israel the victory.

The women welcomed their men back with singing and dancing. Unfortunately their chorus awakened the king's jealousy. From that time onward he eyed David until his selfish emotional response to David's popularity destroyed his soul. So intense was Saul's jealousy that it drove him from one stratagem to another in an endeavor to get rid of his nemesis.

Finally the sand in Saul's hourglass ran out. As Dr. Clarence Edward Macartney remarked, "The same God who had called him to be king over Israel, who had given him a new heart and had sent Samuel to instruct him and to warn him and to pray for him, now answered him not." Then quoting from Proverbs 1:25,28 (KJV) where wisdom is personified as a woman, Dr. Macartney reminded us of the spiritual attrition that can so easily take place in a person's life when he or she turns his or her back upon the Lord: "Ye have set at naught all my counsel, and would have none of my reproof. . . . Then they shall call upon me, but I will not answer; they shall seek me early, but they shall not find me." The same God who says, "Those that seek me early shall find me" (Proverbs 8:17, KJV), also says of those who scorn his love, "They shall seek me early, but they shall not find me."[11]

The late Leon J. Wood in his fine work *Israel's United Monarchy* compelled his readers to recognize the awesomeness of dying without having accomplished anything of lasting value.[12] He compared the size of the land at the beginning of David's reign to the dimensions of the kingdom at the beginning of Saul's reign. They were about the same. Saul had failed to extend Israel's borders. And although he had tried to unite the tribes, he had squandered his energies trying to rid himself of the person whom God had appointed as his successor. Having failed to live up to his potential, Saul passed from this life into the presence of his Maker.

FINAL THOUGHTS

The Power of Influence

It is easy to dismiss Saul as a failure and thereby turn our backs on some of his strengths. Yet many in Israel admired him and were loyal to him. Men whose hearts God had touched followed him and became the nucleus of his army. Samuel, who had anointed him with oil, loved him dearly. Even after God rejected Saul, Samuel continued to pray for him. And David, in spite of Saul's relentless persecution of him, remained unfailingly loyal to the king—even after Saul gave Michal to another! Jonathan, who bore the brunt of his father's wrath and was excluded from his father's counsels because of his love for David, died on mount Gilboa defending Saul.

In Saul we see a man of great potential. His natural powers were enhanced by the Spirit of God. Initially he was very successful. He stands therefore as an example of what God can do through an individual. But his life also serves as a warning; it illustrates how we can negate and nullify the work the Lord desires to accomplish through us. We too have been given certain natural gifts. And when God the Holy Spirit came to indwell us at the time of our conversion, our potential was increased. We became men and women of influence in our homes, schools, offices, factories, hospital wards, or barracks. However, only to the extent that we remain obedient to the Lord is He able to use us.

Dr. Macartney developed an important thought from Samuel's words when the prophet and Saul first met.

> There is an invisible prophet standing before every young man and every young woman, and he says to you, "For whom is all that is desirable in the world? It is not for thee?" God intends the best for you. He has called you, as Paul said, to "glory and

honour and immortality." Will you also intend it for yourself? Will you choose that great destiny, as well as be called to it— and strive and suffer for it? As Jesus said, "Many are called but few are chosen."[13]

The Place of Testing

The writer of Hebrews reminded us of the inevitability of God's testing:

> Have you forgotten the exhortation, which discourses [addresses] you as sons: "My son, do not make light of [the] discipline of [the] Lord, nor faint [when you are] being reproved by Him; for whom [the] Lord loves He disciplines, and scourges every son whom He receives." For you endure discipline; God is dealing with you as with sons; for what son [is there] whom a father does not discipline? But if you are without discipline, of which all have become sharers, then are you illegitimate and not sons of the Father (Hebrews 12:5-8).

God knows what is in the heart of each of us. He tests us to show us our weaknesses and imperfections so that we might draw on Him for His strength. And through these times of trial we are gradually conformed to the image of His Son. Saul was tested. He failed as we often do. In his case, however, failure was not followed by repentance.

> He blamed the people, just as Aaron blamed the people for making the golden calf, although he had told them how to make it. When he was rebuked by Samuel for his transgression and was told that his kingdom would be given to David, a man better than he, Saul said, "I have sinned." No person in the Bible ever said that as often as Saul did, and he said it sometimes with tears. But soon after he said it, he turned back to his old ways. He was convicted for the moment, but he did not repent.[14]

When Saul met Samuel for the last time in the home of the spiritist at Endor, there was no remorse but only a fearful anticipation of judgment. God had withdrawn from Saul. And when he fell on his sword in an attempt to end his life, his act was not preceded by a prayer for the Lord to receive his spirit.

The Penalty of Self-will

God sought in many ways to mold the will of Saul into harmony with His own. He gave him instruction through Samuel, who taught him the duties of a king and warned him of the danger of disobedience. The Lord also chastened both Saul and the people. He allowed the land to fall into the hand of the Philistines to impress upon him his own weakness and dependence. Yet Saul deliberately disobeyed Him. The king feared the people more than he feared the One who had appointed him a ruler over His inheritance.

God's love is indeed boundless in its yearnings and self-sacrifice for the good of man. But His love is limited in its gracious and beneficent designs by the eternal laws of righteousness and the perverse will of man. The wise man said, "He who is often reproved and hardens his neck shall suddenly be destroyed, and that without remedy" (Proverbs 29:1).

The same God who inspired the pen of Solomon instructed Ezekiel to speak to His people and say to them, "'As I live,' says Yahweh, 'I have no pleasure in the death of the wicked; but rather that the wicked turn from his way and live: turn, turn from your evil ways; for why will you die?'" (Ezekiel 33:11)

Even the Lord Jesus Christ, who embodied the love of God as He walked this earth, wept over Jerusalem and lamented, "If you had known in this your day the things which belong to your peace! But now they are hidden from your eyes" (Luke 19:41-42).

Notwithstanding the boundless and unutterable love of God, it is possible for men and women to perish as a result of their self-will. It is possible for people, through stubborn and persistent disobedience, to drive away the Spirit of God and to fall into a condition in which it is impossible to renew them again to repentance. Tragedies such as that of Saul are not uncommon. Pastors who counsel families encounter such tragedies all too often. Far better it is to say with David, "Do not cast me away from Your presence, and do not take Your Holy Spirit from me" (Psalm 51:11).[15]

> So Saul died for his trespass which he had committed against Yahweh, because of the word of Yahweh which he did not keep; and also because he asked counsel of a medium...and did not inquire of Yahweh. Therefore He killed him, and turned the kingdom over to David the son of Jesse (1 Chronicles 10:13-14).

Under David, as recorded in 2 Samuel, God sovereignly established his kingdom and righteousness characterized his reign. And as valuable as this history is to us, it but sets the stage and prepares our minds for the time when "great David's greater Son" will set up His rule and reign over the kingdoms of the world.

NOTES

Preface

1. C. C. Ryrie, *Basic Theology* (Wheaton, IL: Victor, 1987) 43-44.

Introduction

1. D. Waitley, *Secrets of Greatness* (Old Tappan, NJ: Revell, 1983) 30.
2. G. L. Archer, Jr., in *A Survey of Old Testament Introduction* (2d ed., Chicago: Moody, 1974, p. 273) states, "For some reason the text of 1 and 2 Samuel seems to have been more poorly preserved in the Masoretic recension than any other book of the Bible." W. F. Albright in *Samuel and the Beginning of the Prophetic Movement* (Cincinnati: Hebrew Union College Press, 1961, 28 pages) discusses the supposed textual discrepancies. See P. A. H. deBoer, *Oudtestamentische Studien* 6 (1949) 1-100, and A. v. d. Kooij, *Nederlands Theologisch Tijdschrift* 36 (1982) 177-204, for lengthy critiques of the problems found in the Masoretic text. S. R. Driver in *Notes on the Hebrew Text of the Books of Samuel* (2d ed., Oxford: Clarendon, 1966, iv-lxxxiii) provides a most extensive discussion of the problem and favors using the Septuagint to emend the Masoretic text. Other approaches are taken by J. D. Shenkel, S. Pisano, and E. C. Ulrich, Jr. Shenkel compares the Masoretic text of 1 and 2 Samuel to the books of Chronicles. Pisano and Ulrich compare the Masoretic text with the Dead Sea scrolls. See Shenkel, *Harvard Theological Review* 62 (1969) 63-85; Pisano, *Additions or Omissions in the Books of Samuel* (Göttingen, W. Germany: Vandenhoeck and Ruprecht, 1984) 295 pages; and Ulrich, *The Qumran Text of Samuel and Josephus* (Missoula, MT: Scholars, 1978) 278 pages.
3. Cf. J. M. Boice, *Standing on the Rock* (Wheaton, IL: Tyndale, 1984) 202 pages; N. L. Geisler and W. Nix, *A General Introduction to the Bible,* 2d ed. (Chicago: Moody, 1986) 724 pages. See *The Minister's Library* by C. J. Barber for additional works on the importance of a sound understanding of Bibliology (Chicago: Moody, 1985-1987, I:67-71 and II:16-20).
4. *The Babylonian Talmud,* ed. I. Epstein (London: Soncino, 1935) Baba Bathra, 14b. Eusebius Pamphilius in his *Ecclesiastical History* (VIII:25:2) and Eusebius Hieronomus (otherwise known as Jerome) in his *Profatio in Libros Samuel et Malachim* of the Vulgate edition of the Bible make the same assertion.
5. C. C. Ryrie, *Ryrie Study Bible* (Chicago: Moody, 1978) 409.
6. The unity of Samuel is further attested by the fact that in the Masoretic text there is a note at the end of 2 Samuel referring to our 1 and 2 Samuel as the entire "Book of Samuel" and identifying our 1 Samuel 28:24 as the central verse.
7. R. H. Pfeiffer, *Introduction to the Old Testament* (New York: Harper, 1948, pp. 339-341) follows K. Budde, *Die Bücher Richter und Samuel, ihre Quellen und ihr Aufbau* (Tübingen: Mohr, 1892, pp. 167ff.). Cf. M. H. Segal, *Jewish Quarterly Review* 55 (1965) 318-339; 56 (1965) 137-157.
8. O. Eissfeldt, *Einleitung in das Alte Testament* (Tübingen: Mohr, 1934) 306.
9. A. R. S. Kennedy, *Samuel,* New Century Bible (Edinburgh: Jack, 1905) iv-l. Cf. H. H. Rowley, *The Growth of the Old Testament* (London: Hutchinson's, 1960) 66-67; R. W. Klein, *1 Samuel,* World Biblical Commentary (Waco, TX: Word, 1983) xxvi-xxxii; and P. K. McCarter, Jr., *1 Samuel,* Anchor Bible (Garden City, NY: Doubleday, 1980) 5-11.
10. Cf. Archer, *Survey of Old Testament Introduction,* 284-287; R. K. Harrison, *Introduction to the Old Testament* (Grand Rapids: Eerdmans, 1969) 696-714.
11. Archer, *Survey of Old Testament Introduction,* 272-273.
12. C. F. Keil and F. J. Delitzsch, *Biblical Commentary on the Books of Samuel,* trans. J. Martin (Grand Rapids: Eerdmans, 1986) 11-13.
13. Ibid., 2-12.

14. F. M. Cross, *Bulletin of the American Schools of Oriental Research* 132 (1953) 15-26; cf. F. M. Cross and S. Talmon, eds. *Qumran and the History of the Biblical Text* (Cambridge: Harvard University Press, 1975) 415 pages.
15. J. Bright, *Interpretation* 5 (1951) 452-454.
16. This is the view of the majority of conservative scholars. Cf. L. J. Wood, *Distressing Days of the Judges* (Grand Rapids: Zondervan, 1975) 88-89. For a fuller discussion than is possible here see C. J. Barber, *Judges: An Expositional Commentary* (Neptune, NJ: Loizeaux, 1990) 15-17.
17. Popularized by I. L. Jensen in *Jensen's Survey of the Old Testament* (Chicago: Moody, 1978) 183. Followed in most study Bibles and books of outlines.
18. A. P. Stanley, *Lectures on the History of the Jewish Church* (London: Murray, 1875) I:332-336. Cf. G. Oehler, *Theology of the Old Testament* (Minneapolis: Klock, 1978) 355-361; J. D. Pentecost, *Things to Come* (Grand Rapids: Zondervan, 1964) 433-445. For a listing of relevant journal articles see W. G. Hupper, *An Index to English Periodical Literature on the Old Testament and Ancient Near Eastern Studies* (Metuchen, NJ: Scarecrow, 1987) I:471.
19. Cf. K. L. Barker, *The NIV: The Making of a Contemporary Translation* (Grand Rapids: Zondervan, 1986) 106-110; T. Ishida, ed. *Studies in the Period of David and Solomon* (Winona Lake, IN: Eisenbrauns, 1982) 109-138. Ryrie in his *Basic Theology* (47-48) says: "This is a military figure which pictures *Yahweh* as the Commander of the angelic armies of heaven as well as the armies of Israel (1 Sam. 17:45). The title reveals the sovereignty and omnipotence of God and was used often by the prophets (Isaiah and Jeremiah) to remind the people during times of national crisis that God was their Leader and Protector."
20. D. F. Payne, *I and II Samuel* (Philadelphia: Westminster, 1982) 4.
21. C. J. Barber and J. D. Carter, *Always a Winner* (Ventura, CA: Regal, 1977) 7.
22. S. Ridout, *King Saul: The Man After the Flesh* (New York: Loizeaux, n.d.) 294 pages. Saul's primary problem was his external orientation, which made it easy for him to be motivated by the fear of man. The doctrine of the fear of the Lord is one of the most neglected and misunderstood in all of Scripture. For a concise summary of the evidence see C. J. Barber, *Dynamic Personal Bible Study* (Neptune, NJ: Loizeaux, 1981) 139-147. Cf. J. Murray, *Principles of Conduct* (Grand Rapids: Eerdmans, 1957) 229-242.
23. A. Maclaren, *The Life of David Reflected in the Psalms* (Grand Rapids: Baker, 1955) 261 pages; W. G. Blaikie, *David, King of Israel* (Minneapolis: Klock, 1981) 381 pages.
24. In a private communication W. W. Wiersbe (whose wisdom and Biblical expertise I greatly respect!) has drawn my attention to the fact that the great British Reformed Bible teacher D. M. Lloyd-Jones in *Romans: An Exposition of Chapter 8:5-17; The Sons of God* (Grand Rapids: Zondervan, 1975, pp. 1-52) has argued that the persons described in these verses are (1) unsaved individuals, not carnal Christians, and (2) true believers who are under the control of the Holy Spirit. Lloyd-Jones has made no provision for "fleshly" Christians (1 Corinthians 3:1) but divides all people into two groups (not four as Paul does in 1 Corinthians 2:14–3:3). But the word *flesh* can refer to the "fallen, ego-centric human nature" of the believer, which is not eradicated at the time of conversion as C. E. B. Cranfield, another Reformed scholar, has shown in his magisterial work entitled *A Critical and Exegetical Commentary on the Epistle to the Romans,* International Critical Commentary (Edinburgh: Clark, 1975) I:370-372,385-387. Further corroboration on the terminology used by Paul comes from the pen of the late H. C. G. Moule, whose exposition on *The Epistle to the Romans* in the Expositor's Bible Commentary series (reprinted by Klock, 1978) lays stress on the *mind* or moral affinity of the individual, not that person's eternal state (205-217). Cf. W. G. T. Shedd, *Commentary on Romans* (Minneapolis: Klock, 1978) 233-236.
25. Wood, *Judges,* 31,343-346. Cf. C. J. Barber, *Judges,* 14-18.
26. D. J. Wiseman, *Tyndale House Bulletin* 14 (1964) 8ff.; *Zondervan Pictorial Encyclopedia of the Bible,* ed. M. C. Tenney, 5 vols. (Grand Rapids: Zondervan, 1975) IV:910-912.
27. W. C. Kaiser, Jr., *Quest for Renewal* (Chicago: Moody, 1986) 27.
28. Ibid., 53-64. Cf. C. J. Barber and J. D. Carter, *Always a Winner,* 23-33.
29. See the discussion of '*īš gibbôr ḥayil* in *Ruth: An Expositional Commentary* by C. J. Barber (Neptune, NJ: Loizeaux, 1989) p. 154, n. 6.

30. *Macmillan Bible Atlas* by Y. Aharoni and M. Avi-Yonah, rev. ed. (New York: Macmillan, 1977) 80, 82. Cf. D. J. Wiseman, ed. *Peoples of Old Testament Times* (Oxford: Clarendon, 1973) 53-78; R. A. S. Macalister, *The Philistines: Their History and Civilization* (London: British Academy, 1913) 136 pages; E. E. Hindson, *The Philistines and the Old Testament* (Grand Rapids: Baker, 1971) 184 pages.

31. *Encyclopedia of Archaeological Excavations in the Holy Land,* ed. M. Avi-Yonah and E. Stein, 4 vols. (Englewood Cliffs, NJ: Prentice-Hall, 1975-1977) II:408-417; *New International Dictionary of Biblical Archaeology,* ed. E. M. Blaiklock and R. K. Harrison (Grand Rapids: Zondervan, 1983) 207-208.

32. *Encyclopedia of Archaeological Excavations* I:121-130; *New International Dictionary of Biblical Archaeology,* 75-76.

33. *Encyclopedia of Archaeological Excavations* I:103-119; *New International Dictionary of Biblical Archaeology,* 73-74.

34. *New International Dictionary of Biblical Archaeology,* 205-207; *Zondervan Pictorial Encyclopedia* II:658-659.

35. *New International Dictionary of Biblical Archaeology,* 173; *International Standard Bible Encyclopedia,* ed. G. W. Bromiley, 4 vols. (Grand Rapids: Eerdmans, 1979-1988) II:47-48.

36. *Macmillan Bible Atlas,* 78. Cf. C. J. Barber, *Judges,* 142-148; Wood, *Judges,* 106-109,278-287; Wiseman, *People of Old Testament Times,* 230,233.

37. *Macmillan Bible Atlas,* 6, 52. Cf. *New International Dictionary of Biblical Archaeology,* 319-320; Wiseman, *People of Old Testament Times,* 229-258.

38. *New International Dictionary of Biblical Archaeology,* 170-171; *Zondervan Pictorial Encyclopedia* II:201-205.

39. *Macmillan Bible Atlas,* 6, 10, 52-54. Cf. *New International Dictionary of Biblical Archaeology,* 319-320; Wiseman, *Peoples of Old Testament Times,* 229-258.

40. A. T. Olmstead, *History of Assyria* (Chicago: University of Chicago Press, 1964) 45-144; Wiseman, *Peoples of Old Testament Times,* 156-178; *Ancient Near Eastern Texts Relating to the Old Testament,* ed. J. B. Pritchard, 2d ed. (Princeton: Princeton University Press, 1955) 274-300.

41. J. A. Wilson, *The Burden of Egypt* (Chicago: University of Chicago Press, 1965) 225-229,255-256,314-318; G. Steindorff and K. C. Steele, *When Egypt Ruled the East* (Chicago: University of Chicago Press, 1963) 11-23; *Ancient Near Eastern Texts,* 217,269-300; Wiseman, *Peoples of Old Testament Times,* 79-99.

42. W. F. Albright, *Yahweh and the Gods of Canaan* (Garden City, NY: Doubleday, 1968) 293 pages; K. M. Kenyon, *Amorites and Canaanites* (London: British Academy, 1966) 80 pages.

43. Cf. Wood's excellent discussion of these issues in his *Judges,* 390-391.

Chapter 1

1. *Rāmātayim* means "double height" or "twin peaks" (i.e., hills). The location of Elkanah's home has been debated for centuries. Eusebius of Caesarea in his *Onomasticon* (32:21-23), followed by Jerome in his introduction to the Latin Bible, and in more recent times McCarter (*1 Samuel,* 47) sought to locate the village in the region of Rentis, about 16 miles east of Tel Aviv. Based on 1 Samuel 1:19 and 7:17, others have preferred a Benjamite location, possibly er-Ram. Identification is complicated by the fact that more than one city or village west of the Jordan river bore this name. Most cartographers locate Samuel's birthplace within the tribe of Benjamin, not Ephraim. Cf. McCarter, *1 Samuel,* 47; *Macmillan Bible Atlas* (west southwest of Geba and north of Gibeah in the territory of Benjamin) 2, 80-82 (and for a town with a similar name in Naphtali, 71-72). B. J. Beitzel in the *Moody Atlas of Bible Lands* (Chicago: Moody, 1985, pp. 34,51-52) identifies another town of the same name between Benjamin and Hebron. The term *Ephraimite* is derived from *pārah,* "to be fruitful."

2. Elkanah is described as a descendant of Zuph, after whom the area had been named. In 1 Samuel 9:5 the territory is called *'ereṣ ṣûp,* "the land of Zuph," Samuel's home. See S. R. Driver, *Notes on the Hebrew Text,* 3ff.; J. Mauchline, *1 and 2 Samuel,* New Century Bible (Greenwood, SC: Attic, 1971) 43.

3. Shiloh is located about 18.5 miles north of Jerusalem. See *Encyclopedia of Archaeological*

Excavations IV:1098-1100. For a discussion of the Shilonite priesthood see M. A. Cohen, *Hebrew Union College Annual* 36 (1965) 59-98; J. Kjaer, *Journal of the Palestinian Oriental Society* 10 (1930) 87-174; and J. Robertson, *Bulletin of the John Rylands Library* 32 (1949) 25.

4. *Zondervan Pictorial Encyclopedia* II:521-526. Klein (*1 Samuel,* 7) believes this special visit to Shiloh was for the purpose of sacrificing peace offerings to the Lord. See also M. Haran, *Vetus Testamentum* 19 (1969) 11-22.

5. W. Eichrodt, *Theology of the Old Testament,* trans. J. A. Baker (Philadelphia: Westminster, 1961) I:192-194. See also W. Dryness, *Themes in Old Testament Study* (Downers Grove, IL: InterVarsity, 1979) 46-47; W. H. Brownlee, *Bulletin of the American Schools of Oriental Research* 26 (1977) 38-46; J. P. Ross, *Vetus Testamentum* 17 (1967) 76-92; *Theological Wordbook of the Old Testament,* ed. R. L. Harris, G. L. Archer, Jr., and B. K. Waltke, 2 vols. (Chicago: Moody, 1980) II:749-751 (#1865).

6. God's original intent was for a man and woman to live together in a unique and lasting relationship (i.e., as husband and wife for life). This is indicated in such Scriptures as Genesis 2:18,23-25; Mark 10:8-9. The text of 1 Samuel 1:2,4-5,19 plainly intimates that Hannah and Peninnah shared similar rights and status as Elkanah's wives. Peninnah was not his mistress. Their social standing was sanctioned by divine precept (Deuteronomy 21:15) as well as social precedent (Genesis 16:2-3; 25:6; 29:18,25,30; 30:1-5; Judges 8:30). Apparently each came under the same lifelong *covenant* of marriage (Malachi 2:14) although Hannah had "seniority" because she was Elkanah's first wife. For a thorough discussion of these issues within the *Sitz im Leben* of the times see L. M. Epstein, *Marriage Laws in the Bible and the Talmud* (Cambridge, MA: Harvard University Press, 1942) 3-76; and E. Neufeld, *Ancient Hebrew Marriage Laws* (London: Longmans, Green, 1944) 118-132.

7. W. G. Blaikie, *The First Book of Samuel* (Minneapolis: Klock, 1978) 6-11. Some scholars have a penchant for introducing cultic elements (generally associated with the fertility rites of different peoples in the ancient Near East) into the Bible stories. An illustration of such a practice may be found in J. T. Willis's articles in *Studia Theologica* 26 (1972) 33-61 and *Catholic Biblical Quarterly* 35 (1973) 139-154.

8. Apparently Peninnah's provocation occurred only when she and Hannah were together at the annual feast. There is no indication in the text that her bickering and belittling occurred at any other time. Elkanah's comforting of Hannah (1 Samuel 1:8) appears to have been a special appeal in light of infrequent though well-known circumstances rather than a frequently rehearsed statement. If Hannah had heard these words of reassurance each time Peninnah picked on her, they would long since have lost their impact, for oft-repeated statements tend to diminish in significance the more they are used. When the infrequency of the provocation is correlated with the difficulty of locating Ramah in Ephraim (1 Samuel 1:1) and the mention of Samuel's home apparently being in Benjamin (7:17; 9:5), the conclusion drawn is that Elkanah may well have maintained two residences. Given the topography of the land occupied by the sons of Israel, these two residences may well have been only a few miles from each other. To go up to Shiloh yearly from *his city* (1:3,21) Elkanah would obviously depart from the city within the territory of Zuph. In the New Testament Bethlehem is looked upon as the city of Joseph and Mary, but this did not prevent them from living in Nazareth. First Samuel 1:19 adds tacit evidence of a separate residence for Hannah. It speaks of the place to which they went as "their house," not one shared with Peninnah and her children. None of this information is conclusive in and of itself. It does however point to certain facts that have often been overlooked. Cf. W. Deane and T. Kirk, *Studies in First Samuel* (Minneapolis: Klock, 1983) I:2,10,18. For a description of Ramah see E. Robinson, *Biblical Researches in Palestine* (London: Murray, 1856) I:458,576, II:8-10. For a discussion of Peninnah's character see E. Lipinski, *Vetus Testamentum* 17 (1967) 68-75.

9. M. Noth, *Die israelitischen Personennamen im Rahmen der gemeinsemitischen Namengebung* (Stuttgart: Kohlhammer, 1928) 63.

10. L. M. Epstein, *Marriage Laws,* 19,23,32-33,293-294; Neufeld, *Ancient Hebrew Marriage Laws,* 97,137,202.

11. Blaikie, *First Book of Samuel,* 10-12.

12. *Mānā 'aḥat 'appāyim* has no acceptable translation. It is usually rendered "a double portion" and signifies special favor (Genesis 43:34). See S. R. Driver, *Notes on the Hebrew Text*, 6. For a discussion of *'pym* (from *'appāyim*, "nose" or "face") see D. Auerbach, *Vetus Testamentum* 24 (1974) 350-354, and F. Deist, *Vetus Testamentum* 27 (1977) 205-209.

13. Cf. C. J. Barber and J. D. Carter, *Always a Winner*, 10-21; C. J. Barber and A. A. Barber, *You Can Have a Happy Marriage* (Grand Rapids: Kregel, 1984) 55-56.

14. Cf. P. R. Ackroyd, *I and II Samuel*, Cambridge Bible Commentary (Cambridge: University Press, 1971) 24. Eli was sitting at the *mĕzûzat hêkal Yahweh*, "the doorpost of the temple of Yahweh."

15. F. B. Meyer (*Samuel the Prophet*, London: Morgan and Scott, n.d., pp. 14-17) has a different analysis of Hannah's prayer from the one presented in this chapter. For Hannah's defense of herself before Eli (1 Samuel 1:15) see G. W. Ahlstrom, *Biblica* 60 (1979) 254; Klein, *1 Samuel*, 8-10.

16. *Zondervan Pictorial Encyclopedia* V:90-91.

17. *The Mishnah*, trans. H. Danby (London: Oxford University Press, 1933) Nedarim, 264ff.

18. Since Eli spoke as God's representative to His people, Eli's benediction was in effect God's own word of reassurance to Hannah. Cf. Pentecost, *Things to Come*, 433.

19. There are three distinct levels of faith or belief. The first level is a purely cognitive one. A person may give mental assent to certain propositional statements and believe them to be true. Salvation does *not* take place at this level, for we read in Scripture that Satan's emissaries also believe and tremble (James 2:19). The first level of belief, therefore, involves assent to the truth without conformity to it. The second level of faith or belief is the one at which conversion takes place. At this level we not only give mental assent to certain truths but also intimate our preference for them by embracing them, relying on them, and placing our entire confidence for the future in them. At this level, preference is clearly discernible (Acts 16:31; John 20:30-31; Galatians 3:22). The third level of faith or belief is the one at which we see a marked dedication or commitment. At this level the individual gives himself/herself unreservedly to Christ and willingly devotes his/her life to Him. This is the level at which spiritual growth takes place (Hebrews 10:39; 11:6). In the passage before us Hannah must have understood Eli's benediction to imply the granting of her prayer. The Hebrew *ûpānêhā lō'hāyû-lāh 'ôd*, "she no longer had a sad face" (1 Samuel 1:18), reflects her inner assurance. Against all indications to the contrary, she believed God's word through His spokesman.

20. The word *knew* in 1 Samuel 1:19 is a Biblical euphemism for sexual intercourse. The Lord "remembered" Hannah and gave her conception. The role of God in this act of creation (though interpreted in a cultic context) has been discussed by W. Schottroff in *Theologisches Wörterbuch zum Alten Testament*, ed. G. J. Gotterweck and H. Ringgren, in process (Stuttgart: Kohlhammer, 1970-) I:507-518.

21. The Hebrew is very picturesque. It literally reads, "At the coming round of days" (i.e., at the turn of the year, when a year had passed). S. R. Driver (*Notes on the Hebrew Text*, 16) believes that Elkanah and his family attended annually the New Year's (Rosh Hashanah) festival.

22. There appears to be a couple of wordplays in Hannah's statement at the time of the birth (1 Samuel 1:20). The first is on the verb *s'l*, "to ask, request" and *hû' sā'ûl lĕyahweh*, "he is dedicated to Yahweh." The second is connected with the name Hannah and Elkanah had given their son. *Š̌ ĕmû'el kî miyyahweh š̌ ĕ'iltîw* ("Samuel because from Yahweh I requested him") has led some to interpret Samuel's name to mean "asked of God." Contrary views have been proposed by S. R. Driver (*Notes on the Hebrew Text*, 16-17) and McCarter (*1 Samuel*, 62).

23. Nursing an infant normally lasted for three years in ancient Near Eastern societies (see Apocrypha, 2 Maccabees 7:27; *International Standard Bible Encyclopedia* III:568).

24. D. Zeligs, *Psychoanalysis and the Bible* (New York: Bloch, 1974) 97-100. Few books have challenged my thinking as much as this one, and with few works have I found myself in such hearty disagreement.

25. See the discussion of how to provide a sense of security in C. J. Barber and A. A. Barber, *Your Marriage Has Real Possibilities*, (Grand Rapids, Kregel, 1984) 93-113; and

in C. J. Barber and G. H. Strauss, *The Effective Parent* (San Bernardino, CA: Here's Life, 1980) 147 pages.

26. C. R. Swindoll, *You and Your Child,* 2d ed. (Nashville: Nelson, 1977) 27-48.

27. The preferred reading is "with a three-year-old bull." Other translations, however, read "with three bulls." Elkanah may indeed have taken other animals to Shiloh for sacrifice but it is highly unlikely that he would take *three* bulls. The bull in the text was a special one and was probably intended as a whole burnt offering. It would symbolize Samuel's complete dedication to the Lord. Other offerings also indicated their gratitude to God for His goodness to them. Cf. Keil and Delitzsch, *Biblical Commentary,* 27; Mauchline, *1 and 2 Samuel,* 49.

28. J. Hall, *Contemplations on the Historical Passages of the Old and New Testaments* (London: S.P.C.K., n.d.) 154.

29. The majority of scholars (e.g., S. R. Driver, *Notes on the Hebrew Text,* 22-23; J. Hall, *Contemplations on Historical Passages,* 154; McCarter, *1 Samuel,* 57-58) believe that Eli, or perhaps Elkanah, is the "he" referred to in 1 Samuel 1:28b. Others emend the text to read "she" (i.e., Hannah). The structure of the Hebrew text, however, is against such a forced interpretation. It seems more in keeping with what has been revealed of Samuel thus far, together with the grammar of the text itself, as well as with what is to follow, to conclude that Samuel is the one who bows and worships the Lord. This interpretation also fits better with Han-nah's statement that immediately precedes 1:28b, "I have also dedicated him to Yahweh" (1:28a), for 1:28b then shows Samuel's acceptance of his destiny. Those who object that he was too young to understand what was taking place manifest a distinct lack of understanding of child psychology. At no time is it easier to instill in a child a deep and lasting internal God-consciousness than in the first three years of life.

30. The service of women in the tabernacle/temple is well-documented (Exodus 38:8; Psalm 68:11; Luke 2:36-38). Some of these women were not necessarily virtuous (1 Samuel 2:22; 2 Kings 23:7), but others of their number would have made suitable foster mothers for young Samuel. Cf. J. M'Clintock and J. Strong, *Cyclopedia of Biblical, Theological, and Ecclesiastical Literature* (Grand Rapids: Baker, 1968) IV:818-820.

31. Deane and Kirk, *Studies in First Samuel* I:19; C. J. Barber and J. D. Carter, *Always a Winner,* 17-18.

32. See D. N. Freedman, *Pottery, Poetry, and Prophecy* (Winona Lake, IN: Eisenbrauns, 1980) 243-261; R. W. Klein, *Concordia Theological Monthly* 41 (1970) 674-687; T. J. Lewis, *Journal of Biblical Literature* 104 (1985) 105-108; G. R. O'Day, *Current Trends in Theology and Mission* 12 (1985) 203-210.

33. Blaikie, *First Book of Samuel,* 36. He has a fine exposition of this song of praise on pages 26-36. Cf. Meyer, *Samuel the Prophet,* 18-20.

34. Blaikie, *First Book of Samuel,* 36.

35. M'Clintock and Strong, *Cyclopedia of Literature* X:816-819.

Chapter 2

1. P. Miller, *Jonathan Edwards* (Amherst, MA: University of Massachusetts Press, 1981) 13-14,35-37,40,127-130,201-208,214,228-230; O. E. Winslow, *Jonathan Edwards* (New York: Farrar, Strauss and Giroux, 1973) 5-30,40-43,49-50,74-77,113-117,128-132,136,218, 291ff.,307-308,332-335,342-343; R. L. Dugdale, *The Jukes* (New York: Putnam's, 1910) 121 pages.

2. *Shārat,* "serving," indicates that at a very early age Samuel was being presented to the reader as a priest. Cf. W. Gesenius, *Hebrew and English Lexicon of the Old Testament,* ed. F. Brown, S. R. Driver, and C. A. Briggs (Oxford: Clarendon, 1962) 1058; *Theological Wordbook* II:958 (#2472); N. L. Tidwell, *Vetus Testamentum* 24 (1974) 505-507; and D. M. Gunn, *Vetus Testamentum* 24 (1974) 505-507.

3. Deane and Kirk, *Studies in First Samuel* I:19.

4. *Zondervan Pictorial Encyclopedia* II: 332-333.

5. Meyer, *Samuel the Prophet,* 28.

6. *Theological Wordbook* I:111 (#246).

7. H. W. Wolff, *Expository Times* 12 (1952-1953) 533-554. See also H. W. Hertzberg, *I and II*

Samuel, a Commentary, Old Testament Library, trans. J. S. Bowden (Philadelphia: Westminster, 1964) 36. *Yāda,* "to know," as H. C. Alleman and E. E. Flack in their *Old Testament Commentary* (Philadelphia: Muhlenberg, 1948, I:379) remind us, "is a very meaningful term" (cf. Hosea 4; 6:6; 8:2; 13:4). When used negatively (as here) it implies "the absence of a knowledge of God that opens the door for unfaithfulness and disloyalty, swearing falsely, deception, murder, stealing, adultery, acts of violence, idolatry, and eventually, rejection of the truth."

8. Deane and Kirk, *Studies in First Samuel* I:24.
9. Ibid.
10. Blaikie, *First Book of Samuel,* 39.
11. Meyer, *Samuel the Prophet,* 28.
12. C. J. Barber, *Judges,* 14-17; Pentecost, *Things to Come,* 433-445.
13. A few of the works published in this genre of literature in recent years are: U. Cassuto, *The Goddess Anath* (Jerusalem: Magnes, 1971) 194 pages; J. Gray, *The Legacy of Canaan* (Leiden: Brill, 1971) 348 pages; A. S. Kapelrud, *Baal in the Ras Shamra Texts* (Copenhagen: Gad, 1952) 156 pages; idem, *The Violent Goddess* (Oslo: Universitetsforlaget, 1969) 156 pages; the numerous works of E. O. James including *The Cult of the Mother Goddess* (London: Thames and Hudson, 1959) 300 pages; S. N. Kramer, *The Sacred Marriage Rite* (Bloomington, IN: Indiana University Press, 1969) 170 pages; M. H. Pope, *El in the Ugaritic Texts* (Leiden: Brill, 1955) 116 pages.
14. Blaikie, *First Book of Samuel,* 41-42.
15. Keil and Delitzsch, *Biblical Commentary,* 38; A. P. Stanley, *History of Jewish Church* I:323,339-340.
16. Blaikie, *First Book of Samuel,* 45-47.
17. Hertzberg (*I and II Samuel,* 37) notes a change in the text of 1 Samuel 2:29 from second person plural to second person singular, indicating that God was personally holding Eli responsible for not dealing decisively with the sins of his sons.
18. There is no mention of an Aaronic priest from Eli's time until Ahijah, his great-grandson in the days of Saul (1 Samuel 14:3). Later on, the house of Zadok was substituted for the house of Abiathar (1 Kings 2:27,35; cf. 1 Chronicles 12:26-28). Cf. Hertzberg, *I and II Samuel,* 38; M. Noth, *Vetus Testamentum* 13 (1963) 390-400.
19. Hertzberg, *I and II Samuel,* 38-39; A. F. Kirkpatrick, *The First Book of Samuel,* Cambridge Bible for Schools and Colleges (Cambridge: University Press, 1888) 62-63.
20. J. Hall, *Contemplations on Historical Passages,* 156.
21. Josephus (*Antiquities of the Jews* V:10:4) claims Samuel was twelve years old at the time. Eli would have been ninety years of age (c. 1077 B.C.). For a detailed analysis of the structure of 1 Samuel 3, showing the contrasts intended by the Biblical writer, see W. G. E. Watson, *Biblische Zeitschrift* 29 (1985) 90-93. The passing of the mantle of authority from Eli to Samuel has been treated by J. T. Willis in *Theologische Zeitschrift* 35 (1979) 201-212, though not without Willis's usual emphasis on the cultic elements he believes lie behind the narrative.
22. *Zondervan Pictorial Encyclopedia* III:865-866.
23. J. G. Janzen, *Journal for the Study of the Old Testament* 26 (1983) 89-96. Cf. *International Standard Bible Encyclopedia* III:967-968.
24. Kirkpatrick, *First Book of Samuel,* 67. Cf. R. Gnuse, *Zeitschrift für die alttestamentliche Wissenschaft* 92 (1982) 379-390; idem, *The Dream Theophany of Samuel* (Lanham, MD: University Press of America, 1984) 278 pages; M. Newman, *Israel's Prophetic Heritage,* ed. B. W. Anderson and W. Harrelson (New York: Harper and Row, 1962) 86-97; L. W. Batten, *Journal of Biblical Literature* 19 (1900) 32-33; G. R. Driver, *Journal of Theological Studies* 32 (1931) 365; idem, *Journal of Theological Studies* 32 (1931) 365-366; and J. T. Willis, *Theologische Zeitschrift* 35 (1979) 201-212.
25. C. J. Barber and G. H. Strauss, *The Effective Parent,* 95-106; Blaikie, *First Book of Samuel,* 55.
26. Kirkpatrick, *First Book of Samuel,* 63-65,67.
27. Josephus, *Antiquities of the Jews* XVII:6:5 and XVII:8:2; idem, *Wars of the Jews* I:33:7-9; S. Perowne, *Herod the Great* (London: Hodder and Stoughton, 1956) 167-175.
28. D. S. Schaff, *History of the Christian Church,* ed. P. Schaff (Grand Rapids: Eerdmans, n.d.) VI:693-694.

29. J. H. Merle D'Aubigne, *History of the Reformation in England* (Edinburgh: Banner of Truth, 1963) II:474. Too little attention is paid the fine works of this evangelical scholar! Years ago Victor Thomas, a pastor under whose ministry I sat, said, "No one can read D'Aubigne and remain the same." He was right.
30. Meyer, *Samuel the Prophet,* 32.
31. J. Elliot, *The Journals of Jim Elliot,* ed. E. Elliot (Old Tappan, NJ: Revell, 1978) 361.

Chapter 3

1. An entire literary corpus has grown up around "the ark narrative." Most scholars view these chapters as a separate segment of Israel's history inserted here by an editor. Many believe that it was originally a part of 2 Samuel 6. And then there are those who connect the plague of rodents with a much later era (possibly Sennacherib's invasion). For a detailed discussion of the viewpoints see A. F. Campbell, *The Ark Narrative* (Missoula, MT: Scholars, 1975) 6-54. Other important treatments include P. D. Miller, Jr., and J. J. M. Roberts, *The Hand of the Lord* (Baltimore: Johns Hopkins University Press, 1977) 119 pages; L. Rost, *Das kline Credo und andere Studien zum alten Testament* (Heidelberg: Quelle und Meyer, 1965) 119-253. Also see A. F. Campbell, *Journal of Biblical Literature* 98 (1979) 31-43; P. R. Davies, *Journal of North Semitic Languages* 5 (1977) 9-18; D. M. Gunn, *Vetus Testamentum* 24 (1974) 286-317; J. Dus, *Vetus Testamentum* 13 (1963) 333-337; L. I. Conrad, *Journal of the American Oriental Society* 104 (1984) 281-287; O. Margolith, *Vetus Testamentum* 33 (1983) 339-341; J. B. Geyer, *Vetus Testamentum* 31 (1981) 293-304; J. Wilkinson, *Expository Times* 88 (1977) 137-141; D. W. Thomas, *Journal of Theological Studies* 11 (1960) 52; and M. Delcor, *Vetus Testamentum* 14 (1964) 137-154.
2. Deane and Kirk, *Studies in First Samuel* I:28-29.
3. The Septuagint adds that "in those days the Philistines gathered together to make war against Israel." Josephus (*Antiquities of the Jews* V:11:1) supports this view. Cf. Klein, *1 Samuel,* 41 (but the chronology he cites is faulty); McCarter, *1 Samuel,* 103.
4. *Macmillan Bible Atlas,* 84. Cf. A. D. Baly, *The Geography of the Bible* (San Francisco: Harper and Row, 1974) 13,97-98,130-134; Robinson, *Biblical Researches in Palestine* II:457-459; W. M. Thomson, *The Land and the Book,* 3 vols. (New York: Harper and Brothers, 1886) II:604-607.
5. Deane and Kirk, *Studies in First Samuel* I:37.
6. Deane (ibid.) observed, "[The Israelites] misused the history of these wonders to delude themselves into the idea that the Lord's presence was so inseparably united to this material symbol that He would always give success to those who possessed it, and that by putting it in jeopardy they could compel Him, as it were, to come to their rescue. But if this were so, what would become of God's moral government of the world? Is it feasible for God's people to constrain Him to side with them without regard to their fitness of His favor? Should God sanction this trust in the externals of religion where there was no conformity to His will?" This same tendency is often found today when leaders in the Christian community establish schools or engage in various outreach ministries; some claim, "The Lord told me to do such-and-such," and then believe that because God's honor is at stake, He is obligated to make the venture a success.
7. Yahweh is said to be enthroned above the cherubim (Psalm 99:5; 132:7; 1 Chronicles 28:2). Cf. W. F. Albright, *Biblical Archaeologist* 1 (1938) 1-3; R. deVaux, *Ancient Israel: Its Life and Institutions,* trans. J. McHugh (New York: McGraw-Hill, 1961) 298-300; F. M. Cross, *Canaanite Myths and Hebrew Epics* (Cambridge, MA: Harvard University Press, 1975) 35-36. See also *Theological Wordbook* I:454-455 (#1036).
8. Kirkpatrick, *First Book of Samuel,* 71.
9. Ibid.; cf. K. M. Kenyon, *Archaeology of the Holy Land,* 5th ed. (Nashville: Nelson, 1985) 183ff.; *Documents from Old Testament Times,* ed. D. W. Thomas (London: Nelson, 1958) 38.
10. Blaikie (*First Book of Samuel,* 67-69) graphically describes the battle as well as the fate of Eli's sons. We have dated these events in 1069 B.C. For a fuller discussion see W. F. Albright, *Archaeology and the Religion of Israel* (Baltimore: Johns Hopkins University

Press, 1942) 103ff.; H. Kjaer, *Journal of the Palestinian Oriental Society* 10 (1930) 87-114; M. Tsevat, *Journal of Bible and Religion* 32 (1964) 355-358; idem, *Hebrew Union College Annual* 32 (1961) 191-216; cf. L. M. Eslinger, *Kingship of God in Crisis* (Sheffield, England: Almond, 1985) 161-186.

11. Deane and Kirk, *Studies in First Samuel* I:39.
12. *Theological Wordbook* I:314-315 (#722). Cf. 2 Samuel 1:2. See also Homer, *Iliad* 18:23; Virgil, *Aeneid* 12:609-611.
13. M. Tsevat, *Journal of Bible and Religion* 32 (1964) 355-358. For a summary of Eli's ministry note the comments of J. Hall, *Contemplations on Historical Passages,* 157-158.
14. Cf. the treatment of the shekinah glory in C. J. Barber, *Theological Students Fellowship Bulletin* 7 (1975) 17-20.
15. These include (1) assurance of God's presence (Exodus 25:8; 40:34-35; cf. Psalm 74:2); (2) evidence of God's attributes (e.g., holiness, power, protection, etc.; cf. Exodus 19:18 and 24:16-17; Numbers 20:6); and (3) knowledge of God's will (i.e., His guidance; cf., Exodus 13:18,21-22; 16:7,10; 40:34-38; Numbers 9:15–10:10). When these and other verses are compared with the Jewish Targums, the importance of the shekinah becomes even more startling. Cf. M'Clintock and Strong, *Cyclopedia of Literature* IX:637-639; *Theological Wordbook* II:925ff. (#2387).
16. F. M. Cross and D. N. Freedman, *Bulletin of the American Schools of Oriental Research* 175 (1964) 48-50; D. N. Freedman, *Biblical Archaeologist* 26 (1963) 134-139; *Encyclopedia of Archaeological Excavations* I:103-119; Robinson, *Biblical Researches in Palestine* II:33; Thomson, *The Land and the Book* I:157-161,169-171; Herodotus, *History* II:157.
17. Cf. Miller and Roberts, *Hand of the Lord,* 40-51; P. R. Davies, *Journal of Northwest Semitic Languages* 5 (1977) 9-18; A. F. Campbell, *Journal of Biblical Literature* 98 (1979) 31-43; Eslinger, *Kingship of God,* 187-212.
18. In other accounts Dagon is mentioned as the brother of El. Cf. *Theologisches Wörterbuch zum Alten Testament* III:139-142; Macalister, *Philistines,* 99-114; Mauchline, *1 and 2 Samuel,* 76; S. A. Cook, *The Religion of Ancient Palestine in the Light of Archaeology* (London: British Academy, 1930) 170-171; Kapelrud, *Baal in the Ras Shamra Texts,* 52-56,64-66; and Pope, *El in the Ugaritic Texts,* 5-116.
19. Blaikie, *First Book of Samuel,* 44-46.
20. Klein (*1 Samuel,* 50) discusses the belief in antiquity that evil spirits lived beneath the threshold of houses and temples. Even today some hold to the tradition of carrying a bride over the threshold, believing that if she stumbles or falls when entering her new home for the first time, it will be an evil omen of the future.
21. Deane and Kirk, *Studies in First Samuel* I:46.
22. J. J. M. Roberts, *Vetus Testamentum* 21 (1971) 244-251.
23. Cf. G. R. Driver, *Journal of the Royal Asiatic Society* (1950) 50-51. J. Wilkinson, *Expository Times* 88 (1977) 137-141, believes the most likely translation of *'ōpel* is "hill, mound, swelling, tumor." Cf. Herodotus, *History* II:141. J. Trapp in his commentary on the Bible gave his opinion that the disease was syphilis. The evidence of the Biblical text is against such a view. Josephus (*Antiquities of the Jews* I:6:1) adhered to the belief that the disease was dysentery. Kirkpatrick (*First Book of Samuel,* 77), Mauchline (*1 and 2 Samuel,* 77), and Keil and Delitzsch (*Biblical Commentary,* 60) believe *'ōpel* refers to boils.
24. Cf. Keil and Delitzsch, *Biblical Commentary,* 60-61; G. Cansdale, *Animals of Bible Lands* (Exeter, England: Paternoster, 1970) 132-134; V. Møller-Christensen and K. E. Jordt-Jørgensen, *Encyclopedia of Bible Animals* (Philadelphia: Fortress, 1965) 111; Aristotle, *History of Animals* 6:37.
25. Gesenius, *Hebrew and English Lexicon of the Old Testament,* 979.
26. *New International Dictionary of Biblical Archaeology,* 73-74; *Zondervan Pictorial Encyclopedia* I:352-354.
27. G. E. Wright, *Biblical Archaeologist* 29 (1966) 78-86; *New International Dictionary of Biblical Archaeology,* 205-206; *Zondervan Pictorial Encyclopedia* II:658-659.
28. Robinson, *Biblical Researches in Palestine* II:226-229; G. E. Wright, *Biblical Archaeologist* 29 (1966) 70-86; Y. Aharoni, *The Land and the Book,* rev. ed. (Philadelphia: Westminster, 1979) 270ff.; *New International Dictionary of Biblical Archaeology,* 173; *Zondervan Pictorial Encyclopedia* II:259-260.

29. Cf. J. Wilkinson, *Expository Times* 88 (1977) 137-141.
30. *Theological Wordbook* II:871 (#2236).
31. Deane and Kirk, *Studies in First Samuel* I:51; S. R. Driver, *Notes on the Hebrew Text,* 53-55; B. O. Long, *Journal of Biblical Literature* 92 (1973) 489-497. Cf. Exodus 7:11; Isaiah 2:6; Daniel 2:2.
32. For further illustration of this point see W. H. Stephens, *The New Testament World in Pictures* (Nashville: Broadman, 1987) 229-232,262 (#s 456-470,525).
33. Blaikie, *First Book of Samuel,* 79.
34. Robinson, *Biblical Researches in Palestine* II:18,223-225 and III:153. Cf. F. M. Cross and G. E. Wright, *Journal of Biblical Literature* 75 (1956) 202-206; Y. Aharoni, *Bulletin of the American Schools of Oriental Research* 154 (1959) 35-39; W. F. Albright, *Bulletin of the American Schools of Oriental Research* 173 (1964) 51-53; *Encyclopedia of Archaeological Excavations* I:248-253.
35. Thomson, *The Land and the Book* I:543. Cf. J. Gray, *Archaeology and the Old Testament,* 415; and for a discussion of the route from Ekron to Beth-shemesh, see J. A. Emerton, *Archaeology and the Old Testament,* 199-202.
36. The Septuagint claims that it was the sons of a man named Jeconiah who "rejoiced not among the men of Beth-shemesh because they saw the ark"—perhaps fearing its presence might bring the plague upon them. Cf. S. R. Driver, *Notes on the Hebrew Text,* 59.
37. The Masoretic text reads, "seventy men fifty thousand men." There is no conjunction between the first "men" and "fifty," as one might expect. This is most unusual. This is the only place in the entire Hebrew Bible where such a phenomenon occurs. Josephus (*Antiquities of the Jews* VI:1:4) says that only seventy men were killed. Most scholars believe it impossible that a village the size of Beth-shemesh could have more than 50,000 inhabitants. Whatever the answer to the problem, the Biblical text states that it was a "great slaughter" (1 Samuel 6:19).
38. Y. Aharoni, *The Land of the Bible,* trans. A. F. Rainey, rev. ed. (Philadelphia: Westminster, 1979) 224-227,287,301; J. Blenkinsopp, *Journal of Biblical Literature* 88 (1969) 143-156; *New International Dictionary of Biblical Archaeology,* 280-281; *Zondervan Pictorial Encyclopedia* III:825-827. Psalm 132 looks back on King David's plans to build the temple. Verse 6 of the Psalm (where *jaar,* "wood," is probably an abbreviation of *jearim,* "woods") may reflect his bringing of the ark to Jerusalem.
39. Cf. J. J. Von Allmen, *Vocabulary of the Bible* (London: Lutterworth, 1966) 36; cf. *Theological Wordbook* I:132 (#285); L. O. Richards, *Expository Dictionary of Bible Words* (Grand Rapids: Regency Reference Library, 1985) 130-132. (See Deuteronomy 33:29; Psalm 32:1; 33:12; 65:4; 84:4; 144:15.)
40. Meyer (*Samuel the Prophet,* 37) writes: Israel "remembered the wonderful scenes in which the Ark had played a part; how the waters of the Jordan had fled before it, and the walls of Jericho had fallen down. Its going forth, in the words of the great lawgiver, had always meant the scattering of Jehovah's foes. They did not realize that God's very present help depended not upon the presence of a material symbol, but on moral and spiritual conditions."
41. J. Hall (*Contemplations on Historical Passages,* 157) describes the events with particular vividness: "What a spectacle was this, to see uncircumcised Philistines laying their profane hands upon the testimony of God's presence! To see the glorious mercy-seat under the roof of an idol [temple]! To see the two cherubim spreading their wings [beneath the sightless stare of Dagon]. . . . Security and presumption attend ever the threshold of ruin. God will let them sleep in this confidence; in the morning they shall find how vainly they have dreamed. Now they begin to find they have gloried in their own plague, and overthrown nothing but their own peace."

Chapter 4

1. Benjamin Disraeli, in a speech before Parliament, June 24, 1870.
2. *Macmillan Bible Atlas,* 92.
3. Meyer, *Samuel the Prophet,* 60; cf. Blaikie, *First Book of Samuel,* 86-87.
4. Kirkpatrick, *First Book of Samuel,* 87; cf. A. Edersheim, *Bible History: Old Testament* (Grand Rapids: Eerdmans, 1954) IV:27.

5. The Biblical writer often provided his readers with a foreview or summary of what happened over an extended period of time (e.g., 1 Samuel 4:1a) only to digress and deal with a specific event (4:1b–7:1) before returning to his previous thought (i.e., the ministry of Samuel, 7:2b).

6. Keil and Delitzsch, *Biblical Commentary*, 71.

7. R. P. Smith, *The Expositor* 3 (1876) 241-251,342-355,401-414; idem, *The Expositor* 4 (1877) 35-46; cf. Hupper, *Index to English Periodical Literature* I:116-117.

8. *Macmillan Bible Atlas*, 85. The circuit is depicted in the form of an oval, as if Samuel went from Ramah to Gilgal, then to Bethel, and from Bethel on to Mizpah before returning to Ramah. This is plainly incorrect. The sequence of the text implies that Samuel more than likely followed the valleys, going first northward to Bethel, then turning east and going on to Gilgal, and finally turning back and taking in Mizpah on his way home.

9. *Nāhā 'ahā   re*, "to turn after" the Lord. They "went into mourning toward Yahweh." Cf. Blaikie, *First Book of Samuel*, 87; S. R. Driver, *Notes on the Hebrew Text*, 61-62; Kaiser, *Quest for Renewal*, 56; Mauchline, *1 and 2 Samuel*, 83.

10. Blaikie, *First Book of Samuel*, 87-89.

11. Klein (*1 Samuel*, 67-68) appears obsessed with the idea of a holy war. Certainly this was in Samuel's mind when he said, "And Yahweh will deliver you from the hand of the Philistines," but it is unwise to make such an idea the central thought of all that follows. Spiritual reconciliation with a holy God of necessity had to precede His intervention on their behalf. For a discussion of the role of intercessory prayer as a special function of a holy war, see G. von Rad, *Old Testament Theology*, trans. D. M. G. Stalker (New York: Harper and Brothers, 1962) II:51-52; P. D. Miller, *Vetus Testamentum* 18 (1968) 100-107.

12. Deane and Kirk, *Studies in First Samuel* I:63. The location of Mizpah has been hotly disputed in recent years. The majority of modern scholars favor Tell en-Nasbeh, eight miles north of Jerusalem (cf. *Encyclopedia of Archaeological Excavations* III:912-918). Others believe Mizpah to be mount Scopus, just north of Jerusalem and the site of a modern university (cf. Kirkpatrick, *First Book of Samuel*, 88). The most plausible location, however, is Nebi Samwil, approximately five miles northwest of Jerusalem (cf. *Archaeology and the Old Testament*, 329-342; Kaiser, *Quest for Renewal*, 58). Robinson (*Biblical Researches in Palestine* I:460-461) and Thomson (*The Land and the Book* I:67-68,72,77,79) offer helpful descriptions of Nebi Samwil.

13. Cf. Leviticus 16:29,31. Yōm Kippur was the only fast in Israel's calendar. The solemnity of this convocation at Mizpah is indicated by the fact that Samuel proclaimed a solemn fast. Cf. C. J. Barber and J. D. Carter, *Always a Winner*, 33 (note 8); *Zondervan Pictorial Encyclopedia* II:501-503. Fasting can easily deteriorate into an external rite. The Pharisees fasted twice a week (supposedly to show how spiritual they were). When a person really fasts in the Biblical sense, he/she becomes oblivious to the passing of time. Because he/she is so intent upon prayer and so in earnest, a meal may be missed without the individual being aware of it. Only afterward does he/she feel hungry (cf. Matthew 4:2, "He then [at the end of the forty days] became hungry").

14. Confession can likewise become a routine. Cf. *International Standard Bible Encyclopedia* I:759.

15. Cf. L. I. Conrad, *Journal of the American Oriental Society* 104 (1984) 281-287; Edersheim, *Bible History* IV:28; Hertzberg, *I and II Samuel*, 67; Klein, *1 Samuel*, 67; McCarter, *1 Samuel*, 144; G. F. Moore, *Judaism* (Cambridge, MA: Harvard University Press, 1966) II:44-46; *Talmud*, Tosefta Sukkah, 3:3; 5:1-4; 50a.

16 Kaiser, *Quest for Renewal*, 59; cf. Keil and Delitzsch, *Biblical Commentary*, 73.

17. Kaiser, *Quest for Renewal*, 60.

18. *'Al-tāhărēš mimmennū mizzĕ'ōq*, "Do not keep silent from us, from crying out," shows their desperate need. They implored Samuel to pray for them. *Wayya'ănēhū Yahweh... wayyar'ēm Yahweh*, "And Yahweh answered him...and Yahweh thundered," shows God's sovereignty in answering Samuel's prayer (cf. Jeremiah 33:3). Cf. Cross, *Canaanite Myths*, 147-194; Kaiser, *Quest for Renewal*, 53-54.

19. For a fuller discussion of these issues, see C. J. Barber and S. Aspenleiter, *Through the Valley of Tears* (Old Tappan, NJ: Revell, 1987) 101-112.

20. *'Ôlâ kālîl,* "whole burnt offering." These words are more or less synonymous.
21. Josephus, *Antiquities of the Jews* VI:2:2.
22. Blaikie, *First Book of Samuel,* 98-100.
23. Ibid., 107; cf. B. C. Birch, *Rise of the Israelite Monarchy* (Missoula, MT: Scholars, 1976) 11-21; Hertzberg, *I and II Samuel,* 69; Keil and Delitzsch, *Biblical Commentary,* 75; Mauchline, *1 and 2 Samuel,* 69; A. D. H. Mayes, *Israel in the Period of the Judges* (London: SCM, 1974) 147 pages; idem, *Israelite and Judean History,* Old Testament Library (Philadelphia: Westminster, 1977) 285-331.

Chapter 5

1. John Naisbitt, *Megatrends* (New York: Warner, 1982).
2. Blaikie, *First Book of Samuel,* 109.
3. Apparently the average longevity of God's people during this period was between thirty-five and forty years. Life was hard. During periods of apostasy when the Lord withheld the rain, the people had great difficulty eking out an existence. If we add to this difficulty the heavy taxation of some foreign power, we can well see how only the rich (who had servants to do menial work for them) could enjoy a normal life expectancy. The fact that Samuel was now in his sixties, but had neither riches nor servants, shows God's reward of His servant's righteousness (Psalm 91:16; Proverbs 3:16; 4:10; 9:11; 10:27). See also J. Pedersen, *Israel,* 4 vols. (London: Oxford University Press, 1940) I-II:230-232,315-316,327-328.
4. Josephus, *Antiquities of the Jews,* VI:3:2; cf. A. Wiser, *Samuel: seine geschichte Aufgabe und religiöse Bedeutung. Traditionsgeschichte Untersuchungen zu 1. Samuel 7–12* (Gottingen: Vandenhoeck und Ruprecht, 1962) 30-31.
5. *Macmillan Bible Atlas,* 90. For a description of Beersheba see Thomson, *The Land and the Book* I:297-299; II:94,125,599; III:211,356,653,660; J. Perrot, *Israel Exploration Journal* 5 (1955) 17-40,73-80; idem, *Syria* 34 (1957) 1-38; 36 (1959) 6-119. Cf. *Encyclopedia of Archaeological Excavations* I:160-168.
6. Edersheim, *Bible History* IV:31-32.
7. In 1 Samuel 8:3 the use of *bĕdarkô,* "his [Samuel's] way" ("way" is singular, not plural as in most versions), and the expression *wayyittâ 'ahărê habbāṣa',* "turned aside to private gain," imply that Joel and Abijah had not previously demonstrated these weaknesses.
8. Abijah's name may have been inadvertently omitted from the text of 1 Chronicles 6 by a copyist. Cf. McCarter, *1 Samuel,* 156.
9. *'Attâ,* "So now," is a very unusual form of expression. Cf. Mauchline, *1 and 2 Samuel,* 72.
10. Cf. A. J. McClain's masterful description in *The Greatness of the Kingdom* (Grand Rapids: Zondervan, 1959) 556 pages (noting in particular pages 96-100). For a further discussion of the institution of the monarchy see Birch, *Rise of the Israelite Monarchy,* 11-108; J. Bright, *A History of Israel,* 3d ed. (Philadelphia: Westminster, 1981) 184-190; R. E. Clements, *Vetus Testamentum* 24 (1974) 398-400; T. N. D. Mettinger, *King and Messiah* ([Sweden]: Gleerup, 1976) 342 pages; D. J. McCarter, *Interpretation* 27 (1973) 401-412; A. D. H. Mayes, *Zeitschrift fur die alttestamentliche Wissenschaft* 90 (1978) 1-19; I. Mendelsohn, *Bulletin of the American Schools of Oriental Research* 143 (1956) 17-22; M. Noth, *History of Israel,* 2d ed. (London: Black, 1960) 164-167; and A. F. Rainey, *Ras Shamra Parallels* II:69-107 (which provides a necessary corrective to certain of Mendelsohn's ideas).
11. Blaikie, *First Book of Samuel,* 111-112.
12. C. J. Barber and J. D. Carter, *Always a Winner,* 24ff.
13. M. Henry, *A Commentary Wholly Biblical on the Books of the Bible* (Old Tappan, NJ: Revell, n.d.) II:321.
14. *Lekol 'aš er y'meru 'leyok,* "to everything that they may say to you," seems to imply that God is not going to resist the desire of the people any longer. He knows the intent of the elders and He knows that they are determined to have their own way.
15. *Mimmĕlōk 'ălēhem,* "from ruling over them," intimates their rejection of Yahweh as their *melek,* "king."
16. S. L. Harris, *Vetus Testamentum* 31 (1981) 79-80. *'Ak kī-hā'ēd tā'îd bāhem,* "But you

shall solemnly warn them" (1 Samuel 8:9), legally places before the nation the nature of their offense and its consequences.

17. Klein (*1 Samuel,* 76) and McCarter (*1 Samuel,* 157-158) deal with the play on words in 1 Samuel 8:10.

18. Keil and Delitzsch, *Biblical Commentary,* 84; deVaux, *Ancient Israel,* 123-124,221,224.

19. Cf. Exodus 18:21; Deuteronomy 1:15. From 1 Samuel 22:7 it is evident that Saul appointed most of his officers from the tribe of Benjamin. Even David fell prey to nepotism, for he assigned to key positions in his administration his own brothers and the sons of Zeruiah, his sister. Cf. Josephus, *Antiquities of the Jews* VI:12:4. '*Asar,* "tenth," is from '*eser,* ten," and is referred to in Deuteronomy 14:22-29; 26:12-15.

20. Those designated "servants of the king" (2 Kings 22:12; 25:8) were not slaves, but people appointed to positions of high honor. Cf. I. Mendelsohn, *Bulletin of the American Schools of Oriental Research* 143 (1956) 19-20. All of this highlights Paul's use of the term *doulos,* "slave" (of Christ), in the New Testament.

21. Blaikie, *First Book of Samuel,* 116-117. Cf. L. J. Wood, *Israel's United Monarchy* (Grand Rapids: Baker, 1979) 67-76.

22. The *Lō',* "No" (1 Samuel 8:19), is emphatic. Cf. S. R. Driver, *Notes on the Hebrew Text,* 68; McCarter, *1 Samuel,* 156.

23. The Masoretic text is most interesting. *Bayyōm hahū',* "on that day," occurs twice for emphasis (1 Samuel 8:18). It underscores the future powerlessness of the king who does not walk after the law of the Lord and who is unable to help them in time of need. Such impotence is diametrically opposed to their experience with Yahweh of hosts during the period of the judges. He had answered their prayers whenever they had called upon Him (e.g., 1 Samuel 7:9).

24. Mauchline, *1 and 2 Samuel,* 74.

Chapter 6

1. J. Gill, *A Complete Body of Doctrinal and Practical Divinity* (London: Tegg, 1839) II:110. God's providence is evidenced in three ways: (1) divine preservation by which He sustains all creatures in their distinctive natures and powers; (2) divine cooperation by which God not only sustains but is actively involved in all the things that His creatures do; and (3) divine government by which God fulfills His purpose for His creatures by guiding and leading them.

2. Meyer, *Samuel the Prophet,* 71; cf. Deane and Kirk, *Studies in First Samuel* I:79.

3. Deane and Kirk, *Studies in First Samuel,* I:80; Klein, *1 Samuel,* 80; P. W. Lapp, *Biblical Archaeologist* 28 (1965) 2-10; McCarter, *1 Samuel,* 173; Noth, *Israelitischen Personennamen,* 225,227; Wood, *United Monarchy,* 104-109.

4. For a discussion of '*īš gibbōr ḥayil,* "mighty man of valor," see McCarter, *1 Samuel,* 173.

5. *Encyclopedia of Archaeological Excavations* II:446-450; Robinson, *Biblical Researches in Palestine* I:455; J. B. Pritchard, *Gibeon: Where the Sun Stood Still* (Princeton, NJ: Princeton University Press, 1962) 176 pages; *New International Dictionary of Biblical Archaeology,* 213-214.

6. Robinson, *Biblical Researches in Palestine* II:118 and III:286; A. P. Stanley, *Sinai and Palestine* (London: Murray, 1889) 213ff.; W. F. Albright, *Bulletin of the American Schools of Oriental Research* 52 (1933) 6-12; P. W. Lapp, *Biblical Archaeologist* 28 (1965) 2-10; *New International Dictionary of Biblical Archaeology,* 212-214.

7. C. J. Barber and J. D. Carter, *Always a Winner,* 46-58.

8. The literature on Saul has become quite extensive. Two bibliographies reflect the proliferation of works in this area: Hupper, *Index to English Periodical Literature* I:96-97; and Eslinger, *Kingship of God,* 491-508. Other works include J. A. Sanford, *King Saul, the Tragic Hero* (New York: Paulist, 1985) 144 pages; D. M. Gunn, *The Fate of King Saul* (Sheffield, England: Journal for the Study of the Old Testament, 1980) 181 pages. By far the most satisfactory treatments, however, are Deane and Kirk's *Studies in First Samuel* and Blaikie's commentary on the *First Book of Samuel.*

9. *Bāḥur wāṭōb,* "tall and good looking"—the external criteria that are sure to please those who judge according to appearance. Cf. Homer, *Iliad* III:227; Virgil, *Aeneid* VII:784. Tacit support is to be found in the change in pronoun in 1 Samuel 9:12-13. The young

women evidently found Saul so handsome that they ended up speaking directly to him ("you" is singular, not plural) and this led some rabbinic writers to conjecture that if it had been possible the young women would have liked to detain Saul.

10. Cf. C. E. Macartney, *Chariots of Fire* (Nashville: Abingdon, 1951) 150-159; and Hupper, *Index to English Periodical Literature* I:77.

11. Cf. Birch, *Rise of the Israelite Monarchy*, 30-31; idem, *Journal of Biblical Literature* 90 (1971) 55-58; idem, *Catholic Biblical Quarterly* 37 (1975) 447-459; N. Habel, *Zeitschrift für die alttestamentliche Wissenschaft* 77 (1965) 297-323; Klein, *1 Samuel*, 83ff.; McCarter, *1 Samuel*, 165ff.

12. Blaikie, *First Book of Samuel*, 121.

13. *Macmillan Bible Atlas*, 86; Baly, *Geography of the Bible*, 177-181; M. Bic, *Vetus Testamentum* 7 (1957) 92-97 (with a rebuttal by H. J. Stobbe, pages 362-370); Klein, *1 Samuel*, 86; Mauchline, *1 and 2 Samuel*, 93-94.

14. The use of *tĕš ūrâ*, "gift," is rare, occurring only in 1 Samuel 9:7 in the Masoretic text. Cf. S. M. Paul, *Biblica* 59 (1978) 542ff.

15. A shekel weighed approximately .403 ounces. For the literature on weights and measures in the ancient Near East see Hupper, *Index to English Periodical Literature* I:417-427 and J. A. Thompson, *Handbook on Life in Bible Times* (Downers Grove, IL: InterVarsity, 1986) 167-172.

16. Samuel is referred to by several titles: a *rō'eh*, "seer" (*Theological Wordbook* II:823-824 [#2095]); a *nābî*, "prophet" (*Theological Wordbook* II:544-545 [#1277]; S. Shaviv, *Vetus Testamentum* 34 [1984] 108-131); and as an *'îš h ā-'ĕlōhîm*, "man of God" (R. Hallevy, *Journal of Near Eastern Studies* 17 [1958] 273-244).

17. For a discussion of *bāmâ*, "high place," see Albright, *Archaeology and the Religion of Israel*, 103-107; idem, *Vetus Testamentum* Supplement 4 (1957) 242-258; C. C. McCown, *Journal of Biblical Literature* 69 (1950) 205-219; S. Iwry, *Journal of Biblical Literature* 76 (1957) 225-232; G. E. Wright, *Biblical Archaeologist* 7 (1944) 65-77; P. H. Vaughan, *The Meaning of "Bama" in the Old Testament* (Cambridge, MA: Cambridge University Press, 1974) 90 pages; deVaux, *Ancient Israel*, 284-288; and *Theological Wordbook* I:113 (#253).

18. The Hebrew of 1 Samuel 9:15 is most picturesque. *Gala 'ozen*, "revealed," literally means "uncovered [Samuel's] ear" and conveys the idea of either moving aside his hair or lightly pushing back the hood of his cloak. Cf. Deane and Kirk, *Studies in First Samuel* I:79.

19. *Nāgîd*, "rule," conveys the idea of keeping within certain bounds. See McCarter, *1 Samuel*, 178; W. Richter, *Biblische Zeitschrift* 9 (1945) 71-84; *Theological Wordbook* II:550 (#1289).

20. The Hebrew has "leg" and could refer to either the front or the back legs. Because Saul was being honored in a significant way, the hindquarters are most probable. In accordance with custom his portion would have been the thigh.

21. The term *kol-ḥemdat*, "every treasure" (1 Samuel 9:20), has received extensive discussion. See Klein, *1 Samuel*, 89; Mauchline, *1 and 2 Samuel*, 96; McCarter, *1 Samuel*, 169-170,179; H. P. Smith, *A Critical and Exegetical Commentary on the Books of Samuel*, International Critical Commentary (New York: Scribner's, 1902) 63.

22. I do not concur with the judgment of McCarter (*1 Samuel*, 180) that in giving Saul the *'et-haššôq*, "thigh," Samuel was conferring upon him priestly status. Cf. S. R. Driver, *Notes on the Hebrew Text*, 75-77; Klein, *1 Samuel*, 90; Josephus, *Antiquities of the Jews* VI:4:1.

23. Cf. Thomson, *The Land and the Book* I:39; J. Kitto, *Daily Bible Illustrations* (Grand Rapids: Kregel, 1981) I:472,642-643.

24. Blaikie, *First Book of Samuel*, 142-143.

25. For an explanation of *naḥālātô*, "[Yahweh's] inheritance," see P. K. McCarter and R. B. Coote, *Bulletin of the American Schools of Oriental Research* 212 (1973) 20-21. Klein's view (*1 Samuel*, 90) is unreliable. Cf. Birch, *Journal of Biblical Literature* 90 (1971) 55-58; N. Habel, *Zeitschrift für die alttestamentliche Wissenschaft* 77 (1965) 297-323; A. D. H. Meyes, *Zeitschrift für die alttestamentliche Wissenschaft* 90 (1978) 1-19; J. Muilenburg, *Vetus Testamentum* 9 (1959) 347-365. The expression, "Has not Yahweh anointed you ruler," is a Hebraism for stating something certain.

26. The location of Rachel's tomb is disputed. The tomb near Bethlehem, which is shown

to tourists, was built by the Crusaders. For a concise discussion see *New International Dictionary of Biblical Archaeology*, 383; *Zondervan Pictorial Encyclopedia* IV:25-26.

27. Cf. J. M. Miller, *Vetus Testamentum* 25 (1975) 145-166; A. Demsky, *Bulletin of the American Schools of Oriental Research* 212 (1973) 26-31.

28. J. Milgram, *Israel Exploration Journal* 22 (1972) 33-38; cf. Hupper, *Index to English Periodical Literature* 1:242-246.

29. Deane and Kirk, *Studies in First Samuel* II:29; cf. J. M. Miller, *Vetus Testamentum* 25 (1975) 145-166; S. R. Driver, *Notes on the Hebrew Text*, 80; Klein, *1 Samuel*, 91; Mauchline, *1 and 2 Samuel*, 98-99; H. P. Smith, *Critical and Exegetical Commentary*, 69-70.

30. *Zondervan Pictorial Encyclopedia* IV:311-324.

31. L. J. Wood, *Bulletin of the Evangelical Theological Society* 9 (1966) 125-137; cf. pages 157-158.

32. Blaikie, *First Book of Samuel*, 151. Cf. H. Tawil, *Journal of Biblical Literature* 95 (1976) 405-413.

33. Deane and Kirk, *Studies in First Samuel* II:31-33; V. Eppstein, *Zeitschrift für die alttestamentliche Wissenschaft* 81 (1969) 287-304; H. N. Malony, *Journal of Psychology and Theology* 9 (1981) 326-334; S. B. Parker, *Vetus Testamentum* 28 (1978) 271-285; and J. Sturdy, *Vetus Testamentum* 20 (1970) 206-231.

34. Kennedy, *Samuel*, 70; cf. Wood, *United Monarchy*, 105-107.

35. Deane and Kirk, *Studies in First Samuel* I:92.

36. D. R. Ap-Thomas, *Vetus Testamentum* 11 (1961) 241-245, wrongly identifies the uncle as the Philistine deputy (1 Samuel 10:5).

37. Cf. Birch, *Catholic Biblical Quarterly* 37 (1975) 447-457; N. Habel, *Zeitschrift für die alttestamentliche Wissenschaft* 77 (1965) 297-323; J. Lindblom, *Vetus Testamentum* 12 (1962) 164-178; and G. Wallis, *Zeitschrift für die alttestamentliche Wissenschaft* 64 (1952) 57-61; *Zondervan Pictorial Encyclopedia* III:988.

38. Cf. S. R. Driver, *Notes on the Hebrew Text*, 117; H. G. May, *American Journal of Semitic Languages and Literatures* 56 (1939) 44-69; Deane and Kirk, *Studies in First Samuel* I:95; Blaikie, *First Book of Samuel*, 102.

39. Cf. Josephus, *Antiquities of the Jews* VI:4:6.

40. For the background of the term "sons of Belial" (1 Samuel 10:27) see *Zondervan Pictorial Encyclopedia* I:513. By their actions they showed contempt for Saul. Inasmuch as he now stood in the line of the theocracy, they were in reality spurning God and His selection of Saul as their first king. The giving of a "gift," *minḥā* (10:27), was a token of homage/loyalty on the part of those who recognized Saul's right to rule over God's heritage. Their free and willing presents to a Benjamite (the smallest of the tribes) was indicative of their desire (1) to follow the man of God's selection and appointment and (2) to contribute toward national unity. To refuse to give a present was tantamount to rebellion and was regarded by the men of Israel as equivalent to treason (1 Samuel 11).

41. The Hebrew *hāraš*, "keep silent" or "[was] as one being deaf," is further indication of Saul's mature self-control.

42. The "Cyrus Cylinder," an ancient Near Eastern document, was discovered in the nineteenth century. It depicts the Persian monarch as a polytheistic politician. To the advantage of Biblical scholars, it provides a summary of his benevolence toward captive peoples living in his domain. In it Cyrus tells how the Babylonian god Marduk chose him to lead his annual procession, thus "declaring him to be the ruler of all the world.... Without any battle, he made him enter his town Babylon, sparing [the city] any calamity.... I returned to sacred cities on the other side of the Tigris, the sanctuaries of which have been in ruins for a long time, the images which used to live therein and established for them permanent sanctuaries. I also gathered all their former inhabitants and returned them to their habitations." For the full text see *Ancient Near Eastern Texts*, pages 315-316.

Chapter 7

1. J. M. Boice, *Foundations of the Christian Faith* (Downers Grove, IL: InterVarsity, 1986) 199-206; Ryrie, *Basic Theology*, 222-226; H. C. Thiessen, *Lectures in Systematic Theology*,

rev. V. Doerksen (Grand Rapids: Eerdmans, 1979) 105,124-125; W. H. G. Thomas, *Principles of Theology* (London: Longmans, Green, 1930) 156-160.

2. While some may be inclined to tone down the presence of sin in the world and look upon it as the "law of human limitations," experience has shown that justice cannot prevail without the sanction of force. Furthermore, as the late Bernard L. Montgomery has reminded us in his book *The Path to Leadership* (London: Collins, 1961, pages 15-16), in addition to the ideal of human love, there is also the fact of human corruption. Each one of us therefore at times encounters violent and abusive people as well as the immoral and the unjust, and they have to be treated with the kind of wisdom that we glean from God's Word.

3. W. F. Albright, *Archaeology of Palestine* (London: Penguin, 1954) 120-121; *New International Dictionary of Biblical Archaeology*, 213.

4. Zeligs (*Psychoanalysis and the Bible*, 122-128), reading back into this early period of Saul's life his later external locus of control, believes that he was indecisive and lacked both vision and motivation.

5. The name *Nā'h‿ āsh* may mean "serpent" or be derived from the Akkadian *nahšu*, "magnificent." Cf. Noth, *Israelitischen Personennamen*, 230; Pedersen, *Israel* I-II:221,241. His capital was Tabboth-ammon, modern Amman. Josephus (*Antiquities of the Jews* VI:5:3) believes he was killed by Saul in battle (1 Samuel 11:11).

6. F. M. Cross, *Ancient Library of Qumran and Modern Biblical Studies* (Garden City, NY: Doubleday, 1958) 133-134; idem, *Biblica* 35 (1954) 263-266; idem, *Harvard Theological Review* 57 (1964) 281-299; cf. E. Lohse, *Die Texte aus Qumran* (Munchen: Kosel, 1971) 198 pages; D. Edelman, *Zeitschrift für die alttestamentliche Wissenschaft* 96 (1984) 195-209; Ulrich, *Qumran Text*, 166-170.

7. Noth, *History of Israel*, 167; cf. idem, *Zeitschrift des deutschen Palastina-Vereins* 69 (1953) 28-41; T. K. Eves, *Westminster Theological Journal* 44 (1982) 308-326.

8. The leading Ammonite deity was *Mo'lek*, "Molech." Cf. J. Gray, *Journal of Near Eastern Studies* 8 (1949) 72-83; Albright, *Archaeology and the Religion of Israel*, 156-159; E. Dhorme, *Anatolian Studies* 6 (1959) 57; R. deVaux, *Studies in Old Testament Sacrifice* (Cardiff: University of Wales Press, 1964) 73-90; N. H. Snaith, *Vetus Testamentum* 16 (1966) 123-124.

9. Cf. T. Longman, *Westminster Theological Journal* 45 (1983) 45-82.

10. *Yāḇeš gil'ād*, "Jabesh-gilead," is usually located on one or the other of the banks of the Wadi Yabis. Several ruins in the area make identification difficult. *Macmillan Bible Atlas*, 87,90. Cf. N. Glueck, *The River Jordan* (New York: McGraw-Hill, 1968) 92-94,101-103,110-112,127-128,132-139; idem, *Bulletin of the American Schools of Oriental Research* 89 (1943) 91; G. L. Harding, *The Antiquities of Jordan* (London: Lutterworth, 1959) 39,64; Noth, *Zeitschrift des deutschen Palastina-Vereins* 58 (1935) 230-235; *Zondervan Pictorial Encyclopedia* III:381-382.

11. Y. Yadin, *The Art of Warfare in Biblical Lands*, 2 vols. (New York: McGraw-Hill, 1963) I:203.

12. Deane and Kirk, *Studies in First Samuel* II:47-48.

13. Saul's leadership qualities deserve special consideration. A careful analysis of the text will reveal some interesting points in relation to his patience/timing; capacity for moral indignation; ability to size up a situation, develop a viable plan of action, communicate his plan in a convincing manner, and motivate others to follow him with confidence; his magnanimity or largeheartedness in overlooking an offense; and, finally, his ability to enjoy the results of the victory with his men and give praise where due. Important data on these facets of leadership may be obtained from C. J. Barber and G. H. Strauss, *Leadership: The Dynamics of Success* (Greenwood: Attic, 1982) 118 pages; and J. O. Sanders, *Spiritual Leadership* (Chicago: Moody, 1967) 43-69.

14. The Biblical description of Saul's anger in 1 Samuel 11:6 is most interesting. *Wayyihar 'appô mĕ'ōd* literally means "and his nose [i.e., anger] burned greatly." Cf. *Theological Dictionary of the Old Testament*, ed. G. J. Botterweck and H. Ringgren, trans. J. T. Willis, in process (Grand Rapids: Eerdmans, 1974-) I:348-360; *Theological Wordbook* I:58 (#133).

15. Cf. Judges 19:29-30. Zeligs (*Psychoanalysis and the Bible*, 127) believes that Saul was symbolically separating himself from his father's influence and control. The discussions of G. Wallis, *Zeitshrift für die alttestamentliche Wissenschaft* 64 (1952) 57-61, and R. Polin, *Harvard Theological Review* 62 (1969) 227-240, are worth noting.

16. The Bezek mentioned in this passage is not to be confused with the one in Judah (cf. Judges 1:4-5). This city is probably ancient Khirbet Ibziq, about thirteen miles northeast of Shechem and approximately fifteen miles west of Jabesh-gilead. For a discussion of *paḥad* in the expression "dread of Yahweh" (1 Samuel 11:7) see *Theological Wordbook* II:720-721 (#1756).
17. Blaikie, *First Book of Samuel,* 176. Cf. Yadin, *Art of Warfare* I:263-267; R. Gale, *Great Battles of Biblical History* (London: Hutchinson, 1968) 40-43; C. Herzog and M. Gichon, *Battles of the Bible* (New York: Random, 1978) 63-73.
18. Deane and Kirk, *Studies in First Samuel* II:54.
19. R. Kittel in *Great Men and Movements in Israel* (New York: Ktav, 1968, pages 98-102) states that three separate sources or traditions have been blended together to form the anointing-selection-enthronement of Saul. He misses the point of *ûnĕhaddēš... hammĕlūkā,* "renew the kingship" (1 Samuel 11:14). Cf. Keil and Delitzsch, *Biblical Commentary,* 113ff.
20. D. J. McCarthy, *Treaty and Covenant,* 2d ed. (Rome: Biblical Institute Press, 1978) 141; J. Muilenburg, *Vetus Testamentum* 9 (1959) 347-365.
21. Klein, *1 Samuel,* 112-116.
22. Blaikie, *First Book of Samuel,* 182; cf. E. A. Speiser, *Bulletin of the American Schools of Oriental Research* 77 (1940) 15-20.
23. Blaikie, *First Book of Samuel,* 194.
24. The Hebrew for "Barak," *brk,* is very similar to "Bĕdān," *bdn,* and may have arisen as a result of a scribal error. Cf. McCarter, *1 Samuel,* 211. Y. Zakovitch, *Vetus Testamentum* 22 (1972) 123-125, emends the text to read *ben-dān,* "son of Dan," shortened to *bedan,* and believes that the reference is to Samson.
25. Cf. Josephus, (*Antiquities of the Jews* VI:6:6) who cites only Jephthah and Gideon.
26. Cf. Keil and Delitzsch, *Biblical Commentary,* 117-118.
27. Deane and Kirk, *Studies in First Samuel* I:113-114.
28. Ibid. I:114. Cf. J. J. M. Roberts, *Vetus Testamentum* 2 (1971) 244-251.
29. H. Taylor and G. Taylor, *Hudson Taylor's Spiritual Secret* (Chicago: Moody, n.d.) 152.

Chapter 8

1. D. Reisman in *The Lonely Crowd* (New Haven, CT: Yale University Press, 1970, pages 6-25) offers an excellent summary of the dynamics of those whose locus of control lies outside themselves. He attributes the change from an inner-directed approach to life to an other-directed stance to social/cultural phenomena. What Reisman ignores is the fact that this shift is also related to the decline of Christianity in the West.
2. For a careful study of Saul's character, see W. L. Humphrey, *Journal for the Study of the Old Testament* 6 (1978) 18-27; 18 (1980) 74-90; 22 (1982) 95-117.
3. Some writers have persisted in referring to this verse as a "regnal formula" (cf. 1 Kings 14:21; 22:42). In reality such a device only became popular decades later. Furthermore it was not used of David, Saul's successor, who was surely worthy of a "regnal" introduction if such a literary device had been in vogue at the time. First Samuel 13:1 is best understood, therefore, as a summary heading covering Saul's reign. For a dissenting point of view see Klein, *1 Samuel,* 124; also see R. Althann, *Biblica* 62 (1981) 241-246.
4. For a discussion of the problems see Deane and Kirk, *Studies in First Samuel* I:117-119; S. R. Driver, *Notes on the Hebrew Text,* 96-97; Hertzberg, *I and II Samuel,* 103; Josephus, *Antiquities of the Jews* VI:14:9; Klein, *1 Samuel,* 122-123; Keil and Delitzsch, *Biblical Commentary,* 122-124; McCarter, *1 Samuel,* 222; Mauchline, *1 and 2 Samuel,* 111; H. P. Smith, *Critical and Exegetical Commentary,* 91; Wood, *United Monarchy,* 122-123.
5. The similarity between *Gib'ā,* "Gibeah," *Geba',* "Geba," and *Gib'ōn,* "Gibeon," in the Hebrew Bible has led P. D. Miller in *Vetus Testamentum* 25 (1975) 145-166 to argue that all the references are to the same place. He errs, however, as 1 Samuel 13:15 and 16 distinguish between Geba and Gibeah. Cf. L. A. Sinclair, *Biblical Archaeologist* 27 (1964) 56ff.; G. E. Wright, *Biblical Archaeologist* 29 (1966) 70-86.
6. The literature on Jonathan is not very extensive. Cf. Hupper, *Index to English Periodical Literature* I:58.

7. Cf. E. H. Merrill, *Bible Knowledge Commentary* (Wheaton, IL: Victor, 1985) I:443-444;
    Noth, *History of Israel*, 176-178; J. H. Stobbe, *Theologische Zeitschrift* 21 (1965) 269-280;
    P. D. Miller, *Catholic Biblical Quarterly* 36 (1974) 157-174.
8. N. K. Gottwald in *The Tribes of Yahweh* (Maryknoll, NY: Orbis, 1979, pages 419,423-
    424) states that Saul was referring to those of his own race who had joined forces with
    the Philistines (cf. 1 Samuel 14:21). Such a view fails to explain why such people would
    desert the Philistines before the battle and flee across the Jordan river (cf. 1 Samuel
    13:7). Cf. Hertzberg, *I and II Samuel*, 104; H. P. Smith, *Critical and Exegetical Commen-
    tary*, 91-92; Hupper, *Index to English Periodical Literature* I:158-160.
9. 1 Samuel 4:9. For a brief resume of the usage of *'ibrî*, "Hebrews," in the Masoretic text
    see *Zondervan Pictorial Encyclopedia* III:65-66.
10. Deane and Kirk, *Studies in First Samuel* II:66-71, noting in particular pages 69-71.
11. Ibid. I:119.
12. Cf. Edersheim, *Bible History* IV:57-58; J. C. Geikie, *The Holy Land and the Bible* (Lon-
    don: Cassell, 1887) II:171-177. In light of the descriptions given by these writers—who
    thoroughly investigated different sites associated with events mentioned in the Bible—
    the comments of Klein (*1 Samuel*, 135) seem very out of place.
13. Most commentators suspect a copyist error, for the number of chariots exceeds the
    number of men to ride in them. Normally two men were assigned to a chariot, but
    records from antiquity indicate that there were sometimes three. Cf. *Ancient Near
    Eastern Texts*, 172,183-184; J. J. Davis, *Birth of a Kingdom* (Grand Rapids: Baker, 1970)
    55; Yadin, *Art of Warfare* II:250,336. For Israel's response to this invasion see J. Naveh,
    Israel Exploration Journal 13 (1963) 74-96; J. A. Sanders, ed. *Near Eastern Archaeology
    in the Twentieth Century* (Garden City, NY: Doubleday, 1970) 299-306.
14. R. Morosco, *Journal of Psychology and Theology* 1-2 (1973) 43-50.
15. Blaikie, *First Book of Samuel*, 210-211.
16. Samuel's instructions on this occasion are not to be confused with the prophet's words
    of 1 Samuel 10:8, which were given many years earlier. Although Gilgal was plainly
    visible to the Philistines, it was a place hallowed for Saul by memorable links with the
    past. Samuel may well have had in mind the strengthening of Saul's faith in the Lord
    when he commanded the king to wait for him there.
17. J. Hall, *Contemplations on Historical Passages*, 173ff.; Meyer, *Samuel the Prophet*, 111-
    114; Merrill, *Bible Knowledge Commentary* I:444. Cf. Blaikie, *First Book of Samuel*, 212;
    Deane and Kirk, *Studies in First Samuel* I:125; Klein, *1 Samuel*, 127. It should also be
    noted from 1 Samuel 14:35 that Saul built an altar and offered sacrifices on it without
    censure of any kind. Other Old Testament men who were not priests but erected al-
    tars include Gideon (Judges 6:24), Manoah (Judges 13:19-20), David (2 Samuel 24:18-
    25), and Elijah (1 Kings 18:31-32).
18. Deane and Kirk, *Studies in First Samuel* I:125-126; cf. Birch, *Rise of the Israelite Monar-
    chy*, 80-83.
19. Samuel was a master in the art of communication. Repeatedly in direct discourse he
    used words for emphasis. Here his *ṣiwwâ*, "command," is linked with *miṣwâ*, "com-
    mandment." *Šāmartā 'et-miṣwat Yahweh 'ĕlōhêkā 'ašer ṣiwwāk*, "You have not kept the
    commandment of Yahweh your God, which He commanded you," plainly indicates
    that God's communiqué to Saul through Samuel was meant to be obeyed. When God
    chose Saul as Israel's first king, His plans exceeded Saul's fondest expectations (1
    Samuel 13:13b).
20. David is introduced for the first time, but not by name. The words *'îš kilbābô*, "a man
    according to His own heart," underscore God's sovereign choice of Saul's successor.
21. Montgomery (*Path to Leadership*, 11ff.) wisely observed, "Leadership is based on truth
    and character. A leader must himself be the servant of truth, and he must make the
    truth the focus of a common purpose. He must then have the force of character nec-
    essary to inspire others to follow him with confidence.... Then a leader must have
    infectious optimism, and the determination to persevere in the face of difficulties. He
    must also radiate confidence, relying on moral and spiritual principles and resources
    to work out rightly even when he himself is not too certain of the material outcome. He
    must have a sound judgment in which others will have confidence, and a good
    knowledge of human nature. He must be able to see his problems truly and [as a]

whole. Self-confidence is a vital component of his make-up....When all is said and done, the true leader must be able to dominate, and finally to master, the events which surround him." From this brief statement it will be seen that Saul's leadership had undergone a serious decline in the years following the events of 1 Samuel 11–12.

22. For an excellent discussion of the "rejection syndrome" see M. B. Hodge, *Your Fear of Love* (Garden City, NY: Doubleday, 1972) 14-50. An understanding of the dynamics involved will help to explain Saul's actions in 1 Samuel 14.

23. *Macmillan Bible Atlas*, 88.

24. There is extensive literature on Israel's plight as a result of the fact that they lagged centuries behind the other nations in the manufacturing of iron implements. Among the more reliable discussions is W. G. Dever's in *Hebrew Union College Annual* 40-41 (1969-1970) 139-204. Cf. Gottwald, *Tribes of Yahweh*, 419,761 (footnote 335); Mauchline, *1 and 2 Samuel*, 114.

25. The word *pĕsîrâ*, "price" (?) (1 Samuel 13:21), is unique, being used only here in the Old Testament. For a discussion of the cost of having different implements sharpened see J. Bewer, *Journal of Biblical Literature* 59 (1942) 45; W. G. Dever, *Hebrew Union College Annual* 40-41 (1969-1970) 182; W. R. Lane, *Bulletin of the American Schools of Oriental Research* 164 (1961) 21-23; E. A. Speiser, *Bulletin of the American Schools of Oriental Research* 77 (1940) 19; Thomas, *Documents from Old Testament Times*, 229-230.

Chapter 9

1. Source unknown.

2. Evidence that Saul had become conditioned to thinking of himself on a par with Kish's servants is to be found in 1 Samuel 9:7-8,10 where he, though a son, identified himself with the servant by the use of the word "we" (cf. Galatians 4:1,3,7). The servant also had come to regard himself as Saul's equal (cf. 1 Samuel 9:8,10). He did not offer Saul the money to give to Samuel, but stated that he would give it to the seer and so be the person to whom credit would ultimately be due. From the subtle clues given to us in the text, it would seem as if Kish's rule of his home was authoritarian. His influence on Saul could only have been detrimental, and it should not surprise us that Saul would later manifest the same traits as his father. The only corrective available to Saul was the controlling power of the Holy Spirit.

3. Defense mechanisms take several different forms. *Repression* is the most common form and is the basis on which the others operate. In repression a person experiencing an unacceptable impulse (e.g., anger, adulterous thoughts, jealousy) subconsciously forces those thoughts out of his awareness and into his unconscious mind. *Projection* is another common form of defense (cf. Genesis 3:12-13). When experiencing an impulse that threatens one's sense of worth or esteem, an unconscious transfer of the unwanted emotion takes place and the blame is projected onto someone else. This was Saul's strategy in 1 Samuel 13:11-12 and 15:15. *Displacement* likewise is a means of transferring one's feelings to another. A mother, for example, may not want to show her anger toward her son (even though his actions through the day have called for discipline). She remains calm, but when her husband comes home she finds some pretext to lash out at him. This means of handling pent-up feelings may explain Saul's actions in 1 Samuel 14:43-44. He did not show any anger toward Samuel (for all the people held Samuel in high honor) but acted in a very punitive way toward Jonathan. *Reaction formation* involves repressing a feeling that is inconsistent with one's sense of esteem (e.g., dislike for a person) and then professing the exact opposite. Saul felt awkward and uncomfortable in Samuel's presence. He might have felt as Ahab did when he spoke of Micaiah, "He never has anything good to say about me" (1 Kings 22:8,18).Saul's use of this defense mechanism may be seen in the affable greetings he gave Samuel (1 Samuel 13:10; 15:13). *Intellectualization* is another subtle defense. When using this mechanism, a person will hide unacceptable feelings and/or behavior behind a smoke screen of intellectual analysis or high-sounding words or phrases. This is done to avoid the pain of facing reality head-on. *Rationalization* is the substitution of "respectable" motives for "unrespectable" ones. An example of this in Saul's behavior

may be found in several of his statements; perhaps the clearest one is in 1 Samuel 15:15 where his emphasis is on "to sacrifice to Yahweh your God." *Sublimation* is the only constructive defense mechanism. It involves channeling one's inner emotional tensions into some appropriate form of action (e.g., exercise). Jonathan did this when he suggested to his armorbearer that they go to the Philistine encampment and see what the Lord might do for them there (1 Samuel 14:1,6-14).

4. The ephod was frequently used to determine the will of God. Cf. M'Clintock and Strong, *Cyclopedia of Literature* III:248-249.

5. *Zondervan Pictorial Encyclopedia* IV:224.

6. Blaikie, *First Book of Samuel,* 78-79. We are not to conclude from 1 Samuel 13:22—"So it came about on the day of battle"—that the Philistines actually drew up in formation ready to launch an attack upon the Israelites. No specific battle is mentioned. It seems preferable to regard this verse as bringing to a conclusion the digression of 13:19-22. Furthermore the Hebraism may best be understood in a general sense as meaning, "So whenever there was a battle" (cf. Deane and Kirk, *Studies in First Samuel* I:130-131).

7. An expression used in the form of a slur (cf. 1 Samuel 17:26,36) and drawing a sharp distinction between those who are believers and beneficiaries of the covenant, and those who are not (cf. Jeremiah 6:10; 9:25-26).

8. C. R. Conder, *Tent Work in Palestine* (London: Palestine Exploration Fund, 1880) II:112-113.

9. Deane and Kirk, *Studies in First Samuel* I:133-134.

10. J. Naveh, *Israel Exploration Journal* 13 (1963) 74-96; Sanders, *Near Eastern Archaeology,* 299-306.

11. Note Jonathan's words, "For Yahweh has given them into *the hands of Israel*" (1 Samuel 14:12, emphasis added). He did not say "*our* hand," as well he might. Instead he revealed his motives, which were for the national good. Cf. G. R. Driver, *Zeitschrift für die alttestamentliche Wissenschaft* 80 (1968) 174-183.

12. The Masoretic text is most descriptive. *Ḥerdat 'Elōhîm* literally means "a shuddering from God" (1 Samuel 14:15).

13. The Masoretic text reads, "Bring the ark of God here" (1 Samuel 14:18). While it is true that the ark of the covenant might temporarily have been moved from Kiriath-jearim to the camp of Saul for safekeeping, it is also most unlikely that the Philistines would have taken it again as part of the spoils of war, for we may be sure they did not want to repeat the mistakes of the past. According to 1 Samuel 6:21-7:2 the ark remained in the house of Abinadab until the time of David. For a discussion of whether the ark or the ephod is meant (cf. 1 Samuel 14:3) see P. R. Davies, *Journal of Theological Studies* 26 (1975) 82-87; and Wood, *United Monarchy,* 134-135.

14. The discussion of Deane and Kirk (*Studies in First Samuel* II:85) is most apropos.

15. *Macmillan Bible Atlas,* 88-90.

16. Josephus, *Antiquities of the Jews* VI:6:6.

17. *Zondervan Pictorial Encyclopedia* I:312-325. The Old Testament has nine different nominal forms and one verbal form to describe the spoils of war taken by soldiers as compensation for their services (cf. Numbers 31:53; Judges 14:19; 2 Samuel 2:21; 2 Kings 21:14; Isaiah 42:22; Jeremiah 30:16). The victor could seize anything that he could carry or cart away (cf. Genesis 14:11; 2 Chronicles 20:25) including women and children (Deuteronomy 20:14), cattle (Deuteronomy 2:35; 1 Samuel 14:32; 2 Chronicles 15:11; Jeremiah 49:32), clothing (Joshua 7:21; Judges 5:30; 2 Chronicles 20:25; 28:15), and jewelry and precious metal (Joshua 7:21; Judges 8:24-25). The only exception to this normative policy was the *ḥerem,* or "ban" that was placed on "devoted things" (cf. Numbers 21:2-3; Deuteronomy 7:2-6; 20:17-18; Joshua 6:21; 8:26; 10:28; 11:11). Cf. W. C. Kaiser, Jr., *Hard Sayings of the Old Testament* (Downers Grove, IL: InterVarsity, 1988) 106-109; Pedersen, *Israel* III-IV:1-32; deVaux, *Ancient Israel,* 255-257; *Theological Wordbook* I:324 (#744a).

18. The teaching of Scripture on blessing and cursing is very extensive. Basically both are the prerogative of God (and His representatives on earth). Cf. *International Standard Bible Encyclopedia* I:837-838. For a fuller discussion of these issues see deVaux, *Ancient Israel,* 143, 290ff.,408; H. M. Buck, *People of the Land* (New York: Macmillan, 1966) 147,253ff.

19. Blaikie, *First Book of Samuel,* 230-231.
20. *Debaš,* "honey," is a symbol in the Bible of God's blessing (cf. Deuteronomy 32:13; Psalm 19:10; 81:16; Ezekiel 16:13). The material presented by H. B. Tristram in *Natural History of the Bible* (London: S.P.C.K., 1889, pages 322-326) is worth noting. Cf. *Theological Wordbook* I:181-182 (#400a).
21. Deane and Kirk (*Studies in First Samuel* I:138) have an excellent discussion of this passage. Ridout (*King Saul,* 152-154) also has some notable comments, but his tendency to see types in these incidents introduces a subjective element into his interpretation and application of the text. For an elaboration of Jonathan's supposed sacrilege see J. Blenkinsopp, *Catholic Biblical Quarterly* 26 (1964) 423-449. For the superstitious element in handing down a judgment in cases involving a curse see E. F. D. Ward, *Zeitschrift für die alttestamentliche Wissenschaft* 89 (1977) 1-19.
22. There is tacit evidence in Jonathan's statement to support the view that Saul had reigned for a fairly lengthy period of time and not for only two years as some scholars maintain.
23. Deane and Kirk, *Studies in First Samuel* I:139.
24. In the New Testament the Lord Jesus Christ plainly stated that the needs of man are to be placed above ceremonial requirements (Mark 2:23-28). Since the time of creation God has shown concern for His creatures (cf. Psalm 36:6; 104:14-15; 145:16). Saul, as God's representative, should have done the same.
25. Deane and Kirk, *Studies in First Samuel* I:140.
26. Wood (*United Monarchy,* 136) points out that Jonathan had unknowingly disobeyed Saul's order but that this was only a secondary reason for God's refusal to reply to Saul. Cf. A. Toeg, *Vetus Testamentum* 19 (1969) 493-498.
27. Oaths are meant to be kept. At summer camps and special meetings young people as well as adults, in the flush of enthusiasm after dedicating their lives to Christ, may make promises about serving the Lord on the missionfield or giving a specified amount of money to a worthy cause. A failure to keep these commitments may result in feelings of guilt that cause a spirit of hopelessness and discouragement to descend upon the believer. Such feelings may eventually lead to an inner sense of worthlessness because of having "failed the Lord"; the individual may even give up the Christian life all together. Broken vows and unkept promises also hinder our prayers. If we are unable to keep commitments we have made to the Lord because circumstances have changed, we should confess our failures and ask the Lord to release us from our promises. Only in this way can we be safeguarded from the kind of defeat that dogged the footsteps of King Saul. Some vows should never be made. When a parent tells a child, "Promise me that you will never see him/her again," the parent uses his/her position of authority in an ill-advised way that deprives the child of his/her growing autonomy. Instructing one's offspring and instituting wise precautions are totally different from extracting a promise. Cf. Hupper, *Index to English Periodical Literature* I:509ff.
28. T. R. Preston, *Journal for the Study of the Old Testament* 24 (1982) 27-46.
29. D. Jobling, *Journal of Biblical Literature* 95 (1976) 367-376; W. L. Humphrey, *Journal for the Study of the Old Testament* 22 (1982) 95-117.
30. Hupper, *Index to English Periodical Literature* I:58.
31. Blaikie, *First Book of Samuel,* 230-231.
32. F. F. Fuller, "Personalized Education for Teachers" (unpublished paper, Research and Development Center for Teacher Education, University of Texas at Austin, 1970, 65 pages).
33. We are prone to look at the notable people portrayed in the Bible as larger than life. This may well be the impression many have of Jonathan. It is easy for us to conclude that in spite of the teaching of such passages of Scripture as Romans 15:4 and 1 Corinthians 10:11 his example is unattainable today. A study of the life and character of General Charles Gordon, however, will show many points of similarity that are at once interesting and important. *The Journals of Major-General C. G. Gordon* (London: Kegan Paul, Trench, 1885, 587 pages) are well-deserving of careful attention. Modern biographers are intent upon pointing out weaknesses of all heroes, so an attempt to discredit Gordon is to be found in C. C. Trench's *The Road to Khartoum* (New York: Norton, 1979, 336 pages). More reliable treatments come from older authors, some of

whom were Gordon's contemporaries. While not perfect, Gordon does provide an illustration of the kind of qualities Jonathan possessed.

Chapter 10

1. G. A. Smith, *Historical Geography of the Holy Land,* 25th ed., revised (London: Hodder and Stoughton, 1931) 282; Baly, *Geography of the Bible,* 159; Wiseman, *Peoples of Old Testament Times,* 125,232.
2. L. Woolley and T. E. Lawrence, *The Wilderness of Zin* (New York: Scribner, 1936) 62ff.; H. C. Trumbull, *Kadesh-Barnea* (London: Hodder and Stoughton, 1884) 28,67-69,305,358; Y. Aharoni, *Israel Exploration Journal* 8 (1958) 26ff.; 10 (1960) 23ff.,97ff.; idem, *The Land of the Bible,* 57-60,102-103,138-140,201,215-216; N. Glueck, *Rivers in the Desert* (New York: Grove, 1959) 113-116,124-133; A. Negev, *Cities of the Desert* (Jerusalem: Hebrew University Press, 1966) 28 pages.
3. God often reveals His attitude toward certain transgressions by judging the offenders and making examples of them so that others will fear the Lord and obey His commands. For instance see what happened to the man who cohabited with a Moabitess as a part of a religious ceremony (Numbers 25:1-3,6-8); Achan, who took things that were devoted to the Lord (Joshua 7:16-26); and Ananias and Sapphira, who connived together to lie to the apostles (Acts 5:1-11).
4. Because the Masoretic text contains a seemingly needless repetition—"the voice of the words of"—the majority of scholars have used this verse as an example of variant manuscript traditions being superimposed on one another. If this were the case, then the work of the supposed editor can only be regarded as sloppy. On the other hand these expressions can also be seen as repetition for the sake of emphasis. Saul needed to be thoroughly cognizant of the seriousness of the task the Lord was entrusting to him. If this latter argument is correct, then the repetition can be seen to underscore God's sovereignty and reinforce the argument of the book of 1 Samuel.
5. *Yahweh Ṣĕbā'ōt* (1 Samuel 1:3,11) is a name for God which lays stress on His absolute power, might, majesty, and supremacy. Cf. E. Jacob, *Theology of the Old Testament* (London: Hodder and Stoughton, 1958) 43-64. In the writings of the later prophets it was used to describe Yahweh's relationship to His people as their Savior and protector.
6. The *ḥerem,* "ban," ("utterly destroy" in 1 Samuel 15:3) was the term used for a holy war. Everyone and everything was to be destroyed (i.e., was "devoted to destruction") or dedicated to the Lord. References to this practice include Exodus 34:13; Deuteronomy 7:2; 20:10-17; Joshua 6:17-21. Cf. Kaiser, *Hard Sayings,* 106-109. Klein (*1 Samuel,* 149) wrote: "According to the prescriptions of Deut. 20:12-15, distant cities, outside the land of Israel, were only to have their men put under the ban, while the women, children, livestock and other spoil could be saved. But in 1 Sam. 15, a total ban is ordered for a distant people, Amalek. This may reflect the intense hatred felt for Amalek and/or the need for defense against their raiding activities." For an example of a holy war on the part of a pagan society see *Ancient Near Eastern Texts,* 320.
7. To us the complete destruction of every living thing seems barbaric. For a discussion of the issues see Deane and Kirk, *Studies in First Samuel* I:145-149.
8. Blaikie, *First Book of Samuel,* 242-243; cf. Deane and Kirk, *Studies in First Samuel* I:148.
9. *Tela'im* may possibly be identified with Telem in Joshua 15:24, a city south of Ziph, which was itself about thirty-two miles south of Hebron.
10. Cf. Klein, *1 Samuel,* 150; A. Kempinski, *Biblical Archaeology Review* 7 (1981) 52-53.
11. F. C. Fensham, *Bulletin of the American Schools of Oriental Research* 175 (1964) 51-54.
12. Havilah cannot be identified positively. McCarter (*1 Samuel,* 261) believes it to be somewhere on the western edge of the Arabian peninsula. Cf. J. A. Montgomery, *Arabia and the Bible* (New York: Ktav, 1969) 38-40.
13. This Carmel is in southern Judah, seven miles south southeast of Hebron, and is not to be confused with mount Carmel to the north from whose summit Elijah looked out on the Mediterranean sea. Cf. *Macmillan Bible Atlas,* 92.
14. God's removal of Saul from being His appointed representative underscores the teaching of human responsibility and provides its own illustration of 1 Corinthians 9:24-27. Cf. J. B. Payne, *Bibliotheca Sacra* 129 (1972) 321-325.

15. Deane and Kirk, *Studies in First Samuel* II:108-109; cf. I:153.
16. See M. Sternberg, *Hebrew Union College Annual* 54 (1983) 48-52, for a discussion of Samuel's mastery of the art of communication.
17. Saul was obviously shaken by Samuel's words; cf. H. H. Rowley, *Vetus Testamentum* 1 (1951) 67-68. To convince the people of his zeal for the Lord (and show them how wrong he believed Samuel to be) he hunted down witches and banished them from the land (cf. 1 Samuel 28:3). And to demonstrate how undeserving he was of the opprobrious term *idolater* he broke Israel's treaty with the Gibeonites (2 Samuel 21:1-11). An extensive body of literature has grown up around the subjects of idolatry and witchcraft. For further information on the Biblical data dealing with idolatry see J. J. Davis, *Moses and the Gods of Egypt* (Grand Rapids: Baker, 1971) 196-204; H. C. Leupold, *Exposition of Isaiah* (Grand Rapids: Baker, 1968) I:79-86; F. J. Delitzsch, *Biblical Commentary on the Prophecies of Isaiah*, trans. J. Martin (Grand Rapids: Eerdmans, n.d.) I:119-127; J. M. Boice, *The Minor Prophets* (Grand Rapids: Zondervan, 1983) I:13-14,61-62,67-69. For information on witchcraft see G. Bush, *Leviticus* (Minneapolis: Klock, 1978) 212-213,216-217,219; R. K. Harrison, *Leviticus,* Tyndale Old Testament Commentary (Downers Grove, IL: InterVarsity, 1980) 202,205,207-208; S. H. Kellogg, *Book of Leviticus* (Minneapolis: Klock, 1978) 411-412,418-426; G. J. Wenham, *Book of Leviticus,* New International Commentary on the Old Testament (Grand Rapids: Eerdmans, 1978) 272,278; G. Bush, *Numbers* (Minneapolis: Klock, 1981) 71-85; G. J. Wenham, *Numbers,* Tyndale Old Testament Commentary (Downers Grove, IL: InterVarsity, 1981) 79-85; P. C. Craigie, *Book of Deuteronomy,* New International Commentary on the Old Testament (Grand Rapids: Eerdmans, 1976) 259-261; J. A. Thompson, *Deuteronomy,* Tyndale Old Testament Commentary (Downers Grove, IL: InterVarsity, 1974) 210-213.
18. Cf. Deane and Kirk, *Studies in First Samuel* II:92; Ishida, *Studies in the Period of David and Solomon,* 109-138.
19. The quotation has been taken from Benjamin Franklin's *Poor Richard's Almanac* and reveals how well-read he was in the classics. The essence of this statement, though not the exact wording, is to be found in Cicero's *De Legibus* III:2:5 and also in Dionenes Laertius's *Solon* I:60. Cf. Deane and Kirk, *Studies in First Samuel* II:110-111; S. Yonick, *Rejection of Saul as King* (Jerusalem: Franciscan Printing Press, 1970) 68 pages.
20. Two thoughts are worth noting. First, the term *hehĕzîq bakkānāp,* "he caught hold of the hem," shows Saul's desperation. He took firm hold of the prophet's *mĕ 'îl,* "robe"; he exerted strength to detain Samuel. Second and perhaps more importantly, throughout the ancient Near East to grasp the hem of another's garment was a sign of submission. Saul must have fallen to his knees to do this, for he was much taller than Samuel. He apparently wanted to plead with the prophet and his act of grasping the hem of Samuel's robe tacitly indicated his willingness to submit to the prophet's authority. Cf. R. A. Brauner, *Journal of the Ancient Near Eastern Society* (of Columbia University) 6 (1974) 35-38; F. J. Stephens, *Journal of Biblical Literature* 50 (1931) 59-70; *Ancient Near Eastern Texts,* 560-562.
21. Blaikie, *First Book of Samuel,* 250. Did Samuel sin in worshiping with Saul? P. N. Greenhow, *Grace Journal* 11, 2 (1970) 34-40, states emphatically that he did. Greenhow's reasoning, however, unwittingly reveals the conventional level of his thinking; cf. L. Kohlberg, *Essays in Moral Development,* vol. 2 of *The Psychology of Moral Development* (San Francisco: Harper and Row, 1984) xxix,41-72.
22. Blaikie, *First Book of Samuel,* 250-251; cf. S. Talmon, *Vetus Testamentum* 11 (1961) 456-457; R. G. Bratcher, *Bible Translator* 22 (1971) 167-168.
23. We see the evidence of this kind of reasoning in 1 Samuel 15:30-34 (noting in particular verse 31). Saul set aside Samuel's words and made plans for establishing his dynasty!
24. J. G. Whittier, *101 Famous Poems,* rev. ed., comp. R. J. Cook (Chicago: Contemporary Books, 1958) 149.

Chapter 11

1. The literature on the life of David is very extensive. Hupper (*Index to English Periodical Literature* I:87-90) provides a listing of journal articles through 1969-1970. *The Minister's Library* (I:101-104; II:63-66) draws attention to the most important works

that have been published in the last two hundred years. Of particular value for their scholarship are D. M. Gunn's *The Story of King David* (Sheffield: Journal for the Study of the Old Testament, Supplement 6, 1982, 164 pages with an extensive bibliography taking up pages 142-153) and K. W. Whitelam's *The Just King* (Sheffield: Journal for the Study of the Old Testament, Supplement 12, 1979, pages 71-148, with a bibliography comprising pages 277-302). Both works however are steeped in the latest redaction criticism. The most valuable works for the lay Bible student and/or expository preacher are W. G. Blaikie's *David;* W. J. Deane's *David: His Life and Times* (London: Nisbet, n.d.) 222 pages; F. W. Krummacher's *David, King of Israel,* trans. M. G. Easton (Minneapolis: Klock, 1983) 540 pages; A. Maclaren's *David;* F. B. Meyer's *David: Shepherd, Psalmist, King* (London: Marshall, Morgan and Scott, 1953) 160 pages; W. M. Taylor's *David, King of Israel* (Grand Rapids: Baker, 1961) 443 pages.

2. *Zondervan Pictorial Encyclopedia* V:1058.
3. Cf. M. Kessler, *Catholic Biblical Quarterly* 32 (1970) 543-554; J. J. Jackson and M. Kessler, eds. *Rhetorical Criticism* (Pittsburgh: Pickwick, 1974) 43-67; J. T. Willis, *Zeitschrift für die alttestamentliche Wissenschaft* 85 (1973) 294-314; A. Wiser, *Vetus Testamentum* 16 (1966) 325-354.
4. Deane and Kirk, *Studies in First Samuel* II:121; cf. Edersheim, *Bible History* IV:79-80.
5. Kaiser, *Hard Sayings,* 65.
6. For a discussion of this issue see Blaikie, *First Book of Samuel,* 255-256; Krummacher, *David,* 3-4,13-15; Deane and Kirk, *Studies in First Samuel* I:159; Edersheim, *Bible History* IV:82-83; Wood, *United Monarchy,* 146-147.
7. Cf. Murray, *Principles of Conduct,* 126ff.,139-140,146-147.
8. Cf. N. Geisler, *Ethics: Alternatives and Issues* (Grand Rapids: Zondervan, 1971) 13-20,87, 122-123; J. Fletcher, *Situation Ethics* (Philadelphia: Westminster, 1966) 26-39,73,89-95.
9. Deane and Kirk, *Studies in First Samuel* II:124.
10. Blaikie, *First Book of Samuel,* 257-258.
11. The birth order of children is important. A mother tends to favor the last born. Cf. K. Leman, *The Birth Order Book* (Old Tappan, NJ: Revell, 1984) 82-95.
12. Josephus, *Antiquities of the Jews* VI:8:2.
13. Blaikie, *First Book of Samuel,* 270.
14. Deane and Kirk, *Studies in First Samuel* I:160-161; S. J. Dragga, *Journal for the Study of the Old Testament* 38 (1987) 39-46.
15. Blaikie, *First Book of Samuel,* 260-261; A. F. Campbell, *Australian Biblical Review* 34 (1986) 35-41.
16. N. P. Lemche, *Journal for the Study of the Old Testament* 10 (1978) 2-25; R. L. Ward, "The Story of David's Rise" (unpublished doctoral dissertation, Vanderbilt University, 1967, 234 pages.
17. Cf. Blaikie, *First Book of Samuel,* 267; Edersheim, *Bible History* IV:83-84; M. F. Unger, *Unger's Commentary on the Old Testament* (Chicago: Moody, 1981) I:385; R. P. Gordon, *Vetus Testamentum* 37 (1987) 39-49; L. J. Wood, *The Holy Spirit in the Old Testament* (Grand Rapids: Zondervan, 1976) 126-144.
18. Cf. M. F. Unger, *Biblical Demonology* (Wheaton, IL: Scripture, 1955) 27,132,154.
19. Saul's experiences—prior to ascending the throne as well as with the Lord and Samuel—affected the way he thought about himself and impaired his organizational skills and judgment of people and events. The tangible losses (his dynasty and the right to rule) were interwoven with his loss of self-confidence and sense of worth. The emotional pain accompanying such feelings fluctuates, but in a person of Saul's temperament it would also lead to imbalance in thinking and impairment of the ability to function effectively. For a reliable discussion of these issues see A. D. Hart's *Depression: Coping and Caring* (Arcadia, CA: Cope, 1981) 230 pages; idem, *Counseling the Depressed,* Resources in Christian Counseling (Waco, TX: Word, 1987) 275 pages.
20. The value of music therapy should neither be downplayed nor ignored. Appropriate sounds and/or rhythm can help a depressed person respond and be willing to develop healthy attitudes. It is a nonthreatening means of communication leaving the sufferer free to reflect upon his/her feelings, develop creativity, and when feeling better recover a renewed sense of personal esteem. Perhaps eventually the sufferer can enjoy the music in the company of others and in this way express his/her feelings

nonverbally. For a discussion of these issues see H. L. Bonny and L. M. Savary, *Music and Your Mind* (New York: Harper and Row, 1973) 165 pages; C. H. Cornill, *Music in the Old Testament,* trans. L. G. Robinson (Chicago: Open Court, 1914) 25 pages; E. Feder and B. Feder, *The Expressive Art Therapies* (Englewood Cliffs, NJ: Prentice-Hall, 1981) 249 pages; J. Stainer, *The Music of the Bible* (London: Novello, Ewer, 1914) 186 pages. A very important discussion of music in our contemporary culture is to be found in A. Bloom's *The Closing of the American Mind* (New York: Simon and Schuster, 1987) 68-81.

21. Blaikie, *First Book of Samuel,* 256-266.
22. Cf. Deane and Kirk, *Studies in First Samuel* I:102.
23. Cf. B. Peckham, *Zeitschrift fur die alttestamentliche Wissenschaft* 97 (1985) 190-209; the discussion of love in P. R. Ackroyd, *Vetus Testamentum* 25 (1975) 213-214; J. A. Thompson, *Vetus Testamentum* 24 (1974) 334-338.
24. J. T. Brady, *The Heisman: A Symbol of Excellence* (New York: Atheneum, 1984) 154-157.
25. M. Lomask, *Aaron Burr* (New York: Farrar, Strauss, Giroux, 1982) 476 pages.

Chapter 12

1. Cf. C. J. Barber and J. D. Carter, *Always a Winner,* 95-104.
2. Most preachers I have heard or whose books I have read resort to subjectivism and describe the "giants" we face as lust or sensuality or greed or any inordinate desire of the flesh (Galatians 5:19-21). Such a ploy distorts the context and destroys the meaning of this passage.
3. Examples of this kind of warfare are not hard to find. They are found in Matthew Arnold's story of Sohrab and Rustum; Homer's account of the fight between Paris and Menelaus in the *Iliad* III:340ff.; Homer's account of the fight between Hector and Ajax in the *Iliad* VII:206ff.; etc. There is also the story of Sinuhe, an Egyptian, fighting a man from Retenu (cf. *Ancient Near Eastern Texts,* 20). Livy I:23 also provides an example of this kind of warfare. And a Hittite parallel to the story of David and Goliath is to be found in H. A. Hoffer's article in *Catholic Biblical Quarterly* 30 (1968) 220-225. For a fuller discussion of these issues see R. deVaux, *The Bible and the Ancient Near East* (Garden City, NY: Doubleday, 1971) 122-135; T. A. Boohart, *Reformed Review* 38 (1968) 220-225; S. J. deVries, *Journal of Biblical Literature* 92 (1973) 23-36.
4. Keil and Delitzsch, *Biblical Commentary,* 181-185; cf. Klein, *1 Samuel,* 173; A. M. Honeyman, *Journal of Biblical Literature* 67 (1948) 13-25; H. Jason, *Biblica* 60 (1979) 36-70. Some commentators (e.g., McCarter, *1 Samuel,* 284ff. and Mauchline, *1 and 2 Samuel,* 136-137) have sought to discredit this story by either linking it with the account mentioned in 2 Samuel 21:16ff. or implying that material from the later account was included in the story of David to build his credibility. None of these arguments is persuasive and the Biblical account needs no defense.
5. Edersheim, *Bible History* IV:87; cf. Hertzberg, *I and II Samuel,* 148-149.
6. We know from 1 Samuel 14:52 that there was war continually between the Israelites and the Philistines. Most of these battles were border skirmishes such as the one recorded in 23:1ff. The Bible mentions three full-scale battles between these two countries during the reign of Saul, of which the one mentioned in 1 Samuel 17 is the second.
7. Goliath is described as six cubits and a span tall (i.e., about nine feet and nine inches—from which we derive our description of a person as being "ten feet tall"). A cubit was the distance from a man's elbow to the tip of his middle finger, but as the length of a man's arm differed from person to person, the usual length was about eighteen inches. Cf. D. D. Luckenbill, *The Annals of Sennacherib* (Chicago: University of Chicago Press, 1924) 34; A. Segre, *Journal of the American Oriental Society* 64 (1944) 73-81; R. B. Y. Scott, *Biblical Archaeologist* 22, 2 (1959) 22-39.
8. Yadin, *Art of Warfare* I:196-197; II:354.
9. Idem, *Palestine Exploration Quarterly* 86 (1955) 58-69; idem, *Art of Warfare* II:355.
10. Mention of iron as well as bronze in 1 Samuel 17:5-7 shows that the Philistines still retained the use of bronze and had not fully entered the iron age. Cf. J. J. Bimson and D. Livingstone, *Biblical Archaeology Review* 13 (1987) 40-53,66-68, noting in particular pages 46-47; J. Strange, *Scandinavian Journal of the Old Testament* 1 (1987) 1-19.
11. Deane and Kirk, *Studies in First Samuel* II:142-143.

12. There appears to be a discrepancy between 1 Samuel 16:6-10 and 17:12 on the one hand and 1 Chronicles 2:15 on the other. It seems likely that one of Jesse's sons died and so was not taken into consideration by the chronicler.
13. Blaikie, *First Book of Samuel,* 279-280.
14. Hertzberg, *I and II Samuel,* 150-151.
15. There are three possible interpretations of David's statement. Cf. Deane and Kirk, *Studies in First Samuel* II:155-157; Keil and Delitzsch, *Biblical Commentary,* 180-181. The Apocrypha, Psalm 151, reads: "I was small among my brethren, and youngest in my father's house: I tended my father's sheep. My hands formed a musical instrument, and my fingers tuned a psaltery. And who shall tell my Lord? The Lord Himself, He Himself hears. He sent forth His angel, and took me with the oil of His anointing. My brothers were handsome and tall; but the Lord did not take pleasure in them. I went forth to meet the Philistine; and he cursed me by his idols. But I drew his own sword, and beheaded him, and removed reproach from the children of Israel."
16. Cf. A. R. Ceresko, *Catholic Biblical Quarterly* 47 (1985) 58-74; P. M. McCarter, Jr., *Journal of Biblical Literature* 99 (1980) 489-504.
17. *Iliad* III:340ff.; VII:206.
18. A. Deem, *Vetus Testamentum* 28 (1978) 349-351.
19. Deane and Kirk, *Studies in First Samuel* II:152-154.
20. Cf. N. P. Lemche, *Vetus Testamentum* 24 (1974) 373-374; C. J. Barber and J. D. Carter, *Always a Winner,* 128-129. Because Goliath's sword was later found at Nob (1 Samuel 21:8-9) the majority of commentators are inclined to emend the text from *be'oholo,* "his tent," to *be'oholi,* "tent [of Yahweh]." Cf. Klein, *1 Samuel,* 181; Mauchline, *1 and 2 Samuel,* 135. Deane and Kirk (*Studies in First Samuel* II:165-167) offer a different, plausible explanation.
21. For a discussion of *nepeš Yĕhônātān niqšĕrâ bĕnepeš Dāwîd,* "the soul of Jonathan was knit [bound] to the soul of David," see P. R. Ackroyd, *Vetus Testamentum* 25 (1975) 213-214; J. A. Thompson, *Vetus Testamentum* 24 (1974) 334-338. Also see Aristotle's definition: friendship is "a single soul living on two bodies" (Diogenes Laertius, *Aristotle* V:20).
22. Edersheim, *Bible History* IV:94.
23. Deane and Kirk, *Studies in First Samuel* II:170-171.
24. Cf. Maclaren, *David,* 37-48.
25. B. Larson, *There's a Lot More to Health Than Not Being Sick* (Waco, TX: Word, 1984) 74.

Chapter 13

1. J. Thurber, *The Thurber Carnival* (New York: Modern Library, 1957) 47-51.
2. Deane, *David,* 24ff.; Deane and Kirk, *Studies in First Samuel* I:168.
3. Blaikie, *First Book of Samuel,* 296-297.
4. Deane, *David,* 25.
5. Claudian, *In Rufinum* I:1:12.
6. This was the custom (cf. Exodus 15:20-21; Judges 11:34). Cf. Deane and Kirk, *Studies in First Samuel* II:173; Meyer, *David,* 49; C. E. Macartney, *Great Portraits of the Bible* (New York: Abingdon, n.d.) 152. *Tuppîm* are probably tambourines and *šālī šîm* may be three-stringed instruments (although some have identified them as triangles).
7. For a more extensive discussion of jealousy than is possible here see K. F. Bernard, *Jealousy: Its Nature and Treatment* (Springfield, IL: Thomas, 1986) 165 pages. A helpful analysis of jealousy as a manifestation of pathological narcissism is to be found in O. Kernberg, *Internal World and External Reality* (New York: Aronson, 1985) 135-153. Meyer (*Samuel the Prophet,* 155-160) treats Saul's jealousy at length. The Hebrew *'ălāpîm,* "thousand," in juxtaposition with *rĕbābôt,* "myriad" (but usually translated "ten thousand"), is a standard poetic expression contrasting the two figures (cf. Psalm 144:13).
8. Cf. N. P. Lemche, *Journal for the Study of the Old Testament* 10 (1978) 2-25; J. van Seters, *Journal for the Study of the Old Testament* 1 (1976) 22-29; R. P. Gordon, *Tyndale Bulletin* 31 (1980) 37-64.
9. The unusual Hebrew construction *'ăšar hû' maśkîl mĕ'ōd,* "that he was very successful" (1 Samuel 18:15), serves to emphasize why David prospered. It was because Yahweh was with him.

10. Cf. W. L. Moran, *Catholic Biblical Quarterly* 25 (1963) 77-87; Deane and Kirk, *Studies in First Samuel* II:178.
11. J. J. Gluck, *Zeitschrift für die alttestamentliche Wissenschaft* 77 (1965) 72-81.
12. J. C. Geikie, *Hours with the Bible* (London: Hodder and Stoughton, 1882) III:152-153; Maclaren, *David,* 70-85.
13. G. W. Coats, *Journal of Biblical Literature* 89 (1970) 14-26.
14. The *mōhar* or "bridal price" has received a full discussion in deVaux, *Ancient Israel,* 32-33; Neufeld, *Ancient Hebrew Marriage Laws,* 100-110; Pedersen, *Israel* I-II:67-70.
15. *Lērō',* "fear," in the Masoretic text is most irregular. Cf. S. R. Driver, *Notes on the Hebrew Text,* 155.
16. Blaikie, *First Book of Samuel,* 301.
17. Deane, *David,* 29.
18. Deane and Kirk, *Studies in First Samuel* I:173. Cf. Josephus, *Antiquities of the Jews* VI:11:1-4; C. J. Barber, *Worldwide Challenge* 6 (1979) 34-36.
19. Cf. I. Boszormenyi-Nagy and G. M. Spank, *Invisible Loyalties* (New York: Brunner/Mazel, 1984) 37-51,151-165. W. M. Taylor (*David,* 76) wrote of Jonathan: "I do not know many instances in which we have such a manifestation of prudence and principle combined, as we have in the case of this expostulation of Jonathan with his father. Prudence did not go so far as to make him silent about the sin which Saul was purposing to commit; principle was not so asserted as to arouse his father's indignation. Neither was weakened by the other; but both were so admirably inter-blended as to produce the result on which his heart was set."
20. Cf. Deane and Kirk, *Studies in First Samuel* I:173-174; W. M. Taylor, *David,* 75ff.
21. Josephus, *Antiquities of the Jews* VI:11:4.
22. Ibid. For a discussion of the teraphim see S. Smith, *Journal of Theological Studies* 33 (1932) 33-36.
23. Deane, *David,* 31-32; C. J. Barber and A.A. Barber, *You Can Have a Happy Marriage,* 67-79.
24. A. Malamat, *Journal of the American Oriental Society* 82 (1962) 146. Samuel is described in 1 Samuel 19:20 as *'omēd niṣṣāb,* "standing in the position of authority," and *niṣṣāb 'al,* "presiding over" the *qĕhillat hannĕ bīm,* "the assembly." This is significant, for in our day many influential preachers and others with a large radio or television following have spoken of the need for accountability. They have not given their listeners any guidelines, however, and this has led certain zealous groups to assign arbitrarily a younger believer to an older Christian who is supposed to disciple the neophyte. Some of the results of this practice have been disastrous. The word translated "standing" (in the assembly) looks at Samuel's divine appointment. He was also "presiding" over the students. This looks at his acceptance by them. They willingly subordinated themselves to his authority. There was no coercion. Only as these Biblical principles are maintained can there be appropriate accountability!
25. Deane and Kirk (*Studies in First Samuel* I:169) observed that "Saul's old magnanimity which he had showed towards enemies in his early days had been ruined by years of brooding and discontent, and the evil temper to which he had given way at times utterly displaced the old affection for the gallant friend and soothing minstrel, and left nothing in its place but a feeling of rancorous envy and jealousy."
26. Cf. Blaikie, *First Book of Samuel,* 320-323; D. R. Hillers, *Bulletin of the American Schools of Oriental Research* 176 (1964) 46-47; G. R. Driver, *Zeitschrift für die alttestamentliche Wissenschaft* 80 (1968) 174-183; A. Wenim, *Biblica* 64 (1983) 1-19. For a discussion of *hesed* see K. D. Sakenfeld, *The Meaning of Hesed in the Bible* (Missoula, MT: Scholars, 1978) 82-90.
27. The phrase "he [Saul] intends evil" (1 Samuel 20:7) is very important and occurs only here and in 20:9,33; 25:17; Esther 7:7. It looks at the unfavorable treatment of someone who formerly stood in a good relationship to the person now harboring evil designs in his heart.
28. Cf. J. Wozniak, *Biblische Zeitschrift* 27 (1983) 213-218.
29. Cf. *New York Times* (August 8, 1984).
30. In the *TV Guide* (March 29, 1986) Mary Murphy showed that Marcia's experience was not unusual. In fact this kind of harassment is common.

31. For a clearer understanding of the levels of friendship see C. J. Barber and S. Aspenleiter, *Through the Valley of Tears,* 139-179,207.
32. Blaikie, *David,* 54.

Chapter 14

1. A. H. Maslow, *Motivation and Personality,* 2d ed. (New York: Harper and Row, 1954) 369 pages. Note in particular his discussion on pages 59-95.
2. Ibid., 185ff.
3. Edersheim, *Bible History* IV:114 (note 1). Edersheim reasoned that Doeg, who influenced Saul, is the Cushite referred to in this Psalm. Cf. Kitto, *Daily Bible Illustrations* I:710-711 for a contrary point of view.
4. David's dire hunger is tacitly confirmed in 1 Samuel 21:8. If he had gone home to Michal after visiting Naioth, he surely would have had some weapon(s) in his possession when he fled to Nob. And even if someone had given him food, he still faced a long journey to Gath and had no means of knowing when or where his next meal might come from.
5. Blaikie, *First Book of Samuel,* 329; cf. Kitto, *Daily Bible Illustrations* I:697-701.
6. Blaikie, *First Book of Samuel,* 329-331; Edersheim, *Bible History* IV:112.
7. Blaikie, *First Book of Samuel,* 331.
8. Kitto *(Daily Bible Illustrations* I:697ff.) believes the sabbath was approaching so no one could pursue David to Nob, nor could word be brought back to Saul of his whereabouts.
9. Baly, *Geography of the Bible,* 175,188. Different writers have proposed different sites; cf. Aharoni, *The Land and the Book,* 313,410,416,440; Robinson, *Biblical Researches in Palestine* I:464; Thomson, *The Land and the Book* I:236,434-437. For a clearer understanding of the places David was forced to flee to after leaving Gibeah, see the *Macmillan Bible Atlas,* 92.
10. *Wayyeḥĕrad...liqrā't Dāwī̃d,* "Came trembling...to meet David," indicates his apprehension on seeing the king's son-in-law without an escort. Cf. *Theological Wordbook* I:321-322 (#735).
11. *Leḥem qōdeš,* "holy bread," was the same as the *leḥem happānīm,* "bread of the presence" (cf. Exodus 25:30; Leviticus 24:5-9). Cf. J. A. Grassi, *Novum Testamentum* 7 (1964) 119-122; *Zondervan Pictorial Encyclopedia* V:420-421. The condition of the gift of the bread is that the men accompanying David on his supposed mission "have kept themselves from women" (1 Samuel 21:4). This ceremonial abstinence from sexual intercourse was deemed necessary so that those fighting the Lord's battles could be committed in mind and body to one thing only (namely, the task at hand—"fighting Yahweh's battles").
12. Possibly with yes-and-no answers obtained by consulting the urim and thummim. If this is so, it would have been easy for David to disguise the true intent of his questions. In addition to the other sources of information on the urim and thummim already cited in this work, the following articles are worth consulting: H. E. Dosker, *Presbyterian and Reformed Review* 3 (1892) 717-730; B. Johnson, *Annual of the Swedish Theological Institute* 9 (1974) 23-29.
13. Kitto, *Daily Bible Illustrations* I:699-700. Cf. Blaikie, *First Book of Samuel,* 335; Edersheim, *Bible History* IV:114; Macartney, *Chariots of Fire,* 104-113. *Ne'sār lipnē Yahweh,* "detained before Yahweh," most likely indicates detention for some ceremonial purpose.
14. Cf. Deane, *David,* 43-44.
15. Kitto, *Daily Bible Illustrations* I:701-703; cf. F. Crusemann, *Zeitschrift für die alttestamentliche Wissenschaft* 80 (1980) 215-217; H. S. Gehman, *Journal of Biblical Literature* 67 (1948) 241-243; G. A. Wainright, *Vetus Testamentum* 9 (1959) 73-84.
16. The superscription of the Psalm mentions Abimelech (not Achish). Some have conjectured that this was the Hebrew equivalent of the hereditary title used by the Philistines. Edersheim *(Bible History* IV:115) identified Psalms 59, 7, 56, 34, 52, 142, and 54 (listing them in chronological order) as dating from the period of David's persecution by Saul. Cf. Maclaren, *David,* 49-143.
17. Cf. Robinson, *Biblical Researches in Palestine* I:481-482; G. A. Smith, *Historical Geography of the Holy Land,* 229ff.; Thomson, *The Land and the Book* I:145,330-335,338; Albright,

Bulletin of the American Schools of Oriental Research 15 (1924) 3-4. For a brief discussion of David's mighty men see H. G. M. Williamson, *Oudtestamentische Studien* 21 (1981) 164-176.

18. Cf. L. M. Epstein, *Marriage Laws*, 3-76; Neufeld, *Ancient Hebrew Marriage Laws*, 118-132. See also the comments on Elkanah and his wives (chapter 1, note 6). There can be no doubt that God's ideal has always been for one man and one woman to live together in harmony for life. There are times however when circumstances (as here in the case of David) make this impossible. Some preachers whom I have heard do not hesitate to accuse David of adultery. They overlook his own testimony (recorded without any intimation of divine disapproval; contrast 2 Samuel 11:27) in Psalm 18:20-24 and 31:19-22. They are also guilty of interpreting the Bible in accordance with western culture.

19. David showed respect for the king of Moab by using the general name for God, *'Ĕlōhîm*. By his words he also expressed his sincere reliance on the Lord for the future. Cf. Blaikie, *First Book of Samuel*, 344.

20. Edersheim, *Bible History* IV:118.

21. This forest is not mentioned elsewhere in the Bible. Some Bible scholars believe it was near Khirbet Khoreisa, about two miles from Ziph. If this is so, David and his men were close at hand and could deliver the people of Keilah without having to travel any great distance. Cf. *Macmillan Bible Atlas*, 90,92.

22. B. Mazar, *Vetus Testamentum* 13 (1963) 310-320; D. W. Thomas, *Journal of Theological Studies* 21 (1970) 401-402.

23. E. Fromm, *The Nature of Man* (New York: Macmillan, 1968) 173; cf. M. Buber, *Good and Evil* (New York: Scribner's, 1953) 111.

24. Blaikie, *First Book of Samuel*, 345; W. M. Taylor, *David*, 104,106-108; Deane and Kirk, *Studies in First Samuel* I:183-184.

25. Blaikie, *First Book of Samuel*, 346.

26. Thiessen, *Lectures*, 82,119.

27. Deane and Kirk, *Studies in First Samuel* I:184.

28. T. Veijola, *Revue Biblique* 91 (1984) 51-87. Keilah was prominent in the Amarna period (1369-1353 B.C.); cf. *Ancient Near Eastern Texts*, 487-489.

29. In this we note that Saul had abandoned a relationship with Yahweh, the covenant-keeping God of Israel. Yahweh had not given him what he wanted, and indeed had taken from him what he wanted most—his dynasty, popularity, and the right to rule the people. *'Ĕlōhîm*, however, in Saul's thinking was a Force who at least appeared to be aiding him in the carrying out of his quest. Saul must have been very disappointed when David escaped. He could only have felt further disillusionment (the kind we have all felt at one time or another when some cherished dream, long prayed for, eluded our grasp). Saul acted irresponsibly, however, never pausing to consider God's will for him (contrast Eli, who meekly accepted the Lord's chastening, 1 Samuel 3:18). David, in contrast to Saul, submitted to the period of discipline God required him to endure and emerged better for the experience. For a contemporary discussion of such experiences see P. Yancey, *Disappointed With God* (Grand Rapids: Zondervan, 1988) 260 pages.

30. David's statement on leaving Keilah, *Wa'ănî hôlēk 'al 'aser 'ănî hôlēk*, "and I am going where I am going" (1 Samuel 23:13), is idiomatic for "I'll go wherever I can" (cf. S. R. Driver, *Notes on the Hebrew Text*, 185-186; Keil and Delitzsch, *Biblical Commentary*, 230; Mauchline, *1 and 2 Samuel*, 160). See also Deane, *David*, 50.

31. The Lord still keeps covenant with those who fear (i.e., reverence) Him. While the promises to Israel are not fulfilled in the church, Christians benefit from the soteriological blessings of the new covenant (Jeremiah 31:31-34; Romans 11:13-24). Cf. Pentecost, *Things to Come*, 116-128.

Chapter 15

1. H. Black, *Friendship* (New York: Revell, 1903) 244 pages; S. Dodds, *Friendship's Meaning and the Heart of God in Nature* (Butler, PA: Ziegler, 1919) 7-43; A. van Selms, *Journal of Near Eastern Studies* 9 (1950) 65-75; C. J. Barber and J. D. Carter, *Always a Winner*, 115-125;

G. Inrig, *Quality Friendship* (Chicago: Moody, 1979) 223 pages; C. J. Barber, *Worldwide Challenge* 6, 2 (1979) 34-36; J. Wazniak, *Biblische Zeitschrift* 27 (1983) 213-218.

2.   Cf. Geikie, *The Holy Land and the Bible* I:357; Robinson, *Biblical Researches in Palestine* I:492,495; Thomson, *The Land and the Book* I:286-288.

3.   *Baḥōrēšâ,* "in the wood" or "in Horesh" (1 Samuel 23:15-18). Most writers point to Khirbet Khoreisa, approximately two miles from Tell Zip, as the location. Conder *(Tent Work in Palestine* II:89) is of the opinion that the dry porous rock in this region could never have supported a forest. Geikie *(The Holy Land and the Bible* I:50-51 and *Hours with the Bible* III:187ff.) is aware of this and reminds us that when trees are cut down, the rainfall in the area diminishes. In the course of time evidence of vegetation vanishes. We must also remember that three millennia have elapsed since David's flight from Saul and considerable climatic changes could easily have taken place in this area during the intervening period.

4.   Neither Hachilah nor Jeshimon can be located with certainty. *Hachilah* means "dark." It may have been situated on a long ridge now known as El Kolah where there is a high hill and a ruin on the summit called Yukin. For a possible identification of *Jeshimon,* which means "a waste, a desolation," see G. A. Smith, *Historical Geography of the Holy Land,* 312-314; Baly, *Geography of the Bible,* 35-38.

5.   Deane and Kirk, *Studies in First Samuel* II:208-209.

6.   Cf. C. J. Barber and J. D. Carter, *Always a Winner,* 122-123. *Wayḥazzēq 'et-yādo bĕyahweh,* "and strengthened his hand in Yahweh" (1 Samuel 23:16), is used of encouraging the fearful. The Lord does not change, but our perception of His interest in us and concern for us may need to be reaffirmed (cf. Nehemiah 6:9).

7.   C. J. Barber and J. D. Carter, *Always a Winner,* 122-123.

8.   It was a widely held practice in ancient times for a new king to kill off all other claimants to the throne (cf. Judges 9:1-2; 1 Kings 15:27-29; 2 Kings 10:11).

9.   The wording in 1 Samuel 23:21 seems to imply that Saul no longer took Jonathan into his confidence as formerly. He does not appear to have been a part of Saul's special force to capture David. Are we to gather from this incidental statement that the king no longer trusted his son and for that reason left him behind? If so, it points to the cost some friendships entail! Also of note is the fact that Jonathan would have had to make a special journey to the barren wastes around Ziph for the sole purpose of meeting with his friend. Furthermore we may be sure that it was only through diligent inquiry that he was able to learn where David was.

10. J. Watt, *Old Testament Characters* (New York: Loizeaux, n.d.) 112-123.

11. C. J. Barber and J. D. Carter, *Always a Winner,* 120.

12. Cf. Romans 12:10; 13:8; 14:13,19; 1 Corinthians 12:25; Galatians 5:13; Ephesians 4:2,25,32; Philippians 2:3; 1 Thessalonians 3:12; 4:9; 5:11,13; Hebrews 3:13; 10:24.

13. Blaikie, *First Book of Samuel,* 359-362.

14. Cf. Baly, *Geography of the Bible,* 198-216; Glueck, *Rivers in the Desert,* 153-163.

15. Deane and Kirk, *Studies in First Samuel* II:209-210; cf. Conder, *Tent Work in Palestine* II:92. The identification of the crag *(hassela',* 1 Samuel 23:23) is confusing and requires further explanation. David and his men were on one slope, and Saul and his elite corps were on the other. Saul divided his forces so that they could circle around and *'otĕrîm 'el* ("come upon," 1 Samuel 23:26) David and his men from both sides. As a result of God's providential intervention, the place was given the name *sela' hammaḥlĕqôt,* "rock of divisions" or "rock of escape" (23:28).

16. Modern 'Ain Jidī. This region served to shelter other Jewish soldiers during the revolts of A.D. 66-70 and 132-135. Cf. Edersheim, *Bible History* IV:125-126; Robinson, *Biblical Researches in Palestine* I:500,504-508; Thomson, *The Land and the Book* III:534; W. F. Albright, *Bulletin of the American Schools of Oriental Research* 18 (1925) 11-15; B. Mazar, *Archaeology* 16 (1963) 99-107; idem and J. Dunayevsky, *Israel Exploration Journal* 14 (1964) 121-130; *Encyclopedia of Archaeological Excavations* II:370-380.

17. Cf. Edersheim, *Bible History* IV:125-126; J. C. Geikie, *Old Testament Characters* (New York: Pott, 1903) 170-173; Thomson, *The Land and the Book* I:312-324, II:316-320, III:354.

18. The euphemism "to cover his feet" means "to defecate" (not to take a nap as Blaikie proposed). David's refusal to kill Saul is discussed by W. Baars, *Oudtestamentische Studien* 14 (1965) 201-215; R. P. Gordon, *Tyndale Bulletin* 32 (1980) 37-64.

19. For a discussion of the "hem of the garment" motif see F. J. Stephens, *Journal of Biblical Literature* 50 (1931) 59-70; R. A. Brauner, *Journal of the Ancient Near Eastern Society* 6 (1974) 35-38; *Ancient Near Eastern Texts,* 560-562. For a more traditional interpretation see Blaikie, *First Book of Samuel,* 366-370.
20. See note 8.
21. Blaikie, *First Book of Samuel,* 363-365.

Chapter 16

1. *Random House Dictionary of the English Language,* s.v. "influence." Used by permission.
2. *The Dramatic Works of William Shakespeare,* ed. S. W. Singer (London: Bell, 1899) VIII:425.
3. R. K. Massie, *Nicholas and Alexandra* (New York: Atheneum, 1967) page vi; see also pages 190-520. Cf. A. DeJonge, *The Life and Times of Grigorii Rasputin* (New York: Dorset, 1982) 363 pages.
4. *Complete Poetical Works of Elizabeth Barrett Browning* (Boston: Houghton, Mifflin, 1900) 430-431.
5. Deane and Kirk, *Studies in First Samuel* II:27. Excellent eulogies of Samuel's life have been given by Edersheim (*Bible History* IV:127-128) and Meyer (*Samuel the Prophet,* 170-177).
6. Josephus, *Antiquities of the Jews* VI:13:5.
7. Meyer, *Samuel the Prophet,* 172.
8. Cf. the descriptions given by Robinson (*Biblical Researches in Palestine* I:126ff.) and Thomson (*The Land and the Book* I:199-200).
9. *Nabal* means "foolish, lacking in sense." Klein (*1 Samuel,* 248) does not believe anyone would call a son by this name and conjectures that it was a nickname given him by others. Cf. J. D. Levenson, *Catholic Biblical Quarterly* 40 (1978) 11-28; Mauchline, *1 and 2 Samuel,* 168.
10. For a discussion of Abigail see C. J. Barber and A. A. Barber, *You Can Have a Happy Marriage,* 81-93; C. E. Macartney, *Ancient Wives and Modern Husbands* (Nashville: Cokesbury, 1934) 123-140; idem, *Great Women of the Bible* (Nashville: Abingdon, 1942) 105-120.
11. Thomson, *The Land and the Book* I:288 (see also pages 290-291). Cf. Blaikie, *First Book of Samuel,* 382-384; Edersheim, *Bible History* IV:129-130; J. Hall, *Contemplations on Historical Passages,* 197-198; Mauchline, *1 and 2 Samuel,* 168-169.
12. Edersheim, *Bible History* IV:130.
13. The King James version preserves the rendering of 1 Samuel 25:21 in the Masoretic text. Cf. G. R. Driver, *Journal of Theological Studies* 8 (1957) 272-273.
14. Cf. Edersheim, *Bible History* IV:130-131.
15. Cf. J. Hall, *Contemplations on Historical Passages,* 199.
16. Edersheim, *Bible History* IV:132.
17. For the laws of inheritance see deVaux, *Ancient Israel,* 53-55,166. For a discussion of the plight of widows see C. J. Barber, *Ruth,* 97-112.
18. Klein, *1 Samuel,* 254.
19. J. D. Levenson and B. Halpern, *Journal of Biblical Literature* 99 (1980) 507-518.
20. Meyer, *David,* 96ff.
21. H. Stanley, *How I Found Livingstone* (London: Samson Low, 1872) 425; see also pages 428-429,431,434. Cf. W. G. Blaikie, *The Personal Life of David Livingstone* (London: Murray, 1882) 354-357; R. Charles, *Three Martyrs of the Nineteenth Century* (London: S.P.C.K., 1906) 149-153; R. Hall, *Stanley* (London: Collins, 1974) 196-198. A woodcut showing the tree under which Livingstone's heart lies buried appears on the frontispiece of H. Stanley's *Life and Finding of Dr. Livingstone* (n.p., n.d.) 335 pages.

Chapter 17

1. W. Manchester, *American Caesar* (Boston: Little, Brown, 1978) 205-241.
2. D. MacArthur, *Reminiscences* (New York: McGraw-Hill, 1964) 117-145.
3. There are many Bible scholars who claim that 1 Samuel 24 and 26 are merely variations

of the same account inserted at different places to serve the purposes of different editors (redactors). Cf. Klein, *1 Samuel,* 236-237. McCarter (*1 Samuel,* 386-387), however, believes that the accounts represent two separate incidents but nonetheless makes provision for different redactors. It is true that there are points of similarity, but there are also major differences. Blaikie (*First Book of Samuel,* 373-374) offers a fine defense of the integrity of the Biblical record. Furthermore it is a principle of Scripture that assurance of a person's integrity or the certainty of an event comes through repeated confirmation (cf. Genesis 41:1-8,25-36). The fact that David twice spared Saul's life proves beyond dispute his loyalty to the king.

4. Cf. F. Bacon, *Essays* (Boston: Little, Brown, 1884) 168-172.
5. R. Thornhill, *Vetus Testamentum* 14 (1964) 462-466.
6. David's words *'al tašḥitēhū,* "do not destroy him," are much stronger than "do not kill him." Cf. J. F. Drinkard, Jr., *Journal of Biblical Literature* 98 (1979) 285-286.
7. The *tardēmot Yahweh,* "deep sleep from Yahweh" (1 Samuel 26:12), recalls passages of Scripture like Genesis 2:21; 15:12; and in a spiritual sense of indifference toward God, Isaiah 29:10.
8. Cf. Deane, *David,* 62-63.
9. Blaikie, *First Book of Samuel,* 391. Cf. Keil and Delitzsch (*Biblical Commentary,* 254-257) who lay emphasis on David's need to find a permanent place of refuge.
10. Deane, *David,* 65.
11. Ibid., 66-67.
12. Different locations have been suggested for Ziklag: cf. Robinson, *Biblical Researches in Palestine* II:390; Thomson, *The Land and the Book* I:232-234; and more recently, Aharoni, *The Land of the Bible,* 347-356. See also the *Macmillan Bible Atlas,* 92-93.
13. The statement, "Ziklag belongs to the kings of Judah to this day" (1 Samuel 27:6), has led the majority of scholars to posit a late date for the composition of the Book of Samuel (see Introduction). In reality, as Keil and Delitzsch (*Biblical Commentary,* 256) show, Achish permanently assigned Ziklag to David, and the writing of what we refer to as 1 Samuel could easily have been accomplished during David's reign in Hebron.
14. W. E. O. Oesterley, ed. *Judaism and Christianity* (New York: Ktav, 1968) I:213-233; T. F. Torrance, *New Testament Studies* 1 (1954) 150-154; T. M. Taylor, *New Testament Studies* 2 (1956) 193-198; N. Levison, *Scottish Journal of Theology* 10 (1957) 45-65; J. Neusner, *Journal of Biblical Literature* 83 (1964) 60-66.
15. The term *yōm,* "day, today," does not mean that David gave a day-by-day accounting to Achish. What was meant is, Where have you been since we last met? David's answer confirms this (1 Samuel 27:10).
16. Meyer, *David,* 91.
17. *Dramatic Works of William Shakespeare* X:5-161.
18. Maclaren, *David,* 130-143.
19. Cf. Proverbs 16:28; 20:19; Matthew 15:19; Mark 7:21-22; Romans 1:28-30; 2 Corinthians 12:20; Ephesians 4:31-32; Colossians 3:8; 2 Timothy 3:3; 1 Peter 2:1-2.
20. *Wall Street Journal* (March 12, 1981) 24. Used by permission.
21. V. R. Edman, *Out of My Life* (Grand Rapids: Zondervan, 1961) 141-143.

Chapter 18

1. G. F. Owen, *The Holy Land* (Grand Rapids: Baker, 1977) 81-88; C. F. Pfeiffer and H. F. Vos, *Wycliffe Historical Geography of Bible Lands* (Chicago: Moody, 1968) 110-116. For a discussion of the route taken by the Philistines when they marched to Aphek, see Owen, *The Holy Land,* 54-70.
2. W. F. Albright, *Zeitschrift für die alttestamentliche Wissenschaft* 3 (1926) 226-234; F. M. Abel, *Geographie* II:470-471.
3. *Macmillan Bible Atlas,* 95.
4. Cf. Edersheim, *Bible History* IV:138.
5. Ibid.
6. Ibid. IV:139.
7. Cf. *Encyclopedia of Religion and Ethics,* ed. J. Hastings (Edinburgh: Clark, 1911) IV:775-830.

8. When the priests of Nob were killed, Abiathar fled to David with an ephod. Priests living in the cities throughout Israel were not included in the massacre. They probably reinstituted the services of the sanctuary, and either Saul (to placate the people) or the person appointed to the titular position of high priest may have commissioned the making of another ephod bearing the breastplate of the high priest. God apparently chose not to reveal His will through this new ephod. Cf. Keil and Delitzsch, *Biblical Commentary,* 260; Edersheim, *Bible History* IV:139 (note 1).
9. Blaikie, *First Book of Samuel,* 406-407.
10. Unger, *Biblical Demonology,* 148-153; Davis, *Birth of a Kingdom,* 96-100. Cf. W. A. M. Beuken, *Journal for the Study of the Old Testament* 6 (1978) 3-17; H. A. Hoffer, *Journal of Biblical Literature* 86 (1967) 385-401; idem, *Theological Dictionary* I:130-134. Additional evidence may be found in the Apocrypha, Ecclesiasticus 46:20.
11. Unger, *Biblical Demonology,* 153ff.
12. Cf. *Theological Wordbook* II:892 (#2303c); *Zondervan Pictorial Encyclopedia* V:395; G. Kittel, ed. *Theological Dictionary of the New Testament* (Grand Rapids: Eerdmans, 1964) I:146-149,657-658; C. Brown, ed. *New International Dictionary of New Testament Theology* (Grand Rapids: Zondervan, 1978) II:205-210.
13. Cf. Klein (*1 Samuel,* 277) and McCarter (*1 Samuel,* 427) for contrary points of view.
14. *Miyyôm 'ăšer hāyîtî lĕpānēkā,* "from the day on which I was [first] before you," invites a critical appraisal believing that nothing negative will be found to blemish the character of the speaker.
15. *Dramatic Works of William Shakespeare* II:417-459.
16. Unless of course Christ returns first (1 Corinthians 15:20-49; 1 Thessalonians 4:17–5:10).

Chapter 19

1. C. Koons, *Beyond Betrayal* (San Francisco: Harper & Row, 1986) 275 pages.
2. Ruff tells his own story in *How to Survive the Coming Bad Years* (San Ramon, CA: Target, 1981) 11.
3. C. J. Barber and S. Aspenleiter, *Through the Valley of Tears,* 224 pages.
4. C. Colson, *Born Again* (Old Tappan, NJ: Chosen, 1976) 351 pages.
5. Robinson, *Biblical Researches in Palestine* II:431-446; Thomson, *The Land and the Book* I:274-279; E. F. Bishop, *Journal of Biblical Literature* 16 (1947) 94-99; G. A. Larue, *Journal of Bible and Religion* 33 (1964) 337-339; P. C. Hammond, *Revue Biblique* 72 (1965) 267-270; idem, *Revue Biblique* 73 (1966) 566-569; idem, *Revue Biblique* 75 (1968) 253-258; idem, *Princeton Seminary Bulletin* (1965) 19-28; idem, *Biblical Archaeologist* 28 (1965) 30-32.
6. Blaikie, *First Book of Samuel,* 417-418.
7. Deane, *David,* 74.
8. Klein, *1 Samuel,* 282; McCarter, *1 Samuel,* 435.
9. Blaikie, *First Book of Samuel,* 423.
10. The Negev was apparently broken up into districts. The Cherithites originally came from the Aegean and at certain times were identified with the Philistines (cf. Ezekiel 25:16; Zephaniah 2:5). A group of Cherithites later made up a part of David's bodyguard (cf. 2 Samuel 8:18; 15:18; 20:7,23; 1 Kings 1:38,44). Cf. Mauchline, *1 and 2 Samuel,* 187.
11. *Hōgĕgîm* is usually translated "making a pilgrimage" or "having a pilgrim feast." The Hebrew *hāg* (1 Samuel 30:16) appears strangely out of place in this context. For explanations of its usage see S. R. Driver, *Notes on the Hebrew Text,* 223; Mauchline, *1 and 2 Samuel,* 188; McCarter, *1 Samuel,* 435.
12. *Hannešep* (1 Samuel 30:17) is usually translated "twilight." McCarter (*1 Samuel,* 435), however, suggests "the first light of dawn." Cf. Job 7:4; Psalm 119:47.
13. K. W. Whiteham, *The Just King: Monarchial Judicial Authority in Ancient Israel* (Sheffield, England: Journal for the Study of the Old Testament, 1979) 95.
14. Klein, *1 Samuel,* 284.
15. Cf. Blaikie, *First Book of Samuel,* 425.
16. Klein, *1 Samuel,* 284-285; McCarter, *1 Samuel,* 436.

17. A. Bloch, *Murphy's Law and Other Reasons Why Things Go Wrong* (Los Angeles: Price, Sterns, Slaon, 1977) 10. Used by permission.
18. See C. R. Swindoll's *Strengthening Your Grip* (Waco, TX: Word, 1982, pages 21-26) for information on reinstating or restoring one's values.
19. O. Chambers, *Christian Disciplines* (Port Washington, PA: Christian Literature Crusade, 1965) I:9,120. Emphasis added.
20. Source unknown.
21. J. Baillie, *A Diary of Private Prayer* (New York: Scribner's, 1949) 67.

Chapter 20

1. Based on a novel by T. H. White entitled *The Once and Future King* (London: Collins, 1958) 677 pages.
2. A. Tennyson, *The Complete Works of Tennyson,* ed. W. J. Rolfe (Boston: Houghton, Mifflin, 1898) 64-68. Archaeologists have excavated what they believe to be Arthur's Camelot. In a nearby churchyard they have found the gravestones of Arthur and Guinevere lying side by side. Tennyson apparently erred in his conclusion when he described Arthur's body being placed in a barge and set adrift to be carried out to sea.
3. Robinson, *Biblical Researches in Palestine* II:318-325; R. A. S. Macalister, *Palestine Exploration Quarterly* 41 (1909) 175; S. Yeivin, *Bulletin of the Israel Exploration Society* 14 (1948) 89; Baly, *Geography of the Bible,* 148-154.
4. Yadin, *Art of Warfare,* I:150; II:353,382-393.
5. Deane and Kirk, *Studies in First Samuel* I:209.
6. Davis, *Birth of a Kingdom,* 108,111ff.; A. P. Stanley, *History of the Jewish Church* II:16,25-26.
7. A. Rowe, *The Topography and History of Beth-shan* (Philadelphia: University of Pennsylvania Museum, 1930) 62 pages; *Archaeology and the Old Testament,* 185-196; *Encyclopedia of Archaeological Excavations* I:207-208.
8. Ish-bosheth had not taken part in the battle. Abner possibly fled the scene of carnage and brought news of the defeat to Ish-bosheth. The two of them accompanied by Ish-bosheth's retainers then crossed the Jordan river in haste and made their way to Mahanaim.
9. G. R. Driver, *Zeitschrift für die alttestamentliche Wissenschaft* 66 (1954) 314-315; G. E. Wright, *Biblical Archaeologist* 29 (1966) 70-86.
10. Cf. D. F. Paine, *I and II Samuel* (Philadelphia: Westminster, 1982) 146.
11. C. E. Macartney, *Mountains and Mountain Men of the Bible* (New York: Abingdon, 1950) 115.
12. Wood, *United Monarchy,* 165-169.
13. Macartney, *Mountains and Mountain Men,* 107-108.
14. Ibid., 110-111.
15. Cf. Deane and Kirk, *Studies in First Samuel* II:267-268.

SCRIPTURE INDEX

PERSON AND TITLE INDEX